Telecommunications Policy
and
Economic Development

Telecommunications Policy and Economic Development

The New State Role

Edited by

Jurgen Schmandt, Frederick Williams, and Robert H. Wilson

PRAEGER

New York
Westport, Connecticut
London

Library of Congress Cataloging-in-Publication Data

Telecommunications policy and economic development : the new state
    role / Jurgen Schmandt, Frederick Williams, and Robert H. Wilson,
    editors.
        p. cm.
    Includes bibliographical references.
    ISBN 0-275-93399-7 (alk. paper)
    1. Telecommunication policy—United States—States.
    2. Telecommunication—Economic aspects—United States—States.
    I. Schmandt, Jurgen. II. Williams, Frederick, 1933-
    III. Wilson, Robert Hines.
    HE7781.T428 1989
    384'.068—dc20   89-16148

Library of Congress Catalog Card Number: 89-16148
ISBN: 0-275-93399-7

First published in 1989

Praeger Publishers, One Madison Avenue, New York, NY 10010
A division of Greenwood Press, Inc.

Printed in the United States of America

The paper used in this book complies with the
Permanent Paper Standard issued by the National
Information Standards Organization (Z39.48-1984).

10 9 8 7 6 5 4 3 2 1

MEMBERS OF THE RESEARCH TEAM

Graduate Students

Janee Briesemeister, College of Communication, co-author, Vermont and Conclusion

Darrick Eugene, LBJ School of Public Affairs, co-author, Florida

Danny B. Garcia, III, LBJ School of Public Affairs, co-author, California

Joellen M. Harper, LBJ School of Public Affairs, co-author, Nebraska

John Horrigan, LBJ School of Public Affairs, co-author, Introduction, Illinois, and Conclusion

Larkin Jennings, LBJ School of Public Affairs, co-author, New York

Amy M. Korzick, College of Communication, co-author, Introduction and Virginia

David McCarty, College of Communication, co-author, Introduction, Florida, and Texas

Darren Rudloff, LBJ School of Public Affairs, co-author, Illinois

Sehba Sarwar, LBJ School of Public Affairs, co-author, Virginia

Harmeet S. Sawhney, College of Communication, co-author, New York

Kerry Strayer, College of Communication, co-author, Washington

Philip Treuer, LBJ School of Public Affairs, co-author, Vermont

David Twenhafel, LBJ School of Public Affairs, co-author, Introduction and Washington

Mahmoud Watad, LBJ School of Public Affairs, co-author, California

Benet Younger, LBJ School of Public Affairs, co-author, Nebraska

Faculty

Jurgen Schmandt, LBJ School of Public Affairs

Frederick Williams, College of Communication

Robert H. Wilson, LBJ School of Public Affairs

Contents

Tables

Figures

Preface

The divestiture of AT&T in 1984 represented the culmination of three decades of technological and structural change in the telecommunications industry in the United States. With the industry no longer the monopoly it once was, telecommunications policy was forced to change. Federal regulation lessened, while the state role increased. During the early 1980s, states were also demonstrating a new interest in economic development as the country's traditional manufacturing base came under pressure from foreign competition. Cutbacks in federal spending and less policy activism at the federal level forced states to undertake new initiatives in a broad range of policy areas, telecommunications among them. The conjunction of these forces has resulted in a flurry of new activity in telecommunications policy at the state level, activity largely undocumented and unexplored. To investigate these developments, the Lyndon B. Johnson School of Public Affairs and the Center for Research on Communication, Technology, and Society (College of Communication), both at the University of Texas at Austin, undertook a year-long study of state telecommunications policy.

The project team consisted of 17 graduate students, 12 from the LBJ School and 5 from the College of Communication. Three faculty members, two from the LBJ School and one from the College of Communication, directed the project. Researchers visited each of the nine states, gaining valuable guidance and insight from a great many people in the public and private sector. The study was conducted as a policy research project, the cornerstone of the curriculum of the LBJ School, which involves student and faculty research on an issue of interest to a client. This project was sponsored by Southwestern Bell Telephone and the Texas Telephone Association. Although important stakeholders in their own right, our clients encouraged us to conduct impartial and scholarly policy analysis of the changing telecommunications environment at the state level. Our preliminary findings were presented in April 1988 at a conference held at the University of Texas. We owe thanks to conference attendees for sharing their thoughts on our initial conclusions and catching some errors in fact and interpretation. Responsibility for any remaining errors rests solely with the authors.

Jurgen Schmandt
Frederick Williams
Robert Wilson

Acknowledgments

The list of people in the states whose help was invaluable is long but bears exposition. In California: Richard Adler, Institute for the Future; Francois Bar, Berkeley Roundtable on the International Economy; Kevin Coughlan, California Public Utilities Commission; William Dutton, University of Southern California; James Fralick, California Department of General Services; Robert Jacobson of California State Assembly Utilities and Commerce Committee; Brenda Lopes, California Department of Commerce; Beverly McDonald, University of California; Patricia Moktarian, Southern California Association of Governments; George Schmitt, Pacific Bell; and Mary Ward, MCI Telecommunications. In Florida: Leon Blue, Information Resource Commission; William Feaster, Florida Telephone Association; Fernando Franco, Eastern Airlines; Edwin Levine, First Florida Bank; H. Frank Meiners, Southern Bell; David Proctor, AT&T of Florida; and Greg Schaeffer, Florida Public Service Commission. In Illinois: Gregory K. Busch, private consultant; Bruce Campbell, Illinois Bell; Mike Farmer, Department of Commerce and Community Affairs; Todd Glenn, Illinois Bell; William McQueen, AT&T of Illinois; Lois Rosen, Labor Coalition of Public Utilities, David Rudd, Illinois Commerce Commission; Nina Shepherd, Information Industries Council; and Gerald Veatch, Illinois Bell. In Nebraska: John W. DeCamp, attorney; Steve McCollister, Northwestern Bell; Stu Miller, Nebraska Department of Economic Development; Norman Osland, Nebraska Telephone Association; and Eric Rasmussen, Nebraska Public Service Commission. In New York: Robert Atkinson, Teleport Communications; Barry Cole, Columbia University; Sharon McStine, Port Authority of New York and New Jersey; Mitchell Moss, New York University; Eli Noam, New York Public Service Commission; Bill Peters, New York City Partnership; Phillip Shapiro, Consumer Protection Board; Neal Vaupel, AT&T of New York; and Joseph Walsh, Jr., New York Telephone. In Texas: Vaughn Aldredge, AT&T of Texas; John Allison, University of Texas; Carol Barger, Consumers Union; Robert Brown, Sugarland Telephone Company; Mark Bryant, MCI Telecommunications; Jo Campbell, Commissioner, Texas Public Utilities Commission; Doug Clark, Southwestern Bell; Philip Diehl, Texas Public Utilities Commission; R.H. Erkel, AT&T of Texas; William Free, Southwestern Bell; Marta Greytok, Commissioner, Texas Public Utilities Commission; Jeffrey Haynes, Texas Telephone Association; Jerry James, ClayDesta Communications; Jon Loehman, Southwestern Bell; Mil Peterson, AT&T of Texas; Lynn Polson, Automated Information and Telecommunications Council; and Dennis Thomas, Chairman of the Texas Public Utilities Commission. In Vermont: Rita Barmann, US Sprint; Richard Cowart, Vermont Public Service Board; Michael Dworkin, Vermont Public Service Board; Philip Hoff, State Senator; Michael Knisbacher, Long Distance North; Gene Laber, University of Vermont; Louise McCarren, Chittenden Bank; Gerald Tarrant, Department of Public Service; and David Usher, New England Telephone. In Virginia: Theodore Adams, AT&T of Virginia; M.E. Blanton, C&P Telephone; Robert Hardiman, C&P Telephone; William Irby, Virginia State Corporate Commission; William F. Marmon, MCI Telecommunications; and Dallas Reid, Continental Telephone Company. In Washington: Victor Ericson, Pacific Northwest Bell; the Honorable Ken

Jacobsen, Washington House of Representatives; and Sharon Nelson, Chairman of the Washington Utilities and Transportation Commission. We would also like to thank those individuals who spoke to the seminar during our study: Donald Dillman, Washington State University; Herbert Dordick, Temple University; Jeffrey Gay, formerly of the Office of Public Utility Counsel; Heather Hudson, University of San Francisco; Joseph Robbins, Bellcore; and Sharon Strover, the University of Texas.

Finally, we acknowledge the help of our editor, Alison Tartt, Ted Melina Raab, who prepared our electronic files for printing the interim report, and our administrative assistant, Susan Roush, who spent many hours preparing the camera-ready copy for this book.

Telecommunications Policy
and
Economic Development

1

Introduction

David Twenhafel, John Horrigan,
Amy M. Korzick, and David McCarty

The telecommunications industry has seen tremendous change in recent years. The forces for change are widespread. Technological innovation, ongoing since the days of Alexander Graham Bell but especially rapid since the 1960s, has pushed back the frontiers of the possible. A move away from strict monopoly regulation--evident in the banking, trucking, and airline industries-- reached the telecommunications industry in 1982 and changed the political context of telecommunications policymaking. The continuing transition of the U.S. economy from a traditional manufacturing base to a service base has created new markets for telecommunications. Telecommunications has been an integral, although often unrecognized, factor in economic development.

The 1984 divestiture of AT&T proved to be a watershed event in telecommunications. In addition to creating a host of new telecommunications companies--seven RBOCs and 22 BOCs--the Modified Final Judgment (MFJ) moved a significant part of the telecommunications policy debate from the federal to the state level. States had always been involved in telecommunications policy decisions-- intrastate regulation was and remains in the purview of each individual state--but had played limited roles. Rate of return regulation was the national norm prior to the MFJ, and most state decisions involved little more than setting local rates. As Charles Stalon has noted, this shift from the federal to the state level necessitates a change in policymaking: "Dramatic changes in both purposes and procedures are going to be necessary if PUC regulation is not to become a meaningless paper shuffle."[1]

In the post-MFJ environment, most of the pressure for policy changes at the state level originated with telecommunications companies. The Baby Bells and AT&T aggressively sought to influence regulatory policies, and their efforts often forced other players to become active. No single pattern applies to all states, however. In some states the policy debates took place within the PUCs; state legislatures took active roles in other states.

Many of the arguments to modify state policies have been couched in the language of economic development. These arguments may be sincere or simply politically expedient--the phrase "economic development" has been used as justification for widely disparate programs and policies--but that telecommunications policies are related to economic development is not to be doubted.[2] Their implications are explored in greater depth below.

Counterarguments to regulatory modifications are based on the varying needs of consumers. Regulatory policies designed to promote economic development may threaten universal service.[3] The needs of small consumers are different from those of large consumers. At the same time Charles Zielinski cautions that maintaining the current policies for promoting universal service may thwart the goals of increasing "economic opportunity and productivity for individuals and businesses in the state."[4] States are grappling with the implications of telecommunications policy for varying policy goals.

In the midst of all this change, state governments are discovering their own importance as telecommunications users, often the largest consumer in the state. Some have begun to develop cogent policies for procurement and use of telecommunications.[5] New teleservices may allow states to provide services more efficiently or perhaps to provide services that otherwise would not be delivered.[6]

The volatile environment is likely to continue for some years. Judge Greene's grip is likely to loosen in the face of FCC, DOJ, and RBOC pressure, thus giving the states latitude over more policy decisions. Moreover, the policy environment is becoming increasingly complex. Technology is continuing to evolve; the stakeholders are many and diverse; specific policies that will benefit everyone are few. Consequently, policymakers will be under heavy pressure from stakeholders even as the targets of policy--both stakeholders and technology--themselves change.

ISSUES IN TELECOMMUNICATIONS REGULATION

Several specific issues central to the debate over telecommunications policy must be dealt with one way or another in each state. The decisions that states make in regard to these issues not only determine the pricing of telecommunications services, but also influence the long-term development of telecommunications infrastructure. They involve questions of economic efficiency and social equity. To a great extent, the significance of these issues has been heightened by divestiture and the FCC's deregulatory philosophy.

This section will discuss in general terms questions of cost allocation, rate of return regulation, and technological innovation as well as related issues such as access charges, cross-subsidization, and depreciation. The intent is to provide the reader a better understanding of the regulatory agenda in the states. Readers already familiar with these issues may wish to move to the discussion on economic development.

Cost Allocation

Discussion of cost allocation involves two different sets of issues: the relationship between local and long distance rates and cross-subsidization between different lines of business or service offerings.

Local and Long Distance Rates

The bulk of the cost of the local telephone network, the local loop, must be incurred simply to connect subscribers to the system. That is, the cost of running a pair of copper wires (or, increasingly, an optical fiber) from the telephone company's central office to an individual residence or business is the same whether that customer subsequently makes a large number of calls or very few calls. In other words, it is "nontraffic-sensitive" (NTS).

Historically, the recovery of NTS costs has raised several problems. One of these is determining what portion (if any) of the NTS cost of the local loop should be recovered through long distance usage charges. The local loop must be used for both local calls and interexchange calls, thus raising the issue of allocation of joint or common costs.[7]

Initially, long distance service made no contribution to local exchange costs. In 1930, however, the Supreme Court determined that some of the NTS costs of local exchanges should be recovered through long distance rates because long distance calls required the use of local loops. This became known as the "separations procedures." The determination of the portion of these NTS costs to be charged to long distance was more or less arbitrary. The final figure was negotiated by AT&T, the independent telephone companies, state regulators, and the FCC. The percentage of NTS costs assigned to long distance was based on the percentage of total calling minutes used for interexchange calls. Over the years, as more interexchange calls were made, they also became more heavily weighted. Thus, an increasing portion of the NTS costs of local subscribers was being "subsidized" by those who made the most long distance calls.[8]

With divestiture, the separations process was replaced by a system of access charges. The two aspects of access charges represent a compromise between two policy goals. The more familiar subscriber line charge (SLC), which appears on everyone's monthly phone bill as "FCC-approved customer line charge," represents the FCC's intention to shift more of the burden of NTS costs to the end user. This policy has the effect of increasing local phone rates and, consequently, has been vigorously opposed by many state regulators and consumer organizations who wish to keep phone rates low. Even Judge Greene has expressed dissatisfaction, saying, saddling "local subscribers with the access costs of interexchange carriers [runs] directly counter to one of the decree's assumptions and purposes;" namely, to keep costs down for the local ratepayer.[9]

The other aspect of access charges, the carrier common line charge (CCLC), continues the subsidization of local rates through usage-based interexchange charges. Interexchange carriers are charged by the local exchange carriers on a per-minute basis for connection to both the originating and terminating local exchanges for every call. In general, then, reductions in access charges create upward pressure on local monthly rates. To the extent that interexchange service is priced above the cost of providing it, an incentive is created for large users of long distance to "bypass" the local exchange company and, thus, the associated access charges.[10] As more and more of these large users bypass the local exchange, by using private microwave, cable, or satellite systems, the subsidy to local rates decreases--again creating upward pressure on local rates. For the most part, bypass has not been perceived by state regulatory commissions as a significant, near-term threat to local rates.

However, the costs of bypass systems continue to decline, thus making it increasingly attractive for users to bypass the local exchange.

Cross-subsidization

A second aspect of cost allocation has arisen as local telephone companies, particularly the BOCs, have been allowed to provide unregulated services and expand into unregulated lines of business. One facet of this issue is separating the joint and common costs of providing both regulated and unregulated services over the same facilities. Another involves accounting separations between regulated and unregulated lines of business. In both instances, the concern is that captive ratepayers of monopoly services might be used to subsidize unregulated services or businesses.

Thus, the allocation of costs among telecommunications services is complicated by the presence of significant joint and common costs. To some extent, decisions regarding cost allocation are relatively arbitrary and, hence, subject to politicization as various players stand to gain or lose from any particular outcome.

Rate of Return Regulation

Another set of issues has to do with the traditional method of regulating telephone companies' rates and earnings: rate of return on investment. The justification for regulating telephone companies' return has been that they are monopoly providers. In the absence of regulation, they could command prices significantly above what a competitive market would allow. Rate of return regulation attempts to make the incentive for investing in a monopoly service similar to that possible in nonmonopoly services. Greatly simplified, this process consists of determining the rate base--that is, the cost of providing service including depreciation and taxes--and adding to that a reasonable profit or a return sufficient to attract the capital necessary for investment.

There are a number of problems associated with this process, but two are particularly relevant to current changes in the policy environment. According to the so-called Averch-Johnson effect, this type of regulation provides an incentive for the firm to overinvest, since its rate of return is based on total capital investment.[11] This may have lead to overcapacity in much of the telephone network, a situation that now skews questions of pricing and competition. It should be noted, however, that the existence of this effect is rather controversial and, in any case, depends upon the cost of capital to the firm being lower than its allowed rate of return.

Another criticism of rate of return regulation is that it discourages operating efficiencies because the benefits of cost-saving techniques flow to consumers rather than providing additional profit to the firm. Some states have moved to price-cap methods of regulation, which allow telephone companies to keep or at least share in the additional revenues provided by increased efficiencies as long as prices are not increased, or are increased only within certain percentages.

A more radical alternative to rate of return regulation is simply to deregulate telephone companies completely. One rationale for this is the theory of contestable markets, which suggests that the mere threat of unrestricted entry and exit by competing firms may be sufficient to preclude such problems as excess profits, inefficient firm operations, and cross-subsidization.[12]

While this theory may not apply to true natural monopolies, the extent of natural monopolies in the telecommunications industry is open to debate. Some even question whether the provision of basic local telephone exchange service is still a natural monopoly.

Issues in the interexchange market are similarly complex. With divestiture, the capital structure of AT&T has changed dramatically. Without its local operating companies, AT&T is no longer the capital-intensive firm that it once was. Few would argue that AT&T enjoys monopoly status in its markets. The rationale for continued regulation of AT&T has shifted to concerns about that firm's position of dominance in certain markets and, thus, its continued ability to control prices. While the extent of AT&T's market dominance--and the need for continued regulation--must be evaluated on a market-by-market basis, it appears that traditional rate of return regulation may no longer be appropriate for AT&T given its new capital structure.

Technological Innovation

One final set of issues for state regulation has to do with technological innovation. The functional life of most telecommunications equipment far exceeds the rate of technological innovation in the telecommunications industry. For example, even while advanced digital switching technologies have been available for some time, electromechanical step-by-step switches continue to function quite adequately in many central offices. This raises two related policy questions. First, at what rate and to what extent should state-of-the-art technologies be integrated into the public network? Second, how should such technological innovation be financed?

The first question addresses the evolution of the infrastructure of the public telecommunications network. As new technologies such as optical fiber and Integrated Services Digital Networks (ISDN) become available, there will be pressure--especially from the telephone companies on behalf of their large users--to incorporate them into the telecommunications network in order to provide the new services which they allow. However, consumer advocates argue that most customers simply want reliable, "plain old telephone service" (POTS).[13] Thus, policymakers must evaluate the need or demand for new services, as well as how widely available they should be, in the context of the cost and availability of basic phone service.

To the extent that policymakers deem the introduction of new technologies appropriate, this raises the question of how to pay for them. For telephone companies to recover the costs of existing technologies, they must be fully depreciated before they are taken out of service and replaced. This means accelerating the rate of depreciation, which in turn creates upward pressure on rates. Policymakers must decide whether the costs of new technologies should be spread across all rate payers or somehow paid for by some subgroup of ratepayers. If consumers truly derive no benefit from advanced technologies, it is unfair to make them pay more than the cost of POTS. However, determining the true costs and benefits of technological innovation involves subjective judgments that make consensus virtually impossible. Policymakers must therefore balance a range of social, political, and economic concerns in deciding whether to allow--or encourage--the application of technological innovation.

TELECOMMUNICATIONS AND ECONOMIC DEVELOPMENT

The link between telecommunications and economic development may be considered in at least two ways, both of which depend upon one's view of economic development. One way to look at economic development is from the perspective of state economic development programs. Such programs involve efforts to retain or attract business to a state or promote the formation of businesses within a state. The second way is to look at economic development as those activities which might promote economic growth, that is, efforts to enhance the productive capacity of the economy. Through this second perspective, telecommunications may be considered most appropriately as a factor of production in the economy. This section will examine the interaction between telecommunications and economic development in these two perspectives and will conclude with a discussion of the policy issues raised by the link between telecommunications and economic development.

Traditional State Economic Development

The recession of 1981-82 and the changing structure of the American economy have caused states to become much more aggressive in economic development.[14] With little prospect of recapturing the manufacturing jobs lost over the last two decades, many states launched new initiatives to diversify their economies. These new initiatives have focused on strengthening the existing economic base, attracting new firms to the state, encouraging the creation of new firms, and providing adjustment assistance to distressed areas and workers.[15]

Industrial recruitment is central to traditional state economic development programs, although states have developed a variety of new initiatives.[16] The focus of industrial recruitment is, of course, on manufacturing. Given that much of the new state economic development activity was stimulated by the closing of manufacturing plants, successful industrial recruitment generates much goodwill for policymakers.[17]

Beyond being good politics, however, state concern with manufacturing is sound economics. Even though the service sector accounted for 95 percent of net new job creation from 1970 to 1984,[18] service jobs exist, to a large extent, as a consequence of manufacturing jobs. Despite manufacturing's declining share of overall employment (about 21 million jobs or 20 percent of the workforce in 1986), manufacturing generates another 40 to 60 million jobs. From one-half to two-thirds of these jobs are in the service sector.[19] Most high-wage service jobs, such as finance, insurance, engineering, design, and communications, are linked directly to manufacturing.[20]

While state policy directed at manufacturing is well placed, states could do more to attract service firms. Most large manufacturing companies have a substantial service component within them; accounting, legal services, and communications are a few examples. The growth of producer services--defined as services, either internal and external to the firm, which aid in organizing the production process--is a significant post-World War II development in America's economic structure.[21] In many cases, the service branch of a firm, like its manufacturing facilities, need not be located near corporate headquarters. This is now made possible, in part, by advances in telecommunications systems. States that are aware of a company's decision to expand its service branch can attempt to keep the service branch nearby. Alternatively, states can try to lure service branches away from the corporate headquarters. One of the many strategies states can employ to attract such firms is an advanced data and telecommunications network.[22] For a corporation with many locations, such links are crucial.

It is worth observing that for the most part, the recruitment focus of state economic development programs is a zero-sum game. States fiercely compete for scarce pieces of a fixed economic pie. Little attention is paid, in these programs at least, to using telecommunications to expand the size of the pie. However, particularly low rates or high quality of service may make one state or locale more attractive than others.

Telecommunications as a Factor of Production

The potential contribution of telecommunications to economic growth is more complex. An historical analogy, that of the railroads and their impact on economic growth, helps illuminate the role telecommunications may play.

There is little dispute that the railroads were vital to American economic growth in the late 19th and early 20th centuries. The production processes of that era required the development of a transportation infrastructure like that of the railroads. Economic growth at the time depended on growing markets and mass production techniques. To take advantage of economies of scale, corporations needed a way to link geographically dispersed demand.[23] The railroads provided that link. Railroads, it should be emphasized, did not create demand, but merely enabled innovations to become economically viable by linking markets and thus permitted firms to realize economies of scale.[24]

Telecommunications serves a similar function in today's economy. The importance of telecommunications, as with railroads, is linked to the nature of production processes. American manufacturing today relies much less on mass production than it once did. Much has been written about the movement of mass-produced goods overseas to countries with low-cost labor.[25] Given the difficulty and undesirability of getting these industries back--American workers' wages would have to be reduced to the low level that caused the movement abroad--the hope for American industrial revival lies in high-value-added, high-technology goods. The types of innovations that telecommunications can support are numerous: automatic teller machines, computer-aided design and manufacturing (CAD/CAM), education, work at home, and many more. Telecommunications will be a crucial part of the infrastructure that will facilitate this revolution.[26]

These innovations will enable the United States to develop flexible production processes, seen by many as the key to American economic revival.[27] Because America can no longer compete in mass-produced goods, it must compete in technologically evolving markets in which quality, rather than price, is most important. Producers must be able to respond quickly to changing markets; the time between design, production, and sale must be substantially reduced. Engineers and sales people must interact constantly to ensure responsiveness to the market. Quick and efficient communication is the key to making such a process function well.

Thus telecommunications should be considered as an important factor of production. As industrial technology has developed, the production process has grown more complex and the organizational and informational tasks in production have grown more important.[28] Informational activity has grown in size as well as importance. By 1980 one-half of all U.S. economic activity was accounted for by information creation and processing. This growth occurred primarily in the business sector; in 1972 business spent $506 billion on printed matter and media, compared with $84 billion by consumers.[29]

Just as the railroads were necessary to link the large markets that made mass production economically feasible, so an advanced communications network is necessary to support the logic of flexible production processes and segmented markets. Thus our changing economy is leading the demand for new telecommunications services. How and when these services will be available is directly influenced by the public policies that affect telecommunications.

Policy Issues

Given the growing importance of telecommunications in the economy, two questions are posed: Have state policymakers recognized the link between telecommunications and economic development? If they have, what policy measures have been or should be taken? In regard to the first question, it is difficult to evaluate how explicitly the link has been made. Because economic development has become so politically popular in recent years, the term has come to mean many things to many people. New jobs, increased gross product, technological innovations, higher wages, and an improved quality of life all could come under the rubric of economic development. Differentiation within these categories is also possible. For example, a region may target specific types of jobs, such as those found in the producer services sector or those offering high wages.

The second question addresses the issue of how states have reacted to the growing economic importance of telecommunications and the changing technology and structure within the industry. Three general approaches have been taken by states. The first preserves subsidies in the regulated prices of telephone companies and opens competitive entry in telecommunications markets. The second preserves subsidies and denies competitive entry in telecommunications markets. The third, a greater departure from the past, removes subsidies in regulated telephone services and opens competitive entry in all telecommunications markets.[30]

Another dimension to the state response to the economic importance of telecommunications is the location in government of the policy initiatives. If the link is unrecognized, state telecommunications policy may be left primarily in the hands of the regulatory agency. But, can or should regulators include economic development considerations in their decisionmaking process?

If the link is recognized, several locations within government could take the lead. State economic development agencies are one possible source of policy initiative. They have expertise and a public mandate. However, state economic development agencies have historically focused on manufacturing and infrastructure development, such as roads, bridges, and sewers. The techniques that bring these development efforts to fruition may not be appropriate to telecommunications. In some states, however, as the strategies for economic development are being cast in broader terms, including policies for technological innovation and human resource development, telecommunications is seen as a potential policy instrument.[31]

State legislatures are another likely source of innovative policy. Legislatures may have standing committees or subcommittees on telecommunications or utilities generally. Moreover, legislators are sensitive to political pressure. Lobbying by the telecommunications industry, large telecommunications users, or other constituents could lead to legislation promoting economic development via telecommunications.

Despite having an historically narrow view of regulation, public utility commissions (PUC) are another possible location within state governments. They may have been directed by the executive or the legislature to implement or study innovative policies. Moreover, commissioners themselves may favor policies linking economic development with telecommunications. In some states, commissioners are elected officials and subject to the same political pressures as legislators. In other states, commissioners are appointed by the governor, perhaps subject to legislative confirmation. Again, the possibility exists for people who recognize the link between economic development and telecommunications to be placed in policymaking positions.

Each of these locations provides both strengths and weaknesses as a center for policy development. Moreover, within each state, these locations are subject to unique traditions and political practices. No single type of location is apt to be best suited to the task across all states.

These policy issues--the recognition of the link, the policy measures taken, and the governmental arms that craft and implement policy--are the central focus of this study. Individual chapters document the approaches taken by specific states and, to the extent possible, evaluate the policy outcomes.

RESEARCH DESIGN

This study focuses on nine states: California, Florida, Illinois, Nebraska, New York, Texas, Vermont, Virginia, and Washington. The states chosen are not, in any sense, a random sample. The overriding selection criterion was the proactive use of state policymaking authority in telecommunications. A review of industry journals yielded an original list of 20 states that had been active and innovative in telecommunications. The research team compiled profiles on these states, with information gathered from both industry literature and exploratory telephone interviews. These profiles revealed the extent of recent state action and identified possible future action.

In addition to proactive policymaking, the selections were made in such a way as to ensure diversity in state economic structure, political environment, and the type and extent of changes in regulatory policy. Furthermore, at least one state from the territory of each RBOC was included.

These criteria restrict the drawing of unqualified conclusions; these states are not likely to be representative of all states. However, the common thread linking all nine states--proactive use of policymaking authority--does allow for some generalization. Indeed, common outcomes in the face of political and economic diversity lend weight to the hypothesis of a link between economic development and state telecommunications policy. Regulatory policies and the regulatory environment among the nine states included in this study are particularly diverse (Tables 1.1 and 1.2). Many policy questions revolve around regulatory methods, pricing flexibility, flexibility in introducing new services, and intraLATA competition.

Table 1.1
Regulatory Flexibility

State	Traditional Rate of Return			Pricing Flexibility*			New Service Flexibility*		
	BOC	AT&T	OCCs	BOC	AT&T	OCCs	BOC	AT&T	OCCs
California	yes	yes	yes	**	**	**	yes	yes	yes
Florida	yes	yes	yes	yes	yes	n.a.	yes	yes	n.a.
Illinois	yes	no	n.a.	yes	yes	n.a.	yes	yes	n.a.
Nebraska	no	no	no	yes	yes	yes	yes	yes	yes
New York	no	no	no	**	**	yes	no	no	no
Texas	yes	yes	no	no	yes	yes	yes	yes	yes
Vermont	yes	n.a.	yes	***	n.a.	yes	***	n.a.	yes
Virginia	yes	no	no	no	yes	yes	no	yes	yes
Washington	yes	no	yes	yes	yes	yes	no	yes	yes

* "Flexibility" is defined as some form of expidited hearing procedure other than a traditional adjudicatory one.
** Limited.
*** Pending.

Source: Compiled from information in individual chapters.

Table 1.2
Regulatory Environment

State	Number of LATAs	IntraLATA Competition	1-Plus IntraLATA for all Competitors
California	10	no	no
Florida	13	yes	yes (miniLATAs)
Illinois	18*	yes	yes (under consideration)
Nebraska	3	yes	no
New York	6	yes	no
Texas	17	yes	no
Vermont	1	yes	no
Virginia	12	resellers only	yes
Washington	4**	yes	no

* Illinois has Market Service Areas (MSAs), not LATAs
** Washington has 2 principal LATAs and small parts of 2 others.

Source: Compiled from information in individual chapters.

The nine states included in this study exhibit diversity as well in the quality of available telecommunications equipment (Figure 1.1). No clear pattern emerges from this data. Some states with large rural areas, such as Nebraska, have relatively few electronic switching offices while others, such as Washington, have almost completely replaced older switches. States with major urban centers, such as Illinois and New York, are similarly disparate.

The states in this study are equally diverse in their telephone subscribership rates (Figure 1.2). Subscribership--the proportion of all households in the state with telephone service--is often used as a proxy measure for universal service. Two of the states in this study, Nebraska and Washington, had decreasing rates between 1985 and 1987, although both states had relatively high rates. Illinois' rate was stable, and the remaining states exhibited increasing rates. In all three years, Texas' subscribership rates were substantially lower than the other eight states.

The role that telecommunications-intensive businesses (TIBS) play in the states is more homogenous (Figure 1.3). New York and California, however show an increasing reliance on information jobs, as defined by Standard Industrial Classification codes. Among the nine states in this study, these two states showed the highest specialization of TIBS with over 20 percent of the state's employment being in these business sectors.

In the midst of technological innovation, this study sought to document state efforts to maintain universal service. The nine states show mixed participation in Link-Up America, an FCC-sponsored program, and in statewide teleassistance programs (Table 1.3).

Table 1.3
State Telephone Assistance Programs

	Link-Up America	Telassistance
California	No	Yes, Lifeline service
Florida	Yes	No
Illinois	No* (on ICC docket)	No
Nebraska	Yes	No
New York	n.a.	n.a.
Texas	Yes	No
Vermont	No	Yes, Lifeline service
Virginia	Yes	Yes, Universal Service Program
Washington	No	Yes, Telephone Assistance Program

Source: Compiled from information in individual chapters.

Data for each state came primarily from three types of sources: industry literature, government documents, and interviews--both telephone and personal --with representatives of major players. Prior to field work in each state, two-person teams researched their state's political and economic backgrounds, became familiar with the telecommunications industry, and identified issues important in the state.

Each team spent one week in the state conducting interviews with representatives from state agencies and private-sector groups. State officials included public utilities commissioners and staff, economic development agency staff, and legislators and legislative staff. Industry representatives included AT&T, other common carriers, Bell operating companies, and independent telephone companies. Other groups with a stake in the process included consumer groups, telecommunications-intensive businesses, and private economic development councils.

ORGANIZATION OF THE REPORT

Each chapter of this report examines one of the nine states. The chapters are similarly organized although the general outline is flexible enough to reflect the uniqueness of each state. In general, each chapter describes the state's socioeconomic characteristics, its telecommunications industry, and the political culture and policymaking environment, with particular attention to major actors and innovative policies. Each state chapter explores how well the link between telecommunications and economic development is recognized and what steps are being taken to capitalize on the link. The state government's role as a user of telecommunications is also discussed. Finally, most chapters have one or two case studies that examine in detail issues of particular interest to individual states. Examples include an analysis of the political processes that enabled innovative legislation to be enacted, the economic development activities of a BOC, and the development of an agricultural information network.

General findings drawn from across the states are presented in the final chapter. The discussion focuses on four principal areas: states as telecommunications policymakers, the link between telecommunications and economic development, universal service, and states as users of telecommunications. The emphasis of the final chapter is not on the similarities and differences among the target states but rather on the effect of their policies. This chapter also includes recommendations for policymakers and thoughts on the future of state telecommunications policy. A glossary of telecommunications terms can be found at the end of this report.

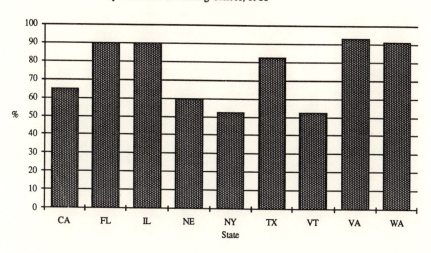

Figure 1.1
Percentage of Total Access Lines Served
by Electronic Switching Offices, 1986

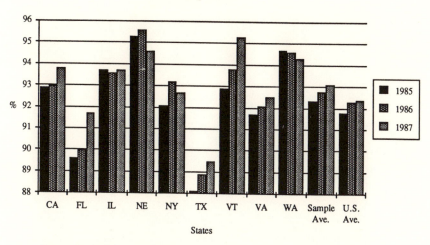

Figure 1.2
Subscribership Rates

Source: Federal Communications Commission, "Telephone Subcribership in the U.S.," February 24, 1988.

Figure 1.3
Employment Shares of
Telecommunications-Intensive Businesses,
1980 and 1984

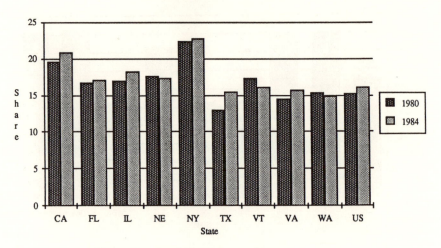

Source: Data from individual report chapters.

NOTES

1.   Charles G. Stalon, "On Barriers to Explicit Policy Making in State PUCs," in Policy Research in Telecommunications: Proceedings from the Eleventh Annual Telecommunications Policy Research Conference, ed. Vincent Mosco (Norwood, N.J.: Ablex Publishing Corporation, 1984), p. 28.

2.   Charles Jonscher, "Assessing the Benefits of Telecommunications," Intermedia, January 1985, pp. 21-24; Sharon Strover, "Urban Telecommunications Investment," in Measuring the Information Society: The Texas Studies, ed. Frederick Williams (Newbury Park, Calif.: Sage Publications, 1988); and Charles A. Zielinski, "From Traditional Economic Regulation to New Policies and Roles in Telecommunications: A Challenge to State Governments," Washington, D.C., 1986. (Working paper.)

3.   Heather E. Hudson, "Divestiture and Deregulation in US Telecommunications: Consumer Policy Issues," Media, Culture, and Society, vol. 7 (1985), p. 71.

4.   Zielinski, "From Traditional Economic Regulation,"p. 24.

5.   See, for example, Automated Information and Telecommunications Council, State of Texas Long-Range Telecommunications Plan (Austin, December 1986).

6.   Joseph M. Chaisson, "State Telecommunications Management," Washington, D.C.: Council of State Policy and Planning Agencies, 1987. (Working paper.)

7.   U.S. Department of Justice, Antitrust Division, The Geodesic Network: 1987 Report on Competition in the Telephone Industry prepared by Peter W. Huber (Washington, D.C.: U.S. Government Printing Office, 1987), p. 3.49.

8.   Zielinski, "From Traditional Economic Regulation," p. 10.

9.   Hudson, "Divestiture and Deregulation," p. 72.

10.   For a detailed summary of the bypass issue, see Robert M. Entman, Issues in Telecommunications Regulation and Competition: Early Policy Perspectives from the States (Cambridge, Mass.: Program on Information Resources, 1985).

11.   H. Averch and L. Johnson, "Behavior of the Firm under Regulatory Constraint," cited in Stephen Breyer, Regulation and Its Reform (Cambridge, Mass.: Harvard University Press, 1982); "Cost-of-Service Rate Making," note 49, p. 404.

12.   Zielinski, "From Traditional Economic Regulation," p. 18.

13.   Carol Barger, Director, Southwest Office of Consumers Union, in a working session at the LBJ School of Public Affairs, University of Texas at Austin, November 6, 1987.

14.   Marianne K. Clarke, Revitalizing State Economies: A Review of State Economic Development Policies and Programs (Washington D.C.: National Governors Association, 1986), p. 11; R. Scott Fosler, ed., The New Economic Role of American States: Strategies in a World Economy (New York: Oxford University Press, 1988); David Osborne, The States Take the Lead (Washington, D.C.: Economic Policy Institute, 1987).

15.   Clarke, Revitalizing State Economies, p. 14.

16.   Ibid., p. 26.

17.   Ibid.

18.   Thierry Noyelle, <u>Beyond Industrial Dualism: Market and Job Segmentation in the New Economy</u> (Boulder, Colo.: Westview Press, 1987), p. 9.

19.   Stephen Cohen and John Zysman, <u>Manufacturing Matters: The Myth of the Post- Industrial Economy</u> (New York: Basic Books, 1987), p. 24.

20.   Ibid.

21.   Thomas Stanback, Jr., Peter Bearse, Thierry Noyelle, and Robert Karasek, <u>Services: The New Economy</u> (New York: Conservation of Human Resources, 1981), p. 49.

22.   Mary Sherry, "Let's Demystify the Service Sector," <u>Economic Development Review</u>, vol. 1, no. 4 (Winter 1987), p. 32.

23.   Michael J. Piore and Charles F. Sabel, <u>The Second Industrial Divide</u> (New York: Basic Books, 1984), p. 66.

24.   Robert W. Fogel, <u>Railroads and American Economic Growth</u> (Baltimore: Johns Hopkins University Press, 1964), p. 237.

25.   See Robert B. Reich, <u>The Next American Frontier</u> (New York: Basic Books, 1983); and Robert U. Ayres, <u>The Next Industrial Revolution</u> (New York: Ballinger Press, 1984).

26.   Ayres, <u>The Next Industrial Revolution</u>, p. 141.

27.   See Piore and Sabel, <u>The Second Industrial Divide</u>; Reich, <u>The Next American Frontier</u>; and Ayres, <u>The Next Industrial Revolution</u>.

28.   Charles Jonscher, "Information Resources and Economic Productivity," <u>Information Economics and Policy</u>, vol. 1 (September 1983), p. 15.

29.   Ibid., p. 13.

30.   Zielinski, "From Traditional Economic Regulation," p. 16.

31.   Jurgen Schmandt and Robert Wilson, "State Science and Technology Policies: An Assessment," <u>Economic Development Quarterly</u>, vol. 17, no. 2 (May 1988), pp. 124-137.

2

California

Danny B. Garcia, III, and Mahmoud Watad

California's economy is diverse, innovative, and propelled by a well-trained and educated work force. The state has the largest manufacturing complex in the nation. Among the fastest growing industries are the telecommunications equipment industry and the telecommunications-intensive services sector, which is growing faster in California than elsewhere in the nation.

Three factors have fundamentally changed the telecommunications environment in the state. The first is increasing competition in the telecommunications industry. In this new environment the state is being forced to assume an active role in deciding the architecture of the industry. Currently the state is moving away from a restrictive regulatory policy to pricing flexibility, exploring alternative approaches to ratemaking and lifting the ban on competition for intraLATA message toll service. How the new approach will affect economic development in the state is not yet clear. Many feel that if the new policy produces lower rates and a greater variety of services, economic development (greater efficiency and productivity) will be fostered.

The second factor is the emerging awareness by large users in the public and private sectors that telecommunications is important to business and government. For example, state government is upgrading its network and implementing fiber optic technology to reduce the cost of services and to improve the coordination and provision of services.

Finally, the state's increased interest in economic development policy has altered the telecommunications debate in the state. As economic growth stalled in California in the late 1970s and 1980s, the state realized it could no longer do without an economic development policy. In this atmosphere of increased concern over economic development, policymakers have exhibited growing awareness of how telecommunications and economic development. may be linked. Recognition of this link is still in an early stage in California, but telecommunications policy is positioned to assume a more prominent role on the state policy agenda in the future.

THE ECONOMY AND THE TELECOMMUNICATIONS INDUSTRY
Economic Profile

California's economy benefits from its many natural resources as well as from a skilled labor force. The state leads the nation in agriculture, manufacturing, mineral production, tourism, banking, and foreign trade. The state's well-developed infrastructure and extensive education and research facilities have made the economy unique in its size, diversity, and potential for innovation.

Education continues to be the State of California's largest budget expense. The total funding level for education in the governor's 1986-87 budget was $21.6 billion (about 55 percent of the total expenditures for that fiscal year).[1] This funding level represents an increase in spending on higher education by 20 percent per student over the previous year's expenditures.

Personal income in California reached $423.6 billion in 1985, 12.8 percent of the total U.S. personal income.[2] Manufacturing and services are the largest sources of income, accounting for 40 percent of total wages, followed by government and trade industries. Net income of $19.3 billion was reported by the 397,854 banks and corporations operating in the state. Manufacturing industries accounted for over one- third of the total net income.[3]

California has the largest manufacturing complex in the nation. According to the 1982 Survey of Manufacturing, value-added goods during that year amounted to $94.4 billion. The state produces goods in microelectronics, biotechnology, telecommunications, and aerospace.[4]

The total nonagricultural employment in 1986 in California was 11,271,000, an increase of 2,434,000 from 1980. The annual employment increase in California between the years 1980 and 1986 was 2.4 percent versus only 1.6 percent for the nation. The share of total employment in the services industry increased from 22.0 percent in 1980 to 24.5 percent in 1986. The employment in finance, insurance, and real estate also increased from 6.3 percent to 6.8 percent during the same period (Table 2.1).

About 4.8 percent of the labor force in California (more than 0.5 million) are employed in the information technology industries (Table 2.2). This is more than twice the share found in the United States as a whole. The employment share in information services is 10.8 percent versus 9.9 percent for the rest of the nation.

Telecommunications Industry

As discussed earlier, manufacturing is an important sector of California's economy. The manufacture of telecommunications equipment, in particular, is very significant. The California Department of Commerce reports that the U.S. telecommunications equipment industry yields sales of $12 billion annually, of which California's share is $1.5 billion.[5] Types of equipment manufactured include private branch exchanges (PBXs), local area networks (LANs), mobile phones, and other equipment.

California is home to 4,451 computer, electronics, and information technology companies, over four times more than the number based in the next highest states, New York and Massachusetts, and 33 percent of the U.S. total. California also leads the nation in its electronics and information technology work force with 556,000 employees, more than that of New York and Massachusetts combined.[6]

Table 2.1
Nonagricultural Employment Shares and Annual
Percentage Change in Employment* for California and
the United States, 1980 and 1986
(total employees in 1,000s, share and change in %)

Sector	Employment Shares 1980		1986		Annual Employment Change	
	California	U.S.	California	U.S.	California	U.S.
Mining	0.4	1.1	0.4	0.8	-0.2	-3.9
Construction	4.4	4.9	4.6	4.9	3.5	1.6
Manufacturing	20.3	22.5	18.3	19.1	0.5	-1.1
Transportation	5.5	5.7	5.1	5.3	1.0	0.3
Wholesale & Ret. Trade	23.1	22.7	24.1	23.7	3.3	2.4
Fin., Ins., Real Estate	6.3	5.7	6.8	6.3	3.9	3.7
Services	22.0	19.6	24.5	23.2	4.6	5.0
Government	18.0	17.9	16.3	16.8	0.6	0.6
Total	9,837	90,657	11,271	99,610	2.4	1.6

* Totals may reflect rounding error.

Source: U.S. Department of Labor, Bureau of Labor Statistics, Employment and Earnings, vol. 34, no. 5 (May 1987), pp. 120-128; idem, vol. 28, no. 5 (May 1981), pp. 120-131.

California has a large internal market for telecommunications equipment.   Californians buy $300 million worth of PBXs annually. California-manufactured PBXs sold for $500 million in 1985, with Rolm Corporation of Santa Clara selling 500,000 lines a year.[7] California makers of LANs, which accounts for one-fifth of the country's total production, include Ungermann-Bass in Santa Clara, Apple Computers in Cupertino, and Sytek in Mountain View.[8]

Table 2.2
Employment Shares and Annual Changes in Employment* of
Telecommunications-Intensive Businesses** for California
and the United States, 1980 and 1984
(share and change in %)

| | Employment Shares | | | | Annual Employment Change | |
| | 1980 | | 1984 | | | |
	Calif.	U.S.	Calif.	U.S.	Calif.	U.S.
Information Services	10.4	9.1	10.8	9.9	3.1	3.2
Finance	3.2	2.8	3.2	2.9	1.5	2.2
Insurance	2.1	2.3	2.0	2.3	0.3	1.0
Real Estate	1.8	1.3	1.7	1.4	-0.4	1.6
Computer/Data Proc.	0.6	0.4	0.8	0.6	11.3	13.1
Other Information Svcs.	2.6	2.1	2.8	2.3	6.9	4.5
Info. Technology Equip.	4.5	2.2	4.8	2.3	2.1	2.4
Research & Development	0.4	0.3	0.5	0.3	3.3	2.9
Media	4.4	3.7	4.8	3.7	2.2	0.5

* Totals may reflect rounding error.

** The Telecommunications-Intensive Business categories are defined by Standard Industrial Classification codes as follows:
    1. Information Services: Finance: SIC 60 (Banking), SIC 61 (Credit), SIC 62 (Commodities); Insurance: SIC 63 (Insurance Carriers), SIC 64 (Insurance Agents); Real Estate: SIC 65; Computer/Data Proc.: SIC 737; Other Information Services: SIC 731 (Advertising), SIC 732 (Credit Reporting), SIC 81 (Legal Services), SIC 891 (Engineering and Architectural Services), SIC 893 (Accounting and Auditing);
    2. Information Technology Equipment: SIC 3573 (Electronic Computing Equipment), SIC 361 (Electronic Distributing Equipment), SIC 365 (Radio and TV Receiving Equipment), SIC 366 (Communications Equipment), SIC 367 (Electronic Components and Accessories);
    3. Research and Development: SIC 7391 (Research and Development Laboratories), SIC 7397 (Commercial Testing Laboratories), SIC 892 (Nonprofit Education and Scientific Research Agencies);
    4. Media: SIC 27 (Printing and Publishing), SIC 48 (Communications), SIC 735 (News Syndicates), SIC 78 (Motion Pictures).

Source: U.S. Bureau of the Census, County Business Patterns, United States (No. 1) and California (No. 8) (Washington, D.C.: U.S. Government Printing Office, 1980 and 1984), Table C.

Fiber optic technology is also very much in evidence in California. Pacific Bell has 6,000 miles, US Sprint has 1,600 miles, MCI has 400 miles along the California Aqueduct, and AT&T has 700 miles. In addition, US Sprint has a San Francisco-to-New York link and a Los Angeles-to-South

Carolina link as part of the first nationwide all-digital fiber optic network. Fiber optic technology will soon allow for transpacific communications, and the California Department of Commerce estimates that calls from Japan to Europe via fiber optic cable will become a reality in 1988.[9] Clearly, such a reliable, state-of-the-art communications link to the Asian markets will have a positive impact on business in California.

Most of the state of California is also served by cellular telephone. The car telephone is considered a practical business tool. Furthermore, the Los Angeles area is the heart of the world's largest cellular network. PacTel Mobile Access has over 50,000 customers.[10] Cellular telephone is also an area of major foreign investment, witnessed by Japan's NEC America plant in Roseville.[11]

Major satellite communications manufacturers, like California Microwave of Sunnyvale, are located in the state,[12] and satellite communication systems are used by universities, businesses, and the state. In addition, the Bay Area Teleport (BAT) makes extensive use of satellites to connect with the Pacific Rim countries and Europe.

Following the breakup of AT&T in January 1984, the state's major provider of telecommunications services became Pacific Bell and 25 other small telephone companies. Pacific Bell, the primary subsidiary of Pacific Telesis Group, the regional Bell company, provides local telephone service to over eight million customers within the 10 LATAs of California.

Table 2.3
Local Exchange Carriers and Access Lines
in California, January 1987

Local Exchange Carrier	Access Lines	Share of Total (%)*
Pacific Bell	13,600,000	80.0
GTE	3,000,000	17.6
Contel	200,000	1.2
Others**	200,000	1.2
Total	17,000,000	100.0

* Totals may reflect rounding error.

** Includes 23 other local exchange carriers.

<u>Source</u>: Pacific Bell, Public Affairs Department, May 3, 1988.

Pacific Bell earned $1.08 billion in income out of $8.98 billion in revenues in 1986. Equal access is available in 73 percent of Pacific Bell telephone exchanges. It also has 12,063,000 network access lines in service, an increase of 433,000 since 1985.[13] The second major provider for local telephone service is GTE of California. It has approximately 3 million access lines in California, which is about 17.5 percent of the total market share (Table 2.3).

Long distance communications are provided by a number of competitive carriers. AT&T dominates with 75 percent of the market share. Other major carriers are MCI, US Sprint, and Allnet.

California's telecommunications manufacturing industry is very healthy and represents a vital portion of the nation's capacity. Telecommunications providers are plentiful and include a cross-section of the nation's largest. In computers and PBX manufacturing as well as construction of fiber optic cables, California is a national leader.

POLICY ENVIRONMENT

The most highly visible political phenomenon to occur in California in recent years, the Proposition 13 tax revolt, signaled the increasingly conservative bent of California politics. The state was known for its massive investments in infrastructure in the late 1950s and 1960s, which doubtless had much to do with its rapid economic growth during that time. Slowing economic growth, the growing burden of government due to Governor Pat Brown's large investments in infrastructure, and the election of Ronald Reagan as governor in 1966 managed to put government on the defensive by the late 1970s and early 1980s. Reagan's successful campaign for governor in 1966 attacked high taxes and large spending programs. Under Reagan's leadership, investment in infrastructure declined, and there were few new policy initiatives.[14] The election of Jerry Brown, although a Democrat, saw no resumption of activist state government. Brown called for an "era of limits" and was more concerned with the environment than with developing the state's economy. Indeed, Brown was concerned that economic growth was having adverse consequences on the environment.

Proposition 13 further limited the latitude for state government initiatives. Passed in 1978, Proposition 13 limited the property taxation powers of local governments. Because of the resulting revenue shortfall at the local level, the state called upon its revenue surplus to aid localities.[15] Naturally this constrained the ability of state government to undertake new initiatives.

Thus by the beginning of the 1980s, Californians' frustration with the growth of government put policymakers on notice: keep the burdens of government light or face an electoral backlash. The election of a Republican governor in 1982, George Deukmejian, further reinforced the growing conservative tendency of California politics. It was in this environment that the state had to deal with the divestiture of the Bell System in 1984. As the "era of limits" required the state to move slowly in other policy areas, so did it require that it move slowly in dealing with divestiture.

REGULATORY POLICY

Although committed to network modernization and efficiency in telecommunications markets, preservation of universal service was the primary policy goal of the California Public Utilities Commission (CPUC) immediately after divestiture.[16] One California administrative law judge referred to universal service as the one beacon to guide policy in the turbulent aftermath of divestiture. Since then, California regulators, like those in other states, have equated universal service with low residential rates; this has required continued subsidization of local rates by long distance service. The concern for universal service, added to a policy environment in which the burden of government had to remain light, explains why California regulators were so concerned with keeping residential rates low after divestiture. California regulators have been relatively more willing to pursue social policy through rate design and have placed less emphasis on new products and technological change than other states.[17]

Telecommunications infrastucture has been linked to social goals by the Intelligent Network Task Force in California. The task force, formed by Pacific Bell, was made up of citizens representing various residential user groups, as well as educators and health care providers. The group's October 1987 report concluded that building sophistication into California's telecommunications system is a necessity of all participants in the information economy if the United States is to avoid developing a society of information "haves" and "have-nots."[18] Recommendations emphasized residential customer use of the intelligent network for access to education, emergency services, security, health care, and even employment through telecommuting. Social goals such as automatic language translation--important in a state like California with a large immigrant population--and services to the elderly and disabled should be and can be achieved through the intelligent network. The task force recommended expanding the definition of universal service to include the intelligent network features. Costs of the network, rates and rate structure were not discussed, although the group supports including intelligent network services in the state's Lifeline program.

The Moore Universal Telephone Service Act, passed in 1983, demonstrates how California telecommunications policy is oriented toward the consumer. The act issued a tax on long distance revenues, which were used to subsidize telephone rates for the disadvantaged and to maintain affordable service and a high rate of telephone penetration (currently 95 percent statewide). State Assemblywoman Gwen Moore, chair of the Utilities and Commerce Committee, introduced more than a dozen new telecommunications bills to the state legislature in 1987. The most important bill is A.B. 389, establishing a research institute for telecommunications and information policy research. Another important bill, A.B. 456, was a telecommunications appropriations act requiring the Telecommunications Division of the Department of General Services to implement at least two regional telecommunications master plans. It was vetoed by Governor Deukmejian.

The CPUC's refusal to allow intraLATA competition is part of the commission's commitment to keep local rates low. By refusing to allow entry into the intraLATA toll market, local exchange companies are able to keep intraLATA rates high; the profits gained from intraLATA toll calls can be used to subsidize local rates, thereby keeping residential rates low. The rationale for adopting this policy reflects the careful approach to policy evident in the state in recent years. The CPUC felt that once competition in intraLATA markets was permitted, there would be no turning back.[19] If competition forced intraLATA toll rates down and local rates up, there would be no way to turn carriers out of the intraLATA toll market. So the commission opted for a policy of delay.

This contrasts sharply with the "least worse off" theory propounded by Illinois policymakers whereby competition was permitted just so damage to the local network and increases in local rates would be minimized.

The CPUC nonetheless recognizes that LECs operate in markets with varying degrees of competitiveness. In 1985 the CPUC conducted a study of the telecommunications markets in the state. It concluded that competition is workable in several segments of the interLATA market. These segments are high-density toll routes and large business applications. In a follow-up study in 1986, these conclusions were reaffirmed; the study also emphasized that local residential service would not become competitive in the foreseeable future.

In the long distance market, the CPUC and FCC have been using a dominant/nondominant regulatory approach, whereby AT&T's prices are controlled on a cost-of-service basis while its smaller competitors are free to set their own prices. Substantial long distance price cuts have occurred due to increased volume and to reductions in the fees of carrier access charges. In 1985 the commission issued an Order Instituting Investigation (OII) to decide whether AT&T should continue to be regulated by the cost-of-service approach or be granted some flexibility. AT&T and the other common carriers argue that the CPUC should permit them to compete within the intraLATA market.

Pressure from the industry, technological change making market entry easier, and California's new interest in economic development have all forced the CPUC to reconsider its traditionally protective regulatory policy.

Alternative Regulatory Framework for LECs

Rapidly changing technology, increasing competition, and political pressures have pushed the CPUC to consider alternative methods of regulating the long distance and local exchange carriers. After the divestiture of AT&T, the CPUC granted the LECs monopoly status for services provided within the LATAs. The main reason for this monopoly was to keep basic telephone rates low and affordable. Since divestiture, basic rates have remained stable, mainly because of the efficiency of the providers in cutting costs. Pacific Bell and other carriers (GTE, Continental) requested more flexibility in pricing and entry for services that are competitive or subject to technological change. In September of 1987, the CPUC held hearings on alternatives to cost-of-service regulation for LECs. The competitors of the LECs agreed that pricing flexibility ought to be granted under certain conditions. Following the hearings, the CPUC adopted a three-phase procedural framework for its new regulatory policy.

Phase I: Pricing flexibility

The pricing flexibility phase will focus on enhanced services such as private lines, Centrex, and special access services; basic residential services, single-line business service, and switched access services will be excluded in this stage. The CPUC will monitor how pricing flexibility for these services affects LECs, their competitors, and customers.

Phase II: Alternative approaches to ratemaking

The second phase will be the consideration of alternatives to the CPUC's current ratemaking structure. The main obstacle here is to prevent cross-subsidization between monopolistic and competitive services within a single carrier. One approach would be to separate revenue requirements for competitive services from revenue requirements for other services.

Phase III: IntraLATA message toll service competition

In this final phase the CPUC will consider lifting the ban on competition for intraLATA message toll service. The main question here is how competitive the service would be if the ban were lifted.

The CPUC's reconsideration of its regulatory policies represents a departure from commission policy of the first few years after divestiture. Whereas protection of universal service has been the commission's overriding goal, two additional goals have come to the forefront of the CPUC's policy agenda. In addition to protecting universal service, the commission now seeks also to maximize the availability of state-of-the-art services and maintain a desirable business climate for the information industry.[20]

New Regulatory Framework for AT&T

Currently AT&T is regulated by the cost-of-service method, which has been used to protect customers from the market dominance of AT&T (which is roughly 75 percent). In July 1987 the CPUC issued a decision allowing AT&T to request changes in regulatory requirements using either of two approaches, the Prediction Approach or the Observation Approach.

Under the Prediction Approach, flexibility in regulation will be granted only in services in which the CPUC could determine beforehand that AT&T has no power to dominate the market. Such an approach is very hard to implement because of the difficulty in measuring the market power of the company. Under the Observation Approach, the effects of regulatory flexibility will be monitored following program implementation rather than predicted in advance.

AT&T followed the Observation Approach and filed on October 30, 1987, seeking regulatory flexibility. AT&T requests that narrow price bands be established around current rates and that it be allowed to adjust prices within these bands. In addition, AT&T requests that it be allowed to introduce new services on the same basis as OCCs by Advice Letter filings effective five days prior to the CPUC approval. On the other hand, AT&T will maintain statewide average rates and will introduce new services on a statewide basis.

The goal of the new regulatory alternatives being examined by the PUC is to encourage the carriers to operate more efficiently while offering more sophisticated and affordable services. The carriers, for their part, are understandably in favor of these initiatives, which are likely to lessen the burden of regulation. They also feel that the freedom to offer enhanced services will discourage bypass.

Bypass

Consistent with its policy of keeping local rates low, the CPUC has attempted to discourage bypass of the local network by large users. Pacific Bell's April 1987 bypass report estimates that losses from service and facilities bypass totalled $381 million in 1987 and will total $491 million in 1988.

Although Pacific Bell has every reason to overstate the amount of bypass of the local network, the CPUC has responded to the bypass threat. First, the commission has ruled that the amounts paid by long distance carriers for access be reduced gradually. While this will increase local rates slightly, the CPUC believes that, with improvements in productivity, revenue increases will offset the increases in local rates. Second, the CPUC has recently given Pacific Bell new flexibility in charging cost-based prices to individual large customers (companies with more than 400 lines) rather than the traditional average-cost rates. This will enable Pacific Bell to compete with new service providers who are attempting to capture the large business market while at the same time discouraging uneconomic bypass of the local exchange.

Encouraging more competition in telecommunications markets and allowing carriers greater flexibility, a trend evident in the other states in this study, seems finally to be sweeping into California. The CPUC's plan to transfer all nontraffic-sensitive (NTS) costs to end users by 1991 indicates a significant departure from policies protective of the status quo since divestiture. The question that remains is why this change has come about. Simply observing that California is finally doing what other states did several years ago is not sufficient. The following section on economic development will show that California's economic problems of the 1970s and 1980s have forced a fundamental reevaluation of how the state should promote economic growth. This change in outlook has been an important environmental factor in the state's move to encourage more competition in telecommunications.

ECONOMIC DEVELOPMENT
The State and Economic Development

Because of California's history of economic vitality and growth, there was little pressure for the state to adopt an economic development policy for many years. Rather than serving as a catalyst for economic growth through targeted programs, state government sought to maintain California's attractiveness as a place to do business. Traditionally, this meant large investments in the physical and educational infrastructure. Much of this investment came under the administration of Governor Pat Brown from 1958 to 1966. Brown invested heavily in highway construction, higher education, and water projects at a rate more than twice that of the population growth during this period. The administrations of Reagan and Jerry Brown saw an end to the massive investments in infrastructure that characterized the Pat Brown years. By 1982, the state was investing only 1.8 percent of its gross product in infrastructure, down sharply from the 2.4 percent level of the late 1960s and early 1970s. It is worth noting that all states curtailed investment in infrastructure during this period.[21]

The relatively poor performance of the California economy in the 1980s (manufacturing employment fell by 3.8 percent in the 1981-82 recession) has prompted the state to take a more aggressive stance toward economic development.[22] Among the agencies established or revived as part of this new effort were the Department of Commerce, the Commission for Economic Development, the California State World Trade Commission, and the California Economic Development Commission (CEDC). The CEDC contracted a study on the implications of telecommunications policy on the state's economy. The thrust of this report, to be discussed more fully below, is that California can no longer afford to lag behind other states in telecommunications policy. Telecommunications markets should be opened to competition while the subsidization of local rates by toll service are curtailed. The state should drive prices toward costs, deaverage rates across geographical areas, permit carriers greater pricing flexibility, and allow carriers more latitude to negotiate contracts with large users.[23]

The State of California does not explicitly link telecommunications with economic development. Personnel in the California Department of Commerce, the California Chamber of Commerce, the CEDC, and other public and private agencies indicate that telecommunications, although recognized as an important industry in the state, is not the target of explicit state economic development policy. The state has, however, begun to recognize the importance of the telecommunications infrastructure to its economic future.

The locus of this recognition has been in the California Economic Development Corporation, which is currently examining the state's economic future in the Vision California 2010 project. The CEDC contracted with Professor Robert Harris of the School of Business of the University of California at Berkeley to report on the relationship of telecommunications with the future of California economic growth. Telecommunications, argues Harris, is important to California's economy not only because of the growing importance of information on economic activity but also because of California's large telecommunications equipment manufacturing sector. Competition should generate more use of telecommunications services, argues Harris, thus stimulating demand for California-made equipment. More competition should also decrease costs of the information services that all businesses are becoming increasingly dependent upon. With location decisions of firms becoming more influenced by availability and costs of telecommunications, greater competition should, by reducing costs, benefit the state's economy.

Harris claims that telecommunications policy must broaden. Regulators, who most often see themselves as guardians of ratepayers' interests, must now see themselves as guardians of citizens as wage earners.[24] Because other states have moved more quickly than California in bringing competition to telecommunications, the state can no longer afford to wait. California is presently stalled in the framework of rate of return regulation and must move toward greater regulatory flexibility and deregulation of services where warranted. The state must, however, move slowly and incrementally in this direction, since immediate deregulation in the presence of cross-subsidies, which keep intraLATA toll rates high, would send the wrong price signals to the market. NTS costs must be moved to the end user, thus ending cross-subsidies and creating a market in which prices reflect costs. Carriers must also be granted the freedom to enter into contracts with large users, be granted depreciation rates that permit network modernization, and be given pricing flexibility.

If all these steps are taken, argues Harris, the economic benefits of the telecommunications network will increase for California. Universal service should, Harris continues, remain a policy goal, but must no longer be promoted through cross- subsidies. California's existing lifeline program, funded through a gross revenue tax on interLATA toll revenues, is a more efficient way to ensure universal service than cross-subsidization. Harris also points out that with technological advances in telecommunications, the state must reconsider the meaning of universal service. If policymakers decide that universal service includes certain enhanced services, direct targeted subsidies may be warranted.[25]

How much impact Harris's report will have on California policy is unclear at this time. The fact that economic development officials have recognized the role of telecommunications in the state's economy is important in itself. Moreover, the CPUC is already considering some of the steps Harris recommends, such as allowing intraLATA competition and placing NTS on end users. Although a direct link between telecommunications and economic development remains distant, the economic development debate in California is being recast to include telecommunications.

Another focus of California economic development efforts has been the attraction of foreign investment. Over 1,100 investments by foreigners have occurred in the past ten years, employing over 300,000 Californians.[26] Whereas no hard evidence is available at this time, examples (like NEC America of Japan locating in Roseville) tend to support the notion that initiatives by the state encourage high-tech development in California. Again, the CEDC has been active in this effort; it recently appointed a task force to promote trade with Pacific Rim countries. The Pacific Rim Task Force is composed of prominent public and private leaders looking for ways to expand trade with this region, which has become more prominent in America's trade structure. Asia, especially Japan, is a large market for telecommunications equipment, one of California's largest manufactures, in addition to being a large producer of telecommunications equipment itself. The General Assembly's Committee on Economic Development and New Technologies held a seminar in 1986 examining ways in which trade with the Pacific Rim influences California's economy. Among the issues discussed was what type of infrastructure, such as ports and education, would be needed to use trade with the Pacific Rim to best advantage.[27] Although the telecommunications infrastructure was not discussed in this seminar, there is awareness in the state that telecommunications will be vital to connect California with global markets.[28]

California's shift from a passive economic development effort to an active one has led to a recognition that telecommunications policy matters to the state's economy. Although, as Harris notes, there is no crisis in telecommunications in the state, the perception that the state must act in economic development has moved the telecommunications policy debate beyond the CPUC. Economic development concerns also seem to have shifted policy debate within the CPUC away from an exclusive concern with universal service. The commission's plan to transfer all NTS costs to end users by 1991 is a case in point. The CPUC is also considering whether to permit competition in intraLATA toll service. How far the commission will go in introducing competition in telecommunications markets remains an open question.

It is now widely recognized that telecommunications is an important infrastructure resource with great ramifications on the development of the state's economy. New work by the Berkeley Roundtable on the International Economy, the Vision California 2010 project, the CPUC, and certain legislators suggests a higher profile for telecommunications on the state's policy agenda in the future.

INNOVATIVE USES OF TELECOMMUNICATIONS: PUBLIC AND PRIVATE

In California innovation can be seen in various uses of telecommunications by the state (including usage and procurement, strategies and planning, and telecommunications programs), in the private sector (Pacific Bell, AT&T, MCI, Bay Area Teleport, Transamerica Corporation, Hewlett Packard, Bechtel Group, and McKesson Corporation), and in other policies (telecommuting). These innovative uses demonstrate advanced thinking in telecommunications use and planning in California.

State Initiatives

Usage and procurement policy

State usage and procurement policy in California has three segments: state networks, strategies and planning, and selected government telecommunications applications.

The Telecommunications Division of the California Department of General Services (DGS) manages and operates the three major state networks: the Public Safety Microwave System; the Automatic Telecommunications Switching System (ATSS); and the Consolidated Exchange Service.

The Public Safety Microwave System serves 15 state, local, and federal agencies at over 250 locations throughout the state, which involve more than 85 urban/suburban areas. The system contains more than 65,000 circuit miles on eight major backbone systems that are used mostly for voice communications only.[29]

ATSS provides service to about 210,000 government telephone users throughout the state in over 120 state, county, and local agency offices. Three network switches in Los Angeles, Sacramento, and Oakland support the system at a total cost of $25.9 million in FY 1985-86.

The University of California System is in the process of implementing a new telecommunications infrastructure. The University of California Intercampus Telecommunication Network will interconnect the nine University of California campuses, the Office of the President, the three physically separate medical centers, and the three national laboratories. The network will be high-capacity, multifunctional, and cost-effective. The network will deliver voice, data, and video communications through a transmission medium that uses digital technology.

As another example of state involvement in telecommunications, the State of California also operates a Consolidated Exchange Service to multiple users in cities, counties, and agencies throughout the state. The Consolidated Exchange Service serves over 90,000 telephones in 46 exchanges at a cost of $36 million per year.[30]

Strategies and Planning

Use of telecommunications by the California state government is officially coordinated through the Department of General Services' Telecommunications Division and the Department of Finance's Office of Information Technology. Unofficially, however, other state agencies, like the

Department of Water Resources, have also helped establish telecommunications usage policy. Friction has often characterized the relationship between General Services and the Office of Information Technology (OIT) as a result of struggles over jurisdiction and control of telecommunications and data processing/data transmission. An attempt was made by the legislature to consolidate the offices, but Governor Deukmejian vetoed the effort at the request of both agencies. Apparently, neither office cared to risk losing its authority. In 1986 the California legislature passed S.B. 1733, which directed DGS to be the manager of the state's telecommunications program, leaving OIT in charge of only the data processing and data transmission part of telecommunications. Therefore, a compromise was reached to appease state personnel, seemingly without high regard to efficiency or effectiveness.

The major achievement in planning efforts so far has been Telecommunications Strategy for State Government, a 1987 Department of General Services report which updated a 1984 version. The first report was written as a response to the divestiture of AT&T and the beginning of deregulation in telecommunications. State personnel felt that old policies would no longer be sufficient in the era of competition. The Telecommunications Division of DGS developed, and is operating under, eight key strategies, the main thrust of which is to upgrade the state networks to digital technology, improve management of telecommunications, improve delivery of state services, and reduce costs. DGS knew that the state could and should no longer depend solely on AT&T for all of its telecommunications needs. Therefore, the state wanted to more effectively and efficiently manage its operations and search for the best telecommunications bargains.

Innovative Public Telecommunications

An innovative network of fiber optic cables has been installed by MCI for the state along the aqueduct system of the Department of Water Resources (DWR). The fiber optic cables run north and south across California from east of the San Francisco Bay Area to just east of Los Angeles. The DWR started negotiations with MCI by offering MCI the right-of-way access that the aqueducts provided if MCI would lay down a set of fiber optic cables for DWR ownership and use. The DWR wanted fiber optic cables to control its many operations, and MCI wanted to expand its long distance network.

When the Telecommunications Division discovered what the DWR was considering, it also wanted access. The Telecommunications Division wants to install fiber optic cables and digital microwave links to connect the north-south network to the main cities of Sacramento, Los Angeles, and San Francisco. In this way California's major government offices and centers of population will be linked with a cost-effective and state-of-the-art telecommunications network that should significantly improve coordination and provision of state services. The innovative aspects of this project include the use of the aqueduct right of way for installation of fiber optic cables and the leadership of the Department of Water Resources instead of the designated Telecommunications Division.

Another fiber optic cable project involves linking 15 major state buildings in Sacramento's capitol mall. The state will soon install fiber optic cables in underground conduits running through the downtown. Services will include voice, data, and eventually video transmission. The innovation in this project is the linking of California government offices together with a high-tech communications system installed in existing conduits.

The California Department of Corrections uses videoconferencing technology in its operations. The Vacaville Medical Facility uses video to examine inmates incarcerated in the state's many distant prisons. Vacaville medical and psychiatric personnel conduct examinations remotely without the expense and security risks of transporting dangerous criminals.

The Northern California Youth Reception Center (NCYRC) has also used videoconferencing to help rehabilitate clients. Poor Bay Area families of the young offenders often cannot afford to visit their children in the distant Stockton facility due to transportation costs and the problem of missing work. Since experts have determined that visits and consultations with family are important steps in the rehabilitation process, locations in San Francisco were chosen for video links with NCYRC to reduce the costs of imprisonment and lessen the costs to society as a result of lost employment and earnings.

The Department of Corrections and the NCYRC are examples of state agencies using telecommunications to improve established services. Other large states with offices distributed widely over a great geographical area could find that videoconferencing programs like California's could help improve their services and save money.

Finally, the fact that the Department of General Services is seeking competitive bids for replacing the current state telecommunications system is of special interest. The state's system, the ATSS and Centrex systems, are leased from AT&T and Pacific Bell. The state wants to abandon these leased analog networks and purchase a digitally switched system. The award for the new system is expected to be made in mid-1988. This digital network would also prepare for ISDN, although it is not now a high priority.

The state of California seems to take a strategy of decentralization in telecommunications usage. Agencies take the initiative in using the network in an innovative ways rather than taking direction from a central authority. In a sense, agencies serve as laboratories for usage, the most innovative of which may serve as models for other agencies in the state.

Private Initiatives

Although Pacific Bell's George Schmitt has admitted that it is very difficult to link California's growth with telecommunications, the company has a policy of trying to keep commercial telephone rates low enough to attract businesses without sacrificing quality. As a result, Pacific Bell feels that private enterprise across the country will get the message that California has low, stable rates and high-quality service, which should be attractive to information-intensive businesses. Schmitt believes that national trends reveal a tendency for less and less concentration of power in big companies and more and more development in small companies. Small businesses in small communities now form the cutting edge in economic development. New businesses do not incur high telecommunications startup costs in California due to low telephone rates. Pacific Bell gained over 400,000 new customers during 1987.[31]

Likewise, AT&T personnel do not stress any form of explicit telecommunications links with economic development policy.[32] AT&T does claim, however, that the proposed implementation of regulatory flexibility will allow it to more rapidly offer better services to businesses at competitive rates without going through time-consuming and inefficient rate cases. AT&T is also offering Software Defined Networks (SDN), which will allow customers to control their own networks and provide cost savings with improved service. However, SDN was the last new service that AT&T was allowed to introduce in California, and this took place in 1985.

MCI Communications Corporation has implemented electronic mail services for Century 21 of the Pacific, a large real estate firm that has property listings and real estate deals from Los Angeles to Guam. MCI's electronic mail service allows Century 21 to be more competitive. MCI's electronic mail is also used to send standardized electronic real estate proposals almost immediately from office to office, thereby handling in just hours matters that formerly took weeks.[33] Accelerating the rate of business in the real estate industry could significantly expedite home and commercial property sales, hasten business relocation, and generally improve customer satisfaction.

The Bay Area Teleport

The San Francisco Bay Area is a well-known center for high-technology and financial services business. Telecommunications is a new area of investment. The Bay Area Teleport (BAT) is a private investment response in this competitive, dynamic region. The BAT, a real estate project based in Alameda and developed by Doric Development and Northern Telecom, is linked to the largest antenna facility in the world, the Niles Canyon Earth Station, and a 3,600-mile regional digital microwave network. This network, linking major cities from Sacramento to San Francisco to Silicon Valley, allows users to bypass the LECs and connect through the BAT and long distance companies and the antenna earth station directly to Europe and Asia.[34]

The development of the BAT, which became operational February 2, 1986, may signify many things. The new regulatory environment has allowed the initial development of the teleport. Although the real estate development to which the BAT is related, the Bay Area Business Park, has been under construction since the early 1970s, the teleport itself was born in the days just prior to and immediately following the divestiture of AT&T, which encouraged the BAT's founders and others to take advantage of new investment opportunities.

The BAT's claims to economic development are of interest. Businesses will be able to communicate with voice, video, and data to both Europe and Japan and all points in between on the same day and through the same location. Furthermore, some observers believe teleports to be future sites of company locations,[35] which has implications for economic development. Interestingly, $200 million is spent annually on telecommunications in the San Francisco Bay Area, which is also home to 34 of the Fortune 1000 businesses. In addition, Silicon Valley, a high-technology hub, is just south of San Francisco. BAT personnel believe that a $50 million market is available to them during the next five years.[36]

In fact, the Bay Area and Silicon Valley are also crucial factors for the development of the BAT. BAT customers include the major domestic providers of long distance telecommunications, financial institutions, government offices, other businesses, and international telecommunications firms like US Sprint International, ITT World Com, and COMSAT International. Whereas no evidence yet exists of any major company locating next to the BAT just to take advantage of the telecommunications technology, most of the firms located on the BAT's business park and real estate complex subscribe to the BAT's services. In an indirect way, then, the BAT has already had an impact on telecommunications use in northern California.

Clearly, the BAT has not been responsible for the past regional economic development in the Bay Area, high-technology-based growth in the area preceded development of the BAT by at least 20 years. Therefore, the argument could be made that the BAT was developed in Alameda to take advantage of existing business rather than to generate new economic development.

The impact of the BAT can be considered to be mixed. The teleport can be lauded as a component of modern regional economic development or criticized as merely a way to bypass the local exchange. Pacific Bell feels quite strongly that the BAT is only a bypasser, an understandable view in that BAT customers are certainly able to bypass Pacific Bell through the BAT's digital microwave network and satellite hookups.[37] Staffers for legislators have given similar arguments.

However, bypass is not the only reason for the teleport's existence. Phase I of the project is the business park, which includes the teleport and companies like Litton Industries Integrated, DEC, Rand Information Systems, and Triton Biosciences, Inc.'s Genetic Engineering Laboratories (the Shell Oil medical research branch). Phase II includes a world trade center, a bank, and incubator space for the startup of high- tech industries. Phase III is an international research complex that will include a new product demonstration center, the University of California Research and Patent Center, and a branch of the Lawrence Livermore Laboratories. The main projects of these phases are expected to be completed within the next ten years.

The three prongs of the teleport--the intelligent park (local area network, shared tenant services), the intelligent region (microwave towers throughout northern California from Sacramento to Silicon Valley), and the earth station antenna complex--are seen by the BAT as an emerging global center for telecommunications and economic development. As noted before, these developments could merely be targeted at exploiting the existing business in the area.

The challenge to achieve economic development, according to a BAT vice-president, is to bring pure research and development to market (the transfer of technology) as quickly as possible, keeping the development of such technology within the region.[38] Discussions with legislative staff in Sacramento verify this view.

Although the BAT is a vehicle for bypass, BAT personnel and others believe that bypass on this scale represents one way to communicate, and therefore conduct business, more powerfully than ever before. Although Pacific Bell may be annoyed at the teleport, companies may use the teleport to their advantage. If proof could be found to show that the teleport has provided a competitive advantage for those firms using it and that, as a consequence, these successful companies have fostered economic growth in the region, then the BAT should be viewed as a link between telecommunications and economic development. Regulatory policy would then (and probably only then) need to be reformed so that other telecommunications providers and private businesses could take advantage of this concept since, it is assumed, society as a whole benefits. However, this is merely an assumption, and the relative novelty of the BAT and teleports in general means that little information is available.

Transamerica Corporation

A popular use of telecommunications in large businesses is to coordinate the often far-flung resources and offices of a corporation through various methods. The Transamerica Corporation, an insurance company headquartered in San Francisco, uses a shared data network to unite its branch offices, thereby saving costs.[39] Doubtless other firms have acted similarly. This is an example of how a large organization can centralize major investments and costs while decentralizing the exploitation of these resources via telecommunications.

Hewlett Packard

Hewlett Packard, one of the original Silicon Valley high-tech companies, has used telecommunications in many innovative ways. For example, engineers in Grenoble, France, work at a computer interface and then send the day's work to their counterparts in Palo Alto, who manipulate the circuit designs and operating codes and then send them back to the engineers in France where the new day is starting.[40] Here telecommunications replaces an older form of communication, mail service, which itself replaces personal travel. Hewlett Packard engineers also use videoconferencing to communicate with colleagues in Geneva, Switzerland.[41] The major consideration here was not the costs saved but rather the speed with which new products could be introduced, which in the rapidly changing high-tech industry is all- important. Hewlett Packard also uses videoconferencing to train employees and allow them to attend college classes. Thus telecommunications technology is used to strengthen employees' skills, a vital asset to the company in this extremely competitive industry.

Bechtel Group

For information-intensive companies that employ field personnel, telecommunications can improve service for both the firm and its clients. Bechtel engineers are linked to company computers by satellites and other lines when they are at a remote project site.[42] This concept has parallels with the Transamerica example discussed earlier, where a large firm with diverse operations centralizes some investments while decentralizing their use. Bechtel also wished to use the ISDN technology; however, lack of a public ISDN forced Bechtel, with AT&T's help, to develop its own ISDN in order to link its computer-aided design and engineering workstations, even though it would have preferred the public network.[43] This is an example of the impact of regulatory policy, set by the FCC, which limited Pacific Bell's capability in instituting a public ISDN (like Project Victoria).

McKesson Corporation

McKesson Corporation of San Francisco is the nation's biggest nondurable consumer goods distributor. McKesson's computerized ordering system requires that customers, rather than McKesson, enter orders, a shift in responsibility from firm to client.[44] Orders are then automatically processed by McKesson. Information gathered by McKesson on its distributions is a source of market data, which McKesson sells to retailers. Retailers who use

McKesson find that switching costs if they consider changing to another distributor. Retailers become dependent on McKesson's system in that they must learn a different system if they decide to work with another distributor.[45] This also makes it difficult for others to compete with McKesson.

McKesson has used telecommunications to improve the quality and speed of service. In the process, McKesson has changed fundamentally the manner in which business is done.

Other Initiatives

Telecommuting

Telecommuting provides an example of how telecommunications can be linked to regional and urban planning. Telecommuting is the phenomenon of working at a location other than the central office but being linked to the central office by means of telecommunications technology. The importance of telecommuting lies in its impact on transportation. As a potential substitute for transportation, telecommuting can reduce traffic congestion, thereby enhancing energy conservation and improving air quality. In the future, if telecommuting becomes widespread, it will play a crucial role in urban and regional planning (land use, office space, and life patterns). Other potential benefits from telecommuting include increasing productivity and bringing mobility-limited people into the labor market. On the other hand, there are several disadvantages, such as isolation and loss of professional interaction in the office.

In California, many agencies and individuals are currently involved in telecommuting pilot projects. The Southern California Association of Government (SCAG) has recognized telecommuting as a partial solution to the traffic problem in southern California. Although there is no quantitative evidence to support their expectations, officials at SCAG estimate that telecommuting has the potential to reduce work-related automobile trips by 12 percent by the year 2000.[46]

SCAG has initiated a pilot project involving 18 employees under the auspices of the Central City Association Telecommunication Task Force. The Telecommuting Subcommittee of the task force is responsible for developing telecommuting pilots in downtown Los Angeles. The members of the subcommittee are carriers (AT&T, Pacific Bell, GTE), government agencies (Los Angeles City Department of Telecommunications, the California Department of General Services), and private companies (ARCO; Sells and Deloitte Haskins).

Another example of a pilot program is the Sacramento state government project. Selected employees will work at home on personal computers and transmit their completed work back to the main office over normal telephone lines. About 200 employees will be involved in this initial pilot project, based on a smaller project with two dozen employees that was considered a success. The state is interested in telecommuting to increase productivity, improve morale, reduce costs (of office space, energy, highway use, employee absenteeism), and reduce traffic.[47] If successful after wider implementation, the California telecommuting program could become a model for planning and reorganizing the workplace.

In Los Angeles, JobLink Watts is a new joint program of the State of California and Pacific Bell, designed to show that telecommunications technology can be used to solve chronic unemployment. It provides computer training and jobs for Watts residents. For example, data entry jobs for commercial banking and other industries are performed at Watts locations rather than the company's downtown Los Angeles headquarters. The program will train and employ a total of 40 participants by the end of 1988.[48]

The City of Los Angeles has conducted a telecommuting pilot experiment. Among the 15 employees who participated in this project, productivity increased by 60 percent and travel decreased by 400 miles. When the program receives full-scale implementation, however, productivity is expected to increase only by 15 percent.[49]

These initiatives suggest that telecommuting has substantial potential for offering solutions to the mounting congestion problems in southern California.

CONCLUSIONS

California demonstrates how a state's growing interest in economic development has altered the terms of the telecommunications policy debate. Whereas universal service was once the paramount policy goal in telecommunications, the state has begun to realize the importance of telecommunications to the economy. While it would be overstating the case to say that California's recent economic problems have caused policymakers to recognize a link between telecommunications and economic development, it is clear that the environment of increased economic development activity has contributed to a broadening of the state's telecommunications policy debate. California once relied on general policies to enhance its economic position. Under these policies the state invested heavily in education, roads, and water projects, assuming that the good business climate which followed would ensure economic growth. As the state's economy matured and growth slowed, these large investments were viewed as a burden on the taxpayer. The result was the taxpayer revolt of the late 1970s and a decline in government activism. This retreat on the part of state government was not sustainable largely because California's traditionally robust rate of economic growth did not continue. The state began, in the early 1980s, to undertake specific economic development initiatives to improve the state's competitive position. These efforts were directed primarily toward high-technology industries and trade with Pacific Rim countries.

At the same time, the state's policy priority in telecommunications moved from the general (the preservation of universal service) to more specific and complex issues (the debate over NTS, intraLATA competition, and methods of regulation). Just as the state realized it could no longer be complacent in economic development policy, it also realized that it could no longer lag behind other states in telecommunications policy. Thus regulators have recently begun to consider policies that will drive prices toward costs and increase competition. The hope is that such policies will result in a more technologically advanced telecommunications network, more efficient use of it, and a better business climate for the information industry.

California is finally undertaking the telecommunications policy steps that other states took several years ago, showing how difficult it is for one state to chart a course contrary to the remainder of the country. The pro-competitive policy initiatives of other states may well have forced the hand of California. With the belief that business location decisions are becoming more dependent on communications costs (although this study has found no empirical evidence of this), California policymakers may have felt they had no choice but to decrease the cost of business service by ending the subsidies to local service. Thus California's policy innovation may be a function of policy innovation in other states. It is worth noting that California seems to have responded not to successful policies in other states but simply to the trend of competition.

Although California is finally taking policy steps that many states took several years ago, it remains to be seen whether California's delay may alter the outcome or emphasis of these policy steps.   California's slow pace in introducing competition to telecommunications markets has allowed it to remain relatively more concerned with equity issues--namely universal service--than states which have moved more quickly toward competition. That California has resisted moves encouraging competition means that it is now more susceptible to rate shock if it quickly ends cross-subsidization.   By delaying the introduction of competition, California has backed itself into a corner, purposely it seems, in which universal service is a first among equals with its new policy goals of network modernization and a desirable business climate for the information industry. It remains to be seen whether increased competition works to the benefit of the telecommunications network of California and the nation.   What is clear is that the wave of competition has rendered telecommunications policy aimed only at the preservation of universal service a thing of the past.

NOTES

1.   California Department of Finance, Economic Report of the Governor 1986, SRI:86, S0840-3 (Sacramento, 1986).
2.   Ibid.
3.   Ibid.
4.   U.S. Department of Commerce, Bureau of the Census, Census of Manufacturing, California, 1982 (Washington, D.C.: U.S. Government Printing Office, 1982), p. PA.-12.
5.   California Department of Commerce, Telecommunications Industry: Equipment, prepared by the Institute for the Future (Menlo Park, May 1986).
6.   California Department of Commerce, The Californias: Telecommunications (Sacramento, n.d.). (Pamphlet.)
7.   Ibid.
8.   Ibid.
9.   Ibid.
10.   Ibid.
11.   Ibid.
12.   Ibid.
13.   Pacific Telesis Group, Annual Report, 1986 (San Francisco, 1987), p. 10.
14.   R. Scott Fosler, ed., The New Economic Role of American States: Strategies in a Competitive World Economy (New York: Oxford University Press, 1988), p. 218.
15.   Richard P. Nathan and Fred C. Doolittle, ed., Reagan and the States (Princeton, N.J.: Princeton University Press, 1987), p. 334.
16.   Roger G. Noll, "State Regulatory Responses to Competition and Divestiture in the Telecommunications Industry," in Antitrust and Regulation, ed.Ronald E. Grieson (Lexington, Mass.: D.C. Heath and Co., 1986), pp. 181-182.
17.   California Public Utilities Commission, Competition in Local Telecommunications: A Report to the Legislature (San Francisco, May 1987), p. 77.
18.   The Intelligent Network Task Force, Task Force Report, October 1987 (San Francisco: Pacific Bell, 1987).
19.   Noll, "State Regulatory Responses," pp. 79-80.
20.   Ibid., p. 90.
21.   Fosler, The New Economic Role, p. 215.
22.   Ibid., p. 232.
23.   Robert Harris, California Telecommunications Policy for the Twenty First Century : A Report to the California Economic Development Corporation (Berkeley, CA: University of California), pp. 39-42.
24.   Ibid., p. 24.
25.   Ibid., pp. 40-41.
26.   Interview with Brenda Lopes, Business Development Specialist, Office of Business Development, California Department of Commerce, Sacramento, January 11, 1988.
27.   California Legislature, Committee on Economic Development and New Technologies, "The Pacific Rim and the Competitive Future of California's Industries," Sacramento, 1986.

28. Harris, p. 15.
29. California Department of General Services, <u>Telecommunications Strategy for State Government</u> (Sacramento, March 1987), p. 4.
30. Ibid.
31. Interview with George Schmitt, Vice-President - Regulation, Pacific Bell, San Francisco, January 15, 1988.
32. Interview with Earl Foreshee, Vice-President, AT&T Communications of California, San Francisco, January 14, 1988.
33. MCI Communications, <u>MCI Communications Corporation Annual Report 1986</u> (Washington, D.C., 1987).
34. Bay Area Teleport, <u>Backgrounder</u>, April 1987. (Press release.)
35. Ibid.
36. John Harrison, "Teleport by the Sea," <u>Telephony</u>, July 13, 1987.
37. Interview with Schmitt.
38. Interview with Steve Wade, Assistant to the President, Bay Area Teleport, Alameda, January 15, 1988.
39. Francois Bar and Michael Borrus, <u>From Public Access to Private Connections: Network Policy and National Advantage</u>, paper presented at the Fifteenth Telecommunications Policy Research Conference, Airlie House, Virginia, September, 1987 (Berkeley: Berkeley Roundtable on the International Economy, University of California at Berkeley, 1987), p. 11.
40. Ibid.
41. Ibid., pp. 11, 13.
42. Ibid., p. 12.
43. Ibid., p. 18.
44. Ibid., p. 14.
45. Ibid.
46. Interview with Patricia Mokhtarian, Senior Planner, Telecommunications and Richard Spicer, Director, Southern California Association of Government, Los Angeles, January 5, 1988.
47. California Department of General Services, <u>Telecommunications Strategy for State Government</u>, p. 17.
48. Correspondence with Treva D. Metoyer, President, Joblink Watts: Telecommunications Project, Lynwood, March 25, 1987.
49. Interview with Susan Herman, Director, Department of Telecommunications, City of Los Angeles, Los Angeles, January 5, 1988.

3

Florida

Darrick Eugene and David McCarty

When telecommunications in Florida is examined, three policy findings warrant particular notice. First, telecommunications demand in the present environment is driven by the recent population growth and is expanding into existing capacity rather than requiring additional investment. Consequently the local exchange companies that overbuilt in the early 1970s are now able to keep local rates low. Second, telecommunications regulatory legislation is notably absent in Florida's regulatory environment. The Public Service Commission has achieved a high degree of respect, and the telcos feel that they will receive fair hearings. Consequently, there is little statutory regulation. However, Florida's Public Service Commission is one of the three largest in the country. This contributes to the high degree of regulation the commission is able to support.

Finally, although an explicit policy linking economic development to telecommunications does not exist, factors regarding the method of telecommunications regulation and management do imply linkages. These factors concern how the degree of regulation affects the telephone industry's ability to provide services and how telecommunications can be managed to facilitate the training and education of Florida's population. Furthermore, Florida seems to offer a clear paradigm for relating telecommunications to economic development in that economic growth is driving developments in the telecommunications industry. This relationship is exhibited by the economic position of the telcos and the innovations implemented by telecommunications-intensive businesses.

THE ECONOMY AND THE TELECOMMUNICATIONS
INDUSTRY
The Economy of the State

Florida's economy has historically depended on several industries subject to economic factors beyond the state's control: construction, agriculture, and tourism. Construction is seasonal, and slowdowns are experienced by all industries in the state. Agriculture is sensitive to extremes of weather. Tourism is directly related to the overall U.S. economy; as national inflation rates rise, the number of tourists in the state declines.

Tourism plays a major role in the state's economy. In 1986, an estimated 33.7 million tourists accounted for $17.6 billion in travel expenditures and $1.028 billion in sales tax collections. The effect of tourism on Florida's consumer market is about the same as one million additional residents, and in 1985 tourism-related sectors employed more than half a million persons.

Table 3.1
Nonagricultural Employment Shares and Annual
Percentage Change in Employment* for Florida and
the United States, 1980 and 1986
(total employees in 1,000s, share and change in %)

Sector	Employment Shares 1980		1986		Annual Employment Change	
	Florida	U.S.	Florida	U.S.	Florida	U.S.
Mining	0.3	1.1	0.2	0.8	-1.7	-3.9
Construction	7.5	4.9	7.4	4.9	4.5	1.6
Manufacturing	12.8	22.5	11.2	19.1	2.1	-1.2
Transportation	6.1	5.7	5.3	5.3	1.9	0.3
Wholesale Retail Trade	26.1	22.7	27.0	23.7	5.5	2.4
Fin., Ins., Real Estate	7.1	5.7	7.3	6.3	5.7	3.7
Services	22.8	19.6	26.2	23.2	7.9	5.0
Government	17.2	17.8	15.1	16.8	2.1	0.6
Total	3570.5	90,657	4,589	99,610	4.8	1.65

* Totals may reflect rounding error.

Source: U.S. Department of Labor, Bureau of Labor Statistics, Employment and Earnings, vol. 34, no. 5 (May 1987), pp. 120-137; idem, vol. 28, no. 5 (May 1981), pp. 120-28, no. 5 (May 1981), pp. 120-131.

Both in Florida and the United States as a whole, trade and services are the two largest industries in terms of employment (Table 3.1). In Florida, government is the third largest employer while manufacturing now ranks fourth. From 1970 to 1985 private-sector employment in Florida grew 102.1 percent compared with 37.7 percent nationally.[1]

The state is now trying to reduce its economic dependence on industries affected by climate, the national economy, and other factors beyond the state's control. By strengthening the manufacturing sector, government officials are trying to achieve a balance among tourism, agriculture, and manufacturing, especially high-technology manufacturing. Although agriculture remains a key element in the Florida economy, manufacturing has grown tremendously. Between 1980 and 1985, manufacturing employment increased 12.9 percent in Florida compared with 4.2 percent nationally. Florida ranks third in the nation in the growth of new manufacturing jobs.[2]

In particular, Florida has sought growth in high-technology manufacturing. Two major federal government programs--space and defense-- have helped provide a high-technology base in the state. According to one analysis, "Florida's industrial sector has shifted from being a construction-driven and therefore volatile sector to one driven by technology closely allied to the recession-immune defense industry."[3] Total defense spending in Florida amounted to $9.7 billion in 1985. The state now boasts 1,867 high-technology firms, accounting for 27.3 percent of the state's manufacturing jobs. In 1985 electrical and electronic equipment represented the largest single manufacturing sector. The manufacturing of machinery, which includes the manufacture of office equipment and computers, was the fifth largest sector and printing and publishing was second.[4]

Florida's growth in per capita income since 1970 almost equals national growth (Table 3.2). The absolute difference between the dollar figures is diminishing as Florida's growth rate increases. When compared with the national average of 12.1 percent in 1980, Florida has a higher percentage of individuals living below the poverty level, with 13.5 percent. However, the unemployment rate is normally lower than the national rate.

Table 3.2
Per Capita Personal Income
in Florida and the United States,
1970, 1980, and 1985
(Current Dollars)

Year	Florida	Percentage of U.S.	United States
1970	3,779	95.8	3,945
1980	4,038	96.9	4,167
1985	13,397	99.6	13,451

Source: Florida Department of Commerce, Division of Economic Development, The Florida Economy--An Analysis of the Economy and Its Industrial Structure (Tallahassee, January 1987), p. 83.

Table 3.3
Employment Shares and Annual Changes in Employment* of
Telecommunications-Intensive Businesses** for Florida
and the United States, 1980 and 1984
(share and change in %)

| | Employment Shares | | | | Annual Employment Change | |
| | 1980 | | 1984 | | | |
	Florida	U.S.	Florida	U.S.	Florida	U.S.
Information Services	10.9	9.1	11.3	9.9	4.6	3.2
Finance	3.3	3.1	3.6	3.3	6.4	3.3
Insurance	2.1	2.3	2.1	2.3	3.1	1.0
Real Estate	2.5	1.3	2.3	1.4	2.2	1.6
Comp./Data Proc.	0.4	0.4	0.5	0.6	15.0	13.1
Other Information Svcs.	2.5	2.1	2.8	2.3	9.0	4.5
Information Technology	2.1	2.2	2.3	2.3	5.0	2.4
Research and Development	0.1	0.2	0.2	0.3	7.2	2.9
Media	3.7	3.7	3.4	3.7	2.2	0.5

* Totals may reflect rounding error.

** The Telecommunications-Intensive Business categories are defined by Standard Industrial Classification codes as follows:
    1. Information Services: Finance: SIC 60 (Banking), SIC 61 (Credit), SIC 62 (Commodities); Insurance: SIC 63 (Insurance Carriers), SIC 64 (Insurance Agents); Real Estate: SIC 65; Computer/Data Proc.: SIC 737; Other Information Services: SIC 731 (Advertising), SIC 732 (Credit Reporting), SIC 81 (Legal Services), SIC 891 (Engineering and Architectural Services), SIC 893 (Accounting and Auditing);
    2. Information Technology Equipment: SIC 3573 (Electronic Computing Equipment), SIC 361 (Electronic Distributing Equipment), SIC 365 (Radio and TV Receiving Equipment), SIC 366 (Communications Equipment), SIC 367 (Electronic Components and Accessories);
    3. Research and Development: SIC 7391 (Research and Development Laboratories), SIC 7397 (Commercial Testing Laboratories), SIC 892 (Nonprofit Education and Scientific Research Agencies);
    4. Media: SIC 27 (Printing and Publishing), SIC 48 (Communications), SIC 735 (News Syndicates), SIC 78 (Motion Pictures).

Source: U.S. Bureau of the Census, County Business Patterns, United States (No. 1) and Florida (No. 11), 1980 and 1984 (Washington, D.C.: U.S. Government Printing Office, 1980 and 1984), Table 1B.

In the area of communications the state again has recorded impressive growth. Between 1970 and 1985, employment in communications sectors grew 60.0 percent, and transportation, communications, and public utilities represented 5.2 percent of Florida's total employment in the latter year.[5] For telecommunications businesses, growth in employment shares has been experienced in all sectors except media (Table 3.3). For information services, employment shares not only increased from 1980 and 1984 but also were above the U.S. average for both years.

Profiles of Telecommunications Companies

The state of Florida is divided into ten LATAs. Thirteen local exchange companies (LECs) and about 90 interexchange carriers (IXCs), including resellers, provide telephone service. In addition, the major urban areas have competitive cellular operators. Customer premises equipment is both manufactured and marketed in the state. There are 183 cable television systems in the state. Furthermore, the state of Florida operates its own, extensive telecommunications network.

The largest LEC in the state is Southern Bell, which serves the entire eastern seaboard as well as the Gainesville and Pensacola areas. In 1986, Southern Bell operated a total of 3.7 million access lines, and had 20,189 employees.

Table 3.4
Local Exchange Carriers and Access lines
in Florida, December 1986

Local Exchange Carrier	Employees	Offices	Share of Access Lines	Total (%)*
SBT&T	20,189	192	3,754,229	59.00
General	10,622	89	1,511,587	23.60
United	4,747	88	813,882	12.80
Centel	1,247	35	208,188	3.26
Alltel	239	27	45,001	0.70
St. Joseph	242	16	18,887	0.29
Others**	544	20	29,386	0.46
Total	37,830	451	6,381,160	100.00

* Totals may reflect rounding error.
** Includes seven other local exchange companies.

Source: Florida Telephone Association, Florida Telephone Association 1987 Directory (Tallahassee, 1987), pp. 8-9. (Booklet.)

General Telephone, the second largest LEC in Florida, operates 24 exchanges around the Tampa area. GTE operates 1.5 million access lines, and 1985 figures showed a total operating revenue of $1.06 billion. The company employed 10,622 persons in 1986.

United Telephone Company of Florida, operating in central Florida, is the state's third largest LEC. The fourth largest LEC, Central Telephone Company, serves the Tallahassee area. The remainder of the state is served by nine smaller LECs (Table 3.4).

The four largest interexchange carriers in Florida are AT&T, US Sprint, MCI, and MicroTel. Most of the other carriers are resellers.

Seven of the 100 largest cable systems in the United States are located in Florida. The largest cable television system in the state serves 143,500 subscribers in Orlando. Another half-dozen systems have at least 60,000 subscribers: Jacksonville (136,000), Pompano Beach (106,801), Pinellas County (94,996), Dade and Broward counties (91,511), Melbourne and Cocoa (74,200), and St. Petersburg (68,000).[6]

As of 1984, ten cable systems in the state offered interactive service. All ten offered security monitoring (narrowband) on their subscriber networks. In addition, one offered utility monitoring, one offered a news retrieval service, and one was conducting a video monitoring experiment with one subscriber. Four of these systems offered interactive video services (wideband) on separate institutional networks (I-nets). Of these four, two also provided data transmission and videoconferencing, with one of these two further providing point-to-point voice transmission.[7]

The State of Florida itself is a major user and operator of telecommunications systems. The state has in place its own voice network, called the SUNCOM Network, with about 135,000 telephones. An additional 115,000 miles of data circuits are currently being leased, but there are plans to shift data transmission to a T-1 (1.544 million baud) capacity digital network backbone that will carry both voice and data. This backbone will be a leased virtual network composed of leased equipment. This virtual network will allow the state to operate and control its own voice and data network while relieving the state of the cost of purchasing the equipment and facilities.

The state government's telecommunications traffic is estimated to be between 75 percent voice and 25 percent data with voice increasing at an annual rate of 6 percent and data at an annual rate of 27 percent.[8]

In addition, the state handles all radio frequency communications for Florida's law enforcement agencies as well as statewide EMS and 911. The total budget for state telecommunications, estimated at $168 million dollars annually, is composed of expenditures for equipment and billing ($90 million) and expenditures for salaries and operations ($78 million). This represents less than one percent of the state budget.[9]

POLICY DEVELOPMENT

Florida has experienced unprecedented population growth during the last decade. It is commonly estimated that a thousand people per day migrate to the state. Population growth has fueled the economy of Florida. This growth is evident in the telecommunications arena; for example, Southern Bell claims that 50 percent of its total access lines were added in the last decade. By deciding to build new facilities in the early seventies, local exchange companies positioned themselves to take advantage of the present population boom. The demand from the current population increase is growing into capacity constructed earlier, and telephone companies are reaping the economic benefits. Consequently, there has been little need for capital investment, telephone rates have remained low, and the regulatory environment for LECs has been relaxed.

Another aspect of the regulatory environment is the strong pro-consumer and pro- LEC orientation of the Florida Public Service Commission (FPSC). This orientation can be traced to a commissioner who saw the breakup of AT&T as harmful to individual ratepayers and did everything to support the local exchange company. Consequently, the commission took measures that focused on access rates as a contribution to the public network and that maintained low basic telephone rates.

Political Culture

Political culture concerns the interaction between agencies, individuals, and societal sectors that influence government policy. In Florida the political culture is determined by a high level of consumer activism, a visible Office of the Public Counsel, and a well-respected PSC.

The most uncommon aspect of the political culture in Florida is the level of consumer activism. This activism is a result of the large number of retirees living in Florida who have ample time to attend hearings and follow issues. This consumer activism played a key role in the defeat of Southern Bell's effort to implement local measured service in 1979.

Policy in the regulatory arena is also affected by the Office of the Public Counsel. The Public Counsel is chosen by the legislature biannually and maintains a high profile where regulatory issues are concerned.

Another interesting aspect of Florida's political culture is the absence of telecommunications regulatory legislation. There seems to be a general agreement among the regulated telecommunications providers to eschew the legislature in matters concerning telecommunications. The prevailing view is that the FPSC, the utility-regulating organization in Florida, is competent and that it is composed of professionals who make the best possible decisions. Although legislation involving shared tenant services (STS will be discussed in a later section) was passed in 1987, it was legislation supported by STS providers and not regulated telcos. In general, involvement in telecommunications regulation in Florida is limited to the regulated telephone companies, the FPSC, and the Public Counsel.

These factors plus the size of the FPSC result in a high degree of regulation in Florida. Florida's commission is one of the three largest public utility commissions in the country. As a result, it can closely monitor all aspects of the telecommunications industry, maintaining a comprehensive regulatory posture.

Although heavily regulated, the local exchange companies are allowed a considerable amount of flexibility. For example, through "limited service offerings" LECs have the ability to introduce new services on a trial basis. "Special assemblies," which have been allowed for many years, allow LECs to offer customer-specific contracts for services which have not yet been tariffed, as long as the LEC can substantiate that the price will exceed cost. "Contract service arrangements," a more recent example of regulatory flexibility, allow LECs to provide existing tariffed services on a similiar basis. That is, a LEC can provide a service such as Centrex on a customer-specific basis at a price below the tariffed rate, providing that it recovers its costs.[10]

The Florida Public Service Commission

Telecommunications in Florida are regulated by the Florida Public Service Commission, which celebrated its centennial in 1987. The agency originally created by the state legislature in 1887 was the Florida Railroad Commission, but legislation in 1911 extended the commission's jurisdiction to include telephone and telegraph regulation.

Before 1978 the FPSC's three commissioners were chosen through statewide elections. Legislation in 1978 changed the number of commissioners from three to five as well as the method of their selection. Commissioners are now appointed by the governor for four-year terms after selection by a nominating committee (also appointed by the governor) comprised of state legislators. The governor's appointments are subject to confirmation by the state senate.

The FPSC is organized into nine divisions: Communications, Electric and Gas, Water and Sewer, Administration, Auditing and Financial Analysis, Information Processing, Records and Reporting, Research, and Consumer Affairs. In addition to these nine divisions and the five commissioners and their assistants, there is an executive director, two deputy executive directors, and a general counsel.

In its method of regulation the FPSC is traditional, regulating utilities' rates of return through quasi-judicial, trial-style rate case proceedings with filing requirements and procedural rules. In a currently pending case, however, AT&T has asked the commission for forbearance of rate of return regulation for two years by substituting rate-cap regulation. The case will be heard in June of 1988.[11]

Significant PSC Decisions

The Florida Public Service Commission has been active in telecommunications regulation over the past several years. The present regulatory environment is greatly impacted by circumstances that resulted from the breakup of the Bell system. The chairman of the commission at that time, Joe Cresse, felt that the Modified Final Judgment would adversely affect local ratepayers. Consequently, he pursued a policy designed to keep local rates low by protecting the LECs. Commissioner Cresse was leery of any proposal that he felt would raise the cost of telephone services; therefore he resisted any effort to tie prices to cost primarily by supporting high access charges. In his opinion, access charges were an appropriate way for the IXCs to contribute to the maintenance of the public network.[12] His regulatory stance has left an indelible mark on telecommunications regulation in Florida as reflected by the following issues before the FPSC.

The most significant regulatory issue concerns the current proceeding on nontraffic- sensitive (NTS) cost allocation. In essence, since 1983 the FPSC has been trying to determine the appropriate level of NTS costs that should be recovered through access charges to the IXCs. Indeed, this issue is of prime national significance, as changes in cost allocation and pricing might substantially alter the structure of the telecommunications network.

The FPSC has "steadfastly resisted" the shifting of these costs--which before divestiture were recovered from toll charges through the separations arrangements--to local ratepayers as a subscriber or customer access line charge (CALC). Initially the FPSC adopted the same minutes-of-use access charge rates filed by the Exchange Carrier Association (ECA), thus keeping this revenue requirement tied to interexchange service.[13] In December 1987, the commission in phase one of the ruling decided to allow NTS recovery to be reduced, on a company-specific basis, by 50 cents per access line per month. However, in order to promote LEC innovation in generating revenue, the commission did not implement an automatic offsetting rate increase.[14]

The only telecommunications legislation passed by the Florida legislature concerned shared tenant service, the offering of equipment and telephone service to tenants of a facility by a nonregulated company. In 1987 the Florida legislature, encouraged by STS providers, voted to allow STS after the FPSC had decided to prohibit STS. However, through negotiation with the legislature, the FPSC imposed some pricing restrictions that were at least in part intended to address the concern that STS created competition for local exchange service. Rather than allowing STS providers to obtain local exchange trunk lines simply at a flat rate, the legislation called for a two-part tariff that would require STS providers to pay 60 percent of the established cost of each telephone trunk line plus 12 cents for each message.[15] Apparently, it was felt that in this way at least some of the advantage of concentrating end users onto fewer local loops would flow back to the LECs and thus to local ratepayers. These provisions apply only to PBX switched systems; smaller key or hybrid key systems with six lines or fewer will be charged the regular flat business rates. The commission did not see these small systems as a threat to the LECs and felt that a bifurcated tariff on such small systems would be punitive.[16] In addition, STS providers must obtain certification and file local service tariffs with the FPSC.[17]

Although the FPSC in general recognizes that LECs are coming under increased competitive pressures--for example, from STS and cellular technologies--the general sense is that "bypass" is not yet significant enough to warrant substantial action. However, when access charges were reduced $59 million in February of 1987, the commission acknowledged that high access charges are one incentive for large users to bypass LECs. Recognizing the potential competitive threat of cellular technologies, the commission has opened a docket on that issue.[18]

Perhaps the first small shot in what might eventually become a move to change the method of telecommunications regulation in Florida has been fired by AT&T. In the previously mentioned case now pending, AT&T has asked the FPSC not to regulate AT&T's rate of return for two years. In return, AT&T would cap rates at mutually agreed-on levels. Now AT&T's rate of return is prescribed by the commission with flexibility allowed between ceiling and floor levels. The proposal would give AT&T much greater flexibility to shift costs and prices and to respond more quickly to specific instances of competition. This case will be decided in June 1988. The related issue of depreciation rates has not yet appeared in Florida, as none of the state's telephone companies have yet requested acceleration of their depreciation rates.[19]

In the area of legislation, a law concerning telephone solicitation is worth noting. Florida has passed a law requiring telcos to offer their customers the option of having a "no telephone solicitation calls" notation published next to their listing in directories and telco directory databases. Solicitation calls to numbers so marked are illegal. The law also requires phone solicitors to state their purpose in calling within the first 30 seconds.[20] This law is sure to have an adverse effect on telemarketing companies. The cost of operation in Florida is likely to increase because additional processing time will be necessary to purge lists of "marked" records of designated individuals. Furthermore, the law will significantly limit the number of potential customers since these calls are perceived as nuisances by most households.

Two final telecommunications issues deserve mention at this point. These are issues having to do with the concept of "open network architecture" (ONA) and "comparably efficient interconnection" (CEI) as raised by the FCC's third Computer Inquiry and the state's possible jurisdiction over video program distribution as raised by the FCC's proposal to eliminate cable and telephone company cross-ownership prohibitions.

The ONA-CEI issue recognizes that LECs would have a competitive advantage in providing "enhanced services" merely because of their ability to house these facilities with local switching offices. Thus far, commission activity in this area has been limited to hearings and approval of some comments to be filed in a Bell Atlantic proceeding. The commission has not articulated any specific policy on this issue, but has recognized in principle that the extra profit or revenue accruing from such a competitive advantage should benefit local ratepayers to some degree rather than company stockholders alone.[21]

Florida has a special interest in the FCC's Notice of Inquiry into cable and telephone co-ownership because of Southern Bell's involvement in the construction of optical fiber systems (including fiber distribution to individual homes) in two Florida communities.[22] Among question raised are those of jurisdiction as well as policy. Again, the FPSC has as yet taken no specific position, but in general it appears to feel that if telephone companies install fiber to residential subscribers, they should be able to distribute video programming services on a common carrier basis with tariffed rates.[23]

The Telephone Companies

As a result of the size and sophistication of the Florida Public Service Commission, the local exchange companies closely monitor any developments in telecommunications regulation. Of the 13 LECs operating in Florida, governmental or regulatory affairs is a part of the organizational structure in five companies; three--General Telephone, Southern Bell, and United Telephone--assign regulatory and governmental affairs to the executive level. Two--Indiantown and Vista-United--monitor this aspect of telecommunications at the managerial level. AT&T and MCI also have regulatory affairs divisions. Furthermore, the Florida Telephone Association serves to represent the general interests of the telecommunications industry. This reflects the level of sophistication exhibited in Florida's regulatory process. Because the FPSC is large and technically adept, it is necessary for the LECs and IXCs to maintain these governmental affairs offices to monitor and promote favorable policies.

Despite the differences in size among Florida's LECs, some issues manage to attract broad appeal. Some of the issues on which the LECs have found common ground are rate of return incentives, profit-sharing arrangements that allow customers and stockholders to share a company's earnings above a predetermined return on equity level, and the adoption of the FCC's Link-Up America plan.[24]

State Telecommunications Management Policy

In 1983 the state created an organizational structure to manage its telecommunications and information needs. This structure consists of the Information Resource Commission and the Joint Committee on Information Technology Resources.

A distinctive aspect of this organizational structure is the separation of the technical data processing and telecommunications functions from the management of these functions. Unlike California, for instance, Florida was successful in developing a separate organization responsible for managing information and telecommunications resources.

This was achieved by the Joint Select Committee on Electronic Data Processing, which was created in 1981 in a political climate in which many legislators felt that spending on computer equipment was out of control. This committee was established to develop recommendations for the legislature on means to improve state development, acquisition, operation, and control of electronic data processing systems.[25] To meet its charge, the committee focused its effort on five critical areas of concern in information technology management: management, purchasing, human resources, telecommunications, and small systems.

A task force approach was employed by the committee to study each of these areas. Each task force was composed of two to five top management executives from major corporations in Florida. Additionally, a university professor who had expertise in the topic of a particular task force was asked to serve on each group. Furthermore, an academician was chosen as the staff director for the committee. With this structure and direction the committee was able to examine the broadest range of telecommunications and information management issues.[26]

One recommendation of the Select Committee in its final report was the creation of a cabinet level commission charged with implementing a comprehensive policy and planning process for information resource management. The statutory authority for the commission as well as for a permanent information resource management committee was established in S.B. 156/H.B. 179. This legislation, passed in 1983, established the Information Resource Commission and the Joint Committee on Information Technology Resources.[27]

The Information Resource Commission (IRC), an executive-level agency, oversees all aspects of information resource management including hardware and software purchasing, telecommunications, and information planning. The primary responsibility of the IRC is the development of the State Strategic Plan for Information Resources Management. The plan would provide a strategic direction for information resource management; establish state goals; provide long-range policy guidelines; and identify the priorities for new SUNCOM Network services to be implemented.[28] Other responsibilities of the IRC include providing technical consultation; reviewing and assessing technical feasibility, cost estimates, and the statewide impact of agency electronic data processing (EDP) and telecommunications plans; certifying that all agency EDP and telecommunications acquisitions are part of the plan; recommending statewide policies and standards; coordinating EDP and telecommunications training; and reviewing and making recommendations on agency budget requests that deal with information resources management.

The second part of this information resource management structure is the Joint Committee on Information Technology Resource. The committee is responsible for recommending to the legislature needed legislation in the area of information technology resource use and management; maintaining a continuous review of the use and management of information technology resources by various agencies; and evaluating the overall influence of resource acquisitions on the productivity and services of state agencies.[29] This committee has been successful in navigating the political seas in order to accomplish its objectives. Because this joint committee is composed of members from both the Senate and the House of Representatives, it has removed much of the politics from the policymaking process.

The Department of State's Public Access System[30]

In Florida, state agencies are investigating the use of telecommunications and information processing technology to provide better service to constituents. Through innovative uses of these technologies, state agencies have focused on improving the efficiency and productivity of their operations. The development of the Department of State's Public Access system is one example of the future of telecommunications and information technology and its use in a public capacity. The Public Access system, developed by the Corporate Affairs Division of the Department of State, allows end users to access the Department of State's (DOS) corporate records database via remote access. The development of this system is of singular importance because of the managerial, technical, and political achievement it represents.

The DOS Public Access system went on line in November 1987. As mentioned earlier, it is a system that allows end users to directly access corporate records filed with DOS's Corporate Affairs Division. Before the implementation of Public Access, this information was obtained either on a walk-in basis or from telephone operators. The increasing volume of inquiries made this system inefficient. A survey taken of telephone users revealed that 85 percent of the calls were going unanswered. Although it cost the state half a million dollars to run this division, it was a source of annoyance for users and managers alike. The management at DOS realized that something had to be done to alleviate this problem. A suggestion was made to allow users to directly access DOS's corporate records and the Public Access system was implemented. With the necessary equipment available, the implementation costs would be minimal. Furthermore, the department selected CompuServe as the public data network. This decision alleviated the concern and necessity of DOS having to purchase its own communications equipment. The major implementation cost was the man-hours required to rewrite the computer programs to enable the users to access the electronic data without jeopardizing the system's security.

With the implementation of Public Access DOS has realized increased productivity and begun to generate revenue. This represents a managerial coup in that a previous cost center was transformed into a revenue-generating center. A subsequent survey found that 45 percent of the telephone calls were being answered, indicating that a caller now has one chance in two of getting through to an operator. Furthermore, Public Access is a revenue-generating project. In February of 1988, CompuServe counted 250 unique users of the DOS database. These 250 users made about 5,000 transactions per day and generated $7,500 per week, of which CompuServe receives 60 percent and DOS 40 percent. This generates about $3,000 per week in revenue for the Department of State and does not yet represent the maximum capacity of the system.

The management considerations made in implementing this system were few but farsighted. The management problem exemplified by the poor connect rate could have been solved by increasing the number of telephone operators or restricting the service to walk-ins only or any number of other options that would not have considered the available technology. However, realizing the options that existing technology would allow, DOS chose one that would be cost effective and efficient by making records available on-line. Another managerial concern involved in the implementation of Public Access was the change in control. Before Public Access, the Corporate Affairs Division controlled all access to corporate documents, which was limited to access via telephone or walk-ins. With the implementation of the on-line system, some control was shifted to the data processing division. Public Access now requires about 40 hours per week of the data processing department's staff time for support and training. However, compared with the cost of hiring additional operators, this cost is minimal. Fortunately for DOS, this change in control has caused no internal strife. This is primarily a result of the enormous positive effect of Public Access on DOS operations.

The success of Public Access has started a kind of multiplier effect with regard to the use of telecommunications and information technology in DOS operations. The Department of State is now considering additional ways to use information and telecommunications technology to enhance the services it provides. For example, DOS will soon implement a two-way transmission process whereby users can request copies of documents via CompuServe; DOS will route these copies through a FAX carrier so that the user receives them via the office FAX machine. This is a direct offshoot of Public Access. Another technological development within the Department of State involves the use of optical disk (OD) technology, which will allow DOS to receive and send information electronically. This will significantly enhance productivity because it will alleviate the time-consuming and repetitive data entry process. Through OD technology the Department of State is moving toward a paperless office. A singular aspect of telecommunications and information resource management that enables Florida to pursue policies designed to enhance services through the use of technology is the information resource management focus in Florida. OD technology is quite expensive. However, the Department of State was allowed to purchase this technology with no opposition from state legislators. This is an outgrowth of the information resources management focus and structure of Florida's state government. The introduction of OD technology was designed as a pilot project by the Information Resource Commission, and the budget and appropriations were approved by the legislature via the Joint Information Resources Management Committee. As a result of the deference given to these government divisions, projects designed to enhance services through technological innovations can be pursued without complications arising due to parochialism or politics.

From the perspective of managers within the Department of State, economic growth has certainly lead to the resulting innovative use of technology. As one manager stated, "If there were no request for the corporate data, there would be no need to develop Public Access." However, the explicit connection between economic development had not been explored by those at DOS. If efficient service provision by state agencies can be regarded as a component of any state's economic development plan, then the efficiency of Public Access qualifies as a link to economic development.

It is interesting to note that Florida is one of the few states that has placed the concern for information resources management at the executive level (South Carolina and Minnesota are the others). The effect of this structure on the use of telecommunications and information technology in state agencies is positive. If the development of the various DOS applications is any indication, the Public Access system represents the type of efficiency and productivity that can be gained from the prudent application of telecommunications and information technology. And the presence of efficiency and productivity in either the public or the private sector is a contribution to economic growth.

TELECOMMUNICATIONS AND ECONOMIC DEVELOPMENT
General Economic Development Policies

Florida's general economic development policy focuses on attracting high-technology manufacturing firms to the state. In addition to other amenities Florida has to offer, an educated labor force is one incentive that is particularly attractive to high-tech companies. Florida takes pride in its continuing education programs, community colleges, and job training programs, and there is broad-based support in the state for them.

Telecommunications Policy Initiatives

In linking telecommunications to economic development two examples have been found: one link that is tangible and in the foreground, the other intangible and part of the background of the economic development landscape. Other ways in which telecommunications can be linked to economic development involve cable I-nets. Finally, views on telecommunications and economic development are present among the various environmental actors in Florida. For instance, both the telecommunications providers as well as the telecommunications-intensive businesses offered their perspective on economic development.

One specific link between telecommunications and economic development exists in East Central Florida. East Central Florida is one of the fastest growing high-tech communities in the United States and is strongly involved in defense and commercial communications, voice and data switching systems, and electro-optics and information systems. A significant component of this growth is the Central Florida Research Park, a cooperative venture between the University of Central Florida and the Orange County Research and Development Authority. Its purpose is to attract high-technology industry to the university-related research park so that a symbiotic relationship can be developed for the mutual benefit of both the company and the university. Opportunities for university-industry relationships in the area of telecommunications have been explored. As of 1985, there were six contracts for telecommunications research in process at the research park.[31]

From a state management perspective, telecommunications is a link to economic development in that it can be used to promote education, serving as the conduit necessary for providing distributed educational resources.[32] Although this focus views telecommunications as a support function, it is very important to Florida's overall economic agenda with education and job training as its cornerstones.

Furthermore, the development of cable I-nets represents another link between telecommunications and economic development. In addition to the enormous savings they offer to the proprietary agency, they can provide a wide range of broadband services at very competitive prices. They represent tremendous potential for business development within cities by offering cost-effective broadband communications services that support voice, video, and data. Once I-nets are established, the cost to connect is usually small and I-nets generally have considerable unused capacity.

Although the Central Florida Research Park represents the only direct link between telecommunications and economic development, an increasing number of companies interested in locating in Florida have begun to inquire about the telecommunications environment.[33] Whether Florida perceives this as a trend worth investigating is not known, but if Florida chooses to promote this aspect of its infrastructure, it could be a great asset.

Regulatory Impact

One way in which Florida can stimulate economic development through telecommunications policy would be to take the lead in assigning the NTS costs to end users and thus letting long distance costs drop. A significant and increasing portion of Florida's economy (most notably tourism and trade) depends on long distance telecommunications. In addition, there is a wide range of "information processing services" and telemarketing services for which geographical location is irrelevant, given economical long distance telecommunications costs.

Telecommunications Company View

To the telcos the paramount concern regarding economic development is their ability to provide any service a business wants--for example, digital networks, fiber installations, information services, WATS, and other enhanced services. Certainly, this would be streamlined for the LECs through further regulatory flexibility.

Telecommunications-Intensive Businesses

Although telecommunications is viewed as a strategic investment by most if not all businesses, it is of nominal importance in decisions to establish a new location or relocate. Of the telecommunications-intensive businesses interviewed in Florida, none had decided to locate in the state as a result of the telecommunications environment.[34] This decision usually turns on factors such as labor cost, tax arrangements, and market demand. Ryder Systems is located in Florida because that is the home of its founder. The telecommunications and information management division of Texas Air is located in Florida because of the climate. The other companies--Florida State University, Florida Power and Light, and Centrust Savings and Loan--are state institutions. However, once the site has been chosen, the provision of quality telecommunications service becomes a high priority.

Bypass

Bypass in Florida does not support Zielinski's claim that firms will pursue bypass when it is economically advantageous to do so.[35] Despite high access charges, firms in Florida were reluctant to bypass. None of the businesses interviewed were at that time bypassing the local exchange company for its long distance service, nor had they implemented such arrangements in the past. The reason for this seemed to have little to do with economics or cost represented by access charges. The primary concern was the vulnerability and dependability of the bypassing arrangement. The firms felt that bypassing the local exchange company with their own equipment would leave them in a vulnerable position if that equipment failed. In the words of one telecommunications manager, they want to avoid putting all their eggs into one basket.[36] Although access charges in Florida are considered high compared with those in surrounding states, bypass is seen as a risky undertaking to be considered only as a supplemental arrangement.

Innovation

The telecommunications-intensive businesses in Florida are oriented toward the future. Several have developed fiber optic arrangements. With the ability of fiber to carry voice, data, and images, these companies will be positioned to take full advantage of integrated services digital network (ISDN) standards and equipment. For Florida Power and Light, the decision was to lay fiber along its existing electricity rights-of-way. Because the utility company is state regulated, it cannot sell or profit from this decision. The fiber will be used to establish a private network for telecommunications that will expand into ISDN when available. It is envisioned that ISDN will allow the company to communicate with and provide enhanced training services to its employees.

Another company using fiber to prepare for future benefits to be gained from telecommunications planning is Centrust Savings and Loan, a state institution. Managers at Centrust decided to connect their new building to the central office with fiber optic trunAmong the telecommunications-intensive businesses, the breakup of the Bell system seems to have produced several benefits--increased technical knowledge, reorganization, and cost advantages.

Divestiture

Among the telecommunications-intensive businesses, the breakup of the Bell system seems to have produced several benefits--increased technical knowledge, reorganization, and cost advantages.

The multivendor environment that expanded considerably in the postdivestiture era has forced businesses to rely on their own knowledge for purchasing and maintenance arrangements. With the breakup of AT&T, companies could no longer rely on a single entity to handle both their service and equipment needs. Telecommunications managers had to make choices based on what they felt would be most beneficial to their firm in terms of quality, dependability, and cost of service. Faced with a mountain of choices, they needed increased technical knowledge. Where previously these telecommunications departments were no more than accounting divisions responsible for supervising billing, these divisions were now expected to supervise the entire purchasing, maintenance, and billing process. As a result, new technical, maintenance, and managerial staff were hired to meet these needs.

Furthermore, firms consistently claimed that the breakup of AT&T has benefited them by reducing the ratio of telecommunications costs to total expenditure. Despite the increased labor costs that divestiture has imposed on firms, savings on equipment and services have resulted in lower telecommunications costs relative to overall costs

CONCLUSIONS

In considering various economic development options, two scenarios involving technology and economics seem plausible. One option focuses on how economic development preceded technological advancement. The other states that economic development is a function of technological advancement. However analyzed, it is certain that technology and economic development are linked in some positive manner. A cursory glance at the development of the railroad, steamship, airplane, and telephone support this notion. But the problem of deciding how this specifically applies to telecommunications involves subtle complexities that support both earlier observations. In Florida, for instance, economic development has been the driving force behind telecommunications. Florida's population change has fueled the economy and created a thriving environment for the local exchange companies. As stated earlier, the LECs in Florida are able to use existing capacity now because of their substantial investment in physical plant during the mid 1970s. Although the evidence in Florida does not lay to rest the debate involving technology and economic development, it does provide a plausible paradigm for the contention that technology follows economic development.

On a less theoretical basis, practical considerations of telecommunications and economic development among telecommunications managers in Florida, although not explicit, do exist. The role of telecommunications in fostering an educated and skilled labor force is seen as the most significant way in which telecommunications is contributing to economic development.[37] This is an outgrowth of Florida's general economic development policy that focuses on attracting high-technology manufacturing firms to the state. In addition to other amenities Florida has to offer, an educated labor force is one incentive that is particularly attractive to high-tech companies. By serving as the conduit for distributive education programs (e.g., community colleges, correspondence courses, teleresearching), telecommunications can contribute to the present economic development agenda.

However, telecommunications does not exist as a distinct component of any economic development agenda. As of January 1988, there was no consideration of the value of telecommunications itself in economic development. Among state agencies, the legislature, and the Public Service Commission, the prevailing telecommunications issues are effective management of the state network and the protection of local ratepayers. They view their responsibility to the maintenance of the public network and to the ratepayer as tantamount. However, telcos and telecommunications-intensive businesses are of the view that a telecommunications environment that can respond to the needs of customers is the best economic development policy. In the opinion of the telcos in particular, an environment with increased regulatory flexibility would be the best economic development program the state as a whole could pursue. It may be some time before these opposing views of telecommunications and economic development meet.

CASE STUDY: CABLE I-NETS

The late 1970s and early 1980s saw a flurry of activity in the franchising and refranchising of cable TV systems. Many of the franchise ordinances included provisions for the development of "I-nets," or "institutional loops." For the most part, these I-nets were separate cable networks (i.e., separate from the regular subscriber network) which connected the cities' schools, fire and police stations, municipal buildings, libraries, and so forth. I-nets usually passed through the cities' central business districts as well. Plans for use, management, operation, and maintenance of these networks varied. Typically, at least half of the capacity was reserved for city use, leaving the cable companies free to use any remaining capacity as they wished.

Early applications included using I-nets to coordinate traffic lights, to provide remote energy management of city buildings, for high-speed data transfer, for videoconferencing, and even to carry telephone traffic. More recently it has been suggested that I-nets can be an economical technology for telephone bypass, linking large telecommunications users directly to IXCs' points of presence. As broadband transmission systems that can be flexibly tailored for specific needs, cable I-nets have tremendous potential for innovative telecommunications applications. Moreover, cities can realize substantial cost reductions by utilizing their I-net capacity efficiently.

Miami and Ft. Lauderdale are two Florida cities that have begun to develop I-net applications for municipal uses. The Ft. Lauderdale system--the older of the two--has supported a variety of applications over the years. The 88-mile I-net (owned and operated by the franchised cable company, Selkirk Cable TV) has 300 megahertz of capacity, split evenly between upstream and downstream channels.

The city currently uses a dozen data links and several video channels. The city assigns the channels through their modems, and Selkirk handles the transmission. Among the video applications, the fire department transmits training programs to the individual fire stations two hours a day five days a week. Whereas in the past it might have taken nearly a month for a given training program to circulate to all shifts at all of the stations via videotape, it now takes only a few days for everyone to see it using the I-net. Another channel carries city council and other city meetings to department supervisors' offices during the day. At night this channel is used to monitor security at the city's sewage treatment plant. Data channels are used for remote control of the plant's operations. By the terms of the franchise, the city is not charged for the use of the I-net (i.e., transmission services), although it is responsible for the modems and terminal equipment.

Broward County, in which Ft. Lauderdale is located, also makes use of this I-net, but it is billed for its use. Selkirk also handles the county's terminal equipment. The county uses the I-net to link its computer center with three other buildings. Four T1 channels are used for data, with another 52 T1 channels used mainly for voice.

In addition to these governmental uses, Selkirk has been involved in a number of private applications. In one of these, a telemarketing operation used the I-net to bypass the local phone company, connecting 250 lines directly to an IXC. Selkirk has also served as subcontractor to lay cable for LANs, including one for IBM. About four years ago several banks expressed interest in I-net applications, and Selkirk ran an experiment with a hospital to transmit magnetic nuclear resonance (MNR) images. The company still receives occasional inquiries but does not actively market I-net services.

In the case of Miami, the city has assumed ownership of the entire I-net. The cable company, Miami Telecommunications, maintains the network under a service contract with the city. Since Miami's cable system is relatively new, applications are only now getting under way.

The primary use of the I-net will be for data transmission. While critical police and fire circuits will use the city's microwave system, all noncritical data are being converted to the I-net. The network will tie together about 30 different locations. Cost estimates show the tremendous potential for savings. Currently all noncritical circuits are handled by the LEC, Southern Bell. Even by renewing Southern Bell's contract at much reduced rates, it would cost $600,481 over the next five years (half the present cost) to remain on the Southern Bell network. By purchasing modems and converting this traffic to the I-net, the city could reduce these costs to $83,060 over the same five years.

The city's voice communication continues to be handled by the Department of General Services and has been limited to basic Southern Bell Centrex service. A study showed that 85 percent of the city's voice traffic was internal (with four locations accounting for 52 percent). A proposal to switch to the I-net, using Rolm equipment, estimated that payback for all equipment would occur in less than three years and that the city's $6 million plus annual expenditures could be reduced by more than half. Apparently concerned that the city would adopt the plan, Southern Bell used a "special assembly" contract to offer an attractive rate on Electronic Switch Services Exchange (ESSX). A new 10-year contract was recently signed, but the terms of the agreement allow the city to reduce voice traffic by 10 percent per year. Thus, the city can phase in a switch to the I-net over the next several years.

Miami also uses its I-nets for fire department training, and audio of city council meetings is run to all city offices. In addition, all fax lines will be put on the I-net in the near future.

One reason that more cable companies in Florida are not involved in bypass is concern that the state's aggressive PSC might construe such operations as "telephone service" and begin to regulate the service on a common carrier basis. Generally, cable companies are very reluctant to be thought of as common carriers. Moreover, because of their protective stance with regard to the LECs, the Florida Public Service Commission might take a strong stance toward cable bypass and undermine its competitive advantage (i.e., through tariffs).

NOTES

1.   Florida Department of Commerce, Division of Economic Development, The Florida Economy (Tallahassee, January 1987), p. 43.

2.   Ibid., p. 1.

3.   David Avery and Frank B. King, "Florida: Sunny with No Clouds," Economic Review 70 (February 1984), p. 73.

4.   The Florida Economy, p. 30.

5.   Ibid., p. 55.

6.   "Cable Stats," Cablevision, September 28, 1987, p. 65.

7.   The Interactive Cable TV Handbook, 4th ed. (Bethesda: Phillips Publishing, Inc.: 1984), pp. 67-80.

8.   Florida High Technology and Industry Council, A Needs Assessment for an Integrated Backbone Statewide Communications Network for the State of Florida, report for the Florida Information Resource Commission, Tallahassee, May 1986.

9.   Interview with Gary Gast, Professional Engineer III, Telecommunications Systems Bureau, Division of Communications, Florida Department of General Services, Tallahassee, January 13, 1988.

10.   Interview with Frank Meiners, Regulatory Affairs Manager, Southern Bell, Tallahassee, January 12, 1988.

11.   Information in this section is from a telephone interview with Beverly DeMello, Public Information Officer, Florida Public Service Commission, Tallahassee, October 7, 1987.

12.   Interview with Meiners.

13.   Telephone interview with Greg Schaeffer, Communications staff member, Florida Public Service Commission, Tallahassee, October 7, 1987.

14.   Interview with Greg Schaeffer, Economist Supervisor, Florida Public Service Commission, Tallahassee, January 11, 1988.

15.   Telecommunications Week, February 2, 1987, p. 7.

16.   Telephone interview with Robin Norton, Planning and Research Economist, Florida Public Service Commission, Tallahassee, December 21, 1987.

17.   Interview with Schaeffer.

18.   Ibid.

19.   Ibid.

20.   Department of General Services, State Telephone Regulation Report (Tallahassee: November 5, 1987).

21.   Telephone interview with Daryl Nall, Communications staff member, Florida Public Service Commission, Tallahassee, October 9, 1987.

22.   Fred Dawson, "Southern Bell Thinks Fiber Can Pay for Itself without Cable TV Revenues," Cablevision, September 28, 1987, p. 16.

23.   Interview with Nall.

24.   Telephone interview with Bill Feaster, Executive Director, Florida Telephone Association, Tallahassee, December 10, 1987.

25.   Florida Legislature, Final Report of the Joint Select Committee on Electronic Data Processing, Tallahassee, July 1983, p. 1.

26.   Interview with Ed Levine, Staff Director, and Karen Fausone, Chief Analyst, Joint Committee on Information Technology Resources, Tallahassee, January 13, 1987.

27. Final Report of the Joint Select Committee on Electronic Data Processing.

28. Telephone interview with Leon Blue, Network Consultant, Information Resource Commission, Tallahassee, November 16, 1987.

29. Interview with Levine and Fausone.

30. The information in this section was obtained from a telephone interview with Tish Beach, Data Center Director, Department of State, Tallahassee, February 22, 1988.

31. Florida High Technology and Industry Council, Telecommunications Science Report (Tallahassee: February 1985), Appendix: University of Central Florida, pp. 1-7.

32. Interview with Levine and Fausone.

33. Telephone interview with Roger Miller, Economic Development Specialist, Florida Department of Commerce, Tallahassee, January 11, 1988.

34. Interview with Henry Fiallo, Telecommunications Manager, Ryder Systems, Miami, January 15, 1988; interview with Fernando Franco, International Systems Manager, Systems One, Eastern Airlines, Miami, January 15, 1988.

35. Charles A. Zielinski, "From Traditional Economic Regulation to New Policies and Roles in Telecommunications: A Challenge to State Governments." Washington, D.C.: Council of State Policy and Planning Agencies 1986. (Working paper.)

36. Interview with Fiallo.

37. Interview with Levine and Fausone.

4

Illinois
John Horrigan and Darren Rudloff

Telecommunications policy in Illinois is driven by a pro-competitive philosophy. The Illinois Commerce Commission and the state General Assembly both realize that telecommunications is no longer a natural monopoly. This realization led to the passage of the Universal Telephone Service Protection Act in 1985. One of the rationales behind the act's passage was that more competition in the industry would benefit the state economically. The act did not, however, result in any initiatives within the state economic development agency to use telecommunications to promote economic development. The only evidence of an association between telecommunications and economic development is in Illinois Bell Telephone's Economic Development Division. It should be emphasized at the outset that the Illinois Bell initiative has a fairly low profile within the state and does not link telecommunications and economic development. It is simply a case where a telecommunications company engages in economic development activity. Little attempt is made to use the telecommunications infrastructure as an economic development instrument.

THE ECONOMY AND THE TELECOMMUNICATIONS INDUSTRY
Economic Profile

The economy of Illinois has undergone a major transition in the 1970s and 1980s. Like its Midwest neighbors, Illinois traditionally has specialized in manufacturing industries. However, the traditional manufacturing states lost significant numbers of jobs in the 1970s as many companies closed their northern plants and reinvested in southern and western states. This employment shift from the Rustbelt to the Sunbelt had significant effects upon the manufacturing economies of Midwest states like Illinois.[1]

The resulting transformation in the Illinois economy is clearly evident in state employment figures (Table 4.1). For example, Illinois suffered annual employment losses between 1980 and 1986 while total U.S. employment was growing yearly. The manufacturing sector in Illinois lost jobs roughly four times more quickly than the United States. Other Illinois sectors experiencing losses were mining, construction, government, and transportation. Illinois did enjoy employment gains in the services, finance, and trade sectors, although the yearly growth rates lagged behind that of the United States.

Table 4.1
Nonagricultural Employment Shares and Annual
Percentage Change in Employment* for Illinois and
the United States, 1980 and 1986
(total employees in 1,000s, share and change in %)

| Sector | Employment Shares | | | | Annual Employment Change | |
| | 1980 | | 1986 | | | |
	Illinois	U.S.	Illinois	U.S.	Illinois	U.S.
Mining	0.7	1.1	0.5	0.8	-3.7	-3.9
Construction	3.9	4.9	3.7	4.9	-1.2	1.6
Manufacturing	25.0	22.5	19.4	19.1	-4.1	-1.1
Transportation	5.8	5.7	5.8	5.3	-0.5	0.3
Wholesale and Retail Trade	23.3	22.7	24.8	23.7	0.7	2.4
Fin., Ins., Real Estate	6.4	5.7	7.3	6.3	1.8	3.7
Services	19.3	19.6	23.6	23.2	3.2	5.0
Government	15.6	17.8	14.9	16.8	-1.1	0.6
Total	4,892	90,650	4,777	99,610	-0.4	1.7

* Totals may reflect rounding error.

Source: U.S. Department of Labor, Bureau of Labor Statistics, Employment and Earnings, vol. 34, no. 5 (May 1987), pp. 120-137; idem, vol. 28, no. 5 (May 1981), pp. 120-128.

As a result of these employment shifts, the employment shares of the various business sectors has changed significantly between 1980 and 1986. The Illinois manufacturing share declined considerably, while the services, finance-related, and trade shares increased. Compared with the United States, Illinois is specialized in the trade, finance-related, and transportation sectors.

Telecommunications Businesses

Many of the increasing number of service businesses rely heavily upon telecommunications in their everyday operations. These telecommunications-intensive businesses (TIBS) can be defined using Standard Industrial Classification (SIC) codes (Table 4.2). Furthermore, state employment levels in the TIBS can indicate how specialized a state's business sector is in telecommunications.

In 1984 Illinois had a larger proportion of its work force in media services and information services than did the nation as a whole. The state's information services employment share was almost two percentage points higher than the sector's U.S. share. Above average employment levels in the finance, insurance, and data processing sectors all helped create this specialization. Of particular note is the rapid employment growth of 47 percent annually in the data processing sector. Chicago's influential financial district undoubtedly explains much of this concentration in information services employment.

Local Exchange Carriers

The primary telephone company operating in Illinois is Illinois Bell Telephone (IBT). As one of the five state companies held by the Ameritech regional holding company, Illinois Bell provides 83 percent of all telephone lines in the state (Table 4.3). Furthermore, Illinois Bell is the primary toll carrier in 7 of the state's 19 market service areas, which include Chicago and most of the other urban regions in the state.

The second largest toll carrier in the state is General Telephone Company of Illinois, a subsidiary of GTE Corporation. General Telephone is the primary toll carrier in six market service areas and supplies 9 percent of the state's access lines. The next three largest telephone companies in the state include Continental Telephone Company of Illinois (Contel), Central Telephone Company (Centel), and Illinois Consolidated Telephone Company. Together, these five telephone companies provide 98 percent of Illinois' telephone lines.[2]

Another important telecommunications presence in Illinois is Ameritech, one of the seven regional Bell holding companies (RBOCs). Based in Chicago, Ameritech has aggressively attempted to expand its horizons beyond basic telephone service since the AT&T divestiture. For instance, Ameritech is vigorously lobbying to remove the restrictions which keep it from manufacturing telecommunications equipment. In addition, Ameritech operates several unregulated businesses that include ADR (software development), Ameritech Publishing (various types of telephone directories), and Ameritech Mobile Communications (cellular phone systems).[3]

Interexchange Carriers

Twenty interexchange carriers offered long distance services in Illinois in 1987, an increase of five carriers from 1986. AT&T Communications of Illinois is easily the largest of these interexchange carriers. As part of the overall AT&T system, AT&T of Illinois provides service nationwide, as well as to several foreign countries. In addition, AT&T of Illinois has 1-Plus dialing capabilities in all of the local exchanges within the state. US Sprint and MCI Telecommunications are the next largest interexchange carriers with both nationwide and some worldwide capabilities. In addition to AT&T, US Sprint, MCI, and five other facilities-based carriers, the state has 12 resellers of long distance services.[4]

Table 4.2

Employment Shares and Annual Changes in Employment* of
Telecommunications-Intensive Businesses** for Illinois
and the United States, 1980 and 1984
(share and change in %)

| | Employment Shares | | | | Annual Employment Change | |
| | 1980 | | 1984 | | | |
	Illinois	U.S.	Illinois	U.S.	Illinois	U.S.
Information Services	10.0	9.1	11.8	9.9	2.9	3.2
Finance	3.4	3.1	3.9	3.3	2.5	3.3
Insurance	2.9	2.3	3.0	2.3	0.0	1.0
Real Estate	1.2	1.3	1.2	1.4	-0.6	1.6
Computer/Data Proc.	0.4	0.4	1.2	0.6	46.5	13.1
Other Information Svcs.	2.2	2.1	2.4	2.3	1.4	4.5
Info. Technology Equip.	2.3	2.2	2.0	2.3	-4.3	2.4
Research and Development	0.4	0.3	0.3	0.3	-4.8	2.9
Media	4.3	3.7	4.2	3.7	-1.6	0.5

* Totals may reflect rounding error.

** The Telecommunications-Intensive Business categories are defined by Standard Industrial Classification codes as follows:
    1. Information Services: Finance: SIC 60 (Banking), SIC 61 (Credit), SIC 62 (Commodities); Insurance: SIC 63 (Insurance Carriers), SIC 64 (Insurance Agents); Real Estate: SIC 65; Computer/Data Proc.: SIC 737; Other Information Services: SIC 731 (Advertising), SIC 732 (Credit Reporting), SIC 81 (Legal Services), SIC 891 (Engineering and Architectural Services), SIC 893 (Accounting and Auditing);
    2. Information Technology Equipment: SIC 3573 (Electronic Computing Equipment), SIC 361 (Electric Distributing Equipment), SIC 365 (Radio and TV Receiving Equipment), SIC 366 (Communications Equipment), SIC 367 (Electronic Components and Accessories);
    3. Research and Development: SIC 7391 (Research and Development Laboratories), SIC 7397 (Commercial Testing Laboratories), SIC 892 (Nonprofit Education and Scientific Research Agencies);
    4. Media: SIC 27 (Printing and Publishing), SIC 48 (Communications), SIC 735 (News Syndicates), SIC 78 (Motion Pictures).

Source: U.S. Bureau of the Census, County Business Patterns, United States (No. 1) and Illinois (No. 16) (Washington, D.C.: U.S. Government Printing Office, 1980 and 1984), Table 1B.

Table 4.3
Local Exchange Carriers and Access Lines
in Illinois, 1986

Local Exchange Carriers	Share of Access Lines	Total (%)*
Illinois Bell	4,860,754	83.0
General Telephone	513,010	9.0
Centel	163,863	3.0
Contel	151,356	3.0
Illinois Consolidated	71,762	1.0
Others**	101,788	2.0
Total	5,862,533	100.0

* Totals may reflect rounding error.
** Includes 51 other local exchange companies.

Source: Illinois Commerce Commission, Annual Report on Telecommunications 1986, (Springfield, January 1987), pp. 4-5.

POLICY DEVELOPMENT
Environment

Belief in the virtue of competition drives telecommunications policymaking in Illinois. State policymakers were quick to realize that the break up of AT&T made the presumption of monopoly on the state level invalid. This pro-competitive environment has led to policy responses by the Illinois Commerce Commission (ICC) and the General Assembly that further enhance competition.

A disposition toward competition has been a characteristic of regulatory policies in the state. In electric utility regulation, the state has moved toward competition, but more slowly than in telecommunications. State policy toward cogeneration of electric power is a good gauge of a commission's attitude toward electric competition. A commission that requires utilities to transport a cogenerator's power favors competition because such transportation threatens the utility's monopoly hold on the service area. In Illinois the ICC does not have the authority to order utilities to transport power, although several state legislators strongly support the idea. The consensus in Illinois is that the state is supportive of competition in electricity, although it is not moving as quickly in that direction as it was under Phil O'Connor, the previous ICC commissioner and a fervent exponent of competition.[5]

The electric power issue yields further insight into the Illinois policy environment and the way this environment interacts with telecommunications policymaking. The state's consumers and consumer protection groups focus most of their energies on electrical issues and rate cases. In particular, they are organized against Commonwealth Edison, an upstate electric company. As a result, they pay little attention to telephone issues, according to various sources in the state. These sources point out that the electric utility issue involves more money, is more visible, and is less complicated than telephone issues. Thus the public has expressed little opposition to phone rate hikes, deaveraging, and local measured service.[6] An Illinois Bell manager offered a slightly different view, claiming that consumer groups are very skilled and organized against Illinois Bell because they are so well organized against Commonwealth Edison.[7]

Initiatives of the Illinois Commerce Commission

Illinois has a tradition of innovation both in telecommunications technology and telecommunications regulation. Dating from the days of the Bell System, Illinois Bell has had a reputation for a sophisticated telecommunications network; since divestiture, Illinois Bell has continued to be a leader in innovation among the BOCs.[8] For example, IBT had the nation's first ISDN demonstration project in 1985 with McDonald's Corporation in Oak Brook, Illinois. Over half of IBT's capital expenditure budget in 1986 went to fiber optic cable and digital switching construction, two key pieces to a state-of-the-art telecommunications network.[9]

The tradition of technical innovation from the private sector has helped establish a telecommunications policy environment open to deregulation and trustful of competition. This environment, along with a recognition by the ICC that regulation of telephone service as a monopoly is no longer viable, has resulted in several commission actions to open telecommunications markets to competition and drive prices to cost. The ICC was the first regulatory commission in the nation to unbundle access from local usage and deaverage access rates across the state. Access costs are usually high for rural areas and low for urban users. Under averaging, urban and rural access costs were averaged and spread among all users in the system. This resulted in urban users subsidizing the high cost of rural service. Averaging also gave large users an incentive to bypass the local network to avoid paying the subsidy to rural users embedded in access costs. Deaveraging was thus a bold move designed to drive prices to cost to the benefit of urban and business users at the expense of rural users.[10]

The commission's other initiative to drive price closer to cost is a plan to transfer all nontraffic-sensitive (NTS) costs to end users in five years. Known as the Alternate Plan, it aims to end the subsidy of local rates by long distance rates.[11] By assigning NTS to long distance service, as has been the tradition, the rates for long distance service have been kept high while the rates for local service have been kept low. The commission has developed this plan with the recognition that it would put upward pressure on local rates. It is worth noting, however, that Illinois Bell is not part of the Alternate Plan because it has already included NTS costs in its rates. Customers of smaller local exchange companies are therefore bearing the brunt of the transition of NTS costs to end users.

A final aspect of ICC regulation worth discussing is its market service area (MSA) concept. The ICC created MSAs before divestiture and uses them instead of local access and transport areas (LATAs). The difference for Illinois is that they have more MSAs (19) than they would have had LATAs under the Modified Final Judgment. This gives Illinois more inter-MSA calling and more competitive zones. With narrower regional calling areas, carriers have an easier time showing that a service is competitive than they otherwise would.[12] (Classification of a service as competitive will be discussed in detail below.)

More than just a tradition of innovation has driven the commission's move toward deregulation. It was also driven by the ICC's chairman, Phil O'Connor, who saw his advocacy of deregulation as a chance to make his mark in the regulatory arena. To do this, O'Connor assembled an economics-oriented staff committed to cost-based (that is, economically efficient) pricing and deregulation. O'Connor's predecessor at the ICC, Michael Hasten, also believed that the present regulatory structure was no longer plausible in an industry becoming more competitive. Illinois' move toward deregulation also occurred in a broader context in which deregulation was gaining both academic and political legitimacy.[13] Deregulation was becoming the fashion not only in telecommunications but also in the trucking and airline industries.[14] O'Connor, Hasten, and an ICC staff committed to competition capitalized on this momentum to push Illinois farther than most other states toward deregulation.

The Illinois Universal Telephone Service Protection Act of 1985

The Illinois Universal Telephone Service Protection Act (UTSPA) of 1985 is the culmination of the state's move toward greater competition. The act authorizes the ICC to deregulate certain telecommunications services through rule making, provides for a reduced level of regulatory oversight for services classified as competitive, reduces the regulatory burden for small telephone companies, and gradually opens up all telecommunications markets to competitive entry.

It is important to recognize that the UTSPA was designed to be a regulatory flexibility law, not a deregulatory effort. Although several states have given regulators more flexibility, officials in Illinois emphasize how the UTSPA was carefully crafted to introduce competition into telecommunications markets, while preserving regulatory oversight of telephone companies.[15] In drafting the legislation, Illinois officials felt that the most rapid dissemination of new telecommunications technologies would come about under conditions of maximum competition. Moreover, officials felt that quick dissemination of new technologies would benefit the state economically.[16] Thus Illinois consciously rejected the dominant versus nondominant regulatory scheme of the Federal Communications Commission. Under that model, the dominant carrier, AT&T, is regulated while other common carriers, like MCI or Sprint, are not. The state did not want to become a cartel manager, nor did it want to regulate only incumbent providers and not new ones. The state felt that regulation only of incumbent carriers would erode their ability to provide basic service. Finally, state officials did not want to delegate the transition to competition to the ICC. Thus, they completely rewrote the Illinois Public Utilities Act of 1921 and produced the UTSPA.[17]

Unlike the Illinois Public Utilities Act of 1921, the UTSPA has a specific statement of legislative findings and policy. The two most important statements of policy embody the trade-off frequently seen in telecommunications regulation, competition and cost-based pricing versus consumer protection and universal service.   One portion of the UTSPA's findings declares that competition can substitute for regulation in many instances.   The second statement declares that consumer protection is the most important objective of the law.   That statement also requires reasonable and nondiscriminatory rates and the promotion of universal service.[18] Conventional wisdom posits that the goals of competition and universal service are irreconcilable. Illinois officials reject that claim, stating instead that competition is the best way to ensure maximum penetration into the residential market.[19]

The UTSPA gives the commission maximum latitude in choosing which services to regulate. In establishing the regulatory structure after divestiture, the UTSPA specifically defines telecommunications and carriers and services, something not previously done in Illinois. Telecommunications services are defined very broadly as offering for sale the transmission of information by any means. Excluded from the definition are the following services: rent, sale, or lease of customer-premises equipment, telephone answering services, and community antenna TV services. The ICC can, through rulemaking, exclude from active regulatory oversight private-line services not used to originate or terminate switched services, cellular radio, and high-speed data transmission.[20]

A telecommunications carrier is defined as any entity that owns or controls facilities or a franchise to provide intrastate telecommunications services for public use. This definition excludes the telecommunications systems of public and private institutions of higher learning, shared-tenant service providers, and local area networks serving closely located buildings affiliated through common ownership. In regard to certification of new carriers, the UTSPA is quite liberal. Interexchange carriers (IXCs) need only show technical, financial, and managerial capabilities to obtain a certificate. Local exchange carriers (LECs) must meet the same standards as IXCs as well as demonstrate that provision of local exchange service will not have a substantial adverse impact on the price or financial viability of the main provider of local exchange service. An important exclusion from both certification requirements is any demonstration of public need by the new carrier.[21]

Perhaps the most innovative aspect of the UTSPA is the section that permits the classification of services as competitive or noncompetitive. All services must have one of these designations under the UTSPA.   The classification of services is made on a service-by-service basis for a geographic area or class of customers. A service is competitive if, in the area in question, the service, its functional equivalent, or a substitute service is reasonably available from more than one provider whether or not any such provider is a telecommunications carrier subject to regulation under the UTSPA. This "reasonably available" test is unique to Illinois and much less rigid than trying to define or quantify competition.[22] The regulatory flexibility law passed by Washington State, for example, requires the presence of "effective competition" before the utility commission grants flexibility. Illinois officials have pointed out that the proper response to effective competition is complete deregulation.[23] The UTSPA is designed to assist in the movement of telecommunications markets to competition. The perception in Illinois is that waiting to be flexible until other forces bring about competition is likely to delay the advent of competition and the benefits that go with it.

Procedurally, there are two routes a carrier can take to get a service classified as competitive. The first is self-classification. A carrier may file tariffs with the commission declaring a service competitive in a specific area. The carrier must also file a long-run marginal cost study (treated as proprietary by the commission) to ensure that the service is not being priced below cost and thus subsidized by a regulated service. The ICC can investigate the proposed classification on its own motion, but cannot suspend the filing pending investigation. The commission can overrule the classification and, if necessary, order refunds of overcharges to customers.[24]

The second route by which a carrier can obtain reclassification is simply through a petition to the commission requesting that a certain service be designated competitive. The commission must rule within 21 days if no hearings are held and 120 days if hearings are held. Until August 1, 1987, this was the only means available to interexchange carriers for reclassification of a service as competitive. After that date, carriers were able to classify a service as competitive without seeking ICC approval prior to doing so. A petition by other carriers that the service is in fact not competitive will prompt the commission to action. The commission also has the option to initiate an investigation into a service classification on its own motion.

Both these routes seek to place the burden of proof of whether or not a service is competitive on the commission, not on the carrier. The speed with which the act requires the commission to act is designed to ensure that carriers compete in the marketplace rather than before the commission in lengthy proceedings.[25] Illinois Bell, however, does not feel the service-by-service classification scheme has worked well. As soon as Illinois Bell declares a service competitive, a rush of other carriers argue before the commission that IBT still has significant monopoly power in that service. The result is what the ICC hoped would be avoided: drawn-out regulatory proceedings. As a result, service-by-service classification has, for Illinois Bell, come to a halt.[26] For this reason, Illinois Bell hopes the commission will approve a social contract scheme in the near future, much like Vermont has done. With the freedom to price services as it sees fit below the ceiling, Illinois Bell feels it could be more aggressive in marketing innovative services. In addition, it would not have to fight regulatory battles before the ICC.[27]

As mentioned earlier (and embodied in the title of the act), protection of universal service is a primary objective of the UTSPA. Under the act, the ICC is required to monitor the level of subscriber penetration in each exchange and report the results to the General Assembly. Should any drop in subscriber penetration occur, some action (unspecified in the law) must be taken to remedy the situation. Thus far, no decline in subscribership has taken place. In 1985, 94 percent of all Illinois homes had telephones, compared with the nationwide figure of 92.2 percent subscriber penetration.[28] In addition, the UTSPA requires all LECs to inform customers, based on calling patterns for the past six months, their least-cost service option. This can be done only for those exchanges whose central offices have been converted to digital switching.

The UTSPA also requires Illinois to participate in all federal programs designed to preserve universal service as long as that participation is cost effective for the state. The commission has determined that participation in the FCC's Link-Up America program is cost effective, and the commission has initiated a proceeding (ICC Case No. 87-0432) to determine criteria for the inclusion of low-income persons in the program.[29] Thus protection of universal service is an active and ongoing concern of the ICC.

The State as a User

Despite the advanced telecommunications network present in the state, Illinois state government currently uses a rather cumbersome telecommunications system. The system is a patchwork of overlapping state agency lines that have developed over the years with little overall planning or coordination. One result of such a system is that state phone users must remember and dial specific codes to place calls to different locations. In effect, callers manually switch and direct the calls to their destinations. In addition, according to Charles Miller, director of telecommunications at the Illinois Department of Central Management Services (CMS), state agencies currently make few, if any, innovative uses of the present telecommunications network.[30]

The state, however, is taking steps to upgrade its telecommunications system. In June of 1987, CMS unveiled a new Strategic Communications Network Plan for the state. A blue-ribbon committee of Illinois government, private industry, and university representatives aided a private consulting firm in preparing the document. The plan's major recommendation is the implementation of an advanced digital transmission trunk line connecting four major nodes in the state, Springfield, Chicago, Champaign/Urbana, and Carbondale. Other cities would connect to these major nodes using lower speed digital lines. The plan also calls for simplified calling procedures, new data capabilities, and the future use of video.[31]

According to Miller, state government is primarily interested in the system because it will reduce costs and increase productivity. However, new innovative uses by state agencies should be possible, considering the new system will have ISDN and other advanced capabilities.[32] The system is expected to cost approximately $150 million and take several years to fully implement. Estimates also suggest that the network will save $62,000,000 in telecommunications costs in its first five years in operation.[33]

CMS adopted the plan and received network proposals from September to December 1987. CMS received eleven bids, which included four complete bids for the entire system and seven partial bids for portions of it. The bidding companies included Illinois Bell, IBM, GTE, AT&T, US Sprint, and MCI. CMS expects to make a decision on a system in June 1988.

ECONOMIC DEVELOPMENT
Public Initiatives

Although Illinois and Chicago have promoted significant economic development activities, they apparently have made no efforts to link economic development to telecommunications. The following is a brief overview of these economic development programs.

The State of Illinois

Illinois' Department of Commerce and Community Affairs (DCCA) is the state's primary economic development agency. Formed in 1979 by combining three related agencies, the department's programs cover the spectrum of economic development activities ranging from small business assistance to export promotion. In addition, DCCA administers several federal programs including the Community Development Block Grant program and the Job Training Partnership program. DCCA is also quite unique among state economic development agencies in that it operates worker training programs in addition to its development activities.

Economic development in Illinois is currently focused on a five-year, $2.3 billion economic development plan called Build Illinois. The program, started in 1985, is primarily focused on improving the state's infrastructure of roads, bridges, and schools. In 1986 the second part of the Build Illinois program, Corridors of Opportunity, was initiated. This program is an attempt to establish areas of targeted economic specialization along key transportation routes. The Build Illinois and the Corridors of Opportunity programs appear to be concentrating on the state's basic infrastructure and traditional manufacturing industries. The programs do not take into consideration the importance of telecommunications services or telecommunications-intensive businesses to the state's economy.[34]

Likewise, DCCA has no other economic development program relating specifically to telecommunications. The agency does maintain a database on available business sites that includes telecommunications information. According to sources at DCCA, individual cases exist where DCCA has referred to prospective businesses specific sites that meet various location criteria including telecommunications. DCCA also frequently simply refers the prospective firm to Illinois Bell or another relevant local exchange company for additional telecommunications information. Thus, DCCA basically treats firms on an individualized basis in regard to telecommunications.[35]

A DCCA marketing manager also points out that traditional economic development activities attempt to attract and expand traditional types of industry, particularly manufacturing. Thus, most economic development programs are aimed primarily at capital-intensive plants, which are the historic strength of the Midwest. Telecommunications-intensive businesses, on the other hand, have developed more recently and are entities considerably different from the more traditional businesses. The information businesses have lower profiles and little public assistance available to them.[36]

This observation has some interesting implications for economic development policy in Illinois. The state is clearly losing its old manufacturing base and moving toward a service-based economy. Indeed, the state has a quite influential financial center in Chicago. Yet the state's economic development efforts primarily target traditional industries. Thus, Illinois may be fighting against irreversible structural change when it could be spending its resources to further develop its strengths in the information industry.

The DCCA marketing manager feels that DCCA will be paying more attention to nonmanufacturing industries in the future. This change will be a gradual and subtle shift in philosophy and not a dramatic change in DCCA policy. An example of this slow shift is a DCCA promotional effort aimed at attracting professional associations to the state. The program, which advertises Illinois as the "Land of Associations," is marketing the state's advantages as a center for national associations of such groups as insurance agents, university professors, and engineers, as well as groups such as the American Heart Association. This type of marketing effort is significant for DCCA because these associations are primarily involved in clerical, telecommunications, and publishing activities instead of other traditional activities such as manufacturing or trade. Thus, while DCCA is firmly entrenched in economic development activities for traditional Illinois business sectors, the agency is showing some new awareness to other types of business activities.[37]

There is considerable evidence that DCCA's main focus on manufacturing is the proper economic development strategy for such an agency. Even though manufacturing employs only 20 percent of the nation's work force, it accounts for another 40 to 60 million other jobs, the vast majority of which are in the service sector.[38] Without a significant manufacturing base, the state will have neither the demand nor the income to support its services. As a result, the state's emphasis on industrial development is probably well placed.

Chicago Economic Development

Like the state of Illinois, the City of Chicago does not appear to have made any link between economic development and telecommunications. The city's Economic Development Department has done nothing to use Chicago's telecommunications network as a development tool.[39] Similarly, the Economic Development Commission, a public and private planning body with linkages to the business community, has not made a linkage between the two issues. This commission is currently developing an economic development strategic plan for Chicago but has not yet raised the issue of telecommunications.[40] It also appears that the commission is concentrating its economic development efforts on traditional manufacturing as opposed to advanced technologies, partly because of real estate interests on the commission.[41]

The lack of public effort to link telecommunications with economic development is consistent with Illinois' free-market approach to telecommunications policy. This is not to say that policymakers, both public and private, do not recognize a link between economic development and telecommunications. Instead of using public means to make this link, Illinois relies upon free competition in the private sector, where efforts in telecommunications and economic development interact more directly. These efforts include the economic development efforts of Illinois Bell, the long distance advertising policy of AT&T, and the activities of the Information Industry Council of Metropolitan Chicago.

Private Initiatives

Illinois Bell

Just as Illinois Bell has led other BOCs in technical innovation, it has also led them in economic development initiatives. In 1978 Illinois Bell was the first Bell company to establish an economic development division. This was a bold move because Bell companies were reluctant to compete with each other for business, fearing that would be a zero sum game for the entire system. Divestiture, of course, has made competition the rule; now 16 of the 22 BOCs have economic development divisions.

The rationale behind Illinois Bell's economic development program is straightforward: the closing or relocation of businesses not only results in hardship for the people of Illinois but a loss of revenue for the phone company. Illinois Bell's primary strategy for economic development is to establish regional organizations to assist communities in attracting and retaining businesses. Illinois Bell has set up four such organizations in Illinois: the

Economic Development Council for the Southwest Suburbs, the Leadership Council of Southwest Illinois, Mid Metro (for western Cook County), and the South Suburban Regional Economic Development Council.[42]

An example of how these regional entities works is Mid Metro. Established in 1983 by Illinois Bell, Mid Metro is a cooperative partnership between businesses (other than Illinois Bell), local government, and educational institutions. To determine what types of economic development initiatives it should take, Mid Metro conducted a detailed survey of leaders in industry, commercial and financial businesses, city government, education, health care, social services, and local telephone management. The survey found that western Cook County was suffering from a decline in population and manufacturing employment.[43] Mid Metro then launched a series of industrial retention visits to encourage existing manufacturing firms to stay in Cook County. Given its broad membership, Mid Metro has tried to communicate the needs of business to local government. The desired result is a local government more responsive to the infrastructure and other needs of businesses in Cook County and of those considering locating there.

There is almost no link between economic development and telecommunications in this regional approach of Illinois Bell. Economic development and telecommunications stand side by side because their interests coincide. There is no effort to promote IBT's telephone network as a reason for service firms (or other TIBs) to locate in western Cook County. Indeed, a major impetus to the establishment of Mid Metro was the decline of manufacturing jobs in Cook County. By Illinois Bell's calculations, one job created increases its annual revenue by $726. A manufacturing job, however, creates an additional 3.2 support jobs; thus the creation of a manufacturing job yields additional annual revenue of $3,049 for Illinois Bell, or more than four times the revenue from a single job. Although it does not disclose its methodology, Illinois Bell took credit for the creation of 9,228 jobs through the third quarter of 1986 for a revenue gain of $16,753,462.[44]

The method by which Illinois Bell maximizes the use of its economic development resources could be a useful model for other states. To give the subject the detail it deserves, this chapter's case study will discuss the process Illinois Bell uses to promote economic development.

AT&T

Another private economic development activity related to telecommunications concerns AT&T. Because AT&T's inter-MSA toll service has been declared competitive, its inter-MSA toll rates are among the lowest of any AT&T division in the country. Even though AT&T's advertising has traditionally been national in orientation, the company is planning an advertising campaign that highlights the fact that AT&T Illinois has such low toll rates. For a company that has not ordinarily engaged in regional advertising, this is a significant development. Although obviously designed to create revenue for AT&T Illinois, it should help create jobs in the state. The strategy is also aimed at other state regulatory commissions; if other states lose business to Illinois' deregulated environment, those states might be pressured to do what AT&T most desires, deregulate.[45]

Information Industry Council of Metropolitan Chicago

Another private economic development effort linked with telecommunications is taking place in Chicago by a group called the Information Industry Council of Metropolitan Chicago. The council is a coalition of companies involved in telecommunications, computer software, microelectronics, and information generation and handling. In addition, universities and government actors are represented. The council's board of directors is quite impressive, with the chief executive officers of Ameritech and Arthur Anderson & Company serving as chairman and vice-chairman respectively. Other board members include the top leaders of Motorola, IBM, Zenith Electronics, AT&T, Bell & Howell Company, Northwestern University, DePaul University, and the University of Chicago.[46]

The council's primary objective is to stimulate information industry growth. To that end, the council has taken several steps. First, it has attempted to bridge gaps between universities and industries to foster greater technology transfer in the information industries. Second, the council has been actively promoting the Chicago area as a leading technological center to attract new businesses.[47] Third, the council co-sponsored a national information industry conference held in Chicago in October 1987. The convention's program, which featured several leaders of Chicago's information industries, included case studies of how leading firms are using new information technologies to gain advantages over their competition.[48] Finally, the council provides information and priorities on information industry matters to a research group called the Institute for Illinois. The goal of this organization is to provide nonpartisan policy suggestions for the Illinois congressional delegation to act upon.[49]

Council sources state that almost all of the requests for assistance that it receives come from software companies. Telecommunications topics, such as new technologies, service availability, and price, are not common issues that the Information Industry Council faces.[50] In addition, large telecommunications users appear to have no problem obtaining and using telecommunications equipment that they need in their businesses.[51] Thus, it appears that the pro-competitive regulatory environment in Illinois does not hinder the economic activities of telecommunications-intensive businesses.

CONCLUSIONS

The Illinois response to divestiture has been to emphasize competition. The philosophy that the marketplace can best maximize the benefits of telecommunications to the economy is present in the Universal Telephone Service Protection Act as well as the private economic development initiatives of Illinois Bell. The drafters of the UTSPA felt that regulation of a monopoly was no longer feasible in an environment of growing competition, and that idea motivated the writing and passage of the act. Other factors contributing to a regulatory environment favorable to competition include the tradition of innovation and technical excellence at Illinois Bell, the pro-deregulation bent of former ICC chairmen Phil O'Connor and Michael Hasten, and the relatively positive image of the telecommunications industry in contrast to the electric utility industry. No evidence was found indicating that the changing structure of the state's economy (the loss of manufacturing jobs and growth of the service sector) was a causal force behind telecommunications policy.

Illinois' favorable view toward competition has made the link between telecommunications and economic development hard to find. The elusiveness of the link is manifest in the economic development program of Illinois Bell in which telecommunications stands next to economic development, rather than being a leading part of the IBT program. IBT has sought to maximize the number of customers it serves using whatever economic development strategies it can employ; telecommunications is not often one of them. The lack of any orientation toward telecommunications in the economic development programs of the DCCA also shows how hard it is to find a link between telecommunications and economic development in Illinois.

Yet one should not confuse the elusiveness of the link between telecommunications and economic development policy in Illinois with the lack of any such link at all. Indeed, the state has deliberately kept this link distant at the policy level, opting instead to let competition in the marketplace substitute for directive state policy. The UTSPA is legislation designed to assist in the transition to competition in telecommunications markets. When it sunsets in 1991, the state can assess how competition has worked and then decide whether to move forward with competition or exercise increased regulatory oversight.

Is such a strategy sound? Given that the strategy is aimed at maximizing the benefits of telecommunications to the economy, it makes sense in Illinois to delegate much of that responsibility to the private sector. Telecommunications is unlike other infrastructure in that it has been traditionally provided by the private sector. This is in contrast to railroads, highways, and dams, all of which have been substantially funded by government. Because the state has no experience in building the telecommunications network and has had control of the network only through regulation, it makes sense to address the emerging importance of the network through regulation. Illinois has chosen the route of less regulation as a means to let large users and telecommunications companies interact with the expectation that this interaction will produce good results. This strategy has been described as "the least worse off theory."[52] Continuing traditional regulation, the theory goes, is bound to have poor consequences on local rates as large users bypass the system. Allowing IBT to compete with new providers not only recognizes the reality of the marketplace, but gives IBT a chance to retain large customers and keep local rates down. Local rates may still rise, as NTS costs are shifted to end users, but the outcome under more competition is not likely to be as bad as under traditional monopoly regulation. Again, Illinois Bell's long history of technical innovation contributes to this trust in the marketplace.

A remaining issue, however, is how well the consumer will be protected in an environment of less regulation. As has been noted, much of the policy intent behind the UTSPA has been to encourage marginal cost pricing of telecommunications services. Given the prior existence of subsidization of residential service by business users, the result of the UTSPA has been to make residential service more expensive and business service less expensive. However, there has been no significant outcry from consumer groups regarding the rising cost of telephone service. Most of the resources of consumer groups has been directed to high electric rates in the state.

The UTSPA, as its name implies, is designed to preserve universal service throughout the state. So far there is little evidence that universal service is on the decline in the state. As noted, Illinois is above the national average for market penetration of telephone service. The ICC is, however, very sensitive to this issue. The UTSPA requires that Illinois participate in all federal programs aimed at preserving universal service. The act also stipulates that any such participation be cost effective for the state. The commission has determined that state participation in the FCC's Link-Up America plan would be cost effective and has opened up a docket (ICC Case No. 87-0432) to examine the criteria for inclusion of low-income persons in the program. It seems that, despite the pro-business thrust of much of Illinois' telecommunications policy, protection of universal service remains a very active concern of the ICC.

In summary, Illinois has chosen to retain much control of telecommunications policy in the Illinois Commerce Commission, subject, as always, to its authority being changed by the General Assembly. The locus of policy has not shifted to the DCCA, even though the telecommunications network has become increasingly important infrastructure in the economy in recent years. There has been little need for a shift in policymaking focus because the state's primary policy response to divestiture has been less regulation. Thus, while Illinois has been quite explicit in its policy response to divestiture, it has not been very interventionist. The state has, through the UTSPA, opted for a policy of introducing competition to telecommunication markets on the theory that such a policy will maximize the benefit of telecommunications to the state. The UTSPA's emphasis on less regulation makes the policy bent less interventionist than other states. It remains to be seen, perhaps when the UTSPA sunsets in 1991 and an assessment of the benefits of competition can be made, whether a more directive role for the state in telecommunications policy will emerge.

CASE STUDY: ILLINOIS BELL AND ECONOMIC DEVELOPMENT

The focus of this case study will be the method used by Illinois Bell to promote economic development in Illinois. By identifying influential business and government leaders in a community and developing a consensus among these leaders to follow through on economic development efforts, Illinois Bell has built an effective program with its limited resources. This type of consensus building and follow-up may serve as a model for other Bell operating companies or other state agencies.

Illinois Bell favors a regional approach in its economic development programs for two reasons. First, it is the most effective way to leverage the company's economic development funds. By mobilizing a large number of key business people in a region, Illinois Bell feels it can get a greater matching-fund commitment from business than if its efforts were more concentrated in many small localities. Second, the regional approach enables Illinois Bell to identify problems specific to the region and concentrate resources on those problems. Thus counterproductive competition among various local economic development entities with different needs is avoided.

Another ingredient Illinois Bell brings to economic development, which the company feels the public sector cannot, is staying power. Whereas public officials and their agenda change with new gubernatorial administrations, Illinois Bell is in a much better position to develop an institutional memory and learn from mistakes. Illinois Bell feels state agencies, with a high turnover in personnel, are unlikely to be able to gain this long-term perspective.

How does Illinois Bell's economic development efforts work in practice? A good example is the company's program in East St. Louis, called Target

2000.[53] In 1977 the president of Illinois Bell made a commitment to develop East St. Louis, a chronically depressed area. Illinois Bell immediately sought out the "movers and shakers" in the business community, not just public representatives but the heads of major companies, unions, and minority groups. The first task was to convince these community leaders to contribute some money to establish a small economic development agency.

The second and more important task was follow-up. Most community leaders are more than willing to set up an economic development agency and hire an executive director. After that, however, there is a tendency to lose interest. Primarily through exhortation, Illinois Bell keeps top community leaders involved and committed to the program. In East St. Louis, Illinois Bell's continued pressure on community leaders helped ensure the program's success.

Illinois Bell also uses its technological resources to maintain community interest. In East St. Louis, the company installed some of its most advanced equipment as part of its commitment to upgrade the community's infrastructure. It must be emphasized, however, that Illinois Bell's economic development work is not ordinarily tied to its network capabilities. The main point here is that Illinois Bell will do what it must to accomplish its economic development goals; in this case, using its network was central to that goal.

What has been the result of Illinois Bell's economic development efforts in East St. Louis? Illinois Bell claims great credit for dramatic economic improvements in East St. Louis; Target 2000 is characterized as the leading force behind redevelopment in the city.[54] The tax base, which was $33 million in 1978, is now $48 million. Illinois Bell literature says nothing, however, about how much the tax base could have grown without its economic development efforts. The broadened tax base has resulted in a drop in the tax rate from 11 percent to 8.4 percent.[55] In addition to overall economic improvement, which means retention and attraction of customers, Illinois Bell has also recently been awarded the telecommunications contract for a major residential development being built.

Another success of Illinois Bell's economic development activities is its Friends of Small Business division. The division attempts to assist small and innovative businesses throughout the state. In 1986 the Small Business Administration awarded the program and its director, Jack Sheehan, a national small business development award.[56] The division and Sheehan are also highly regarded among economic development professionals in Illinois.[57]

There is a final, less tangible component to the Illinois Bell economic development program--the company's supreme confidence in its ability to do its job better than anyone else. This attitude does not reflect an antagonistic attitude toward the state; indeed both Illinois Bell and DCCA acknowledge a cooperative relationship with each other. It is simply that Illinois Bell has been doing its job for ten years, and its employees feel that they have honed their techniques to a science. According to Illinois Bell, the public sector starts with a dream and tries to fund it, whereas Illinois Bell tries to see what funds are available and make the most of them. Certainly a measure of confidence is helpful when trying to leverage scarce funds.

In summing up Illinois Bell's economic development program, it is worth reemphasizing that the company views economic development as a group process. Illinois Bell seeks to bring disparate groups together to foster a cooperative atmosphere that breaks down traditional rivalries. It is also worth remembering that the company's goal is to increase its revenue. By retaining and encouraging expansion of existing businesses and by attracting new ones, Illinois Bell hopes its efforts will ultimately expand its revenue base.

NOTES

1.   Barry Bluestone and Bennett Harrison, The Deindustrialization of America (New York: Basic Books, Inc., 1982), pp. 35-40.

2.   Illinois Commerce Commission, Annual Report of Telecommunication 1987 (Springfield, January 1988), pp. 4-5.

3.   Ameritech, Annual Report 1986 (Chicago, 1987), pp. 16-23.

4.   Illinois Commerce Commission, Annual Report of Telecommunications 1987, pp. 40-46.

5.   Telephone interview with David Rudd, Director of Legislative and Intergovernmental Affairs, Illinois Commerce Commission, Springfield, March 2, 1988.

6.   Interview with Lois Rosen, Executive Staff Director, Labor Coalition of Public Utilities, Chicago, January 7, 1988; interview with Mike Farmer, Regional Marketing Manager, Illinois Department of Commerce and Community Affairs, Springfield, January 5, 1988.

7.   Interview with Todd Glenn, Vice-President of Regulatory Affairs, Illinois Bell Telephone Co., Chicago, January 5, 1988.

8.   Paul Teske, State Telecommunications Regulation (Washington, D.C.: Office of Technology Assessment, 1987), p. 31. (Draft report).

9.   Christine Winter, "Illinois Bell Reaches to High Tech," Chicago Tribune, May 5, 1986.

10.   Teske, State Telecommunications, p. 33.

11.   Illinois Commerce Commission, Annual Report on Telecommunications 1986 (Springfield: Illinois Commerce Commission, 1987), pp. 25-26.

12.   Teske, State Telecommunications, p. 34.

13.   Ibid., p. 35.

14.   Martha Derthick and Paul Quirk, The Politics of Deregulation (Washington D.C.: The Brookings Institution, 1985), pp. 35-57.

15.   Interview with Gregory K. Busch, former Staff Director, Joint House-Senate Committee, Springfield, Illinois, January 3, 1988. (Mr. Busch's committee rewrote the Illinois Public Utilities Act. He is now a private consultant in Springfield.)

16.   Ibid.

17.   Ibid.

18.   David Rudd, The Illinois Universal Telephone Service Protection Act of 1985: A Path to Competition (Springfield: Illinois Commerce Commission, November 1985), p. 4.

19.   Interview with Busch.

20.   Rudd, Illinois Universal Telephone Service, p. 6.

21.   Ibid., p. 11.

22.   Ibid., p. 14.

23.   Interview with Busch.

24.   Rudd, Illinois Universal Telephone Service, pp. 16-17.

25.   Ibid., pp. 18-19.

26.   Interview with Glenn.

27.   Ibid.

28.   Illinois Commerce Commission, Annual Report on Telecommunications 1986, pp. 28- 29.

29.   Telephone interview with Rudd.

30.   Interview with Charles Miller, Telecommunications Director, Illinois Department of Central Management Services, Springfield, January 4, 1988.

31.   Illinois Department of Central Management Services, Strategic Communications Network Plan (Springfield, 1987), pp. ES-1, 3-34.

32.   Interview with Miller.

33.   Illinois Department of Central Management Services, Strategic Communications Network Plan, pp. 3-13.

34.   Interview with Miller.

35.   Illinois Department of Commerce and Community Affairs, Sell Illinois (Springfield, 1986), p. iii.

36.   Interview with Farmer.

37.   Ibid.

38.   Telephone interview with Farmer, March 4, 1988.

39.   Stephen Cohen and John Zysman, "The Myth of a Post-Industrial Society," Technology Review, February/March 1987, p. 56.

40.   Telephone interview with Duane Davie, Chicago Economic Development Department, Chicago, November 18, 1987.

41.   Telephone interview with Paul Borek, Chicago Economic Development Commission, Chicago, November 17, 1987.

42.   Interview with Nina Shephard, Program Director, Information Industry Council of Metropolitan Chicago, Chicago, January 8, 1988.

43.   Illinois Bell Telephone Company, Almost a Decade: Economic Development at Illinois Bell, 1986 (Chicago, 1986), pp. 1-8.

44.   Chicago Association of Commerce and Industry, Chicagoland Development, vol. 14, no. 10 (October 1984), pp. 8-9.

45.   Illinois Bell Telephone Company, Almost a Decade, pp. 1-8.

46.   Telephone interview with Bill McQueen, Vice-President of Regulation, AT&T of Illinois, Springfield, November 18, 1987.

47.   Information Industry Council of Metropolitan Chicago, "The Information Industry Council of Metropolitan Chicago," Chicago, n.d. (Promotional brochure).

48.   Ibid.

49.   Civic Committee of the Commercial Club of Chicago, "Local Information Industry Council to Co-Host National Convention," Chicago, November 13, 1987. (Press release).

50.   Interview with Shephard.

51.   Ibid.

52.   Interview with Bob Riebe, Telecommunications Manager, First National Bank of Chicago, January 6, 1988; interview with James Rayburn, Telecommunications Director, Chicago Mercantile Exchange, January 6, 1988.

53.   Most of the information in this section comes from an interview with Gerald Veach, Manager, Economic Development Division, Illinois Bell Telephone Company, Springfield, January 3, 1988.

54.   Illinois Bell Telephone Company, Almost a Decade, pp. 4-5.

55.   Ibid.

56.   Ibid., p. 4.

57.   Interview with Shephard.

58.   Interview with Busch, Austin, Texas, April 8, 1988.

5

Nebraska

Joellen M. Harper and Benet Younger

Telecommunications policy in Nebraska is of special interest because of innovative legislation passed by the state in 1986. Legislative Bill 835 deregulates telecommunications rates and services while maintaining the telephone companies' territorial franchise on their local exchange areas. L.B. 835 was passed with heavy lobbying by the telecommunications industry and with strong support from then Senator John DeCamp. Much of the rationale behind this legislation was the expectation that it would promote economic development and make Nebraska a telecommunications leader in the United States.

The legislation has not been implemented without opposition, however. The state attorney general, at the request of the Public Service Commission, filed a case with the Lancaster County District Court claiming that L.B. 835 is unconstitutional. The court affirmed the legislation's constitutionality and directed the commission to implement the conditions of the bill. The commission began implementation in April 1987, but the attorney general has filed an appeal with the Supreme Court contesting that ruling. The commission clearly believes that L.B. 835 will be harmful to Nebraska consumers.

Nebraska is dissimilar to most other states: its annual population growth rate is less than half that of the U.S. average; it has a large rural population and is sparsely populated; its economy revolves around agribusiness, only three of the state's eight nonagricultural sectors experienced growth in their share of employment between 1980 and 1986, and annual growth in total employment in the nonagricultural sectors has been well below that of the national rate.

Nebraska is, however, home of numerous large users of telecommunications, specifically many telemarketing firms and reservation centers. The majority of these large users are concentrated in the city of Omaha. Hence Omaha is often referred to as the "800 Capital of the World." These businesses rely heavily on the telecommunications companies for quality and reliable service. It was hoped by many that L.B. 835 would promote the telecommunications industry and provide needed diversification to offset the weakened agricultural industry.

The policy environment in Nebraska surrounding telecommunications and economic development is complex because numerous actors are involved. The state has a unicameral legislature, setting Nebraska apart from other states in its legislative and lobbying processes. The Public Service Commission was a significant player before the passage of the 1986 legislation, but it has now lost most of its regulatory responsibility. Large telecommunications users play only a minor role and are rarely involved directly in the policymaking process. However, they have been used to illustrate the need for legislation or tangible action. There are no consumer advocate groups present in Nebraska, leading one to wonder who is looking out for the best interests of consumers. Finally, a very significant actor in the policy environment is Northwestern Bell, the largest telephone company in the state. It has created its own Office of Economic Development to work with the Nebraska Department of Economic Development to promote the telecommunications industry in the state. The motivation for such efforts on behalf on Northwestern Bell stems from a vested interest in the growth of the state.[1]

The telecommunications industry is a significant portion of the Nebraska economy; therefore the state is aware of the need to support existing telecommunications-intensive businesses as well as to attract new ones. (To a certain extent, the 1986 legislation is an example of this.) However, tangible state efforts to promote telecommunications have been significantly lacking since the former governor, a noted proponent of the telephone companies, left office in January 1987. Although the Department of Economic Development has recently renewed its efforts to promote the telecommunications industry, there is still no explicit action by the state of using telecommunications technology to foster economic development.

AGNET, a computer information network for the agriculture industry, is a specific example of telecommunications technology being used directly to promote economic development in the state. It was developed in Nebraska in 1975 and has since expanded across the United States and internationally. However, the initiative behind AGNET was not from specific state efforts, and there have been no similiar efforts undertaken in recent years.

There are many issues to be considered in relation to the passage and implementation of L.B. 835 in Nebraska. It has implications for the link between telecommunications and economic development, and the impact that promotion of the link can have upon a state's economy. The impact the legislation will have and the fate of L.B. 835 itself are uncertain. Nevertheless, many states are watching the telecommunications story unfold in Nebraska.

THE ECONOMY AND THE TELECOMMUNICATIONS INDUSTRY
Economic Profile

The economy in Nebraska revolves around the agricultural industry. Nebraska ranked fifth in 1985 for total value of its farm commodities. The four leading commodities by value in the state are cattle, corn, hogs, and soybeans.[2] The agriculture industry across the nation has been declining in the 1980s, so

Nebraska is seeking to diversify its economy. Diversification most likely will occur in areas closely related to agriculture, such as food processing.

Table 5.1
Nonagricultural Employment Shares and Annual
Percentage Change in Employment* for Nebraska and
the United States, 1980 and 1986
(total employees in 1,000s, share and change in %)

| Sector | Employment Shares | | | | Annual Employment Change | |
| | 1980 | | 1986 | | | |
	Nebraska	U.S.	Nebraska	U.S.	Nebraska	U.S.
Mining	0.3	1.1	0.3	0.8	2.0	-3.9
Construction	4.6	4.9	3.8	4.9	-2.4	1.6
Manufacturing	15.2	22.5	13.1	19.1	-1.8	-1.1
Transportation	7.6	5.7	6.6	5.3	-1.7	.3
Wholesale and Retail Trade	26.2	22.7	25.8	23.7	0.4	2.4
Fin., Ins., Real Estate	6.8	5.7	7.2	6.3	1.8	3.7
Services	18.7	19.6	22.4	23.2	4.1	5.0
Government	20.8	17.8	20.8	16.8	0.6	0.6
Total	631	90,657	654	99,610	0.6	1.7

* Totals may reflect rounding error.

Source: U.S. Department of Labor, Bureau of Labor Statistics, Employment and Earnings, vol. 34, no. 5 (May 1987), pp. 120-137; idem, vol. 28, no. 5 (May 1981) pp. 120-128.

Table 5.2
Employment Shares and Annual Changes in Employment* of
Telecommunications-Intensive Businesses** for Nebraska
and the United States, 1980 and 1984
(share and change in %)

	Employment Shares				Annual Employment Change	
	1980		1984			
	Nebraska	U.S.	Nebraska	U.S.	Nebraska	U.S.
Information Services	10.3	9.1	11.5	9.9	2.7	3.2
Finance	3.2	3.1	3.5	3.3	2.1	3.2
Insurance	3.9	2.3	3.8	2.3	-0.9	1.0
Real Estate	0.9	1.3	0.8	1.4	-1.8	1.6
Computer/Data Proc.	0.5	0.4	0.8	0.6	15.2	13.1
Other Information Svcs.	1.8	2.1	2.0	2.3	2.7	4.5
Info. Technology Equip.	2.2	2.2	1.8	2.3	-5.1	2.4
Research & Development	0.07	0.3	0.1	0.3	9.0	2.9
Media	5.0	3.7	4.0	3.7	-5.3	0.5
Total	17.8		17.3		0.01	

* Totals may reflect rounding error.

** The Telecommunications-Intensive Business categories are defined by Standard Industrial Classification codes as follows:
    1. Information Services: Finance: SIC 60 (Banking), SIC 61 (Credit), SIC 62 (Commodities); Insurance: SIC 63 (Insurance Carriers), SIC 64 (Insurance Agents); Real Estate: SIC 65; Computer/Data Proc.: SIC 737; Other Information Services: SIC 731 (Advertising), SIC 732 (Credit Reporting), SIC 81 (Legal Services), SIC 891 (Engineering and Architectural Services), SIC 893 (Accounting and Auditing);
    2. Information Technology Equipment: SIC 3573 (Electronic Computing Equipment), SIC 361 (Electronic Distributing Equipment), SIC 365 (Radio and TV Receiving Equipment), SIC 366 (Communications Equipment), SIC 367 (Electronic Components and Accessories);
    3. Research and Development: SIC 7391 (Research and Development Laboratories), SIC 7397 (Commercial Testing Laboratories), SIC 892 (Nonprofit Education and Scientific Research Agencies);
    4. Media: SIC 27 (Printing and Publishing), SIC 48 (Communications), SIC 735 (News Syndicates), SIC 78 (Motion Pictures).

Source: U.S. Bureau of the Census, County Business Patterns, United States (no. 1) and Nebraska (no. 29) (Washington, D.C.: U.S. Government Printing Office, 1980 and 1984), Table 1B.

Nebraska experienced employment growth between 1980 and 1986 in only three nonagricultural sectors: mining; finance, insurance, and real estate

(FIRE); and the service industries. Wholesale and retail sales consistently have claimed the greatest sectoral share of employment. By 1986, the fast-growing service sector had assumed second place, accounting for 22.4 percent of the nonagricultural employment; employment in government represented 20.8 percent of total employment, approximately the same as in 1980. These three sectors accounted for 69.0 percent of the total nonagricultural employment in 1986. Total employment over all of the sectors increased by approximately 23,000 jobs from 1980 to 1986; this represents an annual growth rate in employment of 0.6 percent, which was well below the national rate (Table 5.1).

In 1980 and 1984, Nebraska had a greater proportion of its labor force employed in the information services and media categories of the telecommunications-intensive businesses (TIBs) than the U.S. average (Table 5.2). The computer and data processing portion of the information services category grew significantly between 1980 and 1984, with an annual change in the share of employment of 15.2 percent. The state's share of employees working in the information technology equipment sector equaled the U.S. average in 1980, but fell behind it in 1984. Nebraska trailed the U.S. average for share of employees in research and development in both 1980 and 1984, although there was strong annual growth in this sector between these years, averaging 9 percent per year. However, total employment in TIBs in Nebraska fell between 1980 and 1984.

Telecommunications Companies

Telecommunications providers in Nebraska include Northwestern Bell Telephone Company (a subsidiary of US West), Lincoln Telephone & Telegraph Company, and 36 other local exchange companies. The major companies that offer interLATA services are AT&T Communications of the Midwest, MCI Telecommunications, Lintel Systems Inc., and US Sprint.

Local exchange carriers

Northwestern Bell and Lincoln Telephone & Telegraph serve the majority of the urban population in Nebraska. The remainder of the companies dominate the largely rural areas of the state (Table 5.3). The main sources of revenue for local exchange companies are derived from access charges, revenues from basic exchange service, and revenues from long distance calls originated by their own subscribers (intraLATA toll).[3]

US West is the regional Bell operating company (RBOC) whose territory includes Nebraska and 13 other states. Its subsidiary, Northwestern Bell, serves the Nebraska area and is the largest phone company in Nebraska. US West is well known for its aggressive stance on telecommunications deregulation. As stated in the company's 1986 annual report, "We believe the decision to enter--or not enter--markets should be made by the people who are accountable to their customers and shareowners, not by regulators or judges."[4]

US West has received some strong criticism because of its aggressive stance. Some of the criticism is because of the 1,500-person research center that the company has planned. Some of the states in the US West region complained that the company had created a "bidding war" among them, making deregulation an unstated condition for the center's placement.[5] US West maintains that the regulatory environment was only one of the criteria for determining the location of the research center. Other considerations were education (K-12 and universities), quality of life, business climate, transportation (access, number of flights), and technical initiatives. A spokesman at Northwestern Bell explains that only three questions were asked of states concerning regulatory environment; this is proof that US West was not overemphasizing deregulation or attempting to push deregulation in return for the center's placement.[6] There is some uncertainty over whether Judge Greene's ruling on manufacturing also prohibits research and development by the Bell operating companies.[7] If approved, the site for the research center will be Denver, Colorado.

Table 5.3
Local Exchange Carriers and Access Lines
in Nebraska, 1986

Local Exchange Carrier	Access Lines	Share of Total (%)*
Northwestern Bell	428,202	55.6
Lincoln Telephone & Telegraph	200,050	25.9
General Telephone Co.	43,785	5.5
Great Plains Communications Inc.	24,606	3.1
United Telephone Co.	23,632	2.9
Others **	54,214	6.9
Total	774,489	100.0

* Totals may reflect rounding error.

** Includes 33 other local exchange carriers.

Source: Nebraska Public Service Commission, 1987 Annual Report on Telecommunications to the Nebraska Unicameral Legislature (Lincoln, January 1988), pp. 17-18.

Since deregulation legislation was passed in Nebraska, Northwestern Bell has not increased its rates and maintains that it does not intend to do so in the near future.[8] Nevertheless, US West has stated that if the constitutionality of the Nebraska legislation is upheld by its Supreme Court, it intends to "lower business rates in Nebraska and recover by raising residential rates."[9]

Lincoln Telephone & Telegraph (LT&T) is a subsidiary of Lincoln Telecommunications Company. Other subsidiaries of Lincoln Telecommunications Company are Lincoln Telephone Service and Supply

Company, which distributes telecommunications equipment, LinTel Systems, which provides both long distance telephone services and business equipment, and Alarm Systems of Nebraska.[10] LT&T, supplying the company's local telephone services, is the second largest telecommunications provider in the state. In 1986, LT&T developed a fiber optic facility linking the cities of Lincoln and Omaha, Nebraska's two metropolitan cities. LT&T has set a goal of a completely digital network by the early 1990s, and claims that at the end of 1986 over 75 percent of its customers were served by digital switching equipment.[11]

The Nebraska Telephone Association (NTA) is an organization of Nebraska local exchange companies. The NTA consisted of 39 members in 1986-1987, with a combined total of over 715,000 access lines.[12] Members of the association range in size from Northwestern Bell down to Sodtown Telephone Company, which provides only 78 access lines.

The association, which was established in 1957, is governed by a fourteen-member board of directors. Assisting the NTA in establishing its goals and policy priorities are seven committees: Budget and Laws, Compensation, Mobile Frequency, Regulatory, Safety, Seminar, Small Company, and Legislative.[13] The NTA focuses on three areas: legislative, regulatory (primarily involving the Public Service Commission), and federal (assessing FCC decisions and rulings).

One might expect somewhat of a dichotomy within the association because of the variety and sizes of companies it represents. However, the president of the NTA believes that a strong unity exists. Although at times the needs and interests of one group of companies may be more evident, the general consensus is that working together is of benefit to all.[14]

Interexchange carriers

L.B. 835 detariffed intrastate rates in Nebraska. The long distance companies providing service to Nebraska are AT&T Communications of the Midwest, Lintel Systems Inc., MCI, US Sprint, TeleMarketing Investments Ltd., Dial-Net Inc., Teleconnect Company, Western Union, and United Telephone Long Distance. In addition to these, International Telecharge, Inc., has an application pending to provide service in Nebraska.

Equal access long distance service is available to slightly less than half of Nebraska's lines, as compared with a national average of around 87 percent. Telephone subscribers in equal access areas may select from among the interexchange carriers listed previously. Equal access has been implemented in the communities surrounding Omaha and Lincoln as well as in the Grand Island community, and has been approved for the communities of Gering, Scotts Bluff, and Morrill.[15] Those subscribers to whom equal access is not available are provided with access numbers by their chosen interexchange companies. Subscribers may dial into the chosen system to place long distance calls. Drawbacks to the dial-in systems include the time involved in placing calls, the inferior quality of connections, and a greater probability of dialing errors.

Nebraska is served by AT&T Communications of the Midwest, which is required to provide long distance service to the entire state. Because AT&T is the carrier of last resort, it is required to provide service to the rural, higher-cost areas. Other carriers may choose the areas to which they provide service, so they are able to keep costs down. For this reason, AT&T claims that it "needs every lever it can get to lower costs."[16]

Large Users: 800 Services in Omaha

Omaha, the larger of the two metropolitan areas in Nebraska, is home to many large users. Among them are national health insurance companies and various financial institutions. First National Bank in Omaha processes VISA's credit card transactions, and First Data Resources, founded in Omaha in 1971, is the largest third-party processor of database credit cards in the country. Applied Communications, Inc., designed and developed the automatic teller system (ATM), which is based on telecommunication linkups.[17] However, by far the largest users of telecommunications are the telemarketers and reservation centers who depend on WATS and 800 services.

Omaha has been called the "800 Capital of the World." Certainly Omaha and the surrounding area are densely populated by telemarketing businesses that are intensive users of 800 and WATS services. These businesses employ a large number of Omaha's work force. The Omaha Chamber of Commerce lists over 60 firms in that city which are involved in telemarketing. Of those businesses, some are direct telemarketers whose daily business involves long distance telephone sales, some are contractors who offer their telemarketing expertise to businesses that are not interested in setting up such activities in-house, several are reservation centers for large business chains such as hotels, and a few provide support services such as software and record-keeping or number-crunching via telecommunications links.

Telemarketing

Direct telemarketing may be conducted by a firm whose primary business is not telemarketing. A producer or distributor may have in-house operations that handle the telemarketing needs of the firm. These services may also be offered by telemarketing contractors. These firms contract with companies on a product-by-product basis. These exclusively telemarketing firms have become expert in their fields, and their experience alone is quite valuable to companies wishing to market products or services. In addition to the expertise offered, firms contracting for these services are freed from the complications involved in handling them in-house: additional bookkeeping, records files, interface with the phone company, office space requirements, and all of the headaches involved in expanding a business into support services.

Inbound telemarketing relies on 800-line services. These services are often based on advertising that includes an 800 telephone number to be called for more information or for ordering a product. This method of marketing is a "scatter shot" approach. Except for design, advertising, or packaging purposes, no target market is defined for the product. The advertising message is delivered to a broad segment of the market in the hopes that some of those who receive the message will respond.

Another, potentially greater use of inbound telemarketing is for handling catalog orders. Any business that issues a catalog of its products today without including an 800 number will probably not be in business tomorrow. Businesses must cater to the desire of consumers to be able to purchase products quickly. Larger businesses may handle these telemarketing needs in-house, but for smaller companies, a telemarketing contractor can answer phones, take orders, and compile all necessary information, leaving the business free to devote its efforts to production and distribution. The contractor transmits to the producer all of the information about each order--the product, the buyer's address, and the method of billing--leaving the producer to simply fill the order.

Outbound telemarketing, which generally relies on WATS lines, is very different from inbound telemarketing. In outbound telemarketing, a strong potential market is targeted. Phone lists that target that market are obtained, and only those customers who are expected to respond are contacted. Outbound telemarketing involves calling each individual in the targeted market, or as many of them as possible. Often outbound telemarketing is used to offer a customer enhancements to services or goods he or she has already bought. For instance, cable subscribers may be offered premium channels, or people with low insurance coverage may be presented with a higher coverage plan. When the contracting company has properly targeted the product and the market, such direct-contact marketing can be highly successful.

Reservation Centers

Many large chain operations, especially hotels, have established "800 Reservation Centers." These centers allow customers or would-be customers to call a single number to make reservations or obtain information about all of a company's outlets. A large number of the telemarketers in Omaha are not direct telemarketers but rather 800 centers for hotel chains. For instance, a caller may contact a reservation center to learn about the rates and amenities at a particular hotel in the chain; to compare hotels in different cities; and to make reservations for a particular hotel. Another advantage of the reservation center is the increased attention the chain receives from travel agents. By having a single number to call, from which an agent may obtain an immediate confirmation, the chain has greatly increased its usefulness to travel agents. The more hotel chains that offer this service, the more the travel industry demands it, until it is unrealistic for any large hotel chain to be without a reservation center. Not only hotel chains but also car rental agencies, moving companies, and even large-scale distributors have found that such operations offer many rewards.

Attractions of Omaha for Telecommunications-intensive businesses

Many of these firms have chosen to locate in the Omaha area for several reasons: the sociological characteristics of the region, its central location, and the support services offered.

The people of Nebraska seem to supply the ideal work force for the telemarketing industry. The lack of a regional accent is desirable in a person answering phone calls from all across the country. The Midwest accent lacks the northern nasal sound, the southern drawl, the Texas twang, and the other regional irritants that may sometimes offend people with other accents. This ability to span the regions of the nation is a boon to the business.

The midwestern work ethic, strong in Nebraska, contributes to an extremely productive work force. Nebraska has a productivity rate demonstrably higher than the national average, a desirable feature for any industry. The lower rate of absenteeism and turnover result in much lower costs to the companies.

Nebraska is also well suited to nationwide telephone answering for its central location. Being in roughly the geographic center of the continental United States, phone centers in Nebraska can operate with relatively normal shifts and still span the four-hour nationwide time difference. This central placement is also ideally suited from the standpoint of costs. Calls need not travel across the entire continent, but only halfway in either direction. Shorter call distance results in lower costs. In a business in which telecommunications costs are the major operating costs, location is very important.

The final group of enticements that Omaha offers to telemarketers are the unmatched support services. Northwestern Bell, the local exchange company for the Omaha area, among others, is committed to working with the telemarketers in every possible way. Northwestern Bell provides critical support service to these businesses. First of all, such a large number of available wires exists that there is never a shortage of that facility. Northwestern Bell will prewire telemarketers' businesses upon request. Prewires can be converted to operating lines within one to two hours, a hookup time that is not equalled by most other companies. Further, Northwestern Bell provides its 800-line customers with a "peg count" each day. The peg count is an hour-by-hour listing of the number of lines in use, the call volume handled, and the percentage of calls not able to reach the telemarketer due to busy lines. This critical information can tell a firm whether it has too many or too few lines in operation, allowing it to hold down excess cost while still meeting the industry standard. This hourly listing also lets businesses know what their peak calling hours are so that they can schedule operators accordingly.

Northwestern Bell has created the 800 Power Group, a division to work with the special needs of the telemarketers. In addition to the services already discussed, this group can provide technical assistance to beginning or would-be telemarketers.

Northwestern Bell is also active in recruiting telemarketers to the area. As part of its economic development program, Northwestern Bell recruits such firms as well as providing communities throughout Nebraska with technical information and expertise needed to begin or attract such enterprises. With all of these incentives, it is no surprise that Omaha is the 800 capital of the world.

POLICY DEVELOPMENT
Political Culture

Nebraska is a microcosm of classic middle America. Nebraskans are proud of their "homegrown" heritage. They tend to be forthright in their opinions and their actions. Nebraskans take a pragmatic approach to problem-solving and consider themselves independent thinkers. They are generally conservative, both morally and politically. A certain distaste for governmental intervention is even expressed in the dealings of the legislature.[18]

This distaste, however, does not translate into strong consumer advocacy. In telecommunications, when a community is strongly affected by an action, a neighborhood association might organize to advocate its interests, but there is no ongoing organization. When the 1986 deregulation legislation was debated in the legislature, an independent lobbyist represented the Council for Fair Telephone Rates. This organization of small businesses did not fight deregulation, but only worked to ensure that its interests were represented. The council is no longer active.[19]

A key source of Nebraska pride is the strong work ethic of its citizens. Nebraska is a right-to-work state. The strength of the work ethic can be measured by the high productivity among Nebraska's businesses. According to the 1982 census of all manufacturers, the state's rate of productivity as measured by the value added per dollar of production worker payroll outranks the national average. Nebraska's rate by this measure is $4.38, whereas that for the United States is $4.04. This is not only a point of pride but also a selling point. Those particularly interested in Nebraska's economic development are quick to point out the strong work ethic and its implication for local employers.[20]

Legislation and Degree of Regulation

In contrast with every other state in the nation, Nebraska's legislature has only one house. The legislature, which is known as the Unicameral, consists of 49 senators. The senators are elected on a nonpartisan basis to serve four-year terms. The Unicameral meets for 90 days in odd-numbered years and for 60 days in even-numbered years.

The more usual bicameral, bipartisan legislative system imparts a series of holds and checks on legislation. The opposition involved and the conferences required to pass legislation help to ensure that all sides to any given issue are represented. As the Unicameral lacks this sort of "insurance," each bill is required to undergo a public hearing before reaching the floor for debate. Even with this check, Nebraska's system lends a distinctive flavor to legislative outputs. The Unicameral may even allow for legislation that might not be possible in the typical partisan and bicameral system.

A prime example of such unusual legislation is L.B. 835, which was passed in April 1986 by 28 of the 49 senators.[21] L.B. 835 originated as a proposal by the telecommunications industry, a product of its frustration with the lengthy processes and delays of the Public Service Commission (PSC). Before deregulation, rate change requests were often caught in the PSC hearing and review process for periods ranging from 9 to 18 months. This situation was the main impetus behind local exchange companies presenting a deregulation proposal to the legislature.[22] Another motivation was that pricing flexibility would allow the telephone companies to combat the problem of large telecommunications users bypassing the system.[23]

Senator DeCamp agreed to promote L.B. 835, one of the two bills concerning telecommunications regulation in the Public Works Committee of the legislature at this time. L.B. 1119, proposing a system of modified regulation (which would place substantial power of review in the hands of the PSC), was being supported by Senator Loran Schmit. At the end of negotiations, L.B. 835 was the bill to come out of the committee.[24]

The industry as a whole was ambivalent about the desired level of deregulation. Working in favor of L.B. 835 were Lincoln Telephone & Telegraph, Northwestern Bell, and the Nebraska Telephone Association. Opposing deregulation were US Sprint, MCI, and, although they are members of the Nebraska Telephone Association, the smaller telephone companies.[25] The bill was the result of careful compromise among the members of the industry. The larger companies wanted the ability to offer new services within a short time period if they saw the demand. All companies were in favor of a more flexible pricing system that would eliminate unrealistically long delays. The smaller companies, however, were adamant about retaining territorial franchise. The two groups compromised. The larger companies acquiesced on the issue of the territorial deregulation, and the smaller companies agreed to support the legislation. Rather than completely deregulate, the proposal would begin by detariffing the industry. Thus, the industry was able to offer unified support for the bill.[26]

There was public hearing and debate on the legislation. However, the bill was redrafted on the floor (via the amendment process), after the public hearing, and this is the version that was passed into law. The final result was the deregulation of basic local service rates and services, with the maintenance of the companies' local exchange areas. If the legislation is not changed or repealed, geographic toll deaveraging can begin in 1991.[27]

The revised process for rate change by a telecommunications company is greatly simplified. Eliminated is the lengthy process within the PSC required for approval: public hearings, commission staff recommendation on the proposed change, and a majority vote of commissioners. All that is required for an increase in basic local service rates is 60-day notice by the company to its customers. In addition, new services can be offered after only 10 days' notice to the commission.[28]

There are two triggers that allow the commission to review a proposed increase in basic local service rates. (The commission has no oversight power except for increases in basic local service.) The PSC may initiate review if a company proposes a rate increase of greater than 10 percent within a 12-month period. (Prior to L.B. 835, smaller companies already were detariffed. The commission may review an increase proposed by a smaller company (fewer than 5,000 access lines) if it is greater than 30 percent within a 12 month period.) The PSC must review a company's rate increase, however, if the customers initiate review. This is done via a petition process. The number of customer signatures required for this type of review varies, depending upon the size of the company. This petition must be submitted within 60 days of the company's rate change notification, and the commission must hold a hearing within 90 days after the filing of the complaint.

A sunset clause within the bill eliminates the option of petitioned review in the year 1991. This clause supposedly was based on the belief that by 1991 the full effects of the changes will be felt. Competition would regulate pricing and the need for governmental intervention would be eliminated. Some of those involved were given to understand that also in 1991 the measure would come up for reevaluation.[29] The implication is that if deregulation has had negative effects, the industry will be reregulated to the necessary degree. Provision for the reevaluation, however, is not included anywhere in the bill, and may or may not occur.

L.B. 835 states that the PSC must assure that a service is not priced below the "actual cost" of providing it. However, this requires the PSC to define "actual cost." The PSC objects to the terminology, maintaining that this standard has never been established. Nevertheless, the district court stated that the PSC is "clothed with the authority to determine the precise meaning of the terms found within the statute."[30]

Opponents of L.B. 835, specifically the Public Service Commission, charge that in the rush to pass a "deregulation" measure within the constraints of a short session, the full content of the bill was not properly considered. The commission argues that the final bill was largely drafted "on the floor" by way of the amendment process. The result, they claim, is vague and faulty legislation. Some areas previously regulated are completely neglected in the legislation, leaving legislative intent open to interpretation. Terms are used without proper clarification, again calling points of legislative intent into question. In the PSC's opinion, these faults undermine the validity and viability of the entire measure.[31]

Senator John DeCamp today openly admits that he "strong-armed" the bill through the legislative process to its final passage.[32] He was and is firmly convinced of its merits, and he actively battled for it. Another key actor in the passage of L.B. 835 was then Governor Bob Kerrey, an active advocate of deregulation.

Nebraska Public Service Commission

The Nebraska Public Service Commission is comprised of six divisions. They are General Administration, Motor Transportation, Warehousing, Rates and Services, Railroad Inspection and Safety, and Communications. Since 1964 Nebraska has been divided into five districts, each of which elects one commissioner to the PSC.[33]

L.B. 835 completely changed the role of the Communications Department of the PSC. The tasks left to the PSC in implementing the bill are the following:

1. Handle consumer complaints in regard to billing, quality of service, and rate increases.

2. Resolve disagreements over access charges between the local exchange carriers and the interexchange carriers.

3. Perform on-site central office testing for service quality.

In addition, the PSC is carrying out a blanket audit on all telephone companies to keep the commission up to date on their status. The commission expects to audit every company by 1990.

In compliance with the Telecommunications Act of 1986 (L.B. 835), the PSC submitted a report on telecommunications to the Nebraska Legislature covering the period of January 1 through October 31, 1987. The report contains three required sections covering all aspects of the telecommunications industry.[34]

1. Review of the quality of telecommunications services offered to consumers in Nebraska.

2. Review of availability of diverse and affordable telecommunications services to all of the people of Nebraska.

3. Review of the level of rates of local exchange companies. Specifically the report addresses quality of service; recent changes in rates, services, and technology; the customer petition process; universal service; and the range of rates offered by the local exchange companies as well as their relative sizes.[35]

The report was somewhat controversial. The telephone companies would have liked to have played a role in the drafting of the report, believing that "it could have been a great report for Nebraska."[36] Because they were not allowed to do so, they claim it is one-sided. The PSC counters this accusation by pointing out that it is the entity required to draft the report, not the telephone companies. However, the report clearly proposes to show the damage that L.B. 835 has done Nebraska consumers:

> This Commission is dedicated to providing the Nebraska consumer with good service at a reasonable cost. Public utility regulation with respect to entry, rates, services, and exit of local exchange carriers, is still very necessary in Nebraska and the Commission warns that the public has been and will be adversely affected by L.B. 835.[37]

The PSC maintains that L.B. 835 has not accomplished any of the goals for which it was intended: Nebraska has not become a model for other states; the legislation has not promoted economic development or diversification; and Nebraska was not chosen as the site for US West's proposed research center. In the opinion of the PSC, all of this indicates that the deregulation legislation has not served its intended purposes and evidently is not the means to strengthen the link between economic development and telecommunications.[38]

One of the main concerns of the PSC is that there will be across-the-board rate increases, given the extent of economic freedom provided the telephone companies. However, since the implementation of L.B. 835, only two companies have raised their rates under the provisions of the bill. A small company, Eastern Nebraska Telephone Company (3,200 access lines), had not raised its rate in 17 years when it proposed an increase of 123 percent to 300 percent in basic local rates for its service area in eastern Nebraska. This greatly exceeded the trigger for review needed for a company of its size, and the PSC received sufficient customer petitions to require a hearing to review the increase. Eastern requested an increase in rates from $4.50, $5.75, and $6.50 to $12.75. The commission audited the company and granted an increase of its basic local service rates to $10.95. The other company was GTE North, Inc. (GTE), with 43,000 access lines. GTE proposed an increase of exactly 10 percent for all its rates and services. The commission did not receive a sufficient number of customer signatures, thus the commission had no power to review the rate change. This change was implemented in December 1987. Although some companies have raised rates for various services, there have been no other increases in basic local service.[39]

The final section of the PSC report draws conclusions about the effects of L.B. 835 and suggests recommendations to the legislature. The principal recommendation of the report is that the legislature reevaluate the legislation on the basis of the contents of the report. The commission's specific suggestions follow:

1. The language of the bill referring to "actual cost" should be deleted or defined by the legislature.
2. The process for new rates should be altered to provide additional power to the PSC to review rates.
3. The legislature should reevaluate the need for complete detariffing where natural monopolies (as in basic local service) still exist.

The commission acknowledges that deregulation of nonmonopoly markets involves the difficult task of defining competition, but holds that "at least this solution benefits both the industry and the subscriber."[40]

The final proposal was that the legislature pass L.B. 380, which was in the Transportation Committee during the 1988 legislative session and which would provide a mix of regulation and deregulation according to the competitiveness of the market. This bill, in the opinion of the PSC, is a far better solution for both the consumers and the telecommunications industry of Nebraska. However, the 1988 legislative session ended without L.B. 380 reaching the floor.

The role of the Public Service Commission has undergone sweeping changes since the passage and implementation of L.B. 835. It is clear that, in the PSC's eyes, Nebraska consumers are at the mercy of monopoly telephone companies. The commission believes that repealing or amending the legislation is the only way it will be able to perform its duties and protect Nebraska's consumers.

Pending Issues

A number of questions have arisen which are related to the state's deregulation of telecommunications. The constitutionality of the bill is currently under scrutiny in the Nebraska Supreme Court. The PSC contends that the Unicameral lacks the authority to deregulate the industry. Some proponents of deregulation believe that L.B. 835 is constitutional and should have gone a step further by defranchising the companies' territorial boundaries. Another concern centering on deregulation is the state of universal service and the affordability of basic service. In recognition of this consideration, the state has opted to participate in the Link-Up America program. Finally, the future of telecommunications legislation is a matter for discussion as Nebraska begins to experience the effects of L.B. 835. These are issues significant to the telecommunications industry and the political environment surrounding it.

Appeal

The most significant issue now pending in Nebraska is the Supreme Court appeal filed by Attorney General Robert Spire on behalf of the Public Service Commission. The appeal concerns the March 1987 Lancaster County District Court affirming L.B. 835 as constitutional. In the wake of that decision the PSC was compelled to implement the conditions of the statute.

In the attorney general's brief, there are three basic objections to L.B. 835:

1. L.B. 835 violates the Nebraska constitution which directs the Public Service Commission "to regulate rates and services for common carriers in Nebraska."[41] L.B. 835 divests the PSC of its constitutionally-granted power. The vast majority of the bill discusses basic local service, and one line says "all other rates and services shall be deregulated." The attorney general states that the PSC must be told the specifics of the deregulation.

2. L.B. 835 deprives telephone subscribers of property without due process as guaranteed by the constitution. This contention is based on the right of customers to a fundamentally fair hearing process. L.B. 835 violates this because of the restrictive time conditions. The petition procedure must be completed by the subscribers within 60 days of being notified of an increase in basic local service. Additionally, the commission has only 90 days to carry out the hearing process after receiving sufficient petitions. The issue here is that the customers could carry out all the procedures correctly, but if the commission is not able to hold hearings within 90 days, the customers have no recourse, and the increase can be implemented.

3. Finally, the attorney general maintains that the evidence indicates that the district court ruling was wrong and unsupported in its conclusions.

The appeal must obtain a five out of seven majority of the votes of the Supreme Court judges in order to overturn the district court ruling and declare the legislation unconstitutional. The telephone companies generally maintain that the appeal is not a genuine concern. They believe that the district court was clear and firm in its decision on L.B. 835.[42] However, the PSC believes that the Supreme Court could overturn the decision, because there is a tendency for district courts to avoid making controversial rulings.[43] An important aspect of the legislation is that it contains a "severability clause," allowing certain portions of the bill to be removed without the repeal of the entire bill. The commission believes that it is likely to be invoked when the Supreme Court reviews the legislation.[44]

From the perspective of the telecommunications companies, a ruling of unconstitutionality for L.B. 835 would be a significant setback for Nebraska. The state would revert to the original processes for rate and service changes until new legislation could be passed, thus removing the pricing freedom currently held by the telephone companies. In addition, repeal of the legislation could be considered a setback for the telecommunications industry across the country, given that Nebraska ideally is setting an example for other states.

Defranchise of Territorial Boundaries

Territorial franchise of the local exchange boundaries was a condition in Nebraska before the passage of deregulation. A controversial aspect of L.B. 835 is that it does nothing to dispose of the territorial franchise condition: telephone companies are forbidden to move into any other company's territory. The only way a company is allowed to enter another's area is by demonstrating to the PSC that there is "need and necessity" to do so because the company is not serving its area adequately.

Opponents of the legislation say that this creates monopoly companies without price restraints. However, the protection of the local exchange boundary was an important aspect of L.B. 835 for the smaller telephone companies, which feared being bought out by larger companies. John DeCamp, the senator who promoted the bill in the legislature, believes that the long-run goal is a system of competition (removing the territorial franchise) and total deregulation that ideally will drive rates down and bring new technology into Nebraska faster.[45] The various telephone companies have different stances on the question of the desired final goal. Nevertheless, since the passage of L.B. 835, there has been no movement toward changing this condition of the bill.

Link-Up America

One major concern about L.B. 835 at the time of its passage was that the cost of basic local service might soar as subsidization was discontinued, thus jeopardizing universal service. The definition of universal service according to the PSC is that "every household has telecommunications service available to it."[46] The commission acknowledges that reducing subsidization will have an effect on subscribers, and possibly on the level of subscriber penetration.

Universal service is an accepted priority for the telecommunications companies and the state. The PSC has decided not to support a Lifeline program for Nebraska at this time. Instead, it has worked with the industry to promote the state's participation in Link-Up America. The PSC made a proposal to the FCC, and the FCC certified it. The program will begin in the summer of 1988.

In this program the federal government assists low-income households. The government will pay up to 50 percent of phone installation charges (up to $30) and absorb interest charges on deferred payments. No matching state funds are required. The advantage of the program is that no new "needs test" is necessary, as it serves those people already identified as being in need by other social programs within the state. To qualify, an applicant must have been without phone service for at least three months; not have been assisted by a similar program for at least two years; and not be a legal dependent upon anyone, unless 60 years or older.

Future Legislation

Senator Schmit proposed three bills in the 1987 session to water down or repeal L.B. 835. L.B. 381 and 382, both of which Schmit proposed to completely undo L.B. 835, were killed in committee. L.B. 380 was held over into the 1988 session. The most significant aspect of the bill is that it requires that local service never be deregulated. The PSC believes that this statute would be much better for Nebraska consumers because, in its opinion, there could never be real local service competition, hence the need for regulation.[47]

L.B. 380 was not advanced to the floor during the 1988 legislative session for a number of reasons, primarily because there is no real interest in new legislation while the appeal still is pending on L.B. 835. According to a spokesman for Northwestern Bell, "If there is something in the constitution that prohibits deregulation, the legislature needs to know the specific problems with this bill before pursuing another."[48]

The 1988 legislative session ended on Friday, April 8, 1988. Because it was a short session, legislation cannot be carried over to next year's session; hence L.B. 380 has been "killed." The PSC has requested that the legislature consider amending or repealing L.B. 835.[49] The only way for this to happen is for brand new legislation to be proposed in the 1989 session.

TELECOMMUNICATIONS AND ECONOMIC DEVELOPMENT
Public Initiatives

The general goal of the economic development program in the state of Nebraska is wealth creation. The Department of Economic Development has chosen to emphasize four strategic areas for its activities: developing economic leadership; maintaining a business climate that encourages investment and expansion; building on Nebraska's strengths (location, productivity of labor, education system); and diversifying the economy in the state most dependent on the food and fiber system.[50] The department emphasizes the need for adding value to Nebraska's produce and promoting nonagricultural sectors.

The Nebraska Center for Telecommunications and Information was created by the legislature in 1984 under Governor Robert Kerrey's administration. In 1986 the center became a permanent division of the

Department of Economic Development.[51] Its goals of "a more diversified economy, more job opportunities for Nebraskans, an improved educational system, and an even better quality of life in the state" are pursued by "a partnership among industry, government, and education."[52] Among the first projects performed by this division was the creation of a database listing Nebraska businesses with technological or communications functions. The database was the source of a "Buy Nebraska" directory intended to link Nebraska buyers to Nebraska suppliers. Another major project of the center was the creation of a curriculum for telecommunications management, which has become a degree program at Kearney State College. Among its other projects, the division functioned as a part of the Educational and Technical Consortium, and prepared and presented numerous seminars to outstate communities concerning the attraction and creation of telemarketing firms.[53]

When Governor Kay Orr took office in January 1987, the original director of the center left to work in the private sector. At that time, the Telecommunications Division went into "hiatus."[54] The new focus of the division is identification of economic development opportunities for the state in terms of the telecommunications industry, especially focusing on recruitment and expansion. Promotion of telecommunications and especially telemarketing through work with the state's educational institutions is also emphasized.

Nebraska's ETV Network, an educational public television system, is another state economic development initiative. Unlike the Center for Telecommunications, ETV represents a long-range contribution to economic development. ETV is legislatively mandated to provide specific varieties of educational programs ranging from supplemental kindergarten material to college credit courses and business and career development training. The statewide ETV Network was not designed with the specific intent of economic development. However, its contributions to a better educated, more informed society may have far-reaching economic impact for the state.[55]

Similarly, AGNET is an application of telecommunications that affects the economy of the state. AGNET is an agricultural information database that may be accessed by any subscriber's computer via a modem and telephone. AGNET builds on Nebraska's agricultural economic base. The interactive database provides farmers and ranchers with current information concerning market prices and futures, weather, and scientific agricultural information and can process all of these variables together with an individual's input to yield extremely useful specially tailored information. AGNET, mandated by the legislature and created through state funding, serves as another fine example of a telecommunications application with long-range, nonspecific economic development. AGNET is discussed further at the end of this chapter.

Private Initiatives

The most significant private initiatives toward promoting the link between economic development and telecommunications have been by Northwestern Bell. Northwestern Bell recently created its own Economic Development Office and gave it three distinct functions. One is dealing with the Public Service Commission on regulation and deregulation matters. Another function is public affairs, which is concerned with generating interest within interest groups, city councils, county boards, advocacy groups, and neighborhood associations. The third and primary function is economic development and the role

Northwestern Bell can adopt to promote it. The staff here works with the state and city economic development offices as well as the numerous chambers of commerce across Nebraska. The Northwestern Bell office may provide or lend resources (e.g., providing a personal computer, giving advice, making speeches, etc.) to assist the state in promotion of economic development in specific areas. This office encourages economic diversification, which is important for Nebraska, given the weakened condition of the agriculture industry. In addition, it works to develop the service and manufacturing industries in Nebraska.

All of these actions stem from the belief that a strong infrastructure is integral to economic development. All parts of Nebraska must be promoted, not only Lincoln and Omaha. A state economy that is highly dependent on one industry cannot effectively attract new business and industry. Thus diversification is encouraged. In addition, Northwestern Bell continues its commitment to the quality of telecommunications it offers in Nebraska. The company plans to invest $100 million per year for the next three years in Nebraska, and expects that fiber optics will be available across the state by 1989.

Northwestern Bell has produced a videotape representing Nebraska and its strongest selling points. The tape is sent to companies who are considering moving their headquarters or expanding their operations, with the goal of showing them all that Nebraska has to offer. Telecommunications is emphasized on the tape because it is not only integral to companies of all sizes, but also a big part of what Nebraska can offer. Deregulation is particularly significant to companies that are large users of telecommunications (because of its effects on costs and prices), as is the established telecommunications infrastructure. However, these aspects are only a part of the big picture in Nebraska, which includes a strong business climate (aided by the 1987 legislation promoting business expansion and investment),[56] a progressive legislature that is responsive to industry needs, strength in natural resources, ample land and space, a stable infrastructure, a central location, and a midwestern work ethic that makes Nebraskans better employees.

A spokesman from Northwestern Bell maintains that when the company was regulated, there was a guarantee of profitability because the PSC set the rate of return. Now the emphasis is on economic development: the company is spending more money itself to encourage others to make their investment in Nebraska. Deregulation makes Northwestern Bell stand on its own, encouraging expansion within Nebraska to ensure the company's growth.

CONCLUSIONS
Telecommunications and Economic Development

The state of Nebraska needs to diversify its economy, lessening its dependence upon the dominant agricultural industry. One strategy would be for the state to invest time, money, and energy in the existing telecommunications industry, such as telemarketing businesses and hotel reservation centers. They are a major portion of the economy in the city of Omaha, and are slowly spreading across the state. This is a growth industry in Nebraska, and one that should be exploited.

To some degree, L.B. 835 is promoting the telecommunications-intensive businesses. The passage of this bill has had some impact on telecommunications costs because of the introduction of competition. (Northwestern Bell decreased the cost of WATS lines, for example.) Service quality has been maintained, as this is one of the few oversight responsibilities belonging to the PSC. Possibly most important, however, is that with L.B. 835 the telephone companies can introduce and implement new services within 10 days of notifying the commission. This means that any new telecommunications needs of these businesses can be acknowledged and supplied almost immediately.

L.B. 835 may be able to encourage economic development, in the sense of promoting existing industry and attracting new businesses. It is already apparent that many of the 800 businesses have seen some lower costs. Also as a result of lower costs (and continued quality of service from the telecommunications providers), L.B. 835 could encourage other types of industry in Nebraska to expand their operations within the state. Finally, the legislation could be the proper signal to all types of large companies outside the state to attract them to Nebraska, safe in the knowledge that their telecommunications needs can and will be met at reasonable rates.

It must be noted that thus far very few of these possibilities have occurred. It has been just over a year since the legislation was implemented, so it is too soon for measurable effects on economic development to have appeared. The initial verdict, however, is that although telecommunications costs and quality are important issues for businesses that are large users of telecommunications, they are not the deciding factor in the decision to expand or relocate.

State Policy

Recognition of the link between telecommunications and economic development and the impact that such a link can have upon a state's economy has important implications for state policy initiatives. Nebraska does not have a specific policy linking telecommunications to the promotion of economic development or, until recently, any type of state policy for the promotion of the telecommunications industry. The Nebraska Department of Economic Development often relies on the Office of Economic Development of Northwestern Bell for expertise and resources. Both of these entities have maintained that deregulation, although important, is only a part of the total package a state must offer. This package includes a strong infrastructure, a diversified economy, a healthy business climate, a progressive legislature, a good location, strength in natural resources, and a growing work force. This type of public- and private-sector consensus-building often is very successful, especially when focused on identifying telecommunications goals and policy strategies. However, it appears that the state needs to develop its own role in the promotion of the telecommunications industry and to recognize the impact that industry can have on the economy of Nebraska and on economic development in the state.

It is impossible to predict at this early stage whether L.B. 835 will prove beneficial or detrimental to the state and its economy (or have any impact at all). Nevertheless, the most significant recent action in Nebraska in the realm of telecommunications was not a state policy at all, but rather an industry proposal to the legislature to remedy an unacceptable situation. The state itself should consider identifying policies that could be successfully implemented and beneficial to specific industries within Nebraska.

The Uncertain Status of L.B. 835

L.B. 835 should not yet be considered permanent and could be replaced or changed in several ways. The Public Service Commission's Supreme Court appeal is still undecided. The commission firmly believes that L.B. 835 is unconstitutional and will be declared as such by the Supreme Court. The industry as a whole, on the other hand, is placing little or no weight on the possibility of the bill being ruled unconstitutional. Nevertheless, the oral arguments of the appeal will not be heard until late 1988 at the earliest.

Bills that would revise or repeal L.B. 835 have not successfully been advanced to the floor. There were bills in committee during both the 1987 and 1988 sessions that did not get the support needed to entitle them to hearing and debate. This does not, however, dismiss the fact that the PSC has requested action from the legislature, either in the form of new legislation or in vast changes in the current bill. New legislation could also be a possibility if L.B. 835 produces negative results. If prices began to rise significantly (a prediction of the commission) and the consumers had limited or no ability to petition for review, the legislature itself could decide that L.B. 835 is too sweeping or that it does not provide adequate safeguards. In any event, telecommunications regulation is an unsettled issue in Nebraska.

Nebraska: The Deregulation Success Story

Passage of L.B. 835 was unique to Nebraska in numerous ways. First, the impetus behind the legislation was the telephone companies' frustration with the extraordinarily long delays for approval of rate increases and new services at the PSC. Second, frustration prompted these companies to take action on their own in the form of a legislative proposal that would remedy the problem. Third, a strong-willed and persuasive senator chose to put his efforts behind this bill (at the expense of his seat in the Unicameral, some would argue). Fourth, the bill was redrafted on the floor via the amendment process, its proponents removing and adding sections as it seemed necessary for its passage. Fifth, the unicameral legislature, already identified as being unique to Nebraska, played a significant part in the passage of L.B. 835. Many people on both sides of this bill have agreed that it might not have been possible to pass such sweeping legislation through a two-house legislature. Finally, the final vote on the bill occurred the day before the session ended. Since it was a "short session," if L.B. 835 had not been passed, it could not have been carried over for consideration during the next legislative session. Hence there was a strong desire to pass it, with the knowledge that the legislature could "clean it up next year."[57]

The passage of L.B. 835 has not caused any significant problems. There have been two increases in basic local service, one of which triggered the new PSC review process and still resulted in satisfactory results. Service quality does not seem to have been affected adversely thus far. In addition, the telephone companies have been able to introduce a variety of new services without having to obtain PSC approval beforehand.

The telephone companies are well aware they are being watched to see whether they will take advantage of the conditions within L.B. 835. They must show restraint to prove the benefits of the legislation. Although nothing significantly beneficial for Nebraska in terms of economic development has occurred since the implementation of L.B. 835, nothing significantly detrimental has occurred either. And one good thing, many argue, is that Nebraska has portrayed an image of being progressive in legislation and responsive to its industries' needs.

It is impossible to predict the future for L.B. 835 in Nebraska. There are many different actors involved, all with their own ideas, problems, and solutions. Although in Nebraska the question of the level of regulation is decided for the time being, it is very likely that the question will surface again. Amid the changing technology and trends in regulation throughout the country, the telecommunications environment is likely to be volatile for years. It is certain, however, that until such time as L.B. 835 is amended, repealed, or affirmed, Nebraska undoubtedly will represent the deregulation success story.

CASE STUDY: AGNET

AGNET[58] is an example of telecommunications technology being used to promote development in the agriculture industry. The idea was first developed in the early 1970s by two University of Nebraska at Lincoln professors, James Kendrick and Thomas Thompson, who built interactive computer models for use by their agriculture students. To discover how theory could be applied to real-world problems, they developed programming concepts that could be used by students who were not computer scientists or programmers. The professors also wanted their students to be able to use the same models in their careers. At that time, there was no telecommunications network available to permit off-campus access to their models. As a result, in 1975 they coined the term AGNET and placed a couple of terminals in a district extension office to test the concept of remote access.

The network, which started in Lincoln, has expanded to serve all of Nebraska, 47 states, parts of Canada, and seven other countries as well. Part of what makes AGNET so valuable to its clients is that custom-fit results are available. The system is able to accept data specific to a client (e.g., cost of labor), to provide current data that affects the client's own operations (e.g., the outlook for production), and to analyze it given specific situations.

Growth and Development of the Network

AGNET was founded in 1975 when terminals were first moved off the University of Nebraska campus. The Cooperative Extension Service (CES) funded the installation of terminals at the Panhandle Station to test interactive computing via telephone lines. Initial funding for AGNET came from the Nebraska County Extension Service ($12,300), the Agricultural Experiment Station ($12,300), and a grant from the Nebraska Bankers Association ($3,000). A few years later, after a period of moderate growth, computer terminals were added in district and county agents' offices, and individual producers and agribusiness firms began using AGNET directly with their own terminals. Subsequent funding came in 1977 when a developmental grant was received from the Old West Regional Commission[59] to extend the network throughout the region to Montana, North Dakota, South Dakota, and Wyoming. When AGNET offices were established in these states, the pool of subject matter experts and programmers expanded significantly, as did the clientele. Since June of 1981, AGNET has not required grants to fund the system. Its full costs of operation are being absorbed by AGNET clients, including educational institutions, governmental agencies, firms, and individual users.

AGNET began as a system of strictly management models. The first departure from this came in 1978 when a communications program was developed. This electronic mail system was initially used by university personnel. Today the mail system allows all subscribers of AGNET to communicate via the network. In 1979 the third component to the AGNET library was introduced. Information programs grew out of the need to obtain accurate results for decision making using current information. For example, the weather database obtains relevant data from 832 stations, with 29 stations automatically transmitting their data directly to the AGNET system.[60]

Philosophies

AGNET has certain philosophies that have formed the foundation of the system, the growth of which can largely be attributed to adherence to these basics:

1. Easy to use. AGNET was one of the first user-friendly systems, so that users did not need to have extensive knowledge of computers in order to use the system.

2. Equal treatment for all clients. This philosophy stems from the belief that no client or group of clients should subsidize other users of the system. Each user of the system pays according to telecommunications cost differences (which are traffic-sensitive) and time spent on the system.

3. Humans are to think, machines to do. Sophisticated computer programs are used to accomplish the repetitive control and supervisory functions of the system, making the system highly cost effective. AGNET is available 24 hours per day seven days a week.

Clients

AGNET's users are divided into the following eight categories, listed in descending order of volume of use: (1) producers, (2) general agribusiness, (3) education, (4) credit institutions, (5) farm managers and consultants, (6) government, (7) nonagricultural firms, and (8) hardware and software vendors. The top three categories account for over two-thirds of AGNET's total clientele. The producer category claims an increasing portion of the client base each year. This category accounted for the greatest network use beginning approximately in 1983. It was at about this time that individual producers increasingly were buying their own personal computers, and thus easily hook up to the system on their own. At the close of 1986, producers claimed approximately 40 percent. There are 1,500 accounts on AGNET, but this is a deceiving figure in that the entire University of Nebraska at Lincoln campus is considered one account.

Types of Programs

AGNET's library of programs is classified into three groups: management models (problem-solving and simulation), communications (electronic mail and conferencing), and information. Growth of the program base developed as a response to a consensus of clients' needs. There are more than 200 programs available. In addition, there are 1,000 reports available on the system, with 350 to 500 being updated daily. These reports cover a vast variety of topics and supply necessary and often the most recent information available.

Technical Developments

Central Data Processing (CDP) and the Division of Communications (DOC), both part of the State of Nebraska Department of Administrative Services, provide the network support for the AGNET system. This has made it a reliable and responsive system. CDP provides dependable computer cycles and high-level technical support. The CDP machines have been replaced seven times since the inception of the AGNET system. In addition, the IBM CMS operating system used by AGNET is continually being upgraded, providing the latest computer enhancements that will assist the client. The DOC acts as vendor and advisor to AGNET, supplying the communications network necessary to provide access to the system for the United States and foreign countries.

Telecommunications technology has changed and advanced rapidly since the beginning of AGNET, thus changing the most efficient and effective methods of linking clients with the system. Those methods have evolved from two dedicated WATS lines to multiplexers (concentrators of phone lines for lower cost). In 1979 national WATS lines were added, and in 1982 AGNET added the data packet networking service, primarily to serve its growing international client base. The system does not seem to have been impacted by the change in regulation in Nebraska.

Summary

AGNET is a prime example of telecommunications being used to promote the agriculture industry. A notable aspect of AGNET is the large number of individual producers using the network to run their farms and businesses. AGNET offers a service that can directly affect a state's economy. It allows all types and sizes of agricultural-related businesses to input their own specific information and conditions; use programs that are able to perform complex simulations; have these programs access all types of current data, such as weather or price information; and obtain an answer or results immediately, thus enabling the business or individual to use the information while it is relevant. Although difficult to measure, this system can impact a state's economy inasmuch as it allows farmers or companies to improve their methods and make their businesses more profitable.

AGNET began as a simple system on the state university campus to meet the education needs of just a few. Use of the network has grown continually since it was created, and now meets the production and education needs of people throughout the world. No one could have been predicted that a university venture could expand to have worldwide applications; the growing telecommunications technology and the opportunity for experimentation have been the conditions that have allowed the system to grow in its capabilities and uses: it is an example of telecommunications being used to promote economic development for the agriculture industry in Nebraska.

NOTES

1.   Interview with Stephen J. McCollister, Business Development Manager, Northwestern Bell, Omaha, January 11, 1988.

2.   Interview with Stu Miller, Director, Division of Research, Nebraska Department of Economic Development, Lincoln, January 14, 1988.

3.   U.S. Bureau of the Census, Statistical Abstract of the United States, 1987, 107th ed. (Washington, D.C.: U.S. Government Printing Office, 1986), p. 633.

4.   Nebraska Public Service Commission, 1987 Annual Report on Telecommunications to the Nebraska Unicameral Legislature (Lincoln, January 5, 1988), p. 19.

5.   US West, Annual Report 1986 (Englewood, Colorado, January 1987), p. 13.

6.   "Region Regulators Slam US West Tactics in `Bidding War' Among States for Research Facility," Telecommunications Weekly, July 27, 1987, pp. 3-4.

7.   Interview with Ken Powers, Vice-President and Chief Executive Officer, Northwestern Bell, Omaha, January 11, 1988.

8.   Johnnie L. Roberts, "Tough Operator: Demanding Further Deregulation, U.S. West is Accused of Applying Undue Pressure," Wall Street Journal, September 14, 1987, pp. 1, 12.

9.   Ibid.

10.   "Should Intrastate Telephone Rates Be Deregulated?" Network World, June 16, 1986, pp. 22-23, 33.

11.   Lincoln Telecommunications Company, Annual Report, 1986, (Lincoln, 1986), pp. 15-18.

12.   Ibid., p. 11.

13.   Nebraska Telephone Association, Directory of Members: 1986-1987 (Lincoln, 1986), p. 20. (Pamphlet.)

14.   Ibid., p. 3.

15.   Letter from Norman A. Osland, President, Nebraska Telephone Association, Lincoln, April 25, 1988.

16.   Telephone interview with Chris Dibbern, Staff Attorney, Nebraska Public Service Commission, Lincoln, April 11, 1988.

17.   Interview with Richard P. Mullican, Assistant Vice-President, AT&T Communications of the Midwest, Inc., Lincoln, January 12, 1988.

18.   Interview with McCollister.

19.   Interview with John W. DeCamp, former Nebraska state senator, Lincoln, January 13, 1988.

20.   Telephone interview with Dibbern, Lincoln, March 3, 1988.

21.   Telephone interview with Miller, Lincoln, March 3, 1988.

22.   Nebraska Public Service Commission, 1987 Annual Report, p. 5.

23.   Interview with Mullican.

24.   Interview with Buzz Bigham, Manager, Public Affairs, US West, Austin, April 8, 1988.

25.   Interview with Osland, Lincoln, January 15, 1988.

26.   Henry J. Cordes, "Commission, NW Bell Hook Up in Debate on Phone-Rate Regulation," Omaha World Herald, March 3, 1987, p. 17.

27.   Interview with Elaine Carpenter, Executive Assistant to the President, The Lincoln Telephone Company, Lincoln, January 13, 1988.

28. <u>Telecommunications Reports</u>, April 21, 1986, pp. 3-4.

29. Telephone interview with Dibbern, April 11, 1988.

30. Interview with Dibbern, Lincoln, January 15, 1988.

31. "Nebraska Drafts Rules Under Deregulation Law; `Actual Cost' Proves to Be Most Difficult," <u>Telecommunications Weekly</u>, August 17, 1987, p. 7.

32. Interview with Dibbern; interview with Eric Rassmussen, Commissioner, Nebraska Public Service Commission, Lincoln, January 15, 1988.

33. Interview with DeCamp.

34. Nebraska Public Service Commission, <u>Biennial Report, July 1, 1984-June 30, 1986</u> (Lincoln, December 1, 1986), pp. 5-19.

35. Nebraska Public Service Commission, <u>1987 Annual Report</u>, pp. 3-4.

36. Ibid, pp. 17-51.

37. Interview with Osland.

38. Nebraska Public Service Commission, <u>1987 Annual Report</u>, p. 54.

39. Interviews with Dibbern and Rassmussen.

40. Telephone interview with Dibbern, April 11, 1988.

41. Ibid.

42. Interview with Dibbern.

43. Interviews with McCollister and Osland.

44. Interview with Dibbern.

45. Ibid.

46. Interview with DeCamp.

47. Nebraska Public Service Commission, <u>1987 Annual Report</u>, p. 29.

48. Cordes, "Commission, NW Bell Hook Up."

49. <u>Telecommunications Reports</u>, April 21, 1986, pp. 3-4.

50. Nebraska Public Service Commission, <u>1987 Annual Report</u>, pp. 52-54.

51. Interview with Miller.

52. There are six divisions within the Department of Economic Development. They are Promotion of Small Business, Community Financing, Research, Tourism, Industry Recruitment, and Telecommunications.

53. Nebraska Department of Economic Development, <u>The Nebraska Telecommunications and Information Center</u> (Lincoln, n.d.). (Pamphlet.)

54. Telephone interview with Miller.

55. Interview with Miller.

56. Interview with Kathryn Stephens, Director of Network Information, Nebraska ETV Network, Lincoln, January 12, 1988.

57. Nebraska Department of Economic Development, Industry Recruitment Division, <u>Jobs for Nebraskans, 1987 Legislation</u> (Lincoln, August 1, 1987).

58. Interview with McCollister.

59. <u>Telecommunications Reports</u>, April 21, 1986.

60. Information for this case study was obtained from interviews with Alfred L. Stark, Supervisor, AGNET, and Thomas L. Thompson, Co-Founder, AGNET, Lincoln, January 15, 1988; and AGNET, <u>AGNET The First Decade</u> (Lincoln, January 1985).

61. The Old West Regional Commission was one of seven identical federal-state partnerships designed to solve regional economic problems and stimulate orderly economic growth.

62. AGNET, <u>AGNET</u>, p. 10.

6

New York

Larkin Jennings and Harmeet S. Sawhney

The importance of New York for telecommunications studies lies in the very nature of its economy. Due to the telecommunications intensity of its economy, the economic impact of telecommunications policy is likely to be most visible in New York. It is therefore difficult to imagine any comparative state-level telecommunications policy project which does not include New York.

Unlike other states, New York exhibits a high degree of awareness and concern about the potential link between telecommunications policy and economic development. This potential link is acknowledged by all the major players. A major reason for this awareness is that in New York, unlike many other states, the economic implications of telecommunications are visible in concrete market developments. A prime example of this visibility is Citicorp's 1981 switch of its credit-processing operations from Huntington, Long Island, to Sioux Falls, South Dakota, which was made possible by advanced data communication technology.

New York State policymakers are very much aware of the impact of telecommunications on its economy--especially the banking, insurance, and financial services industries concentrated in the New York City metropolitan area. This concern has resulted in a policymaking climate which is rather cautious in nature.

At present the state does not possess a unified strategy for telecommunications. But, of all the initiatives taken, the following three areas of activity seem to form an underlying pattern: consensus on the need for public policy initiatives in areas concerning economic development, including those involving telecommunications; measures to reduce telecommunications taxation; and innovation in telecommunications to promote economic development.

The political reality of heterogeneous New York has led to a consensus-building approach. Any major policy initiative is unlikely to succeed unless it has the support of various powerful interest groups.[1] The general practice seems to be to take no major action without at least attempting a consensus. Thus the policymaking process in New York is slow and cautious. In the case of telecommunications, it is not clear whether this approach is the cause or the excuse for the delay in taking major telecommunications policy initiatives. In general, there is a great deal of coordination and cooperation between the various policy-developing bodies, and, where possible, the state seeks to encourage projects with the private sector.

The New York State Public Service Commission (PSC) works closely with the Department of Economic Development when addressing issues that have economic development significance. In addition, the PSC attempts to gather information from all concerned parties when making regulatory decisions. No major players in the telecommunications area in New York State complain of being left out of the regulatory policymaking process. Of course, not all parties are satisfied with each decision, but the processes whereby the decisions at the PSC are reached definitely lean toward the relatively peaceful settlement of issues.

Another concrete step toward establishing consensus involved the commissioning of a large telecommunications study which studied the telecommunications issues in New York. The way in which the study was conducted reflects the consensus-building process in the state. A draft was compiled and then circulated among the major contributors, including 25 corporations, for comments.

Most policy actors in New York believe the biggest irritants to growth in the telecommunications industry are the taxes levied on the industry. The most visible is the real property tax, which taxes telecommunications equipment as real property. In 1987, after sustained criticism of the real property tax, the legislature passed a bill that phases out the real property tax by 1993. The gross receipts tax is another tax under much criticism. However, the amount of revenue involved has restrained action so far.

Both public agencies and joint private and public institutions have been involved in telecommunications innovations geared toward enhancing economic development. A crucial impetus toward innovation in the state is the fear of losing large telecommunications users and the economic strength they give New York State.

THE ECONOMY AND THE TELECOMMUNICATIONS INDUSTRY
Economic Profile

Until 1972 manufacturing was the dominant industry, as measured in relative employment shares in the state. New York State was particularly hard hit by the national recession of the 1970s. Since then, services have overtaken manufacturing as the largest employment sector. New York City's stature as the world's financial center contributes to the higher-than-average share of the finance, insurance, and real estate (FIRE) sectors in the employment base (Table 6.1). FIRE industries contain many telecommunications-intensive businesses (TIBs), indicating a more important role for telecommunications in the state's economy. And unlike manufacturing jobs, service jobs are more vulnerable to relocation as a result of new telecommunications technology.[2]

Service and FIRE industries increased significantly from 1980 to 1986. Wholesale and retail trade also increased its share of the employment market.

The declining importance of manufacturing to the New York employment share also became apparent (Table 6.1).

New York State depends heavily on employment in the information services sector, which grew slightly from 1980 to 1984 (Table 6.2). Large telecommunications users, such as corporate headquarters and banks, need to communicate with offices and clients in other states or countries. This creates a demand for extensive advanced telecommunications services and equipment.

Table 6.1
Nonagricultural Employment Shares and Annual
Percentage Change in Employment* for New York and
the United States, 1980 and 1986
(total employees in 1,000s, share and change in %)

Sector	Employment Shares 1980		1986		Annual Employment Change	
	New York	U.S.	New York	U.S.	New York	U.S.
Mining	.1	1.1	.1	.8	-.6	-3.9
Construction	2.8	4.9	3.9	4.9	8.1	1.6
Manufacturing	20.6	22.5	15.8	19.1	-2.7	-1.1
Transportation	6.0	5.7	5.1	5.3	-1.2	.3
Wholesale & Ret. Trade	20.4	22.7	21.2	23.7	2.4	2.4
Fin., Ins., Real Estate	8.7	5.7	9.6	6.3	3.5	3.7
Services	23.6	19.6	26.9	23.2	4.2	5.0
Government	18.2	17.8	17.5	16.8	.9	.6
Total	7,205	90,657	7,906	99,610	1.6	1.7

* Totals may reflect rounding error.

Source: U.S. Department of Labor, Bureau of Labor Statistics, Employment and Earnings, vol. 34, no. 5 (May 1987), pp. 120-137; idem, vol. 28, no. 5 (May 1981), pp. 120-128.

Table 6.2

Employment Shares and Annual Changes in Employment* of
Telecommunications-Intensive Businesses** for New York
and the United States, 1980 and 1984
(share and change in %)

	Employment Shares 1980		1984		Annual Employment Change	
	New York	U.S.	New York	U.S.	New York	U.S.
Information Services	14.4	9.1	14.9	9.9	2.1	3.2
Finance	5.6	2.8	4.3	6.4	1.9	2.9
Insurance	3.0	2.3	2.7	2.3	-2.3	1.0
Real Estate	1.9	1.3	2.0	1.4	1.4	1.6
Computer/Data Proc.	0.4	0.4	.5	0.6	7.5	13.1
Other Information Svcs.	3.2	2.1	3.3	2.3	2.0	4.5
Information Technology	2.3	2.1	2.3	2.3	3.1	2.4
Research & Development	0.5	0.3	0.4	0.3	-4.0	2.9
Media	5.2	3.7	5.2	3.7	3.7	0.5

* Totals may reflect rounding error.

** The Telecommunications-Intensive Business categories are defined by
Standard Industrial Classification codes as follows:
    1. Information Services: Finance: SIC 60 (Banking), SIC 61 (Credit),
SIC 62 (Commodities); Insurance: SIC 63 (Insurance Carriers), SIC 64
(Insurance Agents); Real Estate: SIC 65; Computer/Data Proc.: SIC 737; Other
Information Services: SIC 731 (Advertising), SIC 732 (Credit Reporting), SIC
81 (Legal Services), SIC 891 (Engineering and Architectural Services), SIC
893 (Accounting and Auditing);
    2. Information Technology Equipment: SIC 3573 (Electronic Computing
Equipment), SIC 361 (Electronic Distributing Equipment), SIC 365 (Radio and
TV Receiving Equipment), SIC 366 (Communications Equipment), SIC 367
(Electronic Components and Accessories);
    3. Research and Development: SIC 7391 (Research and Development
Laboratories), SIC 7397 (Commercial Testing Laboratories), SIC 892
(Nonprofit Education and Scientific Research Agencies);
    4. Media: SIC 27 (Printing and Publishing), SIC 48 (Communications),
SIC 735 (News Syndicates), SIC 78 (Motion Pictures).

Source: U.S. Bureau of the Census, County Business Patterns, United States
(No. 1) and New York (No. 32) (Washington, D.C.: U.S. Government
Printing Office, 1980 and 1984), Table I B.

    The downstate region, consisting of New York City and most of the
surrounding metropolitan area (not all counties are in New York State), depends
more heavily on telecommunications-intensive businesses than the upstate

region. The dependence of the New York City economy on FIRE and other service industries accounts for this difference. This great demand for telecommunications services has resulted in a very sophisticated infrastructure, specially in the New York City metropolitan area. Throughout the state, there are some 9.3 million network access lines; approximately half of these, 4.75 million, are in the city of New York.[3] The greatest concentration of telephone services in the world can be found in New York City, in particular, at the southern tip of Manhattan Island, the financial capital of the world. In the three wire centers that serve the approximately two square miles of the financial district, some 427,000 access lines are served. This is about the number of such lines in a city the size of San Francisco. Further, the wire center at 104 Broad Street, the principal one among the three for service to the financial district, supplies some 200,000 of these 427,000 access lines and furnishes yet another 800,000 private services, making it the world's largest wire center, with almost 1,000,000 pairs terminated.[4] On a typical day, the statewide network of New York Telephone handles in excess of 105 million calls.[5] A little over half of these, some 56 million, are within the city of New York; the so-called downstate LATA, which includes the city of New York, accounts for about 84 million of the 105 million calls. According to Ken Phillips, vice-president of Citicorp, the Manhattan Central Business District has more than "twice the telecommunications switching capacity of the average foreign country, more computers than a country the size of Brazil, and more word processors than all the countries of Europe combined. Capital investment by business users in private telecommunications systems, communicating word processing systems, computer mainframes, minis, and micros is currently in the billions of dollars and is growing annually."[6]

Telecommunications Industry Profile

NYNEX, the Baby Bell for New York State and New England, is an aggressive company, seeking to provide more services and products in order to expand its financial base. NYNEX often leads the industry nationwide in petitioning the FCC for greater freedom in the gray areas of federal regulation so as to provide new and innovative services. In addition, NYNEX was the first Baby Bell to receive a patent, underscoring an attempt to duplicate at least part of the function of the highly successful Bell Labs. In April 1988 NYNEX opened its new Science and Technology Center at White Plains. It cost $70 million and employs 200 scientists, engineers and support staff. This center plans to study artificial intelligence, voice recognition and applications software for computerized information systems. It is the first independent research endeavor among the former Bell Telephone Companies.[7]

New York Telephone (NYTel), the New York state phone company for NYNEX, has 90 percent of New York access lines and resembles its parent in approach and objectives (Table 6.3). NYTel has made significant contributions to the state's telecommunications infrastructure. Statewide more than 120,000 fiber miles exist with over 150,000 fiber miles planned for year end 1988. This represents the largest fiber optic network of any local telephone company in the nation. Statewide, by year end 1988, approximately 178 digital switches will be deployed. This figure has sky rocketed since 1976, when NYTEl became the first Bell Telephone Company to install a digital switch, a No. 4 ESS.[8] A disproportionately large component of the revenue is from a few large users.

Approximately 35 percent of New York Telephone's revenues come from less than 1 percent of its customers. The largest customer is the state government, and the second largest, the city government.[9] Many large users in New York City employ bypass technology for a growing part of their telecommunications needs.

Table 6.3
Local Exchange Carriers and Access Lines
in New York, 1986

Local Exchange Carrier	Share of Access Lines	Total (%)*
New York Telephone	8,980,000	90.5
Rochester Telephone	480,000	4.8
Continental Telephone	230,000	2.3
Others	230,000	2.3
Total	9,920,000	100.0

* Totals may reflect rounding error.
** Includes 51 other local exchange carriers.

Source: New York Telephone Association, Basic Facts, New York, 1987.

In the interexchange market, OCCs compete with AT&T in markets covering 96 percent of the population. Equal access exists in 60 percent of the exchanges; in areas of unequal access an 11 percent discount on the access rates is in place. For AT&T, access charges constitute 64 percent of the total cost of providing the service.[10] The OCCs increased their share of access minutes purchased from NYTel from 9.1 percent in 1985 to 17.3 percent in 1986, an increase of 90 percent. The OCCs' share of access minutes in the New York city metroLATA was 26.5 percent.[11]

Of the 1,050,000 private line loops in service in New York, AT&T provides only about 213,000 or 20 percent of the service lines.[12] At least four other companies offer interLATA private line services within New York. Ten competitors also offer interstate private lines, which are often used to carry intrastate traffic as well as interstate traffic. Easy entry exists for resellers: 49 entered in 1986.[13]

Although Fortune 500 companies maintain a high profile in New York City, small business is very important as well. More than 98 percent of the city's companies are small, employing almost half of all private-sector workers. Hence, from the economic development point of view their telecommunications needs merit in-depth study.

POLICY DEVELOPMENT
Environment and Political Culture

In keeping with New York's tradition of strong governors, Mario Cuomo has provided a firm sense of direction in managing the state's economy. Now in his second term and very much the dominant politician in New York State, Governor Cuomo believes in an active state role in the area of economic development. Mario Cuomo's power also stems from his wide margins of victory in the last gubernatorial election and the tradition of active governors with strong personal appeal, such as Nelson Rockefeller and Hugh Carey.

The legislature consists of two chambers, the Republican-dominated Senate and the Democrat-dominated Assembly. The Assembly constituencies tend to be dominated by metropolitan regions, especially New York, which tend to be Democratic, whereas in the larger Senate constituencies the impact of metropolitan populations is diluted; therefore they tend to be Republican. With this distribution a pro-business legislative effort is likely to succeed since it would be compatible with the Republican ideology as well as favorable to metropolitan Democrats whose important constituents are businesses.[14] The support of the metropolitan Democrats is rather indirect. They are most interested in jobs, and therefore they tend to support pro-business legislation as long as the interests do not clash.[15]

In its economy and politics, the state is split into upstate and downstate regions. Geographically the downstate region approximates New York and the surrounding metropolitan areas; but its economy constitutes approximately half that of the entire state. The nature of the two economies is very different; upstate is shackled with declining smokestack industries whereas New York City plays host to the emerging Information Age.

All the constitutional powers reside with the state; the powers of the city government are specifically those delegated to it. Since New York is more than just a city, the city government is more than a typical local government. The city government has its own huge administrative machinery, and many state government functions are also found at the city level. For example, the city has its own Office of Economic Development and Office of Energy and Telecommunications. There seems to be no formal mechanism for coordination between the duplicated state and city agencies. Although there is no evidence of their working at cross purposes, firms often must cope with both state and local controls.

Another factor that constrains policymakers is the high degree of interdependence between the New York City region and New Jersey. Downstate is an integral part of the economy of the New York-New Jersey metropolitan region. Both states officially recognized this common destiny with the establishment of the Port Authority of New York and New Jersey. However, there is a marked difference in the costs of doing business in New York and New Jersey.[16] For example, there is a 30 percent difference in the costs of energy in New York and New Jersey. Thus high costs of energy, real estate, labor, and taxes have induced businesses to flee New York into neighboring New Jersey. This situation presents New York's policymakers with a dilemma: the interests of the city must be safeguarded without harming the region as a whole. Hence the city does not play down New Jersey; the stance taken is that if a firm wants to do business in Manhattan, it must pay a premium and the city will strive to provide superior services to justify the costs.[17]

General Economic Development Policy

Governor Cuomo believes in active government initiatives in the area of economic development. In 1986, to further his goal of promoting vigorous government initiatives in economic development, Governor Cuomo created the position of Director of Economic Development. The director and his staff work out of the executive office and coordinate the economic development activities of 22 public authorities and state agencies. This policy was further translated into legislative action through the Omnibus Economic Development Act of 1987. This bill established a new Department of Economic Development to "oversee and streamline the delivery of economic development services."[18] The omnibus legislation authorized $160 million in new money for economic development programs covering a wide range: financial assistance, infrastructure, research and development, tax incentives, export, and other areas.   Critics have dubbed it "Christmas tree" legislation, a patchwork of programs geared to please constituencies.

Due to the high costs of taxes, energy, real estate, and other business overhead, not only do new businesses hesitate to locate in New York but also many have been fleeing to relatively cheaper neighboring states.   This is especially true of New York City; for example, the number of Fortune 500 companies with headquarters located in the city declined from 125 in 1969 to 61 in 1987.[19] Developments in telecommunications technologies have in fact made possible this exodus due to high business costs. Developments in satellite, microwave, and other technologies made possible the speedy, accurate, and inexpensive transmission of information over large distances.   Therefore, corporations are able to save money by relocating back-office operations to areas where costs for land, labor, and taxes are lower than those in New York City. Increased telecommunications costs for a company can be more than offset by savings in other costs of doing business. Hence, one of the main thrusts of the economic development strategy is to reduce the cost of doing business in New York.

Relatively high levels of both direct and indirect taxation contribute to the high costs of production in New York. The state has substantially reduced the personal income tax--once the highest in the nation--from 17 percent in 1986 to the 6 to 7 percent range anticipated by 1990.[20] In a situation of overall high taxation, reductions for all types of taxes cannot occur simultaneously. Thus the governor sought to evolve tax-cut priorities through a consensus among business groups, consumers, and politicians. Major players agreed to give priority to reduction in the personal income tax over the gross receipts tax; this consensus led to the passage of tax reduction legislation in 1986.[21] Consumers obtained tax relief, corporations were able to reduce personnel costs, and politicians benefited from electoral goodwill. The gross receipts tax on utilities, which has pushed both energy and telecommunications costs in New York to uncompetitive levels, however remains unchanged. The importance of the gross receipts tax will be further explained later in this chapter.

In general, New York State approaches change cautiously and, where possible, seeks a consensus among the involved parties, disdaining hasty actions.   According to Joseph Robbins, division manager of Bell Communications Research, perhaps a better approach may be to start small but to get started.[22] The state sees itself as the initiator and prime funder for infrastructure projects that would benefit the economy as a whole. In order to involve the private sector and academia, the state actively seeks and encourages partnerships for joint projects. The responsive private sector itself takes a great deal of initiative and finds a cooperative state. Many of the innovative telecommunications activities in New York, such as the telecommunications research center at Polytechnic University, receives substantial support from both the state and numerous corporations.[23]

TELECOMMUNICATIONS REGULATION

The PSC's philosophical stance and style of functioning, as well as the important issues and the positions of the major actors, not only explain why and how regulatory action and innovation have taken place but also suggest the environment in which future initiatives are likely to be taken.

The PSC was established in 1907. Its origins lie in the Public Service Law, which stipulates guidelines within which the PSC must operate. Some of these guidelines are very precise and often can be constraining. For example, Section 92(2) in the most recent version of the law requires public hearings when a major change in rates is requested. A major change is defined as an increase in aggregate revenues of $100,000 or 2.5 percent, whichever is greater. The Public Service Law can be amended by the legislature.[24]

New York has a strong tradition of inviting experts to join the commission rather than having political appointees. By law, no more than four members of the seven-member commission may belong to the same political party. The commissioners are appointed by the governor but do not serve at his pleasure. Governor Cuomo has appointed six of the seven current commissioners. Two of these, Gale Garfield Schwartz and Eli Noam, are acknowledged experts in the area of telecommunications; other commissioners bring expertise in their areas of specialty. The commission is reputed to be "active." Because of the PSC's structurally induced nonpartisan nature and high level of technical expertise, the PSC outlook, as reflected in decisions, has been based largely on the technical merits of the issues. The critics argue that the approach is excessively theoretical and not practicable.

The PSC has consistently demonstrated an appreciation for the economic implications of regulating telecommunications services. Due to economic development considerations, even before the divestiture when Alfred Kahn was PSC chairman under Governor Carey, the PSC had started deregulating certain services in the early eighties.[25] The approach in New York is cautious pro-deregulation; instead of a headlong rush for deregulation, the attitude is to wait until sufficient competition builds up and then deregulate.

Although the PSC's approach to deregulation is cautious it has taken several innovative steps. For example, New York was one of the first states to allow long distance carriers to provide intraLATA services. Two other major PSC initiatives, the moratoria process and generic proceedings, discussed in a later section, also reflect the postdivestiture regulatory philosophy of the PSC. The moratoria process provides rate and regulatory stability, gives NYTel greater flexibility in its operations and is a possible move away from rate of return to the rate cap method. With generic proceedings, the PSC bundles many issues into one category (competition, for example) and attempts to evolve general principles so as to make the regulatory process more predictable and also reduce the need for case-by-case hearings.

Regulation of Local Exchange Carriers

Universal service and bypass are the two biggest local exchange market issues in New York State. Because of increased monthly charges for long distance access, the fixed rates for many consumers' monthly phone service have increased since 1985, pushing the universal service issue to the forefront. Bypass technologies are employed more in New York City than perhaps anywhere else, leading NYTel to bring it up as a revenue issue.

A commitment to affordable universal service has enjoyed strong support from the PSC since its inception in 1907. The current PSC, faced with a rapidly changing telecommunications industry, desires to establish a strong system of protection for low-income telephone users before dealing with issues concerning Fortune 500 companies.[26] This stems out of a genuine concern for a strong telephone "safety net." There are 80,000 subscribers to NYTel's Lifeline Service, which provides discounts on fixed charges to those on public assistance.[27] This state of affairs is not perceived as adequate by the PSC. After a stronger program is established, more maneuvering room will thereby exist when dealing with the telecommunications needs of businesses. Without primary consumer concerns under control, a sustained effort to enhance the telecommunications environment for providers and large users will meet persistent opposition.[28]

Bypass is often employed by TIBs in New York State. The state itself is an active bypasser. The PSC's position is that bypass should not be discouraged when the vendor of bypass can sell below NYTel's costs, not the regulated price, for providing a comparable service. Such bypass is referred to as "economic bypass." Even the CPB favors economic bypass, not only because of perceived benefits to the economy but also because bypass exerts competitive pressure on the local exchange companies.[29] NYTel counters that, although difficult to quantify, the loss of revenue from bypass is substantial. Revenue from NYTel's top 200 customers is flat, even though the telecommunications pie is growing rapidly.[30] The CPB and Teleport Communications feel that bypass is a bogus issue presented by NYTel as a negotiation ploy.[31] For example, Teleport has been projected as a major bypasser, but only 9 percent of its fiber optic network's business comes from connections between point of presence of long distance carriers and end users; the rest comes from interconnect business and end-user to end-user connections.[32] The counterargument is that it all depends on how bypass is defined; the interconnect business and the end-user to end-user connections also draw traffic off the main trunk service (MTS) network.[33] The CPB points out that bypass does not cut into NYTel's business but takes a small slice of the demand which surpasses supply.[34] There is also much debate as to the reasons for bypass. NYTel takes the position that PSC pricing above costs for NYTel's business services is the motivation for bypass. Hence, it strongly urges that the business subsidy of residential services be reduced if not eliminated.[35] The situation created by artificially high rates is compounded by the regulatory uncertainties. Many large customers bypass to avoid these uncertainties.[36] The CPB and the other actors take the position that other factors like quality, installation time, and reliability--not price--are more important.[37] The biggest problem in the bypass debate is that it is difficult to quantify the revenue loss.[38]

According to Joseph Walsh, Jr., vice-president of New York Telephone, in local exchange markets defined on the residential level there is some competition, and it is likely to grow in the future; but when the local exchange markets are defined on the business level, there is definitely competition.[39] NYTel argues that multimillion-dollar business-to-residence subsidy undercuts its position in markets where there is competition. At the same time, NYTel appreciates the need to subsidize residential rates. To attain the dual objectives of keeping the residential rates low and at the same time not burdening the competitive services, NYTel presents the following plan. NYTel seeks to eliminate the business-to-residence subsidy by pricing and promoting nonessential services and not by raising the residential access line charges to cost. In other words, NYTel would prefer that residential services be self-sustaining.[40] NYTel is highly vulnerable to bypass because less than 1 percent of its customers account for approximately 35 percent of the revenue.[41] NYTel argues that, in the large customer market where there is competition, it should be given flexibility.[42] Technological developments are carrying the threat over to the medium-size customers, too. By joining together to share facilities or by subscribing to shared service providers, medium-size customers can generate sufficient traffic to use alternatives that exist for large customers.[43] On the question of dominance, NYTel argues that one-point-in-time measures like market shares and market concentration are not appropriate for an industry which is undergoing rapid structural changes. In this view, the commission needs to adopt a more "dynamic" approach. The commission is seeking to establish future regulatory policy, not review the past.[44] When there are alternate service providers with staying power, even with a very large market share no one provider can dictate to the market. Thus customer bargaining power should be the key criterion to determine whether there is competition in a market.[45] More important, the regulators should be interested in a healthy market rather than dominance in itself.[46]

NYTel has often been criticized for its poor record in implementing equal access and not being at the leading edge of technology. According to NYTel, if there is anything to complain about, it is due to historical circumstances and not lack of willingness. In the economic slump of the 1970s, NYTel could not upgrade its network. During the same period, growth regions like the Sunbelt made investments in analog-stored control technology, the latest technology at that time. In the 1980s, along with the coming of digital technology, New York's economy picked up. New York could now leap-frog the analog-stored control stage and move directly from electromechanical to digital. Divestiture suddenly made equal access an issue, and NYTel was still saddled with electromechanical switches that could not be converted to equal access. In spite of the fact that electromechanical switches were exempted from equal access and that NYTel met the decree-mandated targets of one third of lines be served by equal access by September 1, 1985, and 100 percent by September 1, 1986, the impression lingers that NYTel was dragging its feet. By 1992 NYTel plans to replace all its electromechanical switches; also by that year it hopes to attain the highest digital penetration among all the RBOCs.[47]

Regulation of Interexchange Carriers

The interexchange market is dynamic because of the large and specialized demands of corporations, most of them located in the downstate region.

Competition is evident, yet determining the degree of competition is as elusive as quantifying bypass.   As in other states, the regulatory issues for interexchange services center around competition and dominance. AT&T believes that due to the long period of traditional regulation, the PSC is unable to distinguish between monopoly and dominance. AT&T argues that it is no longer a monopoly; at worst, it is a dominant player in a highly competitive market.[48] This, AT&T claims, is a situation similar to that in the computer industry, in which IBM has more than 50 percent of the market. What makes the computer industry competitive is not market share but ease of entry.[49] Earlier AT&T was the sole provider; now there are 100 companies buying access, and of these around 50 are certified long distance carriers.[50] The possibility of entering the market as a reseller has lowered the risk and cost of entry. AT&T also contends that its competitors are not small companies but Fortune 500 companies or their subsidiaries; the aggregate assets of IBM, GTE, and ITT exceed $100 billion.[51]

While determining the degree of competition, the PSC does not consider resellers. AT&T contests this on the grounds that resellers provide comparable services to consumers at lower prices or with more customized features than the facilities-based carriers. Resellers often provide a value added by uniquely packaging services and features so as to meet customers' needs otherwise not met. For example, resellers in New York have offered authorization codes, security codes, speech dialing, billing detail reports, and summary reports as value-added features. In some instances competitors have set prices above AT&T's, taking the level of competition from solely price to quality, features, and packaging.[52]   As far as the customer is concerned, the resellers are independent operations.

The PSC staff is of the opinion that no market segment is ready for complete deregulation. Although the toll rates are lower than those in 1984, the PSC contends that the timing, frequency and magnitude of those rate reductions indicate came about due to regulation, not competition.[53] AT&T's dominance is reinforced by the fact that, while the OCCs have been recording losses or only marginal profits, AT&T's intrastate profits have increased uninterrupted, from 16 percent in 1984 to 48 percent in 1986.[54]

AT&T's competitors, MCI and US Sprint, support AT&T's attempts at deregulation, especially the switch from the ROI method to rate caps. When questioned, they take the rather unbusinesslike position that it is a matter of principle.[55] According to the CPB, rate caps make sense only in an industry with rising costs. In a declining-cost industry rate caps can mean that reduced costs due to technological breakthroughs may not be passed on to consumers whereas the rate of return method, by definition, is tied to the cost of providing the service. So AT&T's competitors, who are at present working with very small margins, think that with price caps AT&T will not decrease rates in proportion to reduced costs, thereby relieving pressure on their margins.[56] This is supported by the statement of MCI's president that AT&T's deregulation will improve MCI's profitability.[57] This reasoning is based on the assumption that AT&T, in order to maintain its nonmonopoly status, will not drive competition out of business. The PSC staff is skeptical about this line of reasoning. Even though AT&T's competitors are willing to risk that AT&T will not use its market power to drive out the competition, the PSC staff feels the probability that excessive rates to consumers would result is not a risk worth taking.[58]

There is much debate as to the degree of pressure that is generated on the competition by changes in AT&T rates. AT&T feels that the PSC is using its control over AT&T's rates as a "price umbrella" to indirectly control the market.[59] The staff argues that the reductions in AT&T's rates do not compel competitive response by AT&T's competitors.[60] The facts indicate that long distance customers choose their carriers on cost competitiveness in the interstate market rather than the intrastate. Interstate calls make up 85 percent of the industry's estimated interLATA toll generated by New York State consumers. Interstate tolls are under the purview of the FCC, hence price changes imposed by the PSC have a very limited impact. Larger competitors like MCI and US Sprint, whose main business comes from interstate revenues, are not too sensitive to AT&T's interstate revenue change, whereas others like RCI and TDX, whose pricing strategies are different, are sensitive.[61]

The commission has instituted a generic proceeding to inquire into the nature of competition in New York. It is an attempt to establish general principles so as to increase predictability in a rapidly changing environment and also reduce the expensive, time-consuming case-by-case hearings. The objective of Stage 1 of the proceeding, completed in October 1987, was "to develop an analytical framework for defining and measuring the presence and extent of competition in the various telecommunications markets, and to ascertain facts that demonstrate the existence or future development of effective competition."[62] The proceeding is now in Stage 2, the objective of which is to "develop regulatory policy in response to specific issues listed in the Commission's order instituting this proceeding."[63] The PSC has yet to conclude the hearings, but the following facts give an idea of the degree of competition.

OCCs are competing with AT&T in markets that constitute 96 percent of New York's population.[64] In 1987 63 percent of the lines had been converted to equal access, and this figure is planned to increase to 85 percent by 1990 and 95 percent by 1992;[65] in nonequal access areas competitors get an 11 percent discount on access charges;[66] 95 percent of the consumers can reach multiple competitors on a toll-free basis.[67] Earlier AT&T was the sole intrastate long distance carrier; now there are 50 other common carriers and resellers.[68]

The OCCs increased their share of the access minutes purchased from 9 percent in 1985 to 17.3 percent in 1986, an increase of 90 percent. In the New York metroLATA, the OCCs' share was 26.5 percent in 1986.[69] MCI increased its business customer base in New York from 35,669 to 136,191, or 281 percent, between December 1986, while its residence subscribers increased from 173,267 to 511,697 during the same period.[70] According to AT&T, its competitors have installed sufficient capacity in fiber optics systems alone to absorb nearly all of AT&T's business in New York.[71]

AT&T is making an all-out attempt to move away from rate of return regulation. AT&T claims that rate of return regulation in a situation of partial deregulation results in arbitrary cost allocation between regulated and unregulated services.[72] Unlike other utilities, AT&T has a small rate base.[73] This small rate base, combined with a high revenue-rate base ratio, makes ROI measured as a percentage extremely volatile, so small dollar amounts can cause wide fluctuations.[74] Finally, AT&T argues that because approximately 70 percent (access charges--64 percent, gross receipts--5 percent) of its costs, mainly access charges, are not under its control.[75] Hence the rate of return regulation is less relevant for AT&T than it is for utilities with large capital bases.

Given the obsolescence of rate of return regulation and the existence, in AT&T's view at least, of competitive markets, the company is seeking more flexibility for its operations. AT&T worked out a Joint Proposal with the PSC staff that moves away from the rate of return method of rate setting toward price caps. The commission accepted the concept behind the Joint Proposal but withheld approval until the agreement was modified along suggested guidelines.[76] The commission took great pains to stress that its opinion did not in any manner prejudge the outcome of the generic proceeding on competition.[77] AT&T accepted the Joint Proposal as modified by the commission.[78] In the Joint Proposal AT&T does not to be pursuing enhanced profitability as much as the philosophical acceptance of the price cap concept.

TELECOMMUNICATIONS AND ECONOMIC DEVELOPMENT
Consensus Building

In general there is a high degree of cooperation between the policymaking bodies, and, where possible, the state encourages joint projects with the private sector. Whether it be the PSC, the Department of Economic Development (DED), or the governor's staff, opinions from public and private telecommunications actors are obtained and usually taken into account before decisions are made.

The PSC attempts to gather all interested parties together before ruling on major telecommunications issues. The PSC's immediate priority is to deal with the consumer issues raised by the rapid changes in the telecommunications industry. This stems out of genuine concern and a degree of pragmatism. With a strong "safety net" it will be easier to maneuver when dealing with the telecommunications needs of the businesses.[79] Otherwise, at every turn the same social issues are likely to crop up again and again. In general the PSC attempts to evolve a balanced regulatory package that is agreeable to most of the major telecommunications actors, including consumers.[80]

The compiling of a DED-sponsored report on telecommunications in New York reflects such attempts to build consensus. Because telecommunications decisions were being taken by the PSC and the state legislature on a case-by-case basis without a well-defined long-term perspective, DED hired the firm of Coopers and Lybrand for a comprehensive study on telecommunications in New York.[81] The objective of the study was to look at the way telecommunications affects the economy of New York and to look at the way the state affects those that provide telecommunications services to both residences and businesses in the state.[82] At the very least, the report contains a needs assessment analysis that inventories telecommunications in New York. It appears to be a consensus-building platform for future action.

Tax Reduction

Due to high taxes, New York telephone rates are among the highest in the nation. A 1985 New York State Finance Committee study reported that telephone rates in New York were 50 percent more than the national average and almost 60 percent more than those in the surrounding states.[83] State and local taxes on telephone services are twice the rate in neighboring states of New England and about 90 percent higher than the Northeast and mid-Atlantic regional averages.[84] In 1986, for each dollar paid for telecommunications services, New York State residents paid 18 cents in taxes, while those in New Jersey and Connecticut paid 6 and 12 cents, respectively.[85]

The types of state and local taxes levied on telecommunications services include real property tax, gross receipts tax, and sales tax. Under the real property tax law, all property owned by a "telephone utility" and used in the provision of telecommunications service was historically taxed as real property. This taxable property consisted of the telephones, PBXs and other station equipment installed on customers' premises; the poles, wires, cables, and conduits known collectively as outside plant; switching, carrier, and other central office equipment; and the land and buildings that house central office equipment.

When only the telephone company owned this equipment and other property, the property tax was easily collectible. Because of deregulation, however, and technological advances that began to accelerate in the late 1960s, customers increasingly began to acquire and own equipment that had formerly been provided by the telephone company. Disputes arose over the taxable status of this equipment, and in 1975 the state courts designated customer-owned station equipment as nontaxable "personal property," while station equipment owned by the telephone company remained taxable.[86]

In order to control the rapidly increasing tax burden on telephone service, the legislature had also frozen at the 1974 level the taxable assessments of telephone company central office equipment and station equipment. However, deregulation and competition in the long distance market complicated the impact of this legislation. Since their equipment was installed after 1974, the newer long distance companies initially did not pay real property tax and yet provided services similar to those of NYTel or AT&T.[87]

Another twist was added by the fact that the tax was levied at the cost of reproduction. Much of the earlier network consisted basically of copper wires whereas the later entrants installed newer technology (microwave radio, coaxial cable, and fiber optic cable) at a much cheaper cost, making the practice of levying property tax on reproduction value inconsistent with the changed environment. The tax was levied not only on telephone companies but also on the equipment owned by corporations.

In 1985, a telecommunications property tax law was passed that was scheduled to expire after two years so that its effects could be reviewed before permanent legislation was enacted. The 1985 law removed the property tax on station equipment and modified the 1974 law by continuing the freeze on central office equipment assessments for local exchange companies while extending the property tax to central office type equipment and outside plant owned by other companies. It proved to be extremely difficult, however, to collect the tax on this newly taxable equipment because local assessors could not locate, identify, or value the equipment.

After much criticism from the industry and users, further legislation that was strongly supported by New York City was passed in July 1987. This legislation did two things. First, the law made permanent the nontaxability of station equipment. Second, and more significantly, the law extended the real property tax on central office equipment for two years--1987 and 1988--while freezing the taxable assessments at the 1986 level and providing for a complete phase-out of the tax by reducing assessments 25 percent per year between 1989 and 1992. By 1993, the tax savings from the phase-out is estimated at $140 million for businesses and individuals.[88]

The enactment of the 1985 and 1987 legislation was an important step in reducing the property tax burden on telecommunications service. Even after the tax on central office equipment is completely eliminated, however, local exchange companies will remain subject to a heavy real property tax burden on their outside plant and other real property. Also, as indicated above, outside plant is assessed on the basis of its reproduction cost, which results in high levels of assessed value on which the property tax is levied.

The gross receipts tax is levied on a restricted basis; utilities, including telephone service, come under its purview. In 1917, when the gross receipts tax was replaced by a general state corporate tax on allocated profits, utilities were a notable exception.[89] The regulated monopoly status of the utilities was seen as more than sufficient justification for continuing this form of taxation. Now, however, technologically induced regulatory changes are rapidly eroding this regulated monopoly status of the telephone utilities. Hence the industry has been arguing that the regulatory bodies should stop treating telecommunications companies as traditional utilities.[90]

Numerous studies have recommended elimination of the tax. The governor and the legislature agree that getting rid of the tax is necessary. However, the magnitude of potential lost revenue prevents elimination of the tax. It is estimated that $820.6 million will be collected from gross receipts in 1987-88, and of the total, $246.5 million will originate from the telecommunications industry.[91] It is estimated that if the gross receipts had been replaced in 1986 with a net profit tax, consumers statewide would have enjoyed a rate reduction of almost $600 million.[92] In fact, early this year the Republican-controlled state senate passed a bill that sought to replace the gross receipts tax with an income tax levied on earnings. But it is unlikely to be passed by the state assembly and is also being opposed by the governor.

New York in general is a high-tax state. Since all taxes cannot be reduced at once, for the purposes of tax cuts the various tax categories need to be prioritized. When Governor Cuomo faced a choice between gross receipts and personal income tax, he chose to reduce the latter. The industry feels that in the changed business environment the gross receipts tax is not only archaic but also unfair. Ultimately, they argue, it will have to be phased out.[93]

In New York sales tax is levied on all telecommunications services. The sales tax on information services, due to its unique nature, is of special interest. Both the state and the local governments levy sales tax on information services; the magnitude of state tax is 4 percent of the selling price, and local tax varies between 1 and 4 percent.[94] Although the taxable information services are not well defined by the law, there are a few guiding principles. The tax is to be levied on new information created and not on conversion from one form to another. The tax is applicable only for written information, including that on a computer screen, but not for aural information. The information generated for personal individual consumption is exempted (for example, the report of a detective agency for use by an individual or the report of an investment counselor for a corporation). Corporate services like advertising and the news media's collection and dissemination of information are also exempted.[95]

The definition of "personal information" is often an area of dispute. For example, the Department of Taxation and Finance levies a sales tax on reports of marketing consultants. The industry argues that these are personalized services and should not be taxed. The rationale given by the department is that since consultants use common databases for their work, these are not personalized services. But these definitions are becoming even fuzzier with the advent of electronic delivery systems. For example, the industry has been demanding that computer-to-computer information exchange should not be taxed.[96] With further technological developments the issues involving the definition of taxable information services and the complexities in collecting this tax are likely to get murkier. But at present no attempt has been made to study the long-term impact of this tax and its likely complications in the future. The state does not even know the amount collected through this tax. According to the Research and Statistics Bureau of the Department of Taxation and Finance, the wide variety of businesses providing information services has made it impossible to estimate the taxes collected on such services.[97]

In view of the fact that the telecommunications industry is burdened with extremely high taxes, there is an across-the-board consensus that there should be further reductions. The major constraining factor is the magnitude of the revenues involved. As Joseph Walsh, Jr., vice-president of New York Telephone, put it, the taxes should be reduced, not merely shifted.[98]

Innovations

The state and the private sector, individually and in concert, have implemented a substantial number of telecommunications innovations aimed at promoting economic development. These innovative efforts are best grouped into three categories: regulatory initiatives, innovative joint projects, and state and New York City initiatives.

Regulatory Initiatives

The PSC has attempted to reduce the regulatory uncertainty in the rapidly changing telecommunications environment by instituting generic proceedings. As the name suggests, these proceedings seek to establish general principles rather than decide a particular case. That is, the PSC has attempted to anticipate the potential areas of dispute in the near future and instituted proceedings to establish the principles for their resolution. The proceedings on rate design and access charges have resulted in changes in rates, and at present those on competition and interconnection are in process. The hope is that through the use of generic proceedings the regulatory process will become more predictable and the need for case-by-case hearings reduced.

The moratorium process provides rates and regulatory stability, gives NYTel greater flexibility in its operations, and is a possible move away from rate of return to rate caps. In early 1986 NYTel agreed to implement a general rate increase until mid 1988 at the earliest. Two limited rate increases were allowed--one in August 1986 and another in August 1987--to recover identifiable cost increases such as wages, taxes, and federally managed cost shifts to the state.[99] There was also the provision that if the cost of equity differed by more than one percentage point from the equity allowance in the last major rate case, the August 1987 charge would be adjusted.[100] In August 1986, NYTel was granted an increase of $156 million. In late 1986 the staff of the PSC came forward with a proposal that would extend the general rate case moratorium and would utilize federal tax savings and pension cost reduction to implement a rate reduction in August 1987 (rather than the planned increase).

The proposal also provided for the use of tax and pension savings to accelerate the amortization of unrecovered inside-wire investment. In May 1987 the commission formally adopted a moratorium extension plan that built upon the staff proposal and a modification of the staff proposal which had been negotiated by NYT and CPB. Under the plan, NYTel revenues were to be reduced by $100 million in August 1987; there would be no general increase in rates until January 1, 1991, at the earliest; amortization of inside-wire investment would be accelerated and three inside-related rate elements that, together provided approximately $400 million in revenues would be eliminated. In addition, the moratorium provided for a sharing of any excess of earnings over the company's authorized return.[101]

On September 1, 1988, NYTel implemented the called-for $100 million revenue reduction.[102] The decrease was not apportioned equally to all calls, so the rate design issues were critical. The result was a lowering of rates for calls within the New York Metropolitan LATA. Under the Regional Calling Plan rate zones in the New York LATA were simplified and the prices brought closer to costs.

The PSC and NYTel project the moratorium as a well thought out, coherent strategy. The CPB does not view the three phases as elements of a larger plan but a series of unrelated compromises that found the moratorium a convenient cover. For example, it believes that, by reducing interregion rates and not intraregion rates, the main impact of the Regional Calling Plan was to strengthen NYTel's competitive position in the New York City intraLATA long distance market. In principle, the CPB is against any rate cap in a declining-cost industry. As previously noted, the CPB feels that through the moratorium process decreased costs will not be passed on to consumers whereas rate of return, by its very nature, is tied to the cost of the service.[103]

NYTel believes the process has worked out because consumers have obtained a rate reduction and the company has received much needed flexibility in the rapidly changing telecommunications environment.[104]

Innovative Joint Projects

New York has implemented many joint projects that seek to stimulate economic development through the use of telecommunications technologies. The significance of the telecommunications component in these projects varies.

The Economic Development Zone (EDZ) program, begun in 1986, aims at helping the economically depressed areas of the state. A variety of incentives are offered to attract businesses, especially those planning to relocate out of New York, into these areas. Incentives include tax credits, discounts on energy bills, and other assistance.[105] In 1987 with strong support from the city a telecommunications component was added to the EDZ package by the PSC and NYTel; it entails an across-the-board 5 percent discount on all telecommunications costs.[106] The telephone company would charge less, and the costs would be passed on to the consumers through the rate-setting process. The parties agree that this discount is by no means the mainstay of the EDZ packet but simply an extra inducement. The small percentage of discount coupled with the unlikeliness of telecommunications-intensive businesses locating or relocating in the EDZs make the discount incremental. Therefore, its importance is more symbolic than economic, a gesture signalling the recognition of the importance of telecommunications in economic activities, a first step in the right direction. The discount and the EDZ concept itself are of too recent an origin to be able to evaluate their impact.

The Centers for Advanced Technology (CATs) were created by New York State in 1982 with the objective of improving the interface between basic and applied research. CATs are cooperative research and development centers that bring together New York State, universities, and private industry. Jointly these groups engage in basic and applied research with the aim of harnessing new technologies for the economic good of the state.[107] Currently, every CAT receives up to $1 million each year from New York State. These funds are matched by at least an equivalent amount from private industry.[108]

One of the centers, the CAT at Polytechnic University, focuses on telecommunications. The CAT at Polytechnic University receives $1 million each year from the state, and corporate sponsors are obliged to at least match the state funding. For 1986, corporate grants totaled $1.6 million.[109] A total of 20 corporations, including IBM, GTE, AT&T, and NYTel, contribute to Polytechnic. In 1987 the state legislature authorized continued funding at the $1 million level through the 1995 fiscal year.[110]

No formal evaluation of the CAT at Polytechnic University has been conducted. However, several accomplishments highlight what many in state government regard as a success story. First, Polytechnic developed a model to analyze packet radio systems. A private firm employed this concept in its operations. Secondly, Securities Industries Automation Corporation, instead of relocating to New Jersey, remained in the New York City borough of Brooklyn in large part because of the presence of the CAT's technical support. Finally, Polytechnic's CAT has developed software used by a company located within the state.[111]

Another innovative joint project is the Teleport, located on Staten Island. The Teleport was largely conceived as a strategy to counter the flight of large telecommunications-intensive firms. It is the result of the partnership between New York City, the Port Authority of New Jersey and New York, Merrill Lynch, and Western Union. The teleport concept was conceived by the Port Authority as a measure to enhance the telecommunications infrastructure of the region and at the same time retain businesses by offering cheaper telecommunications-linked relocation sites as an alternative to fleeing New York. The teleport project consists of two components: the real estate component, managed by the Port Authority, and the telecommunications component, managed by Teleport Communications, a partnership between Merrill Lynch and Western Union.[112]

The basic product offered by Teleport Communications is "antenna slips," which can be described as a high quality, high security environment with support facilities (e.g., emergency and uninterrupted power) for satellite earth stations and ancillary equipment.[113] The services offered are flexible. Customers may choose to install their own earth stations in the Teleport, share them with others, or use Teleport Communication's equipment. If a company installs its own earth stations, maintenance may be performed by that company or contracted out to the Teleport.[114]

The original purpose of the Teleport was the earth station business. It was visualized that the Teleport would provide two advantages over the alternatives. First, it would offer an interference-free environment. New York suffers from microwave congestion; there are so many microwave paths rebounding from one dish to another that it is difficult to find interference-free paths, and the C-Band satellites use the same wavelength as the microwaves.

Hence, for transmission to satellites it has been necessary to situate the earth stations servicing New York two to three hundred miles away in New Jersey and Connecticut. The Staten Island site was selected for low interference, which was further eliminated by the wall erected around the site. Second, the Teleport would offer economies of scale and, at the same time, highly flexible service customized to the user's individual needs.[115]

These advantages were not perceived by TIBs to be big enough to switch from the other alternatives. In addition, a new technological development threatens obsolescence of the original concept. The Ku-Band satellites require smaller earth stations, capable of being located on a rooftop, and do not use the same wavelength as microwaves; hence, for these satellites microwave interference is no longer an issue.

A major success story for the Teleport is a 150-mile fiber optic network connecting the Teleport to much of New York City and parts of New Jersey. Of the total business from the fiber optic network, 71 percent is from the interconnect service, which uses the network to connect the point of presence of one long distance carrier to that of another; 20 percent is from connecting end user to end user, a service competing with private line services; and 9 percent connects the point of presence of a long distance carrier to end users.[116]

Another part of the New York City Teleport is real estate. The Teleport site consists of approximately 80 acres surrounding the equipment area. On this acreage corporations may construct their own buildings or use property developed by the Port Authority. The purpose of making real estate available to companies is that the companies can shift their back-office functions to Staten Island instead of nearby New Jersey. Moreover, the Teleport buildings, unlike New York's older buildings, are better suited for computers and sophisticated telecommunications equipment.[117] Those Teleport customers who do not shift office operations to Staten Island may obtain access through the fiber optic links.

The Teleport, which became operational in 1985, is of such recent origin that it is too early to judge its impact. Economic development of the region is an important aspect of the project. An attempt has also been made to revitalize the economically depressed areas of Queens and Brooklyn by extending to them the fiber optic links. Corporations could move their back-office functions to these areas, where real estate and other costs are lower.[118] If the project succeeds, New York will have attained three benefits: a state-of-the-art addition to the city's telecommunications infrastructure; retained the fleeing firms by relocating them within New York City; and revitalized the city's economically depressed areas.[119]

The New York State Education and Research Network (NYSERNet), another joint project, is a high-speed data communications network linking universities, industrial research laboratories, and government facilities in New York State. The goal is to give greater access to "computing and information resources which will aid in improving economic competitiveness."[120] NYSERNet, formed in 1985, is a not-for-profit company formed by a group of New York State educators, researchers, and industrialists. Users of NYSERNet include Columbia University, New York University, Polytechnic University and Cornell University, IBM, Kodak, and Brookhaven National Laboratory.

NYSERNet is the first network of this sort where the facilities are owned by telephone companies--in this case, NYTel and Rochester Telephone.[121] Most of the equipment comprising NYSERNet is donated and maintained by

NYTel, the largest contributor. Rochester Telephone and NYNEX also contribute to NYSERNet's capital. Other contributors include New York State and the National Science and Technology Foundation. Users of NYSERNet pay annual fees from $15,000 to $35,000 to access the system.

NYSERNet is also interesting as a partnership between a not-for-profit company and telephone companies, NYTel and Rochester Telephone. Due to its not-for-profit nature, NYSERNet is exempt from all regulations. This gives it much greater flexibility than the telephone companies. NYTel, NYSERNet's major supplier, was also granted exemptions and waivers for two years (until December 1988) for many of the services it provided to NYSERNet. An extension is under review. Through this partnership NYSERNet has access to NYTel's infrastructure and resources.[122]

Aside from the public relations benefits, the telephone companies are interested in testing whether NYSERNet could be a prototype for a commercial high-speed data network for research purposes. NYSERNet's policy restricts its usage to tasks related to research. Its business objective is to become self-supporting as soon as possible.[123] Operations at 15 NYSERNet locations began in January of 1987 at a data transfer rate of 56 kilobits per second.[124] More than half the network is now operating at 1.54 megabits per second. This is a significant advance over the original rate and makes the network more valuable to the education and research community.[125] Access to NYSERNet also brings access to INTERNET, a federal communications network connecting six supercomputers and research facilities.

The state also looks at NYSERNet as a prototype. The purpose of the NYSERNet trial is to allow the telephone companies to get some idea about the marketplace for this type of service while laying the groundwork for a future commercial high-speed network.[126] In keeping with this approach, NYSERNet brings together businesses, academia, research institutions, and the state; it is an infrastructure resource that would benefit the economy as a whole, especially the smaller establishments which otherwise would not have access to sophisticated supercomputers and other expensive resources. It is also an asset when competing for projects like Sematech and the supercollider.[127]

Thus far, the major use of NYSERNet has been access to the Cornell supercomputer. Linkage to university library systems is the next major step for NYSERNet, although a completion date is not available.[128] At present NYSERNet's services are targeted at the large institutional customers, but market research indicates that individual customers are a vast potential market.[129]

Another effort addressing the importance of the telecommunications infrastructure to economic development is reflected in the work of the New York City Partnership, Inc. The Partnership is a coalition of leaders in business, nonprofit organizations, and institutions of higher learning. In addition, it serves as the New York City Technology Development Organization under the auspices of the New York State Science and Technology Foundation. The Partnership's mission is to promote economic development in New York City. Its assessment of high technology's impact on the city's economic development is documented in High-Tech New York, a study prepared by Booz-Allen and Hamilton. Within its conclusions and recommendations, it points to the need to focus on telecommunications as a critical ingredient for the stimulation and support of the economy's dominant services industry, especially the financial services industry. The Partnership, assisted by Booz-Allen and Hamilton, is now conducting an analysis of the necessary public and private sector actions to address the key issues facing users and providers of telecommunications in New York City.[130]

In New York there are numerous examples where the deployment of fiber optic cable by the telephone company supported local government and business efforts to revive, retain and/or bolster economic development. Three of the most visible ones are: Buffalo, downtown Brooklyn, and Jefferson County (Fort Drum). As in all businesses, the endeavor is to keep pace with the demand while making network decisions. The investment should not be made too early or too late; it should be just in time.[131] But NYTel's investments in Buffalo are not justified by the projected revenue. An attempt is being made to revitalize Buffalo's depressed economy by creating sophisticated telecommunications infrastructure. Buffalo now has 6,000 fiber miles of fiber optic cable. In fact, according to community and business leaders, the availability of fiber optic technology is a major reason why banks and other information-dependent businesses are relocating to or expanding operations in the Buffalo area.[132] Brooklyn, after a 40-year period of economic decline, is now witnessing an economic boom. This boom has been triggered by the spillover of the companies leaving Manhattan due to high rents, a boom in the computer and securities industries, and generous energy and tax breaks. It is projected that by 1990 more than 20,000 new jobs will be created as a result of this activity. NYTel facilitated and also cashed in on this boom by creating a fiber optic ring around the downtown business district in an attempt to provide customers a telecommunications network as sophisticated as Manhattan's.[133] The project was a result of close collaboration between real estate developers, leasing agents, customers, NYTel, and government agencies.[134] By providing a state-of-the-art telecommunications infrastructure, NYTel facilitated the establishment of a major military base which in turn fueled a local economic boom at Fort Drum.[135] In February 1988 NYTel created its own department of economic development. This was also in response to the Omnibus Economic Development Act of 1987, which established the Department of Economic Development at the state level. NYTel's Department of Economic Development would not only interface with state, public, and private agencies involved in economic development but also coordinate and provide a better focus to NYTel's own initiatives. NYTel has approximately one hundred people participating in the activities of various economic development agencies, community boards, and chambers of commerce.[136] It is obvious and reasonable to expect that NYTel is trying to draw mileage from the developmental work it has long since being doing. This is also in keeping with the activities of other BOCs. Now 17 of the 22 BOCs have departments of economic development.

State and New York City Initiatives

New York State government is the largest single user of telecommunications in the state and NYTel's largest customer. The state government spends approximately $160 million a year on telecommunications equipment and services.[137] The state itself is an active bypasser and has an extensive network of its own. Statewide it has a fiber optic network with switching hubs at New York, Albany, Syracuse, and Buffalo. In Albany itself it has CAPNET, a 32,000-line fiber optic and microwave system servicing 59 government buildings in Albany.[138]

Of the $160 million spent on telecommunications approximately $75 million is channelled through the Office of General Services. The remaining amount is spent by individual agencies.[139] Two bills endorsed by the General Procurement Office that would have linked procurement of all state agencies together were rejected by the legislature in 1985. The bills became a victim of turf politics. State agencies successfully lobbied against the bill because they feared a loss of autonomy due to the standardization and sharing of technology. In addition, some agency officials were concerned about unauthorized access to their agency's data.[140]

Neither the General Procurement Office nor the DED links state procurement policy with economic development. The above-mentioned failed legislation, aside from standardizing the network, would have also created a foundation for a move in this direction. Although the state purchases leading-edge if not state-of-the-art technology, it does not consciously use its massive procurement power to bring high technology into the state. Perhaps how the state spends its $160 million telecommunications budget will have a greater impact than programs like NYSERNet, CATs, EDZs, and others.[141]

As a service organization, the government could enhance the delivery of many of its services by the innovative use of telecommunications technologies. Although this idea is realized to a degree, there is not much evidence of its implementation. Perhaps the most innovative application of computer-based communications has been in the area of the state lottery and off-track betting.[142] There could be many more. For example, the state network has 240 circuits between New York City and Albany that are not fully used after 5:00 p.m. These circuits could be leased out to other users, perhaps to provide facsimile service between Albany and New York for services such as interstate "zap mail."[143] This capacity could also be used for educational programs, linking state data processing facilities, and so forth.[144]

When cables for telecommunications networks are laid, very often rights-of-way are a major constraint. In the past, telecommunications companies have used diverse rights-of-way, ranging from railroad tracks to municipal pipelines. Hence, any potential right-of-way is a valuable resource. State and local governments have often underused this resource. New York was the first state to suggest the use of its thruway system, which lies in close proximity to 80 percent of the state's population, as a "digital thruway." From the state's point of view, this proposal has manifold advantages: the thruway system cuts through populated areas; costs of cabling would be relatively lower; the plan would involve a single state agency rather than numerous agencies, local bodies, and private parties; and the system could be a source of revenue.

Although the state obtained federal approval to use the thruway system, it has yet to figure out how this right-of-way is going to be used. It was Governor Cuomo who first proposed such a "digital thruway" in his 1985 State of the State address and is its ardent supporter. According to the governor, the federal approval to use New York's thruway system as a right-of-way "creates an opportunity for New York to significantly expand its communications capacity and enhance its position as the information capital of the world."[145]

After the state government, New York City is the second largest user of telecommunications in the state. There are two city agencies dealing with telecommunications. The Office of Telecommunications Control looks after the city's telecommunications equipment. The impetus behind creating this office in 1982 was to manage and reduce the city's operational costs in telecommunications. The Office of Energy and Telecommunications, created in

1986, looks into planning and policy areas. It also represents the city's interests before the PSC.[146]

The city has formed a 15-agency Telecommunications Working Committee to enhance interagency coordination for procurement and planning for the future. Due to the critical importance of telecommunications in financial services, the city's Office of Corporate Industry and Insurance also takes an active interest in policymaking and infrastructure development.[147]

New York City government has begun serious efforts at evaluating the links between telecommunications and economic development. The efforts of the Office of Energy and Telecommunications and the Office of Business Development indicate a desire by the city to become knowledgeable and active in promoting telecommunications growth. However, aside from lobbying efforts at the state level, New York City has yet to formulate its own telecommunications policy.

The range and number of telecommunications innovations in New York are clearly large; it is perhaps too early to evaluate their economic impacts.

CONCLUSIONS

The loss of manufacturing jobs and the flight of Fortune 500 firms from New York City has created a policy climate that has encouraged the use of telecommunications and to foster economic development. State policymakers realize that the prosperity of telecommunications-intensive businesses, most of which are in the state's growing service sector, is vital to New York's economic health. The concern over firms fleeing New York, added to a very activist approach to economic development within the state, has resulted in a policy environment in which the telecommunications infrastructure plays an important role in economic development policy.

While the telecommunications infrastructure has gained prominence on the policy agenda, universal service remains a major concern. In many ways, telecommunications regulation is a tightrope-walk between universal service and the ruthless demands of the market. The rural versus urban divide, which plagues other states, finds a parallel in the upstate versus downstate split in New York. The Regional Calling Plan somewhat ameliorates this problem by bringing prices closer to costs, but upstate versus downstate issues will continue to trouble New York for the foreseeable future. It remains to be seen how the universal service issue will be addressed as other policymakers, such as economic development officials, enter the policy debate. Nonetheless, the concern for universal service will be an important factor in the policy environment as the state to continues to integrate telecommunications into its economic development efforts.

Although there are few measurable links between telecommunications and economic development, the perception at the state level and in New York City is that the link exists and policy must respond to it. Both the governor's economic development staff and the Department of Economic Development encourage policymaking that exploits the perceived linkage. The active PSC also relates its policies to economic development. New York's active approach to economic development policy has resulted in a variety of telecommunications initiatives that broadly fall into the following five categories: consensus building, tax reduction, regulatory reform, innovative joint initiatives between the public and private sector, and innovative state initiatives.

Most New York State policymakers believe that consensus on major issues in telecommunications would be the ideal foundation for major telecommunications policy initiatives. As yet there are no signs of a consensus emerging nor have any macro-level telecommunications policy initiatives been taken. This makes one wonder whether consensus building is the cause or an excuse for the delay.

Tax reduction represents another type of telecommunications policy initiative policy in New York State, caused by concern over corporate retention. If there is a consensus among all major players, it is in the area of tax reduction. The much-criticized gross receipts tax, which is levied on revenue generated rather than net income, remains intact despite agreement among policymakers that it is outmoded, given the changed economic environment of the telecommunications industry; the restraining factor is the annual revenue of a quarter of a billion dollars generated by the telecommunications component alone.

The PSC's attempts at keeping the regulatory apparatus relevant to the rapidly changing technology have resulted in two major regulatory innovations: moratoria and generic hearings. The moratorium process successfully brought about a system which provides rate and regulatory stability and gives NYTel greater flexibility in its operations. The generic hearings concept employs both policy-consensus rationale and attempts at innovative regulatory behavior. Grappling with a bundle of related issues, rather than a single disputed case, has the potential to eliminate much of the delay and expense normally associated with regulatory hearings. Input from all concerned parties is encouraged, and the generic process has become a permanent feature of the PSC regulatory process. Telecommunications regulation in New York reflects concern over the provision of universal service, fair competition, and economic development.

There has also been a cautious move toward deregulation, a process that started in New York prior to divestiture. The regulators have long been aware of the need for regulatory changes necessitated by technological developments. Hence, unlike some other states, divestiture did not suddenly make deregulation fashionable. The rather cautious approach is to deregulate on a case-by-case basis, only when there is sufficient competition.

The large number of joint projects among public and private entities is another distinctive feature of the telecommunications environment in New York. The Teleport, an effort to stimulate economic growth by enhancing the telecommunications infrastructure of the region, is certainly the largest and most visible joint project. The state-sponsored CAT at the Polytechnic University is another attempt to stimulate economic development by providing state-of-the-art telecommunications infrastructure. Finally, NYSERNet demonstrates how the self-interests of diverse actors can be rallied around an economic development project that relies on the telecommunications infrastructure. NYTel and Rochester Telephone, interested in business growth and good community relations, have provided New York's educational institutions and research facilities with the opportunity to access computer resources otherwise unavailable. NYSERNet may turn out to be the prototype for the high-speed data transmission networks of the future. Downtown Brooklyn, Buffalo and Fort Drum are examples of deployment of fiber optics by NYTel which support and reinforce the economic development efforts of local and state governments.

The state government, like the private sector, has also begun to use of the telecommunications infrastructure to improve the efficiency of operations. Unfortunately, due to turf politics the Office of General Services was not able to push through legislation that would have brought all telecommunications spending under one authority. This would have facilitated much needed standardization and of course better coordination. Neither the General Procurement Office nor the DED links state procurement with economic development. Although the state purchases leading-edge technology, if not state-of-the-art, it does not consciously use its massive procurement power to attract high technology into the state. The annual budget of $160 million for telecommunications services and equipment is a big amount to play with. Through an artful use of this budget the state could easily influence the telecommunications environment in New York.

As a service organization, the state could enhance the delivery of many of its services by the innovative use of telecommunications technology. It is ironic that most innovative applications of telecommunications have been in the state lottery and off- track betting. The digital thruway, which has the potential (however doubtful to some observers) to improve service delivery, may lose momentum if its most powerful sponsor, Governor Cuomo, leaves office.

New York is an example of a state that has responded to economic crisis, namely the loss of manufacturing jobs and the flight of Fortune 500 companies, by increasing economic development activity at the state level. As part of this increased activity, the state has begun to understand the importance of the telecommunications infrastructure to its economy. The result has been a number of policy initiatives, ranging from regulatory reform to joint public and private ventures, which seek to improve the telecommunications infrastructure and thus the economic vitality of the state. The emphasis on consensus, added to the high level of telecommunications expertise within state government, suggests that New York should be able to develop the link between telecommunications and economic development in the future.

CASE STUDY: THE TELEPORT

This case study analyzes the evolution of New York's Teleport project. The Teleport is of special interest in the present study because its main objective is to stimulate economic development of the New York metropolitan area by strengthening the telecommunications infrastructure of the region. The main dimensions of the analysis are the economic development aspect of the project, the dynamics of private-public sector cooperation in a joint telecommunications infrastructure development project like the Teleport, and the regulatory issues raised by the Teleport's fiber optic network.

The New York Teleport Concept

The World Teleport Association defines a teleport as "an access facility to a satellite or other long haul telecommunications medium incorporating a distribution network serving the greater regional community; and associated with, including or within a related real estate or other economic development project."[148] As the definition suggests, there is a great deal of variation from one teleport to another. The New York Teleport has two components: telecommunications infrastructure and real estate. The telecommunications component is managed by Teleport Communications, a partnership between

Merrill Lynch and Western Union; the real estate component is managed by the Port Authority of New Jersey and New York.

The Teleport is much more than an antenna farm. The basic product offered by Teleport Communications is "antenna slips," which can be described as "a high quality, high security environment with support facilities (e.g., emergency and uninterruptable power) for satellite earth stations and ancillary equipment."[149] Microwave congestion in New York City interferes with quality communications and limits new connections. To ensure a quality environment the equipment area is shielded by a 50-foot wall, thus providing a "window through the interference."[150] The security aspect has two components: the physical protection of the equipment and a dual source of power supply from the New York State Grid System and the New Jersey and Middle Atlantic Grid System.[151] The facility has fiber optic links into New York City and New Jersey. The services offered are highly flexible. A company may choose to install its own equipment in the Teleport, share it with others, or use Teleport Communication's equipment, thus providing economies of scale. A company that installs its own equipment may contract the maintenance to Teleport Communications.[152]

The real estate component consists of approximately 80 acres of land around the equipment area. Here corporations can construct their own buildings or buy or rent property developed by the Port Authority. Aside from offering a cheaper relocation site, the new facilities, unlike New York's old buildings, are better suited for computers and sophisticated telecommunications equipment.[153] Those who do not shift their operations to the Teleport premises can have access through the fiber optics links. These links have also been extended into the economically depressed areas of Queens and Brooklyn. It is hoped that access to sophisticated telecommunications infrastructure will persuade businesses to locate or relocate in these relatively cheaper area and in the process revitalize them.[154]

Economic Development and the Teleport

For the present study the Teleport is of special interest because its origins lie in the economic development of the region. The Teleport was conceived by the Port Authority as a project that would not only strengthen New York's telecommunications infrastructure but also, through its real estate component retain firms that might otherwise leave the city. It was through its economic development link that the Teleport obtained the state and city support which facilitated the project. As Robert Annunziata, president and chief operating officer of Teleport Communications, put it:

> The rights of way are not an issue to be taken lightly, either for the project or for the regional economy. In fact, this need has helped create a new source of revenue for other entrepreneurs with rights of way such as the railroads and utilities. I reiterated--particularly in reference to this point--that having the support of your local government for a teleport is most advantageous.[155]

In fact, Teleport Communications itself has been using this argument in its regulatory battles. According to Robert Atkinson, vice-president of Regulatory and External Affairs for Teleport Communications, "We are foremost an economic development project."[156] In the interconnect case discussed later, Teleport Communications has thus distinguished itself from other carriers: "it [Teleport Communications] is absolutely unique in one crucial respect: It is a `partner' in a public economic development project and shares its gross revenues and profits with public agencies. No other carrier can make that statement."[157] As with telecommunications in general, as yet no specific and quantifiable links have been established between the Teleport project and the region's economy. The Port Authority is in the process of completing an in-house study measuring the economic impact of the Teleport; the study is expected to be completed by June 1988.[158]

Even without well-established economic development links, the expectations of economic development are important in the policy development arena:

> In New York, a main component of Teleport is that it is an office park and it will attract to a relatively undeveloped area of the City, a million square feet development initially and as much as 2 million square feet eventually. In turn this will house about 3400 jobs and create another 2,000 jobs in induced employment. This will result in an annual payroll in excess of $ 100 million dollars on Staten Island. And revenues to the localities will total about $ 10 million dollars a year. All of this is extremely welcome as incremental economic development.[159]

At the inauguration of the Teleport this expectation was echoed by the Staten Island Borough President Anthony Gaeta: "This is our Brooklyn Bridge Day. They will come with more than 3,000 jobs generated with the Teleport."[160] The Teleport became operational in 1983 and hence it is perhaps too early to even gauge the degree to which the expectations have been fulfilled.

The Teleport as a Joint Project

The Teleport is also interesting for studying the dynamics of public and private partnership in a major telecommunications infrastructural project. The logical beginning point for such an analysis is the reasons for the formation of the partnership itself. The reason the Port Authority looked for a private--sector partner for the telecommunications component was that it lacked expertise in this area and also the sensitivity to entry into competitive areas.[161] Merrill Lynch joined the Teleport project for two reasons. First, it is the largest nongovernment telecommunications user in New York and was dissatisfied with the service provided by the telephone companies.[162] In 1983 alone, Merrill Lynch spent approximately a quarter of a billion dollars on communications.[163]

Second, for a company in the investment business the project seemed to be a good investment.[164] The dynamics of the partnership are interesting from the economic development angle. The Port Authority's primary interest is economic development whereas Merrill Lynch's is profit: "There is no inconsistency or impropriety in such an arrangement--in fact, the essence of a public and public deal hinges upon the balancing of these diverse interests."[165]

The following example illustrates an instance of how these diverse interests have been balanced. Teleport Communications could not have invested in the fiber optic links in the economically depressed areas of Queens and Brooklyn purely for business reasons. The potential for immediate profit in such an enterprise is remote; hence, there must be other factors that motivated Teleport Communications to invest in these fiber optic links. According to the Port Authority, they were a part of the lease agreement.[166] However, the answer from Teleport Communications was good public relations.[167] It was "part of our cost of doing business in a cooperative endeavor with the public sector."[168] From the tremendous newspaper coverage the launch of the Teleport project attracted, it appears that the understanding on such issues is an implicit, rather than legally binding, factor underlying the agreement.[169] Such a suggestion is reinforced by a statement from Kenneth Lipper, deputy mayor for Finance and Economic Development, at the 1984 World Teleport Association conference:

> It's also politically necessary to bring these cables and these fiber-optic lines into the Outer-Boroughs and into the Outer Regions so that future development could be taking place in those areas. One of the requirements for this transaction was running the fiber-optic cable into downtown Brooklyn and into Queens. This is a fundamental element even though it's sometimes difficult from a profit point of view for the operators to see the immediate benefit. This will help us to develop those outlying areas.[170]

Guy Tozzoli, director of the Port Authority's World Trade Department, was more poetic:

> The Teleport is about technology and frontiers. It is also about something far more basic, more subtle and in some ways less sure. It is about cooperation. Cooperation between partners, cooperation between technical components, cooperationbetween projects.[171]

The Earth Stations and the Fiber Optic Network

Originally the Teleport was conceptualized as a satellite communication operation, with the fiber optic network as an ancillary operation that would feed into the earth station complex. It was visualized that the Teleport would have the following advantages over the other earth stations serving the region:

1. The proximity to the New York and New Jersey market. Staten Island is only miles from downtown Manhattan, whereas other earth stations, due to the microwave congestion, are situated miles away in New Jersey or Connecticut.
2. Unlike other earth stations, the Teleport would serve multiple users, including competing common carriers.
3. The fiber optic network for accessing the markets would eliminate the microwave congestion problem faced by other earth station complexes.
4. With multiple antennas the Teleport will be able to access the entire domestic arc from 67 degrees to 143 degrees west longitude and the Atlantic INTELSAT arc. The Teleport would be the first installation in the region to collocate domestic and international antennas.[172]

The projections have not materialized as envisioned. The majority of the revenue now comes from the fiber optic network and not the earth stations. The core business of Teleport Communications is now fiber optic network and not earth stations. That does not mean that the earth station business is not doing well, the Teleport now houses 16 earth stations, one more than the projected 15. The issues regarding competition in the local network were unplanned for and the utility, other than market access, was inadvertent. As Christopher Levintow, manager of Regulatory Affairs at Teleport Communications, puts it:

> It is important to understand that Teleport Communications does not operate in a vacuum. The dynamics of this fast-paced and exciting business environment implies at a minimum, the requirement to change. Our business plan is not frozen in concrete, we only have responded to the dynamics of our marketplace.[173]

NYTel argues that Teleport's fiber optic network is one of a growing number of competitors.[174] According to NYTel, 64.5 percent of NYTel's 400 largest customer locations are in buildings passed by Teleport's current transmission facilities. Due to the growth of Teleport and other providers of high-capacity services, NYTel's high-capacity market share has fallen to less than 57 percent in the New York City area.[175] Teleport Communications counters by pointing out that only 9 percent of its business from the fiber optic network is a result of bypass--connection between the point of presence (POP) of a common carrier to the end user. Most of its business, 71 percent, comes from interconnect service, POP to POP, and the remaining 20 percent from connecting end user to end user.[176] Taking the intrastate private line market as a whole, Teleport Communications' market share is about two-hundredths of one percent (0.0002).[177] The counterargument is that even interconnect business and end-user to end-user service draws business off the network and hence is bypass; it all depends on how bypass is defined.

The Collocation Debate

A complex regulatory issue has been raised by Teleport's demand that it be allowed to interconnect with NYTel's network and, in order to make that technically possible and commercially feasible, to be allowed to collocate its multiplexing equipment in NYTel's switching facilities, the local serving office (LSO) of NYTel. Teleport Communications also wants the access charges to be "unbundled" so that its customers will not have to pay access for the "local transport" component. The Teleport sees NYTel as having two "divisions": the monopoly division and the potentially competitive division.[178] The monopoly division is comprised of the local switching equipment and the local loop; the potentially competitive division is the local transport. Local transports are the high-capacity links connecting the point of presence of the long distance carrier to the local switching equipment of the local exchange company. Redundancy in these links makes sense from the security and capacity point of view, hence the argument by Teleport Communications that this segment of the local exchange network is potentially competitive. To be able to provide competition it needs "equal access"; in other words, it must be allowed to interconnect to the local network operated by NYTel. According to Teleport Communications competition in the local transport becomes technically and commercially feasible only if Teleport Communications is allowed to interconnect by collocating its multiplexing equipment in NYTel's facilities. Teleport Communications estimates that the LSO to POP market has an annual value of $100 million.[179] NYTel is unwilling to allow this access, however. Its arguments are based on three objections: first, collocation is not sought as a means of implementing a new technology or a new service by Teleport, but only as a means for carving out an exception to the present access charge regime which requires that all interexchange carriers pay a broadly averaged rate for LEC-provided activities;[180] second, the request is unprecedented and in no way should NYTel be forced to use its own facilities to accommodate Teleport Communications equipment;[181] third, it sets a precedent which would lead to many other similar requests for collocation, making the arrangement unmanageable.[182] Teleport Communications counters by pointing out that

1. the "local transport" need not necessarily be a "natural monopoly"; in order to provide competition collocation is essential;[183]

2. it is only reasonable that its customers not be made to pay access charges for the component of the network ("local transport") they do not use;[184]

3. the space required for the multiplexing equipment at NYTel's facilities is only 8 square feet;[185]

4. there will not be many other parties interested in similar interconnection arrangement;[186]

5. New Jersey Bell has agreed to a similar arrangement; although it is not termed collocation, it is effectively the same thing.[187]

Bell Atlantic, in a filing with the FCC, disputes Teleport's characterization.[188] Teleport litigated its collocation proposal before the New York Public Service Commission. The PSC staff of the commission along with NYTel opposed the proposal. The PSC staff commented that "Teleport has misrepresented alleged benefits of the proposal," and it would not be in the public interest to grant that proposal.[189] On May 9, 1988, Administrative Law Judge J. Michael Harrison issued a recommended decision stating:

> Access to interexchange carriers by end users is, and should be subject to competition from bypass alternatives. NYTel's access connections to its own network, however, cannot reasonably be considered a competitive marketplace. It is recommended that Teleport's collocation proposal be rejected.[190]

The case is now pending before the full commission, as is an identical case Teleport Communications has presented to the FCC.[191]

Teleport is a result of not only cooperation between the private and the public sectors but also, through the Port Authority, a bistate organization, cooperation between New York and New Jersey. These two states are competitors and yet have highly interdependent economies. In this context it would be interesting to study over a period of time the differing reactions of two telephone companies, NYTel and New Jersey Bell, toward the Teleport's fiber optic network. With businesses already moving to New Jersey it would be interesting to observe the impact of Teleport Communications' fiber optic network itself and the attitudes of the telephone companies. It would also be interesting to see what political pressures come into play in the resolution of the dispute.

The Skeptics

The Teleport has received a lot of attention and raised many issues; but there are many who doubt the very feasibility of the concept and have dismissed the idea as "Information Age hype." As one such skeptic puts it:

> The popularity of the teleport is not based on any evidence that such a project can stimulate economic development. Rather, the popularity of teleports demonstrates that public investments are often made on the basis of `municipal chic,' not unlike the popularity of building sports stadiums, convention centers and cultural centers a decade ago. Advances in optical fiber technology and in Ku-band satellite technology, enabling small satellite dishes to be built directly next to or on top of the buildings, however, may ultimately limit their appeal of teleports as currently conceived.[192]

Being an innovative and perhaps a daring idea in a rapidly changing, uncertain environment, the Teleport concept provokes reactions--both for and against-- that are more gut responses than seasoned predictions. But there could indeed be a very serious threat of technological obsolescence. Technological developments in very small aperture terminals, especially in Ku-Band satellites, would permit potential Teleport customers to install their own smaller and cheaper discs on their own premises. In addition, the Ku-Band satellites use frequencies that are different from those used by microwaves. Hence, there would be no problem of interference in microwave-congested metropolitan areas.

Future Trends

Depending on regulatory decisions, the operation that could boom is the fiber optic networks. In 1986 the East Lansing Research Association identified the following six trends that are likely to characterize the future of the teleports:

1. Governmental and regulatory influences will increase due to increasing concerns about emissions from the RF fields used to create an interference-free environment.
2. The satellite aspect of teleports will decrease, and the fiber optic business for various interfacings will increase.
3. Teleports will increasingly become network facility managers.
4. Teleports will increasingly become "one-stop" providers of numerous customer needs, including last-mile access, trunking, equipment, repair, and billing.
5. Teleports will serve as ISDN gateways to interface with the largely nondigital local exchange.

6. There will be tremendous growth potential for teleport operators who position themselves as multinational gateways in concurrence with international trends in privatization.[193]

Other interesting developments are also taking place. For one, the former Bell operating companies are also entering the teleport business. Ohio Bell has already acquired a 20 percent stake in Ohio Teleport Corporation, which is building a teleport at Columbus.[194] Merrill Lynch recently announced that based on the success of the New York Teleport, it will be constructing fiber optic networks in a number of other cities including Boston.[195]

Thus we see that the teleports are going to be around but will be undergoing tremendous changes. The teleport concept was conceived in the early seventies at the Port Authority; Arthur D. Little, Inc., submitted its market research report entitled "Assessment of the Teleport Concept" to the Port Authority in June 1981; and the Teleport was inaugurated in 1983. Hence we see that the foundations for the Teleport were laid before the divestiture, which makes one wonder what shape the teleport concept would have taken had there been no divestiture or had it been delayed.

NOTES

1.   Telephone interview with Joseph Schlosser, Manager, Coopers and Lybrand, New York, June 7, 1988.

2.   Interview with Joseph M. Robbins, Division Manager, Regulatory Support/Capital Management, Bell Communications Research, Austin, Texas, April 1, 1988.

3.   Correspondence from L.J. Titman, Director, Network Technology Management, New York Telephone Company, New York, May 20, 1988.

4.   Ibid.

5.   Ibid.

6.   Kenneth L. Phillips, "Telecommunications and New York in the Year 2000," testimony before the New York City Commission on the Year 2000, May 9, 1985, pp. 3-4.

7.   Calvin Sims, "Baby Bells Moving into the lab," New York Times, April 20, 1988, p. D7.

8.   Letter to Robert Wilson from James T. Horris, Managing Director, Economic Development, New York Telephone Company, New York , August 19, 1988.

9.   New York Telephone Company, Brief of New York Telephone Company, Case 29469 (Competition Proceeding), New York, December 18, 1987, p. 4.

10.   Interview with Neal Vaupel, External Affairs Manager, AT&T, New York, January 22, 1988.

11.   AT&T Communications of New York, Inc., Brief of AT&T Communications of New York, Inc. - Proceeding on Motion of Commission to Review Regulatory Policies for Segments of the Telecommunications Industry Subject to Competition (Case 29469), New York, December 18, 1987, p. 6.

12.   Ibid., p. 35.

13.   Ibid., p. 36.

14.   Interview with Luke Rich, Director, New York State Senate Committee on Commerce, Small Business, and Economic Development, Albany, January 19, 1988.

15.   Interview with Robbins.

16.   Office of the Mayor, The New York City Program for Competitive Business Energy Costs, New York, 1987. (Pamphlet.)

17.   Interview with Catherine Hannah Behrend, Director, Office of Corporate and Financial Services, New York City Office of Business Development, New York, January 21, 1988.

18.   New York State Department of Economic Development, Summary of the Strategic Resurgence Fund and Department of Economic Development Components of the Omnibus Economic Development Act of 1987 (New York, 1987), p. 1.

19.   "The Big Apple Regains Its Shine," The Economist, April 18, 1987, p. 80.

20.   Interview with Rich.

21.   Interview with Kevin O'Connor, Assistant to the Director, New York State Office of Economic Development, New York, January 19, 1988.

22.   Interview with Robbins.

23.   Telephone interview with Michael Shimazu, Senior Program Associate, Science and Technology Foundation, Albany, March 1, 1988.

24. Department of Economic Development, Brief on Behalf of Department of Economic Development for Case 29469 (Competition Proceeding), Albany, December 18, 1987, p. 17.

25. Telephone interview with Mitchell Moss, New York University, New York, June 14, 1988.

26. Interview with Eli Noam, Commissioner, New York Public Service Commission, New York, January 22, 1988.

27. Interview with Walsh.

28. Interview with Noam.

29. Interview with Blau, Martinez, Niazi, and Shapiro.

30. Interview with Walsh.

31. Interview with Blau, Martinez, Niazi, and Shapiro.

32. Interview with Robert C. Atkinson, Vice-President, Regulatory and External Affairs, and Christopher D. Levintow, Manager, Regulatory Affairs, Teleport Communications, New York, January 26, 1988.

33. Interview with Robbins.

34. Interview with Philip Shapiro, Intervenor Attorney, New York State Consumer Protection Board, Albany, January 19, 1988.

35. Interview with Walsh.

36. New York Telephone Company, Brief of New York Telephone Company - Proceeding on Motion of the Commission to Review Regulatory Policies for Segments of the Telecommunications Industry Subject to Competition (Case 29469), New York, December 18, 1988.

37. Interview with Blau, Martinez, Niazi, and Shapiro.

38. Interview with Walsh.

39. Ibid.

40. New York Telephone Company, Brief of New York Telephone Company, Case 29469 (Competition Proceeding), New York, December 18, 1987, p. 4.

41. Ibid.

42. Ibid., p. 60.

43. Ibid., p. 5.

44. Ibid., p. 34.

45. Ibid., pp. 20-21.

46. Interview with Walsh.

47. Telephone interview with L.J. Titman, Director, Network Technology Management, New York Telephone Company, New York, May 20, 1988.

48. Interview with Vaupel.

49. AT&T Communications of New York, Inc., Brief, Case 29469 (Competition Proceeding), pp. 25-26.

50. William J. Baumol, Professor of Economics, Princeton University, Direct Testimony, Case 29469 (Competition Proceeding), New York, December 17, 1988, p. 16.

51. Lee J. Globerson, District Manager, Marketing Plans Implementation, AT&T Communications of New York, Inc., Testimony, Case 29469 (Competition Proceeding), New York, April 17, 1987, p. 16.

52. AT&T Communications of New York, Inc., Brief, Case 29469 (Competition Proceeding), p. 16.

53. New York Public Service Department, Staff Brief and Policy Statement to the Administrative Law Judge, Case 29469 (Competition Proceeding), Albany, December 18, 1987, p. 12.

54. Ibid.

55.   Telephone interview with William Ericson, Attorney, MCI, Rye Brook, February 19, 1988.

56.   Telephone interview with Shapiro, February 29, 1988.

57.   "MCI Is Requesting That Rival AT&T Be Deregulated," Wall Street Journal, March 6, 1987.

58.   New York Public Service Department, State Brief, Case 29469 (Competition Proceeding), p. 1.

59.   Interview with Vaupel.

60.   AT&T Communications of New York, Inc., Brief, Case 29469 (Competition Proceeding), p. 14.

61.   Ibid., p. 44.

62.   New York Public Service Department, State Brief, Case 29469 (Competition Proceeding), p. 1.

63.   Ibid.

64.   Interview with Vaupel.

65.   AT&T Communications of New York, Inc., Brief, Case 29469 (Competition Proceeding), pp. 34-35.

66.   Interview with Vaupel.

67.   Globerson, Direct Testimony, Case 29469 (Competition Proceeding), p. 5.

68.   AT&T Communications of New York, Inc., Brief, Case 29469 (Competition Proceeding), p. 36.

69.   Ibid., p. 41.

70.   Ibid., p. 38.

71.   Ibid.

72.   Ibid., p. 17.

73.   Baumol, Direct Testimony, Case 29469 (Competition Proceeding), pp. 23-24.

74.   Compared with NYTel's rate base of $6.4 billion, AT&T's is only $61 million, less than one percent of NYTel's. For NYTel, with revenues of $4.6 billion, the ratio of revenue to rate base is 0.72; for AT&T, with revenue of $466 million, the ratio is 7.64. With this ratio a 5 percent change in expenses on AT&T's rate base would result in a 20 percent change in AT&T's realized return. In contrast, a 5 percent change in the expenses of traditional utilities, such as NYTel, would amount to less than 2 percent on realized return.

75.   Baumol, Direct Testimony, Case 29469 (Competition Proceeding), p. 25.

76.   New York Public Service Commission, Opinion Proposing Modified Settlement, Case 29595, Opinion No. 88-7, March 4, 1988, p. 1.

77.   Ibid., p. 26.

78.   The modified Joint Proposal indicates target earnings of $7.1 million equivalent to an equity return of 14 percent on a rate base of $59.3 million. AT&T will be permitted to retain 100 percent of earnings above $7.1 million up to $7.5 million (equivalent to a 15 percent equity return). Earnings in excess will be shared equally between AT&T and its ratepayers.

79.   Interview with Noam.

80.   Ibid.

81.   Interview with O'Connor.

82.   Joseph Schloesser, in Telecommunications Technology in New York: Policy and Economic Implications (unedited transcript of the technology briefing presented by the New York State Legislative Commission on Science and Technology and the New York Academy of Sciences for the New York

State Legislature, Albany, New York, April 29, 1987), Albany, New York, 1987, p. 21.

83. New York Senate, Senate Finance Committee, Taxation and Telephone Costs in New York State: A Comparative Analysis (Albany, January 1985), p. 2.

84. Ibid., p. 1.

85. Schloesser, Telecommunications Technology in New York, p. 31.

86. New York Senate, Senate Finance Committee, Taxation and Telephone Costs, p. 17.

87. Ibid.

88. Press Release, Office of the Mayor, Wednesday, July 29, 1987.

89. New York Senate, Senate Finance Committee, Utility Taxation: Time for Change (Albany, May 1987), p. 2.

90. Interview with Walsh.

91. Ibid.

92. Ibid.

93. Interview with Walsh.

94. Telephone interview with Jonathan Pessen, Senior Attorney, Law Bureau, New York Department of Taxation and Finance, Albany, February 17, 1988.

95. Ibid.

96. Ibid.

97. Letter to Harmeet Sawhney from Jonathan Pessen, February 19, 1988.

98. Interview with Walsh.

99. The CPB took the Phase 1 ruling to court, arguing that the ruling authorized $150 million worth of unwarranted increases for consumers. The CPB has charged that the prescribed moratorium procedures were not followed. The court ruled against the CPB.

100. New York Public Service Commission, Annual Report 1986 (Albany, 1987), p. 63.

101. Letter to Robert Wilson from Ronald H. Sirch, Managing Director, New York Telephone Company, August 22, 1988.

102. Ibid.

103. Ibid.

104. Interview with Walsh.

105. New York State Director of Economic Development, New York, Opportunities for Businesses, New York, 1987, section 4. (Brochure.)

106. Interview with Dunleavy.

107. New York State Director of Economic Development, New York, Opportunities for Business, section 4.

108. Ibid.

109. Telephone interview with Shimazu.

110. Ibid.

111. Ibid.

112. Interview with Sharon McStine, Administrator, World Teleport Association, New York, January 21, 1988.

113. Letter to Harmeet Sawhney from Christopher D. Levintow, Manager, Regulatory Affairs, Teleport Communications, May 19, 1988.

114. Bruce Hoard, "An Office Park Offers Satellite Services to Firms Fleeing New York," Computerworld, September 28, 1983, p. 77.

115. Interview with McStine.

116. Interview with Atkinson and Levintow.

117. New York Times, May 2, 1983, p. D1.

118. Christian Science Monitor, October 12, 1983, p. 4.

119. Interview with McStine.

120. NYSERNet, Inc., NYSERNet, Inc., The New York State Education and Research Network (New York, 1987), p. 1.

121. Ibid.

122. Telephone interview with Karen Travis, Administrative Manager, NYSERNet, Inc., New York, March 23, 1988.

123. Ibid.

124. NYSERNet, Inc., NYSERNet, Inc., The New York State Education and Research Network (New York, 1987), p. 3.

125. Letter to Robert Wilson from James T. Horris, Managing Director, Economic Development, New York Telephone Company, New York, August 19, 1988.

126. Telephone interview with Travis.

127. Ibid.

128. Telephone interview with Shimazu.

129. Telephone interview with Travis.

130. Interview with Bill Peters, Director, High Technology Business Development, New York City Partnership, Inc., New York, January 25, 1988.

131. Telephone interview with B.R.Wiginton, Director of Economic and Demand Analysis, New York Telephone Company, New York, May 19, 1988.

132. "Availability of Fiber Optics, Advanced Services Spark Business Boom in Buffalo Urban, Rural Areas," The Buffalo News, February 7, 1988, p. 3.

133. Rosemarie Le Goff, "NYTel's Opnet Helps to Reverse Brooklyn's Economic Decline," Telephony, March 23, 1987, p. 39.

134. Ibid., p. 43.

135. Dawn C. Chmielewski, "NYTel Lays First Line: Fiberoptics Arrives in City," Watertown Times, July 23, 1987, p. 18.

136. Telephone interview with Jim Horris, Managing Director, Economic Development, New York Telephone, New York, May 4, 1988.

137. Interview with John P. Heinsohn, Director of Telecommunications, Office of General Services, Albany, January 20, 1988.

138. Ibid.

139. Ibid.

140. Ibid.

141. Interview with Robbins.

142. Mitchell Moss, "A New Agenda for Telecommunications Policy," New York Affairs, Spring 1986, p. 86.

143. Ibid.

144. Interview with Robbins.

145. "Transportation Ruling Permits Fiber Optic Placement on Thruway," Weekly Summary, February 4, 1988, p. 1.

146. Interview with Dunleavy.

147. Interview with Behrend.

148. Telephone interview with Christopher D. Levintow, Manager, Regulatory Affairs, Teleport Communications, New York, May 24, 1988.

149. Letter to Harmeet Sawhney from Christopher D. Levintow, Manager, Regulatory Affairs, Teleport Communications, New York, May 19, 1988.

150. Robert Catlin, General Manager, The Teleport, Port Authority of New York and New Jersey, World Teleport Conference, New York City, February 6-7, 1984, Official Proceedings (Edited Version) (New York: World Teleport Association, 1984), p. 13.

151. Hoard, "An Office Park Offers Satellite Services to Firms Fleeing New York," p. 77.

152. Ibid.

153. Andrew Pollack, "Business Planners Look to Telecommunications," New York Times, May 2, 1983, p. D1.

154. Jim Bencivenga,"Teleport to use Staten Island's Free Air," Christian Science Monitor, October 12, 1983, p. 4.

155. Robert Annunziata, President, Teleport Communications, World Teleport Conference, New York City, February 6-7, 1984, Official Proceedings (Edited Version), p. 85.

156. Robert C. Atkinson, in Telecommunications Technology in New York, p. 72.

157. Robert C. Atkinson and Rosario P. Romanelli, Reply Brief of Teleport Communications - Case 29469 (Competition Proceeding), submitted to State of New York, Public Service Commission, Albany, January 29, 1988, pp. 15-16.

158. Interview with McStine.

159. Jed Marcus, World Teleport Conference, New York City, February 6-7, Official Proceedings (Edited Version), p. 86.

160. Bill Farrell and Owen Moritz, "21st Century Arrives with Staten Teleport," Daily News, June 24, 1983, p. 4.

161. Interview with McStine.

162. Interview with Atkinson and Levintow.

163. Gerald Ely, Chairman, Merrill Lynch Telecommunications Inc., World Teleport Conference, New York City, February 6-7, 1984, Official Proceedings (Edited Version), p. 8.

164. Interview with Atkinson and Levintow.

165. Letter from Levintow.

166. Interview with McStine.

167. Interview with Atkinson and Levintow.

168. Letter from Levintow.

169. Bencivenga, "Teleport to Use Staten Island's Free Air," p. 4.

170. Kenneth Lipper, Deputy Mayor for Finance and Economic Development, New York City, World Teleport Conference, New York City, February 6-7, 1984, Official Proceedings (Edited Version), p. 41.

171. Guy Tozzoli, Director, World Trade Department, Port Authority of New York and New Jersey, World Teleport Conference, New York City, February 6-7, 1984, Official Proceedings (Edited Version), p. 1.

172. Rosario P. Romanelli, President and Chief Executive Officer, Teleport Communications, World Teleport Conference, New York City, February 6-7, 1984, Official Proceedings (Edited Version), p. 19.

173. Letter from Levintow.

174. Interview with Walsh.

175. New York Telephone Company, Reply Comments, Case C-88-C-004 (Interconnection Proceeding), New York, April 15, 1988, p. 10.

176. Interview with Atkinson and Levintow.

177. Teleport Communications, Initial Brief of Teleport Communications, Case 29469 (Competition Proceeding), New York, December 18, 1987, p. 6.

178. Interview with Atkinson and Levintow.

179. Teleport Communications, Initial Brief, Case 29469 (Competition Proceeding), p. 6.

180. New York Telephone Company and New England Telephone and Telegraph Company, Comments of the NYNEX Telephone Companies in Reply to Petition of Teleport Communications for Declaratory Ruling Concerning Interconnection of Facilities at New York Telephone Company Central Offices, Case ENF - 87 - 14 (FCC), New York, May 14, 1987, p. 1.

181. Ibid., pp. 7-15.

182. Ibid., p. 42.

183. Teleport Communications, Reply of Teleport Communications, Case ENF - 87 - 14 (FCC), New York, June 1, 1987, p. 6.

184. Ibid., p. 35.

185. Teleport Communications, Initial Brief, Case 29469 (Competition Proceeding), pp. 18-19.

186. Teleport Communications, Reply Brief of Teleport Communications, Case 29469 (Competition Proceeding), New York, January 29, 1988, pp. 14-16.

187. Teleport Communications, Initial Brief, Case 29469 (Competition Proceeding), pp. 19-21.

188. Bell Atlantic, Comments of Bell Atlantic, Case ENF 87-14 (FCC), Philadelphia, May 14, 1987, p. 2.

189. Public Service Department, Initial Brief, Case 29469 (Competition Proceeding), Albany, January 29, 1988, p. 1 (attachment).

190. Letter to Harmeet Sawhney from Mary Lusco, Director, Docket/Issue/ Management Audit and Regulatory, New York Telephone Company, New York, May 25, 1988.

191. Public Service Commission, Recommended Decision by Administrative Law Judge J. Michael Harrison, Case 29469 (Competition Proceeding), Albany, May 9, 1988, p. 167.

192. Mitchell Moss, "The New Urban Telecommunications Infrastructure," Computer/Law Journal, vol. 6, no. 2 (Fall 1985), p. 324.

193. Gerald J. Hanneman, "An Overview of Teleports in North America," paper presented at Teleport '86, World Teleport Association, Second General Assembly and Congress, Amsterdam, May 1986.

194. F.W. Lloyd, "Federal, State, and Local Regulation of Video and Telecommunications Information Systems--The Actual and the Ideal," Computer/Law Journal, vol. 6, no. 2 (Fall 1985), p. 308.

195. "Merrill Lynch Launches Teleport Unit," Communications Week, January 1, 1988, p. 35.

7

Texas
David McCarty

Texas is rapidly moving into the Information Age. It is crucial that the telecommunications infrastructure in the state be allowed to evolve appropriately. The challenge will be to develop a regulatory framework that will encourage the timely introduction of technological innovations into the public telecommunications network, while preserving the traditional commitment to widely available and affordable service.

Telecommunications regulation in Texas has developed in an adversarial environment. Issues are decided primarily in the context of adjudicatory proceedings and, thus, tend to focus on short-term and narrowly drawn interests. Long-range, strategic policy development appears to be lacking. Nonetheless, decisions made now and in the near future will have lasting effects on the future development of telecommunications infrastructure in the state. It is important that some mechanism be created to foster rational, long-range policy development. In addition, certain modifications to the state's regulatory framework might be necessary to accommodate changes in the telecommunications industry.

Rural issues in Texas present some especially challenging problems. Revitalization of the agricultural sector, as well as the development of related industries such as food processing, depends on quality telecommunications. Regulatory mechanisms such as pooling arrangements have been vital to the financial viability of many rural telephone companies. However, pressures are building within the industry to deaverage costs and deregulate services. To the extent that this might threaten certain rural areas with loss of affordable telecommunications, other mechanisms, such as a high-cost fund, are available to provide targeted subsidies.[1]

Economic development policy in Texas has been fragmented and lacking in focus. As a reflection of increased concern with economic development, a Department of Commerce was established in the latter part of 1987 and has begun to consolidate and coordinate economic development policy and planning at the state level. It is important that this agency, as well as other state, regional, and local agencies, understand the role of telecommunications in economic development. As yet, this linkage has not been made explicit.

One of the most vital factors in economic development is education, and Texas has lagged behind the rest of the nation in this regard. Improved education is especially important in rural Texas. Telecommunications can play a major role in extending educational opportunities to rural areas as well as in delivering training and continuing education programs to all areas of the state. Telecommunications can also enhance delivery of medical and other social services, especially to rural areas. Efforts to apply telecommunications in these areas are just getting underway in Texas.

THE ECONOMY AND THE TELECOMMUNICATIONS INDUSTRY
Economic Profile

During the past decade Texas has experienced both boom and bust. Paced by rising oil prices during the late 1970s and early 1980s and the formation of an advanced technology manufacturing sector, the general economy of the state, banking and real estate in particular expanded rapidly. This economic growth was matched by population growth and shifts in the state's employment base.

The drop in oil prices in 1985, coupled with a continuing farm crisis, led to a severe economic decline. Real estate foreclosures and bank failures increased significantly, and the state was forced to make heavy spending cuts, even while raising taxes. Texas now faces the challenge of moving from an economy based primarily on oil and agriculture to a more diversified economy that takes advantage of a developing base of information and high-tech industries.

The growth of the Texas economy reached a peak relative to the nation around 1981-1982. However, a national recession, followed by a major world slump in energy prices, reversed the economic direction of the state. For example, in 1982 Texas had 6.6 percent of the nation's population and 7.0 percent of the nation's jobs, but by 1986 Texas had 6.9 percent of the population but only 6.6 percent of the jobs.[2] In addition, per capita personal income (real and nominal) was around 7 percent lower than the national average in 1986. Unemployment, which was close to 30 percent below the national average in 1982, was more than 25 percent above the national average in 1986.[3] Much of the reversal in the state's economic fortunes can be traced, either directly or indirectly, to the energy and agricultural sectors. With major slumps in both these areas and a subsequent decline in banking, real estate, and other businesses have also been negatively affected. Social services have suffered budget cutbacks as well

There have been important changes in the employment base: the wholesale and retail trade, finance, insurance, and real estate, and service sectors have grown from 47.9 percent of nonagricultural employment in 1980 to 53.2 percent in 1986 (Table 7.1). Texas' fastest growing export industries have been producer services, which now account for about 40 percent of jobs in the export industries. Manufacturing has declined from 18 percent of nonagricultural employment in 1980 to 14.6 percent in 1986. Production and distribution of goods account for 60 percent of jobs in the state's export industries.[4] Twenty-one percent of all Texas jobs are related to agriculture.[5] Application of telecommunications and information technologies could greatly enhance the productivity and market reach of all these sectors.

Table 7.1
Nonagricultural Employment Shares and Annual
Percentage Change in Employment* for Texas and
the United States, 1980 and 1986
(total employees in 1,000s, share and change in %)

| | Employment Shares | | | | Annual Employment Change | |
| | 1980 | | 1986 | | | |
	Texas	U.S.	Texas	U.S.	Texas	U.S.
Mining	4.1	1.1	9.5	0.8	26.8	-3.9
Construction	7.2	4.9	5.7	4.9	-1.9	1.6
Manufacturing	18.0	22.5	14.6	19.1	-1.5	-1.1
Transportation	6.2	5.7	5.7	5.3	-0.4	0.3
Wholesale & Ret. Trade	24.5	22.7	25.6	23.7	2.9	2.4
Fin., Ins., Real Estate	5.7	5.7	6.8	6.3	5.6	3.7
Services	17.3	19.6	20.8	23.2	5.8	5.0
Government	16.7	17.8	17.0	16.8	2.4	0.6
Total	5,851	90,657	6,581	99,610	2.0	1.6

* Totals may reflect rounding error.

Source: U.S. Department of Labor, Bureau of Labor Statistics, Employment and Earnings, vol. 34, no. 5 (May 1987), pp. 120-137 ; idem, vol. 28, no. 5 (May 1981), pp. 120-128.

Information services, including banking and credit, insurance, real estate, and computer and data processing, grew at more than two times the national average during the early 1980s (Table 7.2). Many of these telecommunications-intensive businesses are well aware of the importance of flexible and cost-effective telecommunications services and, to some extent, have indirectly pushed telephone companies to seek regulatory flexibility and investment in new technology.

Table 7.2
Employment Shares and Annual Changes in Employment* of
Telecommunications-Intensive Businesses** for Texas
and the United States, 1980 and 1984
(share and change in %)

| | Employment Shares | | | | Annual Employment | |
| | 1980 | | 1984 | | Change | |
	Texas	U.S.	Texas	U.S.	Texas	U.S.
Information Services	7.6	9.1	10.0	9.9	8.5	3.2
Finance	2.5	2.8	2.8	2.9	6.6	2.2
Insurance	2.2	2.3	2.2	2.2	1.7	1.0
Real Estate	0.6	1.3	1.1	1.4	60.7	1.6
Computer/Data Proc.	0.4	0.4	0.6	0.6	10.1	13.1
Other Information Svcs.	1.9	2.1	3.4	2.3	4.5	
Information Technology	2.1	2.2	2.2	2.3	2.3	2.4
Research & Development	0.2	0.3	0.2	0.3	2.1	2.9
Media	3.1	3.7	3.1	3.7	2.5	0.5

* Totals may reflect rounding error.

** The Telecommunications-Intensive Business categories are defined by Standard Industrial Classification codes as follows:
1. Information Services: Finance: SIC 60 (Banking), SIC 61 (Credit), SIC 62 (Commodities); Insurance: SIC 63 (Insurance Carriers), SIC 64 (Insurance Agents); Real Estate: SIC 65; Computer/Data Proc.: SIC 737; Other Information Services: SIC 731 (Advertising), SIC 732 (Credit Reporting), SIC 81 (Legal Services), SIC 891 (Engineering and Architectural Services), SIC 893 (Accounting and Auditing);
2. Information Technology Equipment: SIC 3573 (Electronic Computing Equipment), SIC 361 (Electric Distributing Equipment), SIC 365 (Radio and TV Receiving Equipment), SIC 366 (Communications Equipment), SIC 367 (Electronic Components and Accessories);
3. Research and Development: SIC 7391 (Research and Development Laboratories), SIC 7397 (Commercial Testing Laboratories), SIC 892 (Nonprofit Education and Scientific Research Agencies);
4. Media: SIC 27 (Printing and Publishing), SIC 48 (Communications), SIC 735 (News Syndicates), SIC 78 (Motion Pictures).

Source: U.S. Bureau of the Census, County Business Patterns, United States (No. 1) and Texas (No. 45) (Washington, D.C.: U.S. Government Printing Office, 1980 and 1984), Table 1B.

Retail sales figures in the state have moved in tandem with these changes in the economy. Per capita real retail sales grew more rapidly in Texas than in the nation in every year from 1976 through 1981, then lost ground relative to the rest of the nation every year thereafter. Retail sales were 14.6 percent above the nation in 1981 and only 1.3 percent above the nation in 1986. Figures for durable goods declined from 28.6 percent above the nation in 1981 to 1.1 percent below the nation in 1986.[6]

The revenue base of Texas state government depends heavily on sales taxes and severance taxes on oil. The general decline of the economy and dramatic decrease in the price of oil led to declines in fiscal capacity. The Advisory Commission for Intergovernmental Relations fiscal capacity measure for state and local taxes in Texas decreased from 32 percent above the nation in 1981 to 17 percent above the nation in 1984.[7] Real tax revenues in Texas declined by 3.7 percent in 1986 and 2.9 percent in 1987, despite several important tax rate increases during this period. Texas' tax effort, whether measured in per capita terms or as a percent of income, is around 70 to 80 percent of the national average.[8] The advantage is that Texas has maintained its tax competitiveness, a potential factor in attracting new businesses to the state. The cost, however, has been relatively low levels of state social services, including education.

Difficult economic conditions are likely to persist in Texas for some time, thus increasing the need to find innovative and cost-effective ways to stimulate economic development and administer social services. Telecommunications can and does enhance productivity and the delivery of services in both the public and private sectors. A significant telecommunications base already exists in Texas, due to the nature of certain industries in the state. For example, the oil industry is telecommunications-intensive, and Dallas and Houston are major financial centers.

Large users have long recognized the economic importance of modern telecommunications. The Texas state government, itself a major user of telecommunications, has also recognized the advantages of telecommunications in controlling costs and streamlining delivery of social services. More recently, telephone companies and some of the other policy players have begun to see the availability of modern telecommunications services and facilities as necessary for economic development (although evidence of this linkage has not yet been clearly demonstrated). The importance of telecommunications to the development of Texas cities has also been the subject of recent research.[9]

Despite the widespread perception of Texas as an economy on the decline, the state still has enormous potential. The size of the Texas economy is about $300 billion and supports some 290,000 small businesses, which accounted for 70 percent of total jobs in the state over the past five years.[10] Texas ranks second nationally in farm income and third in tourism. The state already has well-integrated transportation and telecommunications infrastructures, and invested more than $800 million in venture capital in 1986 alone.[11]

Telecommunications Industry Profile

Southwestern Bell Telephone, the Bell operating company serving Texas, is only one of the 66 companies providing local exchange telephone service in the state. It is by far the largest, however, accounting for about 77.9 percent of the 8,027,768 total access lines in the state. The next largest local exchange company (LEC) is General Telephone of the Southwest, with about 13.6 percent of the state's access lines. Three other LECs have between 100,000 and 163,000 lines; seven have between 14,000 and 58,000 lines; and all the others have fewer than 10,000 lines (Table 7.3). Local exchange plant investment in Texas totals nearly $17.7 billion, and LECs have been investing a total of more than $1.2 billion annually in recent years.[12]

Even though Southwestern Bell is the largest LEC in the state, it has fewer digital switches as a proportion of all switches than small rural telephone companies. While Southwestern Bell has roughly 20 percent of its central offices using digital switching, companies which have more than 50 percent of their central offices on digital technology are primarily small rural companies. Indeed 14 rural companies now use digital technology for 100 percent of their access lines.[13]

One reason for this disparity is that rural companies did not install electronic switches in the 1970s as Southwestern Bell did, instead relying on older mechanical switches. As these switches have worn out, the smaller companies have replaced them with the latest digital technology. The electronic switches of Southwestern Bell are still useful, although not on the cutting edge of technology. Thus they remain in central offices. Southwestern Bell would argue that unrealistically low depreciation rates, which serve to keep residential rates low, have made upgrading to digital technology economically infeasible for the company.

Table 7.3
Local Exchange Carriers and Access Lines
in Texas, 1987

Local Exchange Carriers	Access Lines	Share of Total (%)*
Southwestern Bell	6,257,000	78.1
General Telephone	1,087,855	13.6
Contel	162,199	2.0
Central Telephone	119,821	1.5
United Telephone	104,154	1.3
Others**	281,607	3.5
Total	8,012,636	100.0

* Totals may reflect rounding error.

** Includes 61 other local exchange companies.

Source: Texas Telephone Association, "Texas Phone Facts," Austin, 1988.

Prior to the AT&T divestiture, Southwestern Bell (and, to a lesser extent, General Telephone) effectively set the regulatory agenda in Texas through its rate change filings. The PUC established de facto policy primarily through its findings in these dockets.

While in some cases the interests of Southwestern Bell and the other LECs have diverged, for the most part they speak together as an industry segment, particularly through the Texas Telephone Association (TTA). For one reason, most independent LECs lack the resources to participate in formal rate proceedings before the PUC. In addition, many issues are common to all the LECs. The independent telephone companies have political clout with legislators, because their employees and executives are relatively more visible in their local communities. Southwestern Bell can take advantage of the independents' political clout through the TTA. Issues on which the LECs' interests might diverge include revenue pooling, deaveraging, access charge structures, and changes in the scope of Southwestern Bell's operations.

As one of the regional Bell holding companies (RBOCs), Southwestern Bell serves four other states besides Texas: Oklahoma, Kansas, Missouri, and Arkansas. Its Texas operations, however, account for 60 percent of the corporation's revenues. The company has not escaped the effects of the general economic slump in the Southwest. While authorized by the Texas Public Utilities Commission (PUC) to receive a 14.2 percent return on equity, Southwestern Bell's earnings have generally only returned about 10 percent. Return on investment has been about 12 percent.[14] In terms of earnings, Texas has been the lowest among the RBOC's five states, a result of both the state's general economic slump and regulatory decisions, according to Southwestern Bell.[15]

While some of the other RBOCs have diversified into a wide range of nontelephone businesses, such as real estate, car rentals, and computer sales, Southwestern Bell has tended to focus on businesses related to its telephone operations. In 1985 the company spent $120 million to expand its Yellow Pages operations nationally.[16] In 1987 Southwestern Bell spent $1.38 billion to acquire cellular telephone and paging operations, making it among the largest cellular telephone and paging operations in the nation.[17] The company is also promoting ISDN services and plans to have 16,000 ISDN telephone lines in service by the end of 1988 to such customers as Shell Oil, Tenneco, and 3M. A subsidiary, Southwestern Bell Telecommunications, markets customer-premises equipment.[18] Still, roughly 90 percent of the firm's earnings are derived from basic voice-transmission services.[19]

Southwestern Bell Corporation, headquartered in St. Louis, has increased revenues from $7.19 billion in 1984 to $8 billion in 1987. The price of a share of Southwestern Bell stock increased 58 percent from 1984 to March 1988. This was the second smallest increase of all the RBOCs.[20]

Given the number of LATAs (17) and the number of competing firms in the state, Texas can be said to have the most competitive interexchange market in the United States. It is the second largest in terms of revenue (about $5 billion a year).[21] The exact number of interexchange carriers (IXCs) operating in Texas is subject to debate, but most estimates place the number around 60 or more. These estimates include "facilities-based" IXCs (that is, they own their own networks), "carriers' carriers," (that is, they only sell capacity or lease facilities to other IXCs) and resellers (that is, they only lease capacity from the IXCs). In terms of number of firms most IXC operations in Texas fall into this last category. AT&T is the only IXC that is fully regulated in Texas, which is one of the major policy issues still being debated (as will be discussed below).

POLICY DEVELOPMENT

Telecommunications policy in Texas has evolved in an adversarial atmosphere. Prior to divestiture, industry interests were relatively unified. Issues were played out primarily between the telephone companies and rate case interveners, with the PUC deciding the outcomes through Final Orders. In the postdivestiture environment, the number of players involved in the regulatory arena has grown significantly. Within the industry, Southwestern Bell, General Telephone, the other LECs, AT&T, and the other IXCs all have their own agendas. In addition, Texas has a strong consumer advocate community, which plays a major role in the regulatory debate. Through 1986, issues were addressed primarily in the context of adjudicatory proceedings (that is, rate cases). Since then, the context has shifted to the PUC's quasi-legislative function of rulemaking.

There is no forum in Texas for the development of coherent, long-range policy to deal with general issues. Instead, the state's policy has been developed through an accumulated body of regulatory decisions, an occasional legislative directive, the personal philosophies of individual regulators, and the political dynamics of the regulatory arena.

Consumer interests represent a significant influence in the political dynamics of telecommunications policy formation in Texas. The maintenance of low local rates has been a major political issue for the PUC. (This helps to explain in part why access charges in Texas are the highest in the nation. Without the contribution of high access charges, local rates would be forced higher.) The Office of Public Utility Counsel (OPC), established in 1983, formally represents the interests of residential and small business customers before the PUC. Consumers Union has also been quite active in representing residential customers on telecommunications issues. In addition, other public interest groups, such as the American Association of Retired Persons, represent consumer positions on some issues.

A link between telecommunications policy and general economic development was articulated in the version of SB 444 that was originally filed. During the subsequent debate, however, most of this language was deleted. Apparently, it was felt that such provisions would have worked too much in the telephone companies' favor and that it was up to the PUC to define and implement policy.

A few Texas cities have promoted their telecommunications infrastructure as an advantage for businesses. For example, San Antonio promoted itself as a "Telecity" during 1985 and 1986, citing its local digital fiber network and global interconnectivity. Dallas, Houston, and Austin, the state capital, have also been involved in the development of intracity optical fiber infrastructure.[22] A new state Department of Commerce may eventually include a focus on telecommunications, but up to this point it has concentrated on other aspects of economic development.

Regulatory Environment and the Texas Public Utility Commission

Texas has the newest public utility commission in the United States. Prior to 1975, telephone utilities in the state were regulated only to the extent that individual cities chose to do so. Companies in rural areas could set rates and standards as they wished. Most cities did not have the resources to evaluate complex rate requests.

During the 1970s, telephone companies became the targets of consumer resentment as a result of several events. General Telephone increased rates substantially for rural subscribers. Southwestern Bell was in the news for misdealings in its relations with city council members in 1974 and was being sued by two employees. In addition, the attorney general alleged that a 1974 intrastate long distance rate increase was "excessive and unreasonable" and initiated court action.[23]

The 64th Legislature responded to this growing public pressure by passing the Public Utility Regulatory Act (PURA) in 1975. The first three commissioners of the new Texas Public Utility Commission (PUC) took their seats that same year. The next year they faced their first major rate case when Southwestern Bell filed a rate request. The commission allowed "a partial increase in rates," but Southwestern Bell challenged the decision in court, claiming confiscatory ratemaking. The subsequent court decisions affirmed the "doctrine of administrative finality," meaning that administrative orders by the new PUC would be difficult to overturn by appeal to the courts.[24]

PURA had to be reenacted in 1983, when it came up for sunset review. Several amendments were also made at that time. One of these established a new agency, the Office of Public Utility Council, to represent residential and small business subscribers before the PUC and the courts. Another was the first real policy statement, which gave the PUC more flexibility to consider the increasingly competitive nature of the telecommunications industry in regulating telephone utilities. While leaving the administrative details to the commission, the legislature explicitly recognized that traditional regulation might no longer be appropriate. Also during 1983, all three commissioners resigned, allowing then Governor Mark White, a Democrat, to appoint an entirely new commission. In 1985 another amendment to PURA transferred jurisdiction over water and sewer utilities to the Texas Water Commission, leaving only electric and telephone utilities under the jurisdiction of the PUC.[25]

Texas has one of the larger regulatory commissions in the United States, commensurate with the large intrastate business, the number of LATAs, and the level of competition. The three commissioners of the Texas PUC are appointed by the governor to staggered six-year terms, subject to confirmation by the Senate. The chair is elected by the commission itself. The commission staff consists of 196 individuals, about three-fourths of whom are professional attorneys, accountants, engineers, or economists. The PUC is divided into five divisions: Hearings, Telephone, Electric, Operations Review, and General Counsel. An executive director oversees all of these divisions in a managerial role. Public information and administration are part of the executive director's office. The Texas PUC's budget for FY 1986 was $7.8 million, down 5 percent from the previous year.[26]

Regulated utilities in Texas are required to file financial and operating reports annually. The form of these audits is prescribed by the FCC, and they must be completed by independent auditors. In addition, 1983 amendments to PURA require that management audits be conducted every ten years, or more often if requested by the commission. The intention of these audits is to identify ways to improve the efficiency of the telephone companies.[27]

In 1983 Southwestern Bell filed an historic rate change application (Docket 5220), requesting a $1.7 billion increase. This included a major increase in local rates. In May 1984 the PUC entered a final order, granting an $800 million increase. Of this amount, $630 million was access tariffs that replaced toll revenues lost to AT&T.[28] Appeals were filed by several parties, however, and it seems that further appeals to the Supreme Court are certain.

The Texas PUC has generally taken the stance that residential rates should be kept low. As a result, local rates in Texas are among the lowest in the United States. The PUC has opposed any subscriber line charge (SLC) at the intrastate level as well as the FCC's intention to shift all of the nontraffic-sensitive (NTS) costs to the end user through the federally imposed SLC.

Access charges to IXCs, on the other hand, are the highest in the nation.[29] Most parties feel that the current level of access charges is too high, but there is no agreement as to what specific level is appropriate. In general, the PUC feels that at least some NTS costs should be recovered through toll or interexchange charges. In addition, the PUC remains unconvinced that bypass is a great enough threat to warrant substantial reductions in access charges. In Docket 6200 in 1986, the PUC acknowledged that the potential for bypass might become a problem in the future, but that for the present Southwestern Bell had failed to document specific revenue losses attributable to bypass.

While local measured service is available in a few non-Bell local exchanges in Texas, in 1986 the PUC placed a moratorium on further LMS offerings. LMS proposals have met with strong opposition from consumer groups, who feel that LMS is an inappropriate method of charging for local telephone service. Lack of support for LMS may also be due to the very low flat rates that prevail in Texas, thus minimizing customers' potential savings from LMS.

Rural telephone companies have a special interest in regulatory matters. Revenue pooling arrangements (based on toll revenues and expenses and administered by the LECs themselves) have been vital to the financial viability of some rural companies. These pooling arrangements, however, have encouraged some small LECs to overinvest. Not only is there pressure to eliminate this pooling, but PUC rulings on toll structures could also negatively impact many of these rural companies.

Because of the low densities, the unit costs of serving rural areas can be quite high. However, because of toll pooling, low-cost Rural Electrification Administration (REA) money, and statewide averaged toll rates, local rates for rural customers have remained low (in fact, generally lower than in urban areas). Investment incentives in rural areas are quite different from those in urban areas. Small telephone companies have had the incentive to invest in new technologies even if the investment could not be recovered from current prices. As a result, many small LECs are already 100 percent digital, for example.

The primary objectives of consumer advocates in Texas are to assure that regulation is fair and balanced and to keep local rates low. In general, consumer advocates are opposed to local measured service (LMS) in Texas, as well as to shifting more of the nontraffic-sensitive costs of telephone service to the end user (local customer). They are also concerned about the erosion of services while rates stay the same.

As a major user of telecommunications equipment and services, the State of Texas plays a significant, if somewhat indirect, role in the regulatory environment. It is significant because of its size and scope: 207,000 miles of dedicated leased data circuits[30] and voice lines extending to nearly every community in the state. It is significant also in that any standards established for the system (for example, requiring digital or ISDN capabilities) would encourage incorporation of these technologies into the public infrastructure. (The state's new telecommunications system is discussed more fully below.)

City governments may participate in regulatory matters that affect municipal telecommunications costs or services, but their presence is usually on behalf of consumer interests. PURA requires that the utility pay the "reasonable costs" of the cities' intervention. This mechanism of funding cities as interveners is unique to Texas and encourages cities to intervene in most cases. Different cities participate in different dockets, but they intervene as a group.

Cities also influence regulatory policy indirectly, by working individually with telecommunications providers to develop local capabilities, both for their own use and to attract businesses. Cities are becoming increasingly important nodes in the telecommunications infrastructure, offering "multiple points of access to alternative communication systems."[31] For the most part, however, cities in Texas are just beginning to promote telecommunications as an economic development tool.

Legislation

In 1987, with the introduction of SB 229 and SB 444, the telecommunications policy debate entered the legislative arena once again. It should be noted that both bills were initiated by the industry: SB 229 by AT&T and SB 444 by the TTA. The two bills were filed within three weeks of each other and were signed by the governor within four days of each other near the end of that legislative session. A variety of reasons have been suggested as to why AT&T and the TTA took their cases to the legislature. Different perspectives are available, as well, regarding the political dynamics at work as these bills evolved. These bills are discussed in detail in a case study at the end of this chapter.

SB 229 essentially began as a bill to deregulate AT&T. As originally filed, the bill met with strong consumer resistance. Even after incorporating a number of consumer protections, including a prohibition against abandonment of service, the bill was nearly dead at one point. In the last few days of the legislative session, however, parties were able to work out enough problems to get the bill passed.

The focus of the bill was on competition in the IXC market and the issue of whether AT&T still had sufficient market power to require continued regulation. The new law defined "dominant carrier" and delineated the PUC's minimal jurisdiction over nondominant IXCs. It also directed the PUC to report to the legislative every other year on the scope of competition.

A primary aspect of the law directed the PUC to initiate an evidentiary hearing to determine the status of interLATA interexchange competition and whether any IXC is dominant in any interexchange service market.[32] The commission was also directed to conduct a hearing to determine what service markets would be appropriate.

Another section of SB 229 called for the commission to develop a methodology for separation of costs among regulated, competitive, and unregulated services offered by the same IXC.

Essential aspects of SB 444 included similar "tests" of competition in local exchange telecommunications and provided for streamlined regulation of LECs in those service markets in which competition was deemed sufficient. It also directed the commission to promulgate rules to encourage the introduction of new or experimental services or promotional rates. This legislation also enabled smaller LECs (those with fewer than 5,000 access lines) to change rates within certain percentages without undertaking full, formal rate cases.

In addition, SB 444 established a telassistance program which was to provide a subsidy to a narrowly defined segment of consumers to reduce the cost of their monthly local telephone bill. It directed the commission to adopt rules for a universal service fund to finance this subsidy.

Pending Issues

One overriding issue articulated by various groups involved in the policy arena is the dilemma of balancing the goal of universal service (often seen as keeping local rates low) against encouraging the development of innovative technologies and services. While not necessarily mutually exclusive, the two goals may often be in real or potential conflict. For example, it has been argued that the majority of new technologies and services (e.g., digital switching, ISDN) benefit only certain users (typically large businesses in urban areas), yet the costs are spread across all users. On the other hand, such technological development may result in declining costs or permit new service offerings, thereby stimulating use of the network and generating additional revenues. This would suggest that rates should decline, or at least not rise any further. It has also been argued that a technologically advanced telecommunications infrastructure may stimulate general business activity in a state or region, thereby benefiting residents indirectly.

The relationship between access charges and local rates is another issue that has not yet been resolved. High access tariffs can be used to keep local rates low. It is often argued, however, that high access charges encourage large users to bypass LECs and that this will result in upward pressure on rates anyway. So far, quantitative data to support this argument have been sparse and controversial. To the extent that an equitable tariff structure might still provide incentives for economic bypass, this might create a niche market for entrepreneurial telecommunications providers.[33]

Most parties agree that access charges should make some contribution to the NTS costs of the local loops (see the Introduction to this volume). The difficult issue is to determine the appropriate level of this contribution. The fact that access tariffs in Texas are the highest in the nation suggests that some reduction in access charges might be appropriate.

Among the specific issues still pending in the Texas regulatory arena are several related to the implementation of SB 444 and SB 229. These two bills established policy, but they left to the PUC the task of determining the procedural rules. Hearings on these rules are currently in progress.

The primary concerns of SB 229 are defining interexchange markets and determining whether AT&T is dominant in these markets vis-a-vis the OCCs. Under the classic definition (the same basic definition used in the legislation), market dominance occurs when a firm has a sufficiently large share of the market to be able to control prices in a manner adverse to the public interest. The argument of the OCCs, then, is that AT&T, if unregulated, could lower prices long enough to drive them out of business (and then raise rates to levels higher than they could in a competitive market). SB 229 includes nine tests of market dominance intended to assess if and when AT&T may face enough competition in a given market to no longer require regulation. As general guidelines, these tests--proposed or supported by the OCCs, OPC, consumers, and Senators Parmer and Edwards--would provide a good base of information from which to make such a determination. However, the PUC was directed to consider all relevant factors, "including but not limited to" the nine specific tests.[34] An auxiliary issue addressed in SB 229 is abandonment of service areas, since deregulation implies freedom to exit unprofitable markets.

Several local exchange issues were addressed in Senate Bill 444. For example, it gave smaller LECs (those with fewer than 5,000 lines, 48 of the 66 LECs operating in Texas) more flexibility in changing rates. This legislation allows them to change rates within certain limits (2.5 percent of total gross revenues or 25 percent in any one service category) merely by posting sufficient notice and filing the new tariffs, thus avoiding the full, formal rate case process. The new tariffs could also be challenged if enough subscribers (5 percent) were to petition against the change (within 60 days). While the PUC must initiate a full rate case review if limits are exceeded or subscriber petition conditions are met, it may initiate such a review on its own motion at any time.

LECs argue that they are increasingly subject to competition in urban markets in a number of ways. For example, shared tenant services take individual customers away from the regulated LECs; alternative vendors can provide LANs and private line services; large users may find it profitable to bypass LECs entirely. The traditional regulatory process, from the perspective of the LECs (and, especially, Southwestern Bell), took so long that regulated LECs could not bid for competitive contracts in a timely manner.[35] It also slowed the introduction of new services. Thus, a central aspect of SB 444 was to "streamline" the regulatory process in cases where competitive services were available.

A related issue addressed in SB 444 was that of potential cross-subsidization of competitive services by the regulated monopoly services. On this point the bill merely stated that such competitive offerings must recover their costs. Concerns about cost allocation and potential cross-subsidization have also been articulated more generally, as regulated LECs diversify into unregulated businesses and services. Consumer interests are concerned that revenues from regulated monopoly services will be used to subsidize risky, unregulated business activities and that the PUC will be unable to detect or prevent such cross-subsidies no matter what specific rules are adopted. Cost-allocation methodologies and the potential for cross-subsidization are also the subject of current PUC proceedings (and have been, in one form or another, since 1976).

These issues demonstrate the tensions and concerns among various interests that are coming into play as a result of recent changes in the telecommunications industry and the need for Texas to stimulate economic development. Most parties agree that modern telecommunications facilities are a prerequisite to attracting business development, especially high-tech, information-intensive businesses. On the other hand, it is not apparent that investment in telecommunications infrastructure alone will necessarily lead to economic development.

Policy concerns are largely over what rate of technological innovation is appropriate for the regulated public network and how to finance this innovation. How these issues are decided will shape the development of telecommunications infrastructure in the state. Large users and telephone companies especially want to be able to take advantage of new technologies and are thus pushing for sophisticated services, expedited regulatory approval, and customer-specific contracts at competitive prices. Consumer interests are concerned that the costs of such innovation will negatively affect residential ratepayers. So far, the politically popular PUC attitude seems to be to go slow so as to protect the captive residential ratepayers.

TELECOMMUNICATIONS AND ECONOMIC DEVELOPMENT

Economic development policymaking in Texas is relatively fragmented in that there is little coordinated planning among the various state-level agencies involved. Local and regional interests, both public and private, have been much more active in implementing economic development initiatives. A Task Force on Business Development and Jobs Creation was formed in late 1986 by Governor Bill Clements, and in January and March of 1987 it issued a number of recommendations. One of the primary recommendations was that the legislature restructure the different agencies dealing with economic development into a single agency to be charged with developing a long-range strategic plan for economic development in the state.[36] A new Department of Commerce was established as a result. This agency has not yet established the linkage between telecommunications and economic development as a priority, as it has focused its efforts on other economic development issues, such as tourism and promotion of small businesses.

Over the past two years Southwestern Bell has become active in economic development. The company's president was co-chairman of the Governor's Task Force, and a Director of Economic Development was recently appointed within the firm. The company, through its employees throughout the state, is becoming involved in chambers of commerce and economic development committees and is helping to develop educational and business opportunities in other ways as well. The company has been educating local chambers of commerce as to the technical capabilities of their cities' infrastructure, upgrading its network interfaces (especially for international traffic), and rethinking policy on extended area service (EAS, or the scope of local calling areas).[37] At this point, most of the chambers of commerce in the major Texas cities have adopted policies articulating the importance of modern telecommunications for economic development.[38]

Important policymakers in Texas have expressed a need to minimize regulation as a way to stimulate economic development. For example, Senator Farabee, who sponsored SB 444, believes that a lesser regulated business economy is more likely to deliver services at competitive rates and lead to state-of-the-art infrastructure in the long run.[39] Dennis Thomas, chairman of the Texas PUC, has indicated that the most important thing regulators can do to further economic development is to "get out of the way."[40] Consumer advocates, however, are fearful that captive ratepayers will end up subsidizing large users in a deregulated environment. They are also skeptical that the market is competitive enough to regulate itself.[41]

As a relatively telecommunications-intensive state, with its oil, banking, and airline industries, Texas provides numerous examples of the application of telecommunications to enhance productivity and innovate services. Many large business users clearly understand the economic importance of telecommunications for their own profitability. The state itself, as a large bureaucracy, has taken some initial steps to improve its efficiency and innovate its delivery of services through telecommunications.

Most players recognize that rural areas pose special challenges in terms of economic development. It has been pointed out that the Information Age will affect agriculture and that the economic vitality of rural areas will depend increasingly on telecommunications. Education, which is another factor crucial for rural development, can also be greatly enhanced through the use of telecommunications.[42] In some cases, telecommunications providers have little financial incentive to serve rural areas because of the high costs. However, in many cases, investment has been encouraged by low-cost REA money and toll pooling mechanisms.

General Economic Development Policy

Texas combines a strong pro-business tradition with a sense of anticorporate populism to create an environment that is conducive to entrepreneurial firms and an attitude that state institutional power should be dispersed. Traditionally, economic development policy in Texas has been diffused among different state agencies and local and regional interests, with each implementing its own planning and programs. As a result, there has been a lack of any strong focus or coherent planning for economic development.

At the state level, the primary role of the Governor's Office has been in allocating some types of federal aid (such as research and development and job training funds) and in attracting high-tech industry. In terms of linking economic development to telecommunications, even the Governor's Task Force made virtually no reference to telecommunications other than to recommend that legislation be passed to streamline utility regulation.[43]

Economic development efforts at the local and regional levels are better defined. Often these efforts involve private as well as public interests and are generally aimed at attracting high-level, high-technology research and development consortia. Among the more visible examples are Austin's successful efforts, with the aid of the state government, to attract MCC and Sematech and San Antonio's cultivation of biotechnology research firms. Among the quasi-public agencies involved in these kinds of development efforts are local chambers of commerce, Texas universities, and regional economic development corporations and foundations, such as the Travis County Research and Development Authority (TCRDA) and the North Texas Commission (NTC). Unfortunately, these regional efforts have sometimes worked against each other and have often failed to take advantage of knowledge and expertise available in other areas of the state.[44]

Another factor hindering economic development that was noted by the Governor's Task Force was inadequacies, both real and perceived, in the state's infrastructure. Thus, in addition to developing a source of strong leadership and statewide coordination of general economic development planning, the task force stressed the importance of remedying weaknesses in such key areas as trucking regulation, international business development, mobilization of technology resources, and investment in venture capital.[45]

Several of the task force's recommendations have been acted upon. In the area of telecommunications policy, the two legislative initiatives discussed in this chapter, especially SB 444, were attempts to streamline regulation and thus make it less costly and cumbersome for telephone companies to provide new and competitive services to large or otherwise sophisticated users. Timely provision of customer-specific services is often mentioned by telephone companies as a primary way in which telecommunications can contribute to economic development.

Telecommunications Policy Initiatives

In a few legislative documents, the link between telecommunications policy and economic development was articulated quite explicitly. For example, in an early version of SB 444, the bill included a specific policy statement relating the development of telecommunications infrastructure to economic development. For example, Sec. 93.(a)(3) stated that regulation

> should allow the state and its citizens to fully participate in the development of new and varied telecommunications services, which will result in new jobs...encourage businesses to locate and expand . . . [and] will place the state and its citizens in the forefront of economic development through its leadership into the information age.[46]

Subsec. (4) continued: "the economic development of the state and the public interest require a modern, technologically advanced telecommunications system." The bill as originally filed also recognized explicitly the change in the telecommunications industry from monopoly to competition. "Competitive service" was defined in the very first paragraph [Subsec. (v)]. Sec. 93.(a)(2) stated that the PUC "should have flexibility to deal with the change from a noncompetitive to a competitive environment" and subsec. (5) read: "the commission should, if consistent with the public interest, consider competition as a factor to determine the variety, quality, and price of telecommunications services." Moreover, this version might have helped accelerate the introduction of new technologies, implying that depreciation rates should be tied more closely to technological obsolescence than to the physical life of the equipment. Sec. 96. (a) found that "a modern technologically advanced telecommunications system can be maintained only if local exchange companies are allowed to use adequate depreciation rates and methods that recognize technological advances in the industry." Most of these policy statements disappeared early in the legislative process, however. One reason was that it was felt that such language would too narrowly restrict the PUC's options for dealing with such issues. It was also felt that these statements assumed competitive conditions that had not been demonstrated and would have established a "pro-LEC" telecommunications policy. This strategy contrasts sharply with Illinois' regulatory reform legislation, which expressly directed the Illinois Commerce Commission to encourage competition. The political climate there was such that worries about "pro-LEC" policies were not relevant. As finally passed, the bill focused more on the specific rules for providing some regulatory flexibility for the LECs.

In directing the PUC to establish an Advisory Committee on Extended Area Service, House Resolution 733 also explicitly articulated a link between telecommunications and economic development: "The cost, quality, and range of telecommunications services in a community is becoming an increasingly important factor in economic development strategies."[47] The need for specific policy directives linking telecommunications and economic development may be debatable. Policy directives focusing on narrow issues may divert attention from broader policy goals.

Long-range planning for the state government's telecommunications system is a primary responsibility of the state's new Automated Information and Telecommunications Council (AITC). Although the AITC and the state's use of telecommunications are discussed in the next section, one point should be made here. A long-term goal of the AITC for the state network is to migrate to ISDN technology. Certainly, this constitutes a policy initiative within the state system, but it also influences general telecommunications policy in that it would encourage the incorporation of such technology into the public network. For example, to the extent that the state would need to communicate with private vendors and contractors via the public telecommunications infrastructure, it would be desirable for the public network facilities serving these providers to be ISDN-capable. In this way, it might signal the PUC to encourage telephone company investment in ISDN technology.

The State as a User of Telecommunications

Several state agencies have begun using telecommunications applications to reduce costs, increase productivity, improve the use of resources, and speed up delivery of services. For the most part, these programs have been developed and implemented individually by the separate agencies. However, with budgets declining and demands for social services increasing, agencies have begun to realize the importance of coordinated, interagency planning and use of telecommunications systems. The traditional dichotomy between voice and data, while still apparent, seems to be dissolving as the need to integrate systems becomes a priority.

The Texas state telecommunications system generates 115,000,000 minutes of long distance voice traffic annually and uses 207,000 miles of dedicated data circuits. The annual cost to operate the system has been approximately $28 million.[48] Due partially to the increasing importance to state services of computer and telecommunications planning and procurement, the legislature formed the Automated Information and Telecommunications Council in 1985. AITC was formed as an outgrowth of the Automated Information Systems Advisory Council, because the legislature felt a need to increase the authority of that agency to incorporate procurement review functions in addition to advisory responsibilities.[49] Most argue that, conceptually, agencies such as AITC can be valuable in terms of providing information and technical expertise and assuring compatibility of systems. There is a danger, however, that such agencies can also become politicized bottlenecks in procurement process, specially if lacking the appropriate technical resources.

In 1986 AITC issued a comprehensive plan with a short-term goal of replacing the existing state telecommunications system. The justification was that an anticipated increase in telephone rates would nearly double the cost of the state's system. A contract for the new system was awarded to AT&T in 1987, but the award was contested by other bidders, who claimed that AT&T's estimates were unrealistic. In February 1988 the State Purchasing Commission upheld the award to AT&T and refused to review another appeal. Cutover to the new system is planned for August 31, 1988. The new system will be leased, rather than purchased, primarily on the grounds of economic feasibility.[50]

Recent AITC telecommunications projects included a four-month study of LMS (which recommended rejection of LMS) and an update of the state's long-range plan. A long-term goal of the AITC plan is to move the network to ISDN technology. This would help to consolidate voice and data applications and provide the network with state-of-the-art capabilities. It would also influence public telecommunications policy, as noted above.

Among the more innovative applications in the use of telecommunications among state service agencies is the Department of Human Services' (DHS) Welnet. The DHS is planning to implement a $12 million statewide collection of local area networks (LANs) designed to automate and streamline the welfare delivery system. Plans are for the network to be operational by spring 1988, initially linking 100 offices throughout the state. Ultimately, the network will grow to 8,500 machines. Welnet is an example of a well-planned, long-term approach to introducing advanced technology into a large public bureaucracy. The primary philosophy of the Welnet concept is to move information and processing power closer to the point where it will be used, that is, at the case worker's desk. Among the ultimate goals are for end users in the field offices to have a generic case file worksheet through which to enter and retrieve data and to integrate databases.[51]

The Texas Education Agency (TEA) plans to increase its use of telecommunications, perhaps shifting most of its communications with Texas' 1,063 school districts to electronic networks. By April 1988 about 650 local education agencies (LEAs)[52] had purchased access to The Electric Pages,[53] a national education network with information published by nine organizations.[54] The Electric Pages was started in 1983 by a private firm in Austin with one publishing organization and 19 LEAs.[55] In 1987 TEA estimated that an electronic communications system between itself and the LEAs would reduce the overall cost of communications and result in a net savings of $2.69 million per year. This projection was based on a pilot study of 15 LEAs over a 17-month period.[56] TEA spends about $1.2 million per year for communication with LEAs, two-thirds of which is for reproduction and postage. In contrast, TEA can communicate and store information on The Electric Pages for $12,000 a year. Similarly, the LEAs' annual communication costs would be reduced from $3.4 million to $340,000 by using electronic communications just ten minutes a day.[57]

TEA established a network on The Electric Pages, TEA-NET, in January 1986.[58] By April 1988, 30 TEA agency divisions were publishing information on TEA-NET. TEA sends much of its correspondence electronically to the participating LEAs, replacing three to four separate mailings a day.[59]

Users are charged a $24 annual ID fee and $15 per hour for long distance usage over an 800 number. Local usage costs $12 per hour. Once in The Electric Pages system, LEAs can access information from networks such as

TEA-NET, send and receive private electronic mail, and participate in electronic conferences.[60]

The cost savings noted above are probably sufficient reason to justify a movement to electronic communications. However, its potential for other uses is particularly important. For example, in 1986, six health teachers from around the state developed a publication on The Electric Pages about preventing school-age pregnancy. In the Spring of 1987 a professor at The University of Texas at Tyler taught a course over The Electric Pages using electronic mail and teleconferencing.[61] Homebound students can also use the network for instructional purposes. Thus, the professional isolation of teachers, the great distances of Texas, and immobilizing handicaps can be easily overcome by use of electronic communication. TEA is encouraging LEAs to migrate toward the electronic system by making some information available primarily on TEA-NET.

The satellite-based TI-IN Network, operated out of San Antonio, is another example of TEA using a private telecommunications network to deliver educational services. About 80 school districts throughout the state use the system. Many of these are in small and rural communities, which cannot afford to hire sufficient teachers to meet their needs. Instructional programming, as well as in-service training for teachers, is distributed via satellite to participating schools. The schools use telephone lines to communicate with the centralized instructors. TEA itself uses the network about two and one-half hours per week to disseminate general information, including a 15-minute weekly news program, to school districts.[62] Instructional programming is produced by the TEA Service Center in San Antonio.

Another Information Age initiative by TEA is to move the state's school districts to all electronic reporting for administrative purposes. The first step in this direction was the establishment of the Public Education Information Management System (PEIMS), which was the information leg of the public education reform legislation of 1984 (HB 72). The primary thrust of PEIMS thus far has been to revise the flow of information between districts and the state by defining a data standard for reporting by districts. This not only streamlines reporting procedures (which typically involve some 40 to 60 different forms over the year), but also gets the districts themselves into information management. The key advantage of PEIMS is that it provides better information on how schools are managed.[63]

PEIMS was not originally mandated or funded to use telecommunications, although it will probably begin to do so in the next two to three years. At present, districts use the mail to send data (in standardized format, but on a variety of media) to one of 20 service centers. There the data are edited and transferred to a standard medium (computer tapes) and then mailed to TEA in Austin. Since time is not a critical factor in the reporting of these data, there is no great incentive to move this reporting to telecommunications.

The Texas Department of Agriculture (TDA) is another state agency that has been using telecommunications to serve its clients and intends to expand its operations. The basic goal of TDA is to improve the profitability of Texas agriculture. Much of this effort has focused on locating international markets and finding resources to help Texas firms develop.

TDA employees scour the international markets for trade leads, often by searching through databases. When leads are found, the information is entered into a database at TDA headquarters in Austin. The program also contains the names of firms and individuals and their specific interests. Trade leads are matched with interests and the database generates letters to be mailed to the specific firms.[64]

TDA recognizes that this system could be upgraded. As a first step, TDA plans to eliminate paper mail, replacing it with electronic communication to the regional service centers nearest the interested firms. In turn, the service centers could notify the firms more quickly. In the longer run, TDA plans to modify its database, making it accessible by individuals.[65]

To foster development, TDA helps firms find necessary resources such as financial information and market analyses. Much of this information must be gathered outside the state or requires laborious research. Again, TDA employees search databases to find the requisite information. In many cases, the only alternative is physical research in a library. Such research would cost TDA about $50 per hour for several hours' work. In contrast, the database searches take only a few minutes and cost less than $100.[66]

Much of TDA's work requires information from other state agencies. This information could be transmitted electronically but is being gathered physically. For example, the Comptroller's Office collects business data classified by SIC codes. To obtain that information, TDA must send an employee to make copies of the Comptroller's magnetic tapes. Similarly, the Department of Labor and the Secretary of State are major sources of information for TDA. It would like to be able to communicate with those offices via data lines.[67]

Other large users of the state telecommunications system include the Department of Highways and Public Transportation, the Department of Public Safety, the Department of Mental Health and Mental Retardation, The University of Texas, and Texas A&M University. The Texas Employment Commission uses automated telephone systems in a few communities to inform applicants of job openings. In Austin this program has been in use for about seven years. Postcards are also mailed to applicants, both as follow-up to the phone calls and as initial contact for the 25 percent of applicants without telephones.

The State of Texas is a large and increasingly sophisticated user of telecommunications and information technology. Many initiatives have only recently started and thus are difficult to evaluate as to their ultimate impact. To some extent, the constraints of the state's budget have helped stimulate greater cooperation between managers of data and voice systems and among different agencies. This has also underscored the need to consolidate redundant networks and databases.

In the area of education Texas seems to be overlooking a promising opportunity. In some cases, the Texas Education Agency has worked with private firms to distribute instructional programming, inservice training, and administrative communications electronically.

At the college and university level, the application of telecommunications for instructional programming has moved a bit more slowly. In 1987 the Texas Select Committee on Higher Education made a unanimous recommendation that the state should pursue the utilization of telecommunications to share instructional resources among all of the state's nearly 100 institutions of higher education. The committee considered the The Association for Graduate Education and Research's (TAGER) closed circuit television system linking universities and corporations in Dallas as a basic model.

The legislature adopted the committee's recommendation and granted authority to develop a plan for implementation. Unfortunately, funding was not appropriated. Two primary reasons were given for this. One, the idea of "distance education" was new to many people, and there was little information available concerning the instructional and cost effectiveness of this approach. Two, at a time when the legislature was having a hard time funding basic teacher salaries, it was difficult to find the money to fund an untested proposal.

The past chair of the committee, now an Austin attorney, has continued to work on the idea by pursuing private funds to develop a pilot project. It is hoped that a successful pilot project will encourage the next legislature to appropriate funds for full implementation.[68]

Telecommunications has been applied to academic computing among 34 of the state universities and research institutes. The 3,000-mile academic computer network, known as the Texas Higher Education Network, or THEnet, links some 500 computers through the digital transmission facilities of ClayDesta Communications, which carries the network's interexchange traffic.[69]

The University of Texas System spent about $100,000 to implement the network. Annual costs of the UT System's thirteen institutions will be approximately $70,000. The Texas A&M System will spend approximately $12,000 annually. The primary advantage will be the cost savings from the universities' not having to maintain redundant computer facilities and staff.[70]

Private Telecommunications Initiatives

Large telecommunications-intensive firms, such as oil companies, insurance companies, banks, and airlines, appear to be well informed about developments in the telecommunications industry and generally have a strong sense that the economic benefits of telecommunications are obvious, although only sometimes quantifiable. For the most part, private firms do not seem to feel that divestiture has affected them strongly, either positively or negatively.

It is in the interest of large users for telephone companies to operate under greater regulatory flexibility. Large users often feel that telecommunications regulation causes unnecessary delays, unfairly restricts telephone company options, and diverts legal and other resources from more productive areas. In spite of this, they are very reluctant to enter directly into the regulatory policy debate for a variety of reasons. For example, they may be concerned about proprietary information being made public or about their resources becoming tied up in regulatory or legislative proceedings. Moreover, large portions of their telecommunications networks may not even be subject to regulatory changes (for example, consumer premises equipment and private or nonregulated transmission links).

Three large users were interviewed for this report: a manufacturing firm, a service firm, and an oil company.[71] The manufacturing firm planned to convert to ISDN technology in the summer of 1988. Its goal was to streamline organizational structures and to permit easier access by employees to the company's numerous databases. By integrating separate and competing communications and data processing staffs, the company felt that ISDN would eliminate an entire layer of support staff. By and large, however, the use of ISDN to consolidate data processing and communications staff in Texas is a rare phenomenon. Only 5.6 percent of large users surveyed in Texas report full integration of data processing and telecommunications functions.[72] This company felt strongly that innovative use of ISDN would also result in a number of efficiencies that could not be anticipated. (This is one of the problems in quantifying potential benefits.) It did not seem to feel that state regulation of LECs had much to do with its ISDN procurement.

The service firm interviewed, an airline company, had a stronger opinion about the effects of regulation on telecommunications procurement. As an example, this firm's spokesperson described the difficulty it was having in getting a particular service for several different locations. Even though the costs would vary from location to location, the service provider, Southwestern Bell, was obligated to charge the same price for each. This was apparently unacceptable to the company and represented an "unnecessary delay" in implementation.

In terms of linking telecommunications with economic development, this respondent pointed out that most large users did not need assistance from state economic development agencies in meeting their telecommunications needs, because they had sufficient expertise in this area within their own companies. However, he noted that it might be helpful for small businesses to have such a resource within state agencies. He pointed out that since most state economic development agencies serve an informational function for business, integrating a telecommunications element into that function should be feasible.

The oil company also intended to implement ISDN in 1988, although its spokesperson offered no specific reasons, aside from the obvious benefits of improved database management and easier employee access to various databases. The main reason for moving to ISDN was a "feeling" that such technology will improve productivity and efficiency within the firm. This respondent discussed the difficulty in both corporate and regulatory arenas of basing decisions on such unquantifiable benefits. Indeed most large users, when purchasing new telecommunications technologies, base the decision on factors such as improved access to branch locations and improved access to clients and customers.[73] It is usually difficult to quantify the benefits of improved access He also felt that the primary effect of regulation was to restrict telephone companies' ability to offer flexible service and facilities packages and to delay implementation.

In all, telecommunications-intensive businesses want the telephone companies to be able to respond to their requests on a competitive basis. Reduced regulation of telephone companies would generally work to the advantage of these large users. These firms do not seem to feel that state efforts to promote ties between telecommunications and economic development have much impact on their business decisions. These large-user interviews underscored the difficulties of quantifying a link between telecommunications and economic development, at either the corporate or the state level.

Public-Private Telecommunications Initiatives

In some cases, the efforts of both public and private entities have been combined in the development of telecommunications projects. One example of this would be San Antonio's efforts to "market" itself as a "telecity." The city has worked with telecommunications providers to build and market a telecommunications infrastructure specifically designed to attract business to the area. Originally conceived as a business park developed around a teleport, the TeleCity concept grew out of an "inventory" of telecommunications facilities and services available in the city. With satellite facilities from an insurance company (USAA), extensive mileage of Southwestern Bell optical fiber in the metropolitan area, and fiber and microwave intercity links, developers discovered a "system in place to link San Antonio with the world."[74] The business park concept failed to materialize precisely because telecommunications capabilities were readily available throughout the city.[75]

Recruitment of high-tech research consortia such as MCC, Sematech, and the superconducting supercollider also involves cooperative efforts among both public and private interests. The recent efforts to attract Sematech to Austin are a good example. In this case, representatives from The University of Texas System, The University of Texas at Austin, the Austin Chamber of Commerce, Southwestern Bell, several microelectronics firms, and a variety of local, state, and federal agencies and offices worked together to locate and prepare facilities, arrange services, and provide funding. The unprecedented degree of cooperation among the many organizations involved, mentioned by Sematech as a primary factor in its decision to locate in Austin, was apparently driven by a general recognition of the seriousness of the state's economic situation.[76]

Public-private interaction can also be seen in the examples of The Electric Pages and TI-IN networks, mentioned above. The Electric Pages was started about five years ago as a private computer network service. The first clients were primarily educational organizations who used the network mostly as a legislative bill tracking service. This is still a major function, although applications have expanded substantially, as noted above. As system operator, The Electric Pages plays two roles: (1) transmission services and (2) development of communications software to make the system more efficient and effective to use.[77]

Another example of cities' ability to develop innovative telecommunications options is the concept of cable I-nets, or institutional loops, required of cable television companies in most recent urban franchise agreements. Typically, I-nets are separate cable systems (that is, built in addition to subscriber networks) which interconnect the schools, libraries, municipal offices, and other public buildings of a community. They generally run through central business districts as well, thus providing access to the business community. I-net applications include distribution of video programming for training, education, and videoconferencing; intracity data and voice communications; and bypass to IXCs. Among these applications, video training and data transmission (primarily by cities) are the most widely used.

Houston, Dallas, and Austin are also involved to one degree or another in this sort of infrastructural development, with MCI constructing intracity optical fiber networks. For the most part, however, cities have been slow to recognize the importance of strategic telecommunications planning and development.[78]

Another area of public-private cooperation is the development of maquiladora--assembly plants in northern Mexico owned by companies in the United States. The need for reliable telecommunications between assembly plants in Mexico and headquarters in the United States has raised some formidable obstacles. The maquiladora phenomenon is not unique to Texas. Other border states, especially California, are also involved. Texas, however, is involved in more of these projects than the other states. Maquiladoras raise several policy issues that will impact telecommunications and economic development in Texas and require further study.

Additionally, IC^2 Institute, a research group at The University of Texas at Austin, has been exploring the tremendous potential of public-private cooperation in nurturing technological development through the "technopolis" concept.[79] According to these researchers, technopolis interactively links the development of technology in both the public and private sectors to promote economic development through new institutional arrangements among business, government, and academia.[80] Three technopolises appear to be developing in Texas: along the Austin-San Antonio corridor, in the Dallas-Fort Worth metroplex, and in north Houston. In each case, large and small technology companies and industrial R&D consortia, assisted by government coordination and funding, have evolved around the nuclei of major research universities. Technology companies may either be attracted from out of state or "homegrown."[81] Clearly, there is a role for advanced telecommunications in the technopolis structure to facilitate communication among the numerous companies and agencies involved.

CONCLUSIONS

Changes in the telecommunications industry have forced reconsideration of regulatory methods in Texas and have placed a growing emphasis on the state's role in deciding issues. The results of these decisions will shape the development of telecommunications infrastructure and, in turn, hinder or enhance the state's opportunities for economic development. A number of conclusions can be drawn from the present research.

Assumptions have been made regarding the link between telecommunications and economic development, but the relationship needs to be better researched. Certainly, it is important that Texas continue its recent efforts to coordinate economic development policy at the state level, consolidate development strategies, and fund promising initiatives. The recommendations of the Governor's Business Development and Jobs Creation Task Force, the establishment of the new Department of Commerce, and the passage of some associated legislation demonstrate a high level of concern. However, these efforts appear to have overlooked a significant element: the link between telecommunications and economic development. Development efforts in many areas, such as agriculture, education, and rural development, could be further enhanced through strategic application of telecommunications.

Moreover, Texas has acquired a growing base of information services over the past several years and has the resources to become an even bigger player in international markets. A modern, high-quality telecommunications infrastructure is vital in both of these areas. The Governor's Task Force noted how "one of the most sophisticated highway systems in the country" was handicapped by regulatory constraints,[82] but did not address how regulation might be hampering the state's sophisticated telecommunications networks. In terms of state-level economic development, it is important to begin to quantify the impact of telecommunications on the general economy. State agencies, as well as telecommunications providers, need to collect and relate the data that might quantitatively demonstrate this link.

It is generally agreed that a modern telecommunications infrastructure is necessary for economic development in that businesses will not locate or develop in areas with inadequate telecommunications. However, it is difficult to argue that even sophisticated, state-of-the-art telecommunications infrastructure, by itself, is sufficient to stimulate economic growth. If other factors are more or less equal, advanced telecommunications may provide a competitive advantage.

At the micro level, information about telecommunications resources should become a component in the state's business development efforts. For example, a system of small business development centers (recommended by the Governor's Task Force but not funded in the last legislative session) could easily incorporate such information to help small businesses identify their telecommunications needs. Southwestern Bell has already begun to work through local chambers of commerce in this regard.

Texas lacks a forum for the cooperative development of strategic telecommunications policy. Just as general economic development planning must be coordinated and streamlined in Texas, so, too, should the development of telecommunications policy be better organized and more efficient. As long as telecommunications issues are decided primarily in the context of adversarial, adjudicatory proceedings, they will inevitably focus on the short-term self-interest of the parties involved. As a result, the long-term welfare of the state as a whole will suffer.

What appears to be needed, then, is some type of strategic telecommunications policy development organization at the state level. This would provide an arena in which policy issues could be anticipated and the various players, proportionally represented, could discuss plans and concerns. It is idealistic to expect that such a forum could achieve consensus on all issues, but it could at least help to clarify issues and encourage compromise. This alone would streamline PUC proceedings and substantially reduce the time and money spent arguing issues in that arena. More importantly, it would provide a framework for developing coherent and progressive telecommunications policy for Texas.

Such an organization should be operated on a continuing basis rather than as a one-time commission or panel. It is clear that substantial changes will continue to occur in the telecommunications industry for the foreseeable future as technologies continue to evolve at a rapid pace and as issues continue to be played out at the federal level. This organization should be advisory to the executive branch and the legislature as well as to the PUC. Its composition should be carefully considered in order that its recommendations not subsequently be co-opted by interests claiming to have been "left out" of the process.

Further modifications to the regulatory framework may be appropriate. Changes in the telecommunications industry have forced reconsideration of regulatory methods. Texas has already moved to provide some regulatory flexibility in both local and interexchange markets. Other states have made even more radical changes, such as detariffing and price caps (or "social contract"). To the extent that telecommunications markets truly are or may become competitive and to the extent that experience in these other states provides favorable indications, Texas may need to consider further change in the regulatory structure.

Certainly there are legitimate concerns. It is important that telephone companies not be allowed to socialize costs by making all ratepayers pay for advanced infrastructure that may only be used by large, sophisticated users.[83]

However, this assumes that residential or small business customers will not benefit from advanced services. If telephone companies are discouraged from installing advanced infrastructure, large users may leave the public network, causing residential rates to increase anyway. Moreover, residential and small business users who may want technologically advanced services will not get them.

Thus, perhaps the single greatest dilemma facing policymakers is how to encourage the development of advanced telecommunications infrastructure (which appears to be at least necessary for economic development) without unduly burdening the captive ratepayer. One approach might be to define a basic or standard level of service and assure that it is universally available at an affordable price, and then let advanced, state-of-the-art technologies be introduced where demand warrants. Prices for these enhanced services could then be structured to recover the increased costs from those who wish to use them.

The first step would be for policymakers to define universal service. Of course, any such definition would need to take into account evolving technology: for example, digital switching to provide enhanced 911 services. Once such a basic service were defined and the telephone company obligated to meet this standard, then other, advanced services could be installed and priced on a demand basis.

This might mean that urban areas, where economies of density and traffic volume are high, would receive new facilities and services before rural areas (especially if pooling arrangements were eliminated). But to install such technologies in areas with no demand and higher unit costs would only increase the burden on general ratepayers. As demand developed in rural areas, it would be feasible then to install the appropriate facilities. This would seem to be a basic cost-benefit decision.

It might also be appropriate for Texas policymakers to consider moving to some form of incentive regulation. One approach might be to grant telephone companies pricing flexibility under a price cap approach, with earnings in excess of allowed rate of return being split between ratepayers and stockholders. This would provide incentive for telephone companies to reduce costs and improve efficiency and also provide a mechanism for ratepayers to share in the savings. It should be noted, however, that consumer advocates, among others, feel that there is no reason to give Texas LECs further regulatory flexibility at this time.

Explicit policies for economic development in rural areas have just begun to be articulated, but have not included a telecommunications component. As with "universal service," the first step in developing coherent policy for rural areas is to decide exactly what is needed. A vague desire to provide "advanced technology" is counterproductive without specific applications in mind and user demand in evidence. In other words, telecommunications policy for rural areas must go hand in hand with economic development policy. Clearly, there is a wide range of possibilities. For example, the Governor's Task Force recommended an obvious priority: development of a food processing industry. As it pointed out, 94 percent of farm and livestock produce grown in Texas is exported to be processed elsewhere.[84] The location of sites for processing plants would involve consideration of telecommunications as well as transportation facilities. Cultivation of global markets, especially high-profit niche markets, requires even more sophisticated use of telecommunications.

Another rural issue is the importance of recognizing the growing pressure within the industry to eliminate subsidies such as revenue pooling. Such arrangements, however, have been critical to the financial viability of some rural Texas telephone companies. Policymakers have begun to develop alternative mechanisms to support those high cost systems where targeted subsidies may be necessary. In other cases, alternative technologies, such as radio or satellite, may be appropriate. In any case, increased traffic will lower unit costs. Thus, economic development will help pay for the development of telecommunications facilities. There is a pressing need for more research, as is being done for rural Washington.

The quality of education in Texas, especially in rural Texas, can be greatly enhanced through application of telecommunications. High-quality education is fundamental to economic development, especially in rural areas. Yet Texas' commitment in this area has been inconsistent at best. Initiatives such as TI-IN and The Electric Pages demonstrate the potential of telecommunications to enhance educational opportunities, both to rural areas and within cities. The Coordinating Council on Higher Education has made a strong case for improved distance education, but funding has not been forthcoming. Certainly, it is difficult to invest in new systems when state revenues are low, but that is when such investments are the most important.

The development of distance education links in rural areas has two advantages. First, there is the potential for improved quality of education. Second, delivery of instructional programming can help pay for the establishment and maintenance of telecommunications links to rural communities. In this way, distribution of education can help "subsidize" telecommunications infrastructure in rural Texas.

In closing this chapter, it is important to make a critical distinction. Much, if not most, of the debate over telecommunications policy has to do with near-term investment in infrastructure. This is by no means trivial. It should be remembered, however, that the real value is in the communication of information. There is more potential for growth in information services than in transmission. Policymakers should therefore focus on what the information needs of Texans will be as the state moves into the Information Age. Only in those terms can intelligent, long-range telecommunications policy be developed.

CASE STUDY: THE EVOLUTION OF SB 229 AND SB 444[85]

This legislation, passed in 1987, addressed both LEC and IXC concerns. Senate Bill 229 directed the PUC to define markets in interexchange telecommunications and to determine which IXCs, if any, were dominant in each market. While not deregulating AT&T as that company had hoped, it did provide a framework for reviewing the need for continued regulation. Senate Bill 444 was more complex and dealt with regulatory flexibility for LECs. This legislation made it easier for small LECs to change rates and for the larger LECs (Southwestern Bell and GTE) to offer flexible pricing for competitive services, with less regulatory delay. It directed the PUC to make rules for the introduction of new or experimental services. It also established provisions for a universal service fund, which was to be the primary vehicle to fund both a tel-assistance program and a Texas high-cost fund.

The evolution of these bills began years earlier. In 1983, in anticipation of divestiture, AT&T initiated legislation that would have led to its deregulation following the breakup. Apparently, as PURA stood in 1983, there was some question about whether AT&T would remain regulated after January 1, 1984. Presumably, AT&T would not have been regulated unless PURA was changed. Rather than deregulate AT&T, the law was changed so that PURA would specifically allow the PUC to maintain the status quo (that is, AT&T would continue to be regulated while the OCCs were not). However, it also required that the PUC initiate a proceeding to define the relevant markets, which was seen as a first step toward eventually deregulating AT&T. This proceeding was initiated late in 1985, with no action coming from that proceeding.

In August 1986 the PUC staff began considering the idea of giving AT&T some pricing flexibility. Again, there were questions about whether PURA would allow the PUC to make such changes outside of a regular rate case. Moreover, rate flexibility was not deregulation, and AT&T was claiming to have lost money in Texas on intrastate traffic since divestiture. SB 229 was filed on January 29, 1987. Although AT&T may have privately appreciated the pricing flexibility that it was granted in the spring of 1987 (after SB 229 had been filed), publicly it was committed to press for deregulation.

Southwestern Bell had also encountered problems since divestiture. For one thing, the company had failed to convince the PUC of the extent to which it was being threatened by the newly competitive telecommunications environment. For example, in Docket 6220, the company's evidence on the impact of bypass was challenged by the PUC staff and subsequently withdrawn.[86] Southwestern Bell had also been unsuccessful in other key rate cases.

Although many small LECs had been doing quite well financially (due at least in part to low-cost REA money, pooling arrangements, and other revenue transfers), others had forgone needed rate increases due to the expense of litigating formal rate cases.

Southwestern Bell and the TTA may have also perceived in 1987 that the timing was right to seek some regulatory flexibility. RBOCs in several other states had achieved some success in this regard (particularly in Nebraska), and there was a sense that the political fallout from these initiatives might make it increasingly difficult to obtain regulatory relaxation in the next few years.[87] Telecommunications markets were also becoming more competitive, yet any new service offerings still had to go through the full rate-case proceedings. The industry felt that the procedures that were in place did not meet the requirements of the new telecommunications environment.[88] It was felt that in order to change these procedures, PURA would have to be changed.

In January 1987 the TTA presented a draft of proposed legislation to streamline regulation of LECs to state senator Ray Farabee. A staff review by Senator Farabee's office found the bill to be unacceptable in that form, but agreed that the new telecommunications environment had created problems that needed to be addressed. (The last substantive amendments to PURA dealing with telecommunications regulation had been written before divestiture.) A telassistance plan, which provided for a subsidy narrowly targeted to disabled heads of households, 65 years of age or older, and living below the poverty level, was added by Farabee's office. The bill was filed on February 17, 1987.

Consumer advocates opposed the whole bill, feeling that it would "completely gut telecommunications regulation in Texas"[89] and that the telassistance plan was inadequate. The bill was also opposed by the cities in their role as consumer advocates.

Parts of the TTA draft were left in the bill as filed, even though they were expected to be controversial. For example, two sections, Sec. 93 and Sec. 96(a), constituted a policy mandate that explicitly related the development of new telecommunications services to economic development and specifically directed the PUC to consider competition and technological obsolescence in streamlining regulation of certain local exchange services.

In negotiations prior to committee consideration, both the PUC and consumer groups took an active role in having most of this language deleted. For one thing, the language was seen as too narrowly circumscribing the PUC's options rather than simply providing a general policy directive. Some felt that it did not address consumer interests adequately and that the public interest was defined essentially in terms of the telephone company's interest.

As it emerged from the Senate State Affairs Committee, SB 444 was a little more balanced in terms of the public interest and articulated a clear, but broader, policy mandate from the legislature that the PUC recognize the growing impact of competition and new technology and make the benefits available to Texas customers in a timely fashion. The bill changed very little from the time it was reported out of committee until it passed in June. Consumer advocates and several small competitors continued to oppose the bill to the very end.

SB 229, on the other hand, followed a markedly different course. The bill was substantially rewritten in late-night sessions during the last few days of the session. During the middle of the session, a number of consumer protections were written into the bill, and AT&T made some compromises with MCI and US Sprint that, while not immediately deregulating AT&T, would have set a date certain for deregulation. That version lost on the Senate floor by one vote.

The bill was virtually dead going into the last few weeks of the session. Senators Hugh Parmer and Chet Edwards, among others, had threatened a filibuster. AT&T (wanting to get something for all its efforts and expense) went to the bill's primary opponents, ClayDesta and Consumers Union, and asked, in effect, what it would take to get the bill passed. MCI, originally opposed to the bill, had come to the conclusion that continued regulation of AT&T was perhaps not really in MCI's interest.

The two bills acquired distinctly different personalities as they evolved through the legislative session. For one thing, the bills themselves were quite distinct. The basic issues in SB 229 were rather plain: Should AT&T be deregulated? SB 444, on the other hand, was much more complex. The players in SB 229 seemed much more confrontational. The image of Clayton Williams, Jr., ClayDesta's founder, in full cowboy regalia, riding his horse up the capitol steps to symbolically defend the citizens of Texas from the faceless, elite, corporate outsiders of AT&T dramatically characterized the debate. In contrast, the quiet management style of SB 444's sponsor was credited with helping to resolve many of the issues in that bill early on, while it was still in committee. Southwestern Bell's clout with legislators via its local managers and its employees' membership in the Communications Workers of America was also a major factor.

The role of consumer advocates was played out somewhat differently in the two bills. Consumer interests were quite active in all phases of consideration and revision of SB 229. Their involvement with SB 444, although still active, was less effective. Basically they did not want the bill to pass, period. They felt that the tel-assistance plan was too narrow and that potential cross-subsidization of new and competitive services by captive ratepayers was not dealt with strongly enough.

AT&T did not get what it had asked for with SB 229. However, a timetable and a method for the PUC to evaluate the issue were issued, and the rules were extended to the OCCs. With SB 444, on the other hand, the legislation proposed by Southwestern Bell and the TTA remained largely intact. In SB 229 consumer interests and the OCCs had been able to win some major concessions, while in SB 444 consumer interests produced only minor changes to proposed legislation.

The passage of SB 229 and SB 444 established a new statutory framework for regulation of telecommunications in Texas. As of this writing, the AT&T dominance hearing is in progress and the specific rules by which these laws will be administered are being developed.

NOTES

1.   Company-specific access charges are another way to target subsidies to high-cost operations that may truly need assistance.   Radio technology may also help to drive down the cost of rural loops. (Jon Loehman, Assistant Vice-President, Rates and Revenues, Southwestern Bell, Austin, written comments on an earlier draft of this chapter.)

2.   AMBAC Indemnity Corp., "Fiscal and Economic Condition of Texas," New York, 1987, p. v.

3.   Ibid.

4.   Ibid.

5.   "Just hold on: Business taxes may lighten soon, Texas official says," Austin American-Statesman, May 28, 1988, p. 2.

6.   AMBAC Indemnity Corp., "Fiscal and Economic Condition of Texas," p. v.

7.   Ibid., p. vi.

8.   Ibid.

9.   Sharon Strover, "Urban Telecommunications: The Policy Planner's Dilemma," Center for Research on Communication Technology and Society, University of Texas at Austin, September 1987.   For a general discussion of this topic, see Mitchell L. Moss, "Telecommunications and the Economic Development of Cities," in William H. Dutton, Jay G. Blumler, and Kenneth L. Kraemer ed., Wired Cities: Shaping the Future of Communications (Boston: G. K. Hall and Co., 1987), pp. 139-51.

10.   "Recommendations of the Business Development and Jobs Creation Task Force," submitted to Governor William P. Clements, Jr., January 1987, p. 2.

11.   Ibid.

12.   Texas Telephone Association, "Texas Phone Facts, 1988," Austin. (Brochure.)

13.   Michael Dowling, Technological Change, Innovation, and Strategy in the Telecommunications Equipment Industry, 1975-86, Ph.D. Dissertation, The University of Texas at Austin, 1988, Chapter 7.

14.   Loehman, written comments.

15.   William Free, Vice-President, Texas Division, Southwestern Bell Telephone, Austin, written comments on an earlier draft of this chapter.

16.   Eric N. Berg, "A Lagging Ma Bell Offspring," New York Times, November 11, 1985.

17.   Eric Hindin, "National Profile and ISDN Top Agenda at Southwestern Bell.

18.   Ibid.

19.   Ibid.

20.   Laurie Hays and Mary Lu Carnevale, "Regional Phone Firms Bend Rules and Invade Each Other's Territory," Wall Street Journal, March 9, 1988, pp. 1, 18.

21.   Don Cooper, "AT&T Will Call on Legislature," Austin Business Journal, July 13-19, 1987.

22.   Strover, "Urban Telecommunications," p. 6.

23. "Public Utility Commission," Regulation in Texas: Its Impact, Processes, and Institutions, Vol. 2, Policy Research Project Report Series No. 76 (Austin, Texas: Lyndon B. Johnson School of Public Affairs, 1986), p. 87.

24. Ibid., p. 88.

25. Ibid., pp. 88-89.

26. Ibid., pp. 89-95.

27. Ibid., pp. 116-17.

28. Loehman, written comments.

29. Information provided by Stephen Kail, District Manager, Regulatory Relations, AT&T, (Austin, n.d.) (Photocopy.).

30. AITC, The State of Texas Long-Range Telecommunications Plan (Austin: Automated Information and Telecommunications Council, December 1986).

31. Strover, "Urban Telecommunications," pp. 2-3.

32. Nine "tests" of market dominance were included to guide the hearings process.

33. Interview with Mark Bryant, Manager, Texas Regulatory Affairs, and Don Price, Staff Administrator, MCI, Austin, May 25, 1988.

34. General and Specific Laws of Texas, 70th Legislature, 1987,chapter 414, Telecommunications--Regulation of Interexchange Carriers, SB 229, Sec. 4, Subsec. 100. (h).

35. Consumer advocates argue that Texas has one of the statutorily shortest regulatory processes in the nation. Interview with Carol Barger, Director, Southwest Office, Consumers Union, Austin, May 25, 1988.

36. "Task Force Recommendations," p. 10. Reorganization of economic development was also discussed in: Speakers Economic Advisory Group, Texas Building for the Future Alternatives for Revitalizing and Diversifying the Economy, Report submitted to: The Honorable Gib Lewis, Speaker of the House of Representatives, January 1987, Part 6.

37. Telephone interview with Mike Edelmann, Director of Economic Development, Southwestern Bell, Dallas, April 21, 1988.

38. Free, written comments.

39. Interview with Ray Farabee, Texas State Senator, D-Wichita Falls, Austin, January 30, 1988.

40. Dennis Thomas, Chairman, Public Utility Commission of Texas, informal class discussion, Austin, October 2, 1987.

41. Telephone interview with Consumers Union staff member, Austin, May 18, 1988.

42. Don A. Dillman and Donald M. Beck, "Information Technologies and Rural Development in the 1990s," paper presented to the Rural Great Plains of the Future symposium, Denver, Colorado, November 3-5, 1987.

43. "Task Force Recommendations," pp. 12, 93-94.

44. Ibid., p. 4.

45. Ibid., pp. 4-5.

46. Senate Bill No. 444, 70th Texas Legislature, filed February 17, 1987, Art. XIV.

47. House Resolution No. 733, 70th Texas Legislature, filed May 29, 1987, p. 1.

48. AITC, The State of Texas Long-Range Telecommunications Plan (Austin: Automated Information and Telecommunications Council, December 1986).

49. Telephone interview with AITC staff member, Austin, Texas, April 21, 1988.

50. Ibid.

51. Interview with Nancy Vaughn, Assistant Deputy Commissioner for Information Systems, and Warren Russel, Section Director for Network Design, Texas Department of Human Services, Austin, February 1, 1988.

52. Education is a responsibility of the state. Thus, school districts are known as local education agencies.

53. Telephone interview with Richard LaGow, Editor, TEA-NET, Austin, April 20, 1988.

54. Telephone interview with Connie Stout, Educational Specialist, Division of Educational Technology, Texas Education Agency, Austin, March 1, 1988.

55. Texas Education Agency Telecommunications Pilot Project Report, National Information Systems, Inc., n.d., p. 6.

56. Ibid., p. 5.

57. Ibid., p. 29.

58. Ibid., p. 10.

59. Telephone interview with Stout.

60. Ibid., p. 13.

61. Ibid., p. 8.

62. Telephone interview with Wanda Jackson, staff member, Division of Educational Technology, Texas Education Association, Austin, April 20, 1988.

63. Telephone interview with George McCollough, Division Director for PEIMS, Texas Education Association, Austin, April 19, 1988.

64. Telephone interview with Sal Valdez, Director of Agricultural and Economic Development, Texas Department of Agriculture, Texas, March 1, 1988.

65. Ibid.

66. Ibid.

67. Ibid.

68. Telephone interview with Larry Temple, Chairman of the Texas Select Committee on Higher Education, Coordinating Board (1985-1987), Austin, May 31, 1988.

69. Tara Parker Pope, "Massive Computer Network Links up UT, A&M Systems," Austin American-Statesman, May 26, 1988, p. B2.

70. Ibid.

71. The manufacturing company and the service company wished not to be identified by name in this report. The oil company was Tenneco.

72. Michael Dowling, Technological Change, Innovation, and Strategy in the Telecommunications Equipment Industry, 1975-86, Chapter 7.

73. Ibid.

74. Telephone interview with Mario Hernandez, Vice-President, San Antonio Economic Development Foundation, San Antonio, February 3, 1988.

75. Ibid.

76. Telephone interview with Izzy Cordova, Area Manager for Facilities, Southwestern Bell, Austin, April 28, 1988.

77. Telephone interview with John Clark, Executive Vice-President, The Electric Pages, Austin, April 28, 1988.

78. Strover, "Urban Telecommunications," p. 6.

79. Raymond Smilor, George Kozmetsky, and David Gibson, "The 'Technopolis' Concept," in Frederick Williams (ed.), <u>Measuring the Information Society</u> (Newbury Park, Calif.: Sage, 1988).

80. Ibid., pp. 2-3.

81. Ibid., pp. 3-5.

82. "Task Force Recommendations," p. 5.

83. Carol Barger, "Let's Talk Telephones," presentation to United Church of Christ, January 15, 1988.

84. Business Development and Jobs Creation Task Force, "Key Points," mimeograph, n.d., p. 4.

85. This case study synthesizes various accounts in an attempt to present a general picture of the development of this legislation.

86. Interview with Philip Diehl, Director of Telephone Regulation, Public Utility Commission of Texas, Austin, May 27, 1988.

87. Interview with Diehl, April 28, 1988.

88. Loehman, written comments.

89. Carol Barger, Director, Southwest Office, Consumers Union, quoted in Anne Marie Kilday, "Phone 'streamlining' bill hit as deregulation in disguise," <u>Houston Chronicle</u>, February 19, 1987.

8

Vermont

Janee Briesemeister and Philip Treuer

The state of Vermont is in the midst of developing an innovative regulatory framework for telecommunications. In June 1987 the legislature passed a statute that allows the state's dominant local exchange telephone company, New England Telephone, and the state's Department of Public Service (DPS), as representatives of the public, to negotiate a "social contract" subject to approval by the Public Service Board (PSB). The contract is an agreement between the industry and the state by which the company agrees to stabilize basic phone rates and modernize plant and equipment in exchange for the elimination of rate of return regulation and the loosening of some regulatory restrictions on competitive services. Replacing rate of return regulation with the new social contract approach is a radical departure from traditional utility oversight. The Vermont social contract is important to study as the first attempt by a state to rewrite the rules on utility regulation.

A second aspect of the legislation also outlines the role of the state as a telecommunications user and planner and implements new procedures to help the state use telecommunications more efficiently. Each of these two aspects of the statute demonstrates an innovative, forward-looking approach to telecommunications regulation and planning. Each was framed with the hope of encouraging business development in the state by encouraging the growth of sophisticated telecommunications services at competitive rates.

As the telecommunications environment is changing, so, too, are state responses to what was once a completely rate-base-regulated monopoly utility. States are challenged by the growing demand for technologically advanced telephone company services that are adaptive to individual users' needs. At the same time regulators are committed to upholding this country's tradition of universal service, which is premised on good-quality basic service at affordable rates. Vermont's new telecommunications law is one of the earliest and most comprehensive responses to that challenge. The law allows representatives of all interests to participate, monitors the results, and provides a mechanism for reregulation if need be. In addition, each state agency, coordinated by the

Office of Telecommunications, will forecast its own telecommunications needs and decide how best to use telecommunications to meet the needs of Vermont's citizens.

The state's telecommunications policymakers have moved quickly in responding to postdivestiture regulation. They have instituted mandatory local measured service (LMS) because they believe it helps residential customers control their phone bills; and they have allowed intraLATA competition in the single-LATA state. Vermont is now about to take a major step, although the wisdom of that move is subject to much debate nationwide. The original round of negotiations between New England Telephone and DPS on the social contract, or the Vermont Telecommunications Agreement (VTA), were concluded in November 1987. The PSB, in reviewing the VTA in the spring of 1988, found the general notion of the contract acceptable, but objected to some of the terms. Unable by law to amend the terms of the contract, the PSB rejected the VTA in July 1988, but left the door open to a revised contract. The VTA was subsequently renegotiated and resubmitted to the PSB in September 1988. A decision is pending.

Vermont's new telecommunications policy is an ambitious one. The state is to be credited for its hard work and careful thought in studying and now in trying to implement a completely new approach to telecommunications regulation. In considering the state's two major goals for its new policy, protection of universal service and economic development, three themes emerge:

1. The social contract is controversial, and there apparently remains some fear in some policymakers' minds that this step is too bold and that the state's social policy goals will be harmed.

2. Even if Vermont's social contract succeeds as envisioned by its proponents, it is not clear whether this approach could be as easily transferred to other states as an across-the-board replacement for rate of return regulation, particularly given the unique policy environment in Vermont.

3. Based on experience in other states, Vermont is on sounder footing in regard to links between telecommunications infrastructure and the efficient delivery of state services, including education.

THE ECONOMY AND THE TELECOMMUNICATIONS INDUSTRY
Economic Profile

Residents of Vermont earn less income than the national average. Per capita income in 1984 was $10,802, compared with $12,789 in the nation as a whole, ranking Vermont 39th among the states. A tight labor market in the New England region is expected to push up wages faster than the U.S. average over the next three years. The State of Vermont is projecting growth in wages at 2.8 percent for 1987, 2.2 percent for 1988, and 2.7 percent for 1989 compared with 2.0 percent or less for the rest of the nation. The percentage of the population receiving public assistance is lower than the national average and has declined steadily since 1975. Housing stock ranks 30th in the country in median value.[1]

In 1986 the workhorses of the Vermont nonfarm economy, as measured by employment, were manufacturing, wholesale and retail trade, and services

(Table 8.1). Each sector employs from 20 percent to 25 percent of the work force and is roughly in line with national averages. Relative to the national shares, only manufacturing and, to a lesser extent, services are showing specialization in Vermont.

Table 8.1
Nonagricultural Employment Shares and Annual
Percentage Change in Employment* for Vermont and
the United States, 1980 and 1986
(total employees in 1,000s, share and change in %)

Sector	Employment Shares				Annual Employment Change	
	1980		1986			
	Vermont	U.S.	Vermont	U.S.	Vermont	U.S.
Mining	0.3	1.1	0.2	0.8	-5.0	-3.9
Construction	5.0	4.9	6.5	4.9	8.5	1.6
Manufacturing	25.3	22.5	21.2	19.1	-0.3	-1.1
Transportation	4.4	5.7	4.2	5.3	1.7	0.3
Wholesale and Retail Trade	20.4	22.7	22.5	23.7	4.8	2.4
Fin., Ins., Real Estate	4.1	5.7	4.7	6.3	6.0	3.7
Services.	22.0	19.6	24.4	23.2	4.9	5.0
Government	18.4	17.8	16.4	16.8	0.7	0.6
Total	1,997	90,657	2,337	99,610	2.8	1.7

* Totals may reflect rounding error.

Source: U.S. Department of Labor, Bureau of Labor Statistics, Employment and Earnings, vol. 34, no. 5 (May 1987), pp. 120-137; idem, vol. 28, no. 5 (May 1981), pp. 120-128.

Construction and finance as well as insurance and real estate (F.I.R.E.) have been the most rapidly growing industries in Vermont. However, the driving forces of Vermont's recent growth are the service and trade sectors. Combined, they account for 70 percent of nonfarm job growth between 1980 and 1986. Manufacturing lost 1,300 jobs during this period but remains an important focus of the state's economic development efforts. Because of Vermont's small population, it can be particularly susceptible to fluctuations from the exit or entry of a single large manufacturing company. According to state projections, overall job growth will continue to exceed that of the United

States in 1987 and 1989, with a temporary slowdown in 1988 to approximately the national average.[2]

Table 8.2
Employment Shares and Annual Changes in Employment* of
Telecommunications-Intensive Businesses** for Vermont
and the United States, 1980 and 1984
(share and change in %)

| | Employment Shares | | | | Annual Employment Change | |
| | 1980 | | 1984 | | | |
	Vermont	U.S.	Vermont	U.S.	Vermont	U.S.
Information Services	7.5	9.1	6.8	9.9	0.4	3.2
Finance	2.4	3.1	2.5	3.3	2.0	3.2
Insurance	2.4	2.3	1.6	2.3	-4.8	1.0
Real Estate	0.7	1.3	0.7	1.4	0.5	1.6
Computer/Data Proc.	0.2	0.4	0.2	0.6	8.2	13.1
Other Information Svcs.	1.8	2.1	1.8	2.3	10.9	4.5
Info. Technology Equip.	5.1	2.2	5.4	2.3	2.1	2.4
Research and Development	0.4	0.3	0.1	0.3	-14.8	2.9
Media	4.4	3.7	3.9	3.7	0.9	0.5
Total	28.3		28.1		-0.0	

* Totals may reflect rounding error.

** The Telecommunications-Intensive Business categories are defined by Standard Industrial Classification codes as follows:
    1. Information Services: Finance: SIC 60 (Banking), SIC 61 (Credit), SIC 62 (Commodities); Insurance: SIC 63 (Insurance Carriers), SIC 64 (Insurance Agents); Real Estate: SIC 65; Computer/Data Proc. : SIC 737; Other Information Services: SIC 731 (Advertising), SIC 732 (Credit Reporting), SIC 81 (Legal Services), SIC 891 (Engineering and Architectural Services), SIC 893 (Accounting and Auditing);
    2. Information Technology Equipment: SIC 3573 (Electronic Computing Equipment), SIC 361 (Electronic Distributing Equipment), SIC 365 (Radio and TV Receiving Equipment), SIC 366 (Communications Equipment), SIC 367 (Electronic Components and Accessories);
    3. Research and Development: SIC 7391 (Research and Development Laboratories), SIC 7397 (Commercial Testing Laboratories), SIC 892 (Nonprofit Education and Scientific Research Agencies);
    4. Media: SIC 27 (Printing and Publishing), SIC 48 (Communications), SIC 735 (News Syndicates), SIC 78 (Motion Pictures).

Source: U.S. Bureau of the Census, County Business Patterns, United States (No. 1) and Vermont (No. 47) (Washington, D.C.: U.S. Government Printing Office, 1980 and 1984), Table 1B.

Rapid structural change has been a cause for concern to the citizens of Vermont in recent years. In January 1988 Governor Madeleine Kunin proposed statewide planning in an attempt to control the negative side effects of economic change. Her proposals, based on the recommendations of a special commission, include requiring towns to participate in regional planning and requiring regions to adhere to statewide planning standards; doubling the property transfer tax to increase revenue; and creating a new state department to assist local and regional planners.[3]

Economy--Telecommunications-Intensive Businesses (TIBs)

Excluding telecommunications providers (i.e., common carriers, other common carriers, and specialized common carriers), there are four categories of telecommunications-intensive businesses in Vermont: information services, information technology, research and development, and media (Table 8.2). Information services is the employment leader, although its employment share in Vermont was significantly below the national average in 1980 and 1984. This sector is expected to grow in the coming years despite an overall relative decline from 1980 to 1984. The decline in insurance employment is largely attributable to reorganization at National Life of Vermont, one of the state's largest employers.

In contrast, information technology, at 5.4 percent in 1984, is more than double the national employment average. IBM, the state's second largest employer (8,000 employees), dominates this category, making electrical equipment the state's largest manufacturing industry.

Telecommunications Providers

New England Telephone, a Bell operating company, is the dominant carrier in the state, but there are also a handful of smaller companies that provide service in predominantly rural areas. Telecommunications providers consist of New England Telephone, the independent telephone companies represented by the Telephone Association of Vermont, the intrastate interexchange competitors, and other providers.

New England Telephone is a subsidiary of the NYNEX corporation, the second largest of the seven regional Bell holding companies. It is comprised of New York Telephone, New England Telephone, and a variety of unregulated businesses. Telephone operations in New York City and Boston alone account for 50 percent of the corporation's total revenues.[4] New England Telephone (NET) serves Massachusetts, Maine, New Hampshire, Rhode Island, and Vermont. NET is by far the largest local exchange company (LEC) in Vermont, serving 252,600 access lines (Table 8.3) and having gross operating revenues of $166.5 million (the allowed rate of return on capital is 10.75 percent; the allowed rate of return on equity is 14.75 percent).[5] NET-Vermont accounts for 1 percent of NYNEX revenues. Of the total access lines, 175,000 are for residential service, 50,000 are for business. The company serves 85 percent of the total access lines in Vermont, including all of the major population centers. Out of a total of 89 NET switching offices 43 are due to be converted to fully electronic switching and to equal access by the end of 1988; all but one of the remaining offices will be converted by 1997. NET also carries approximately 95 percent of the intrastate (intraLATA) traffic in Vermont.[6]

Table 8.3
Local Exchange Carriers and Access Lines
in Vermont, 1986

Local Exchange Carrier	Access Lines	Share of Total (%)*
New England Telephone-Vermont	252,600	85
Continental Telephone Company	29,300	10
Waitsfield-Fayston Telephone Co.	3,600	1
Ludlow Telephone Co.	3,100	1
Others**	6,700	2
Total	295,300	100

* Totals may reflect rounding error.

** Includes 5 other local exchange carriers.

Source: Correspondence with Telephone Association of Vermont, October 7, 1987.

Eight independent telephone companies operate in Vermont. Continental Telephone Company is the second largest LEC in the state, serving 29,200 access lines and 30 exchanges in 1986. It is a wholly owned subsidiary of the Contel holding company, which operates small telephone companies in several states.

Ludlow Telephone Company, Northfield Telephone Company, and Perkinsville Telephone Company are all subsidiaries of Telephone and Data Systems, a multistate company. Total combined access lines for the three companies in 1986 were approximately 6,200.

The remaining carriers are smaller locally owned companies. Franklin Telephone Company, a small family-owned company operating only within Vermont, had 520 access lines in 1986. Shoreham Telephone Company, with 2,600 access lines in 1986, also operates only within Vermont. Topsham Telephone Company, another small, locally owned LEC, served 900 access lines in 1986. Waitsfield-Fayston Telephone Company, which served 3,000 access lines in 1986, is the largest of the locally owned companies. The lobby group that represents the independent telephone companies is the Telephone Association of Vermont. Continental was the only independent to comment separately from the association on Vermont's new telecommunications law.

Several interexchange carriers also operate in Vermont. Long Distance North (also doing business as Burlington Telephone Company) is a privately held Maryland corporation. Burlington Tel was incorporated in the state of Vermont December 30, 1983. The company resells interstate and intrastate MTS and WATS service, primarily to business customers. US Sprint is an interexchange carrier formed through a joint partnership between GTE Corporation and United Telecommunications, Inc. The company provides MTS, WATS, and private line services. US Sprint offers residential and business interstate and intrastate (intraLATA) service primarily in Burlington, the state's largest metropolitan area, although it has begun expansion into other areas of the state.

AT&T provides only interstate interexchange service in Vermont; therefore the company does not fall under the regulation of the PSB. AT&T has a pending application for a certificate to provide intraLATA service in Vermont. Its application states that its intent is only to offer services which are incidental to its interstate software-defined network (SDN) offerings. This will primarily affect users of greater than $50,000 per year in phone bills.[7] It is the only interstate carrier in most areas of the state outside the two major urban centers (Burlington and Montpelier). MCI has a pending application for a Certificate of Public Good and is expected to begin operations in Vermont during 1988.

Comm-Tech Pay Services, Inc., distributes, installs, and maintains customer-owned coin-operated telephones (COCOTs). Comm-Tech successfully petitioned the PSB to open coin-operated phones to competition. A few dozen privately owned COCOTs also operate in Vermont.

Additionally, Vermont is served by 43 cable television (CATV) systems, which the PSB recognizes as potential competitors to the telephone companies. The largest of these are Telesystems, owned by Cox Cable; several franchises owned by Warner Cable Corporation; EMCO CATV, Inc.; and Better TV of Bennington.

POLICY DEVELOPMENT

The small size of the state and the structure of its legislative system give policy development in Vermont a somewhat unique character. It is not surprising to find that the policymaking process in Vermont has been described by one actor as "extremely manageable."[8]

Although Vermont does not have a sufficiently large population to warrant more than one representative to the U.S. House, the state General Assembly is among the largest in the nation, 30 state senators and 150 representatives. Yet none of the legislators has an office or staff funded by the state. It is truly a citizen legislature. The popular line in Vermont is that the deals are made in the halls of the capitol rather than behind closed doors. Even so, this poses many constraints on Vermont lawmakers. There is a great reliance on the committee system and on the advice of experts, including state agencies and regulators. There is also more dependence on the ability of interested parties to work out their differences.

The development of telecommunications policy in Vermont has followed this course. Major legislation that created an innovative approach to telecommunications regulation was passed only after several legislative and citizen committees had studied the issue, and many (but by no means all) of the parties were able to forge a consensus.

State Policy Actors

The Public Service Board is the major regulatory agency in Vermont. Created under Title 30 of the Vermont statutes, it has regulatory oversight of telephone companies (local and intrastate-interexchange), electric utilities, gas utilities, water companies, and cable television systems. The board performs quasi-judicial duties such as hearing rate requests and granting Certificates of Public Good. It is comprised of three board members appointed to six-year terms by the governor. The chair of the board is the only full-time member. The current chair is Richard Cowart, who replaced Louise McCarren when her term expired last year.[9]

On February 1, 1981, the state's Public Service Board was split into two distinct offices, the Public Service Board and the Department of Public Service. DPS handles administrative duties, consumer affairs, and power planning and other energy matters, and represents the public before the PSB in all matters. The latter is by far its largest function and is carried out by the Division of Public Advocacy, headed by the public advocate, Samuel Press. The division reviews every rate filing and policy matter before the PSB and intervenes in proceedings when it believes the request is not in the public interest.[10] Current commissioner of DPS, Gerald Tarrant, is the former public advocate and represented DPS during negotiation of the VTA.

The PSB and DPS derive their power and often their policy direction from the General Assembly. The Senate Finance Committee and the House Commerce Committee are generally the lead committees regarding utility legislation. Although the legislature and, to a lesser extent, the governor were active in the recent debate over new telecommunications policy in Vermont, these initiatives originated with the PSB rather than in the legislature or at the behest of the regulated Bell operating company (BOC), as has been the case in many other states.

State agencies are heavy users of telecommunications, but they have not been directly involved in the formation of telecommunications policy. During recent legislative hearings, most state agencies, including the Agency of Economic and Community Affairs and the state Department of Education, testified that "current telecommunication systems are adequate to serve the needs of the business and education communities."[11] A telecommunications section of the Department of General Services coordinates the installation and replacement of all telecommunications equipment and services for state government and does planning for the telecommunications needs of the state government.

Significant Decisions

The Vermont Public Service Board has been an innovator in telecommunications policymaking, particularly during the time Louise McCarren served as chair. McCarren is well known nationally among regulators and was an active member of the Communications Committee of the National Association of Regulatory Utility Commissioners (NARUC). Described as a "dissenter" on the NARUC committee, McCarren has advocated regulatory schemes and policies that are often untried and sometimes unpopular with other regulators.[12]

Mandatory local measured service is a policy strongly advocated by McCarren, even though it is unpopular in many other states. Although NET asked the PSB to approve optional LMS in 1981, the PSB felt a mandatory service with a cap on the total bill was the best for consumers. Under this policy local users are automatically switched from a flat rate to a rate based on minutes of use. As NET's central offices are converted to electronic switching (the technology necessary to measure phone usage based on minutes per use), the mandatory LMS kicks in. Party lines remain priced at the flat rate, even after the central office change. Customers in NET's other areas pay a flat rate ranging from about $10 to $19 per month (not including end-user access charges, surcharges, etc.), depending on the area of the state in which they live. Under the LMS pricing scheme, Burlington residents pay a dial-tone access fee of $10.93 per month, plus 2 cents a minute during peak calling hours (9 a.m. to 9 p.m.) and 1/2 cent in off-peak hours. However, the total bill cannot be higher than $27.53 a month. Studies have shown that 75 percent of customers pay less in monthly phone bills with LMS while 25 percent pay more.[13] Regulatory decisions regarding intrastate competition made during McCarren's tenure on the PSB appear to have set the stage for the VTA. IntraLATA regulation in Vermont, as in several other small New England states, is somewhat unique with respect to intrastate service. The entire state comprises a single LATA. Thus, in order to allow intrastate competition, intraLATA competition (generally prohibited after divestiture in other states, although recently a growing trend) is allowed as well. New England Telephone then is in direct competition with the intrastate interexchange carriers. The PSB recently rejected a request for intrastate equal access dialing. That means that NET remains the only carrier capable of offering "1-Plus" intrastate service (other carriers pay discounted access charges to compensate). It is not surprising that NET carries approximately 95 percent of the intrastate toll traffic.

Intrastate competition and competition in customer-owned coin-operated telephones were approved in 1986 as a result of Docket 4946. In that docket the PSB took some time to discuss the broader issue of competition in local telecommunications markets, including its own jurisdiction, and the impact of competition on existing carriers. PSB goals were to "compare the economic and societal cost of allowing competition to the expected benefits and to plan a regulatory approach in a mixed market of competitive and noncompetitive services."[14] The PSB concluded that de facto intrastate competition already existed and would continue regardless of any board action, including any attempt to impede it. The PSB also found that competition would put upward pressure on basic local rates and that any benefits of competition would be concentrated among the high-volume users and urban residents.

In allowing competition in the intrastate market, the PSB called upon the General Assembly to set a future-looking regulatory policy:

> It is also necessary that there be substantial regulatory reform to allow the Board the flexibility to make the kinds of pricing changes that will be necessary in the future, including price flexibility, detariffing or risk apportionment schemes.[15]

The social contract approach flourished in this atmosphere. The social contract, an idea first proposed by Louise McCarren in 1985, is the foundation of Vermont's newly enacted telecommunications law. The goal of this "new social contract" is to preserve universal service through an agreement between the regulators and New England Telephone (other companies may negotiate their own contracts later), which essentially gives each side some of what they want: rate predictability for the public and greater flexibility for NET, including entrance into competitive markets and less regulatory oversight. As in most negotiations, each side also gives up something of value. The public relinquishes the traditional regulatory tool--rate of return regulation--while the company loses the ability to recover virtually any and all expenditures through rate cases.

McCarren says the idea grew from her dissatisfaction with the ineffectiveness of traditional regulation since divestiture. Traditional regulation, according to McCarren, does not work in a multiproduct environment with increased competition in some segments and no competition in others. Through a new social contract, McCarren sought to keep the focus on the fundamental goals of regulation while at the same time responding to the changing market: "The most important goal for the state is to shift the risk away from the basic exchange customer. The goal of any rate agreement would be to isolate and limit the risk to basic exchange customers."[16]

McCarren realized the drastic nature of the regulatory shift she was advocating:

> To achieve such an agreement would require legislative approval and a political consensus within the state, difficult but not impossible to achieve. The debate itself will be worthwhile if it focuses on the appropriate role of regulation.[17]

Legislation

In 1985 the Governor's Telecommunications Commission, composed of representatives of business, NET, competitors, consumers, DPS, and the PSB, looked at the notion of a social contract in detail and recommended it favorably.[18] A bill to amend the state's telecommunications statute was introduced to the General Assembly in 1986. Both New England Telephone and the Department of Public Service were initially skeptical of the idea.[19] Tarrant opposed the bill because he did not know enough about the concept or its impact on residential ratepayers. Since NET controlled such a dominant market share, Tarrant was wary of loosening regulation, and he did not find proponents' arguments convincing.[20] There was much debate within NET as to the desirability of the contract as the company carefully studied financial projections. Many were afraid that entering into such a contract might not protect NET for the future. A consensus could not be reached and the bill did not pass.

DPS and NET eventually came to support the contract idea, but for very different reasons.[21] Tarrant of DPS came to see the contract as more than a one-sided benefit to NET. He found room to move beyond McCarren's original idea of rate stability and shape a contract that won additional benefits for consumers. To NET the contract approach is the removal of the regulatory albatross from around its corporate neck. Flexibility is achieved through the detariffing, customer-specific contracts, and the ability to offer rate and service packages quickly. Vermont NET officials believe their future is based on the competitive marketplace, and no matter what regulators do, competitive and technological forces will win out.[22]

Another study committee, the Vermont Seminar on Education, reported to the legislature in December of 1986. Its study of a state educational network was partially funded by business and industry, including NET, Associated Industries of Vermont (a manufacturers' trade group), IBM, several manufacturers, and an electric power company. The group recommended that Vermont develop the specifications for an integrated video, voice, and data telecommunications network to meet a wide variety of needs, using existing telecommunications facilities and incorporating the capacity for future expansion.[23] The Telecommunications Commission supported the use of telecommunications to make education more widely available and to "demonstrate the state's commitment to a strong job training program."[24]

In 1986 the Telecommunications Study Committee was created by the legislature to review Vermont's telecommunications laws and evaluate their ability to protect universal service and react to the competitive environment in a timely manner. The joint legislative committee was chaired by Senator Philip Hoff, who is a former governor of the state. The Telecommunications Study Committee took testimony from providers, consumers, regulators, and planners. Its recommendations, forwarded to the General Assembly in January 1987, are in two parts, to the state as telecommunications user and to the state as telecommunications regulator.[25]

In assessing the first question, the committee heard from various state agencies involved in telecommunications planning. These included the Agency of Development and Community Affairs, Governor's Office of Policy Research and Coordination, Vermont Purchasing Department, Department of Education, Council of State Planning Associations, and the Vermont State College System. The committee found that, while the industry does extensive telecommunications planning, the public sector has not adequately considered state telecommunications needs. It concluded that telecommunications could improve state efficiency in the delivery of services and improve the state's educational system. The committee recommended that the legislature form a study committee on improving state telecommunications efficiency and that all agencies make five- and ten-year plans on telecommunications needs.

The committee concluded that telecommunications service is an important factor in economic development in Vermont. Its report notes that many telecommunications- dependent industries are not location-specific, and may choose to locate in a state that offers the type of lifestyle Vermont does. "These industries need to be informed that new technology may be available to them only in so far as it comports with state planning goals."[26] Legislators also expressed frustration with what they saw as the inadequacies of the present regulatory system to deal with growing competition and the threat to affordable basic service.

Proposed legislation based on the social contract principle was included in the report. The committee expressed two goals for the legislation:

1. Basic telephone service should be available to everyone in Vermont at prices that are affordable to anyone with an income above the poverty level. Those below the poverty level should receive enough assistance to enable them to obtain and keep basic telephone service. Basic telephone service includes a telephone connected to the public network.

2. Vermont should have a publicly accessible telecommunications network that employs the best available and affordable technology. The basic

and advanced services of this network should be available at reasonable prices subject to state planning and goals.[27]

After extensive hearings in House and Senate committees, S.114, introduced by Senator Hoff, was passed into law in June of 1987. S.114 allows DPS and any LEC[28] to negotiate a contract, to be approved by the PSB, regarding provision of basic local service and the elimination of rate of return regulation. An alternative provision allows the PSB to loosen some regulatory oversight of the company based on a determination of competitiveness in markets, regardless of whether the contract is adopted or not.

S.114 consists of three basic policy directions: (1) protect reasonable cost and superior quality of basic local service by permitting the state to enter into a contract with providers; (2) provide benefits of competition through a contract or by reducing or suspending regulation; and (3) strengthen the state's role in telecommunications planning.[29]

The proposed contract is an attempt to balance the goal of universal service with the encouragement of competitive telecommunications markets. Rates and service quality criteria for basic local service are to be guaranteed for the life of the contract, a schedule of plant and equipment modernization is set to maintain network quality, rates and terms for competitor access to the local network are to be set, and many regulatory requirements, including rate of return regulation, are eliminated.

The PSB must approve the contract negotiated by DPS and NET before it takes effect. The statute requires the board to hold hearings and make a determination based on several factors, including whether the agreement is in the public interest, whether the terms and rates negotiated are reasonable, and whether the risk of cross-subsidization between services is addressed.

There is another provision in S.114 that is outside the scope of the social contract and could apply if the social contract is not ultimately approved. With regard to competitive services, the PSB would hold a hearing to determine whether a competitive market exists for a service. In determining whether the market is competitive the PSB must look at whether barriers to entry exist, whether any provider has power to control prices, and whether the public will benefit from competition at least as much as it did under regulation. It must also be assured that the monopoly carrier does not afford itself any special privileges in offering competitive services on the local network. If these competitive conditions exist, the PSB may reduce or suspend any regulatory requirements regarding the service. However, the board retains the ability to reinstate regulation if conditions change.

The Department of Public Service is also responsible for preparing a ten-year plan for state telecommunications policy. The plan must look at state growth and development and must be based on a survey of residents and businesses to determine needs, an assessment of the network itself, and an evaluation of local measured service. The plan must take into account "the need for basic service at affordable rates, improved competition among providers, the needs of the state as user of telecommunications services, and future development of the state."[30]

Finally, the legislation calls for monitoring of the contract by the DPS, which is to report to the legislature. A contract advocate, appointed by the attorney general, is to represent the interests of the public and the state in general during the PSB in hearings on contract approval.

McCarren, originator of the social contract idea, praised the legislation: "[Vermonters] are going to get rate stabilization and fixed, basic exchange rates that are very moderate. The state will be opened up to new technology."[31] The new law is also predicted to be good news for stockholders. Investment analysts at Argus Research Corporation call the social contract "a positive regulatory decision" because it "calls for deregulation of all services categories except basic local service . . . [and] will allow New England Telephone to retain 100% of its telephone rates."[32] Page Montgomery, a consultant on economics and technology, disagrees. Montgomery says NET would have upgraded its central offices to electronic switching even without the legislation. More important, he adds, the costs of providing telephone service are falling, and it is inappropriate to cap rates; rather, rates should be lowered.

> You don't have to be any big-time expert to see that the carriers are laying off people or are reducing their work forces by attrition. New investment in digital switching and fiber optics is cheaper by unit, and in most telephone jurisdictions, business is booming.

Montgomery also predicts that, because Vermont is a small, rural state, the social contract legislation will have little impact on larger, industrialized states.[33]

The social contract approach involves an elimination of traditional rate of return regulation. Under the price cap negotiated in the most recent version of the contract, residential consumers would be assured of no rate increases through the life of the contract. Yet the theory is that the company will have the incentive to manage its operations more efficiently, as any efficiency gains would be retained as profits. There are historical reasons for rate of return regulation of utilities, one being that a monopoly has the power to reap excessive profits when the public has no alternative. The new statute expresses a desire to both protect basic local exchange service and to provide the benefits of advances in telecommunications to Vermont residents.

TELECOMMUNICATIONS AND ECONOMIC DEVELOPMENT
Public Initiatives

Although telecommunications policymaking in Vermont is relatively sophisticated, economic development goals have not been major priorities. This is in part due to the confusion which surrounds the concept of economic development. The concept provokes a variety of interpretations, even in a state as small as Vermont. It is also in part due to the state's recent interest, since divestiture, in using telecommunications as a cost-saving and efficiency-producing tool. The VTA is one such initiative. The VTA has been viewed as a method of streamlining the state regulatory structure in a way that is hoped to provide economic incentives. These incentives, in turn, could stimulate economic activity while at the same time keeping basic phone service affordable. Another initiative, which is gaining visibility through Vermont Interactive Video, is state promotion of telecommunications technology for education. Finally, recognition of significant cost savings is forcing the state government to make better use of its own network facilities. In the process the state may become the leader in bringing new technology to rural areas of the state. The following sections examine each of these initiatives in detail and concludes with a discussion of perceptions concerning the linkages between economic development and telecommunications in Vermont.

Vermont Telecommunications Agreement (VTA)

The VTA was not proposed merely to streamline the regulatory process. It was equally important to policymakers to encourage growth in the competitive areas of the telecommunications industry and provide economic guarantees and incentives to particular groups. For Tarrant, who had primary responsibility for negotiating the terms of the contract for the public, guaranteeing that basic local service and MTS do not subsidize competitive ventures is a primary concern. The position of DPS in contract negotiations was not to thwart competitiveness in the industry, to the contrary. Tarrant believes that regulation is a poor substitute for competition and that the state should take advantage of any chance to promote competition. Not only is competition in the telecommunications industry desirable, it is inevitable. In Tarrant's view, the contract does not attempt to stifle that competition, but allows it to occur while protecting basic subscribers, both business and residential, and new competitors.[34]

Because of changes in federal telecommunications policy and unique features of the Vermont economy, Tarrant and McCarren saw the VTA as a necessity. In 1982 the FCC changed the method it used to allocate nontraffic-sensitive (NTS) costs between interstate and intrastate services. The FCC formula, called the Subscriber Plant Factor (SPF), had been determined on a state-by-state basis prior to 1982. Like other rural states, Vermont has a fairly high proportion of out-of-state calls. As a result, the share of NTS costs attributed to out-of-state calls (43 percent) was much higher than the national average (26 percent); thus, 43 percent of the fixed costs of Vermont's telephone system were paid by charges to interstate carriers. In 1984 the FCC had established a single fixed percentage for every state of 25 percent for allocating NTS costs, to be phased in over an eight-year period. Immediate imposition of the new policy in Vermont would have meant a cost shift of approximately $11 million to $13 million annually to basic service, which would have translated into an increase of $6 per month per subscriber.[35]

Under the version of the VTA, negotiated in November 1987, basic local rates for access to dial tone were to be capped at current levels until 1990, at which time prices could have increased by 35 cents per month (residential) and one dollar per month (business). In 1991 prices could have increased by the same amount. Usage rates for residential business customers in exchanges with local measured service are currently 2.0 cents per minute for peak hours and 0.5 cent for off-peak hours. In 1990 the peak rate could have increased by 0.25 cent to 2.25 cents, which would have been the ceiling rate through 1991. Off-peak rates would have remained fixed. Rates for services related to basic service could also have increased during the term of the contract. For example, during 1990 and 1991 Touch Tone rates could be increased up to 20 percent; private line rates up to 15 percent; and directory assistance by approximately 50 percent.[36]

Additionally, items which presumably will not change under the revised contract include a variety of packages that permit business and residential customers to purchase a block of minutes of use at a discount. There is also a maximum usage charge, which is set so that "no customer will be charged in excess of the usage charges incurred by customers in the 95th percentile of the local usage distribution."[37]

Based on a model of projected earnings developed by NET and modified by DPS and NET, the company will have a shortfall of approximately $11.3 million by 1991. Gene Laber, consultant to DPS, maintains that this estimate is conservative and that "in the absence of the Contract, there is a very high probability that future rate cases filed by NET will seek most or all of an additional revenue requirement from basic local service."[38] Under the contract approximately $5 million of the additional revenue requirement could be collected from basic rates during the course of the contract. If Laber is correct in predicting a minimum shortfall of $11.3 million for NET, one might be justified in asking what is in it for the company. According to NET, its advantages will come from increased pricing and marketing flexibility and freedom from rate of return regulation, which sets limits on profit levels. The company has declined to say what new services it plans to offer under the contract until the PSB approves the VTA.[39] Although the company does not name likely new services, it stresses they are in the offing. In testimony before the board, NET says the contract will allow it to "package, price and promote products and services in a more direct relationship with its customers, to meet the marketplace demand."[40]

The original agreement also permitted a 10 percent increase in MTS over the term of the contract, although the increase could not take effect until 1991. Laber has argued that it is "unlikely" that NET would attempt to recoup the remaining revenue requirement from this source in view of the fact that "MTS rates in Vermont are quite high relative to AT&T's interstate rates for comparable distances."[41]

Advocates of the social contract approach hope that, in addition to maintaining low basic local rates, the VTA will stimulate competition and development of new services. Under the original contract, all NET services are grouped into three categories under the contract: basic local services, price-constrained related services, and unconstrained related services. Although basic local services are fully regulated, as described above, the other two categories provide NET with increased marketing flexibility. Unconstrained related services, which would be fully deregulated after 1989, include custom calling and listing. In addition, NET was free to offer new services immediately. Price-constrained related services would be partially deregulated; these include MTS, WATS, private lines, Centrex, directory assistance, and Touch Tone service. Controls placed on these services were designed to give NET some flexibility while still offering some basic protection to its competitors. For example, NET was required to maintain a 20 percent differential between MTS and WATS service rates. This is meant to be a safeguard to resellers of NET's WATS service. [42]

The contract advocate and the competitive intrastate carriers, US Sprint and Long Distance North, along with future competitors AT&T and MCI, believe the contract will stifle emerging competition in Vermont. The public advocate characterizes competition as the "core of the agreement" and believes the contract is fundamentally flawed in this respect as "NET essentially admits in its direct case that the Company has a dominant and relatively stable position in the nominally competitive intrastate toll market."[43] More startling to the advocate is the "escape clause" written into the contract, which allows NET to unilaterally terminate the VTA if intrastate equal access is mandated by regulators.[44]

Contract opponents identify NET's ability to control access and repackage existing services as new offerings, thereby avoiding the price caps as the primary threats to competition. The competitors and the contract advocate object to the loose definition of new services allowed under the contract. NET would be allowed to package or "bundle" existing services and bypass the contract's pricing restrictions. In their view the new services provision along with NET's control of access combine to strangle competition in Vermont.

The crux of the issue is that the other intrastate carriers are both customers and competitors of NET. As customers, these companies purchase intrastate access from NET in order to provide their competitive services. As the other carriers point out, there is no alternative provider of access and other monopoly services; NET has monopoly control over the bottleneck facilities and, as a competitor, has every incentive to use that control over the bottleneck to its advantage. The carriers' concerns regarding access boil down to three: the VTA is not clear on whether access rates can be increased under the contract; the VTA is not clear on whether introduction of an end-user access charge or similar charge is allowed; and NET has nearly unlimited ability to gain a competitive advantage by bundling monopoly services with competitive services.

Nina Cornell, an economist testifying for MCI, illustrates the potential abuse given NET's dual role as supplier and competitor. Cornell predicts NET will be able to set up competitors in a "price squeeze." In a price squeeze, "NET charges a high wholesale price for a bottleneck monopoly service that a potential competitor might purchase, and then sets a low retail price to customers for their own [competitive] services using an equivalent bottleneck."[45] AT&T offers another example. NET sells both Centrex and PBX trunk lines. Since Centrex and PBX are substantially similar, NET can gain a competitive advantage by pricing Centrex lines at a lower rate than for PBX use.[46]

NET and DPS have negotiated a 20 percent differential between the toll (MTS and WATS) rate and the average premium access charge to protect competitors. However, because the differential is based on an average, there is nothing prohibiting NET from setting some access rates high and others low in order to gain a competitive advantage.

Although NET and DPS predict NET will have an $11.3 million revenue requirement by the end of the contract, MCI's Cornell predicts NET will earn $14.8 million in excess of its projected revenue requirement over the term of the contract.[47] The contract advocate, whose duty is to represent consumers, says consumers and other users do not gain from the contract. Although the term price freeze is often used, basic rates will actually increase $5 million over the life of the contract:

> [The contract] does not justify the price levels and price caps as reasonable in the context of a more open system of regulation. Rather, it starts with the rates for existing services under traditional rate base/rate of return regulation and justified the Agreement by reference to a five year projection similar to the test-year concepts employed in traditional regulation.[48]

US Sprint argues that the social contract is premised on flawed theory because it assumes that rates for basic local service are set at cost.[49] The advocate and most competitors agree that the contract is not drawn in such a way as to prevent NET from subsidizing interexchange services with excess revenues from basic services. The same fear was not expressed by Long

Distance North president Mitch Knisbacher, who agrees with Laber that usage rates are set very close to marginal cost.[50] (This means that the cost of providing an additional unit of service is equal to the market price.)

US Sprint and Long Distance North have an additional concern, service quality to resellers. Long Distance North cites an instance in which NET took 18 months to provide it with a requested service.[51] It points out that the VTA's quality control oversight procedures will treat all consumer complaints with equal weight. As a result, "failure to repair an entire hunt group of access lines--possibly 50, 100, or more circuits--serving 100's or 1000's of long distance customers, is treated the same as the failure to repair a single residential local loop."[52]

Apparently, the PSB agreed at least in part with the critics of the VTA. On July 12, 1988, the Vermont Public Service Board rejected the Vermont Telecommunications Agreement. They accepted the general notion of the contract but found some of the terms deficient. According to Communications Daily, PSB indicated that it would be willing to reconsider the proposal if the following terms were included:[53]

1. The price freeze should remain in effect throughout the term of the contract with no increases permitted in 1990 or 1991.
2. NET should stick to the original $284 million proposal for modernization of the network rather than the $250 million proposed more recently during PSB hearings held in the spring of 1988,
3. The originally proposed 20 percent differential between toll rates for NET intrastate toll and access rates for interexchange carriers for toll should be raised to 33.3 percent.
4. NET should be prohibited from bundling price-capped basic services with new products or services.
5. NET should provide free blocking of 976 services.
6. More information should be available to consumers about new services that are similar to existing price-capped services.

Subsequent to the PSB decision, NET and DPS renegotiated the VTA, which was resubmitted to the PSB in September of 1988. According to Telecommunications Reports, the

> renegotiated plan has been reduced from five years to three and one-half, and New England Tel has agreed not to raise rates during the term of the contract. The telco also agreed to eliminate a provision that would have allowed it to raise basic service rates if an economic downturn or other unforeseen events dramatically affected earnings. Other changes, the company said, address concerns "such as the need for consumer information about rates for regulated products and consumer control in blocking unwanted services."[54]

Education and Telecommunications

Vermont has recently completed the first link in what may soon be a statewide educational video network. Vermont Interactive Video, which links Vermont Technical College with a vocational center in Newport, the most rural section of the state, is a pilot project of the Governor's Telecommunications Oversight Committee. The purpose of the project is to determine the feasibility of educational video for extending access to educational user groups throughout the state.

The video project is the culmination of four years of planning and feasibility studies. Since 1984, a series of working groups, consultants, and commissions have been conducting needs assessments and feasibility studies. The first study was funded by IBM in order to "examine the feasibility of a telecommunications link between VTC (Vermont Technical College) and IBM campuses."[55]

The report concluded that instructional television was both methodologically effective and technologically feasible.[56] Based on that assessment, the governor formed the Vermont Seminar on Education working group to study the feasibility of a statewide educational network. After an initial meeting during the summer of 1985, the group proposed three preliminary goals to be completed by 1990:

1. An appropriate telecommunications system between and among primary/secondary education, vocational education, higher education, business and industry;

2. A telecommunications policy providing Vermont with the capability to respond to existing and future educational needs;

3. A telecommunications system that is accessible within 25 miles of 90 percent of all Vermonters in order to ensure that no person is disadvantaged by his or her place of residence.[57]

A follow-up study by the same group, completed in December 1986, identified three categories of users for an educational network: business and industry; primary, secondary, and vocational education; and higher education. The Vermont Seminar concluded that a strong demand existed for technical training of employees of large corporations such as IBM, General Electric, and Vermont Yankee Nuclear Power Corporation. These corporations and others have repeatedly expressed their concern about their ability to attract or retrain a skilled work force with existing local educational facilities. In the area of higher education the report concluded that "inter-institutional exchange of coursework would allow for more efficient utilization and less duplication of college faculties."[58] For primary, secondary, and vocational schools the report identified two areas of need: the lack of teacher training at the master's level; and the lack of upper-level courses for low-enrollment rural schools.[59] A telecommunications link to the state's 16 regional vocational centers would ensure that 90 percent of the population would be within 25 miles of a facility.

Provision of a statewide network will depend in part on the success of the pilot program that connects Vermont Technical College in Randolph Center with the North Country Area Vocational Center in Newport, a town on the Canadian border. The current network uses a technology called compressed video. Although inferior in quality to broadcast video (rapid movements become blurred), compressed video can be transmitted interactively (i.e., affording two-way communication) over T-1 circuits at much lower cost.[60]

Satellite transmission is also being considered for classes that do not require interactive video. For example, satellite earth stations in remote sites could be used in combination with a two-way audio link at a relatively low cost. Earth stations can also be used to receive out-of-state educational broadcasts. It is very likely that a combination of both technologies will eventually be used.

A telecommunications consultant hired by the state has calculated that a statewide educational network, including facilities, technicians, and maintenance, could be provided over a six-year period at a cost of approximately $10.8 million. Annual operation and maintenance costs after the system is installed would be approximately $2 million. The system would include 16 regional T-1 sites, similar to the current demonstration project at Newport, and satellite receive-only sites at all of Vermont's 425 elementary and secondary schools.[61]

The decision for or against a statewide educational video system will depend in part on the success of Vermont Interactive Video and the perceived benefits in relation to total costs. Should Vermont choose to proceed with tele-education, it could be the state's most explicit and dramatic link between telecommunications and economic development.

State Government as User

The Governor's Telecommunications Oversight Committee, in addition to examining the potential for a statewide video network, had responsibility for examining the government's use of telecommunications. A telecommunications consultant hired by the committee inventoried the government network and concluded that it could save $450,000 per year through more efficient use.[62] The basic problem is that the government, with all its separate agencies, operates as if the telecommunications market were still regulated. In the past, state agencies went separately to the phone company for their telecommunications needs. As NET's largest user, the state could not have bypassed the public network without having a negative impact on basic rates to the general public. However, with the advent of the VTA and price cap regulation, NET would have to absorb the cost of the state leaving the network to any significant degree.

The consultant, Federal Engineering, calculated that the state could save $750,000 per year by coordinating purchases and contracts and by using the full capacity of the state-owned microwave system. In order to achieve these cost reductions, it will be necessary to restructure and increase the Office of Telecommunications staff, currently 4, to a total of 12 at a cost of $300,000 per year. Net savings would equal $450,000 per year.

A little over 70 percent of the savings to the state would come from just two recommended changes. One would be to implement digital service in Montpelier. Currently government offices in Montpelier are connected by an analog Centrex system located in the NET central office. Federal Engineering estimates that by renegotiating a contract for digital Centrex from NET or purchasing its own digital PBX through competitive bid, the state could save $200,000 per year and get better service.

The second change leading to substantial savings would come from greater use of the state microwave system. The system was built 30 years ago for use by the state police. It is an analog system now used for voice, data, and two-way radio communication primarily by the Department of Public Safety and the Agency of Transportation. Because of upgrades to the system, its capacity far exceeds its use. Of 480 circuits only 110 are being used. Transforming high-use portions of the network to a digital system were also recommended. Using this system wherever possible would save the state $350,000 per year.

Other cost-saving recommendations of the consultant include implementing digital service for the Health Department ($50,000), installing a communications link in Montpelier ($1,320), challenging an existing NET tariff ($48,000), and improving system management in Waterbury ($104,000).

Governor Kunin has accepted the consultant's recommendation to centralize state telecommunications in an expanded Telecommunications Division. In January 1988 she proposed a budget that included funds to expand the division by 7 employees (i.e., 4 to 11). Some of the other recommendations are already being implemented and showing concrete results. Hale Irwin, manager of the Telecommunications Division, has seen cost savings in the coordination of purchase, installation, and repair of equipment. Efficiencies in both time and money have come from the use of statewide data bases for budget planning and general purchasing and in linking human services field offices to a central office.

Private Initiatives

Although all the major telecommunications initiatives in Vermont have been undertaken by the state, the private sector has played an important role in all of them. All the commissions, work groups, and committees, with the exception of the General Assembly's Telecommunications Study Committee, that have taken up the issue of telecommunications policy have had many private-sector representatives. Private-sector firms have provided financial support to some of these telecommunications studies. One report, the Vermont Seminar on Education, which recommended a statewide educational network, was funded from private contributions. Another report, examining the feasibility of a VTC-IBM educational video link between Vermont Technical College and IBM, was funded by IBM after the college failed to secure grant funds from the Department of Commerce for a similar project.

Private-sector enthusiasm for public initiatives is primarily limited to services that the private sector is not willing to provide on its own (e.g., education of the labor force). There is less interest in state planning or oversight of the public network. For the moment, the state's concern with the public network, expressed through the VTA, is limited to assuring that NET maintains its existing modernization schedule, service quality, and rate structure. Although S.114 also includes provisions for government oversight of public network planning, there appears to be little private-sector interest in that particular function. NET in particular objects to any interference in what it considers to be its responsibility.

PERCEPTIONS OF ECONOMIC DEVELOPMENT

A wide variety of opinion exists in Vermont about the connections between telecommunications and economic development. Legislators and other policymakers, at one end of the spectrum, tend to see a close link between the two. At the other end are the skeptics, who tend to be individuals in private industry and staff-level public employees. In between the two extremes are individuals who see telecommunications as of marginal importance to the economic development of the state.

Policymakers point to telecommunications as an important aspect of the state's infrastructure. Telecommunications is seen as vital to development of the state's social and governmental services. Video networking is considered the most cost-effective method of providing job training to otherwise inaccessible parts of the state. A state educational network will help to provide specialized services that will increase educational quality at all levels. Creation of an Office of Telecommunications will allow more effective delivery of governmental services at lower cost. In the process, policymakers maintain, these improvements will demonstrate new technologies to small businesses; create demand for telecommunication services, encouraging the phone company to upgrade the system; and demonstrate to companies outside the state that Vermont has a strong commitment to telecommunications.

In contrast, those not as involved in the policy process view telecommunications as one of the less important elements in the infrastructure hierarchy. When private-sector representatives and government officials were questioned about what companies consider most important in deciding whether to locate in the state, the items at the top were always cost of labor, job skills of the work force, and transportation. An economist at the Agency for Development and Community Affairs, an agency that provides assistance to firms interested in locating to Vermont, knew of only one company that had expressed an interest in the quality of the telephone service. The telecommunications system of the state is most often simply taken for granted.

This difference of perception is partly attributable to how one defines economic development and how one views the causal relationship between infrastructure and growth, given the economy of the state. Some, businesses in particular, feel that economic development creates the demand for infrastructure. Policymakers, on the other hand, tend to see infrastructure as a necessary ingredient that needs to be anticipated: economic development is in a sense an uncertain endeavor that should be nurtured.

This is not a strict dichotomy between public sector and private sector, nor are the lines clearly drawn. Gene Laber, the DPS consultant on telecommunications and an advocate of the VTA, expressed the view that economic activity creates the demand for infrastructure and not the other way around.[63] In a similar vein, DPS commissioner Gerry Tarrant feels that upgrade of the public network would have occurred even without the incentive of the social contract.[64] For most people in the private sector, telecommunications infrastructure is simply something that the telephone companies provide as needs arise.

Vermont makes a strong implicit link between telecommunications and economic development. References are frequently made to economic development in the reports of commissions and committees dealing specifically with telecommunications. But Vermont does not have a state economic development plan or any other official document in which an explicit connection is made. The document closest to a state plan is the recently completed report of the Governor's Commission on Vermont's Future.[65] Explicit references to telecommunications are noticeably absent. Implicit references, however, do exist. One in particular is an economic development guideline, which states: "Access to educational and vocational training opportunities must be available to all Vermonters sufficient to ensure the full realization of their abilities."[66] This would seem to acknowledge implicitly the Vermont Seminar on Education working group's recommendation to plan and implement a statewide telecommunications transmission network for integrating educational video.

However, actions speak louder than words. Telecommunications activity on the part of the state seems to mock official policy documents that lack explicit recognition of telecommunications in the state's future. Given current trends and the high level of interest in telecommunications in Vermont, it may just be a matter of time before the state makes an explicit policy link between telecommunications and economic development.

CONCLUSIONS

Most states have identified the inadequacies of using the traditional regulatory tools developed during the early years of this century now that telecommunications utilities operate in both monopolistic and competitive markets. Vermont has chosen to meet the challenge by setting aside the old ways (although keeping them in the wings to be reinstated if needed) and crafting new instruments. These new tools are designed to achieve a balance between the social goal of universal service and the economic (and perhaps political) goal of unfettered competition. Furthermore, the state is attempting to take control of its own telecommunications usage and harness the technology in such a way as to make its own operations more efficient and its services more widely available. Finally, and as importantly, the state has made the explicit assumption that economic development will follow from each of these initiatives.

How successful Vermont's telecommunications initiatives will be remains to be seen. Based on this review of the state's telecommunications policy, three broad themes emerge. The first is quite obvious, the social contract idea is a controversial one. Although the VTA is the product of much thought and consensus, there is no general agreement that the tools developed here will indeed achieve the state's goals. Second, there is a general consensus that the social contract approach is not easily transferable to other states. Even if all the VTA's goals are successfully met, this new regulatory tool may be unique to Vermont. A link is seen between telecommunications and state activities, including the delivery of services and education. This indirect link is the only identifiable one established between telecommunications and economic activity.

Controversy of the Social Contract

Although Vermont's statute is the product of a long and thoughtful process that included much study, debate, and compromise, there are still many, particularly consumer advocates and BOC competitors, who believe the state will fall far short of its goals, particularly its goal of fair treatment of basic ratepayers and its desire to link telecommunications with economic development. Others see Vermont in the vanguard, cutting a path through the jungle of utility rules, regulations, and statutes so broad that telecommunications-dependent business will stream into the Green Mountain State.

Both the state's own efficiency vis-a-vis telecommunications and the lure of business development in a state with high quality-of-life factors were important goals of the joint legislative study committee. Senator Hoff, chair of the committee, chose other committee members based on their existing beliefs that telecommunications and economic development could be linked to benefit Vermont. Hoff himself sees telecommunications as essential to the growth and development of a state like Vermont, which places a strong emphasis on controlled growth. Secondly, he believes that education is crucial to the economic well-being of any state and that telecommunications is necessary to extend the reach of the educational system.[67]

The question facing Vermont is whether the contract approach and price caps in particular are the appropriate means of protecting the public interest. Today many BOCs are asking state regulators, and AT&T is asking the FCC, to eliminate rate of return regulation. The companies believe this type of regulation hinders their ability to introduce new services and technologies quickly and to otherwise respond to the market through rates, services, and promotions.

On the other hand, consumer groups and many large users argue that current rates for basic local service are already much too high. Price caps and automatic adjustments only set in concrete rates that are already unjustified. Not only is telecommunications a declining-cost industry, but current rates reflect cost allocation schemes that may allocate fixed costs disproportionately to monopoly services. Critics also charge that regulatory reform does not automatically correlate to elimination of rate of return regulation and to imposition of price caps.

Competitors to the LEC find even more fault with the social contract. As mentioned above, NET's competitors see many loopholes that they feel will cause basic rates to rise nonetheless. This ability ro raise rates increases the likelihood of cross-subsidy, something the contract attempts to avoid. Furthermore, the competitors are not satisfied that they will be given fair access to NET's network and that they can be assured of high-quality interconnections. The general sentiment seems to be that the contract will be most successful at entrenching NET as the dominant telecommunications provider in Vermont.

Applicability to Other States

No one involved in the formation of the VTA or its enabling legislation feels that Vermont's social contract initiative can be picked up and copied by other states. Indeed, when asked about applying social contracts to other states, most players emphasized Vermont's unique situation in regard to telecommunications, including the SPF factor, LMS, and intraLATA competition, as making such a contract more applicable in their state.

NET officials are understandably reluctant to predict whether the social contract idea will move to other states. Even Senator Hoff, a strong supporter of the idea, admits there is great potential for abuse of social contracts. Because Vermont is such a small state, there is little chance for abuse that would not be brought immediately to the public's attention. Hoff fears other state regulators may be "captured" by the industry they are charged with regulating and approve a contract that favors the LEC rather than balances the needs of the LEC, users, and competitors.

Louise McCarren has done much to popularize the social contract, yet she does not view it as the ultimate response to competition in telecommunications. It is just one of many ideas states may use when they find their current laws inadequate to deal with the market. The idea worked especially well in Vermont because of the openness and manageability of the political process. Yet she emphasizes the contract is just one part of Vermont's total policy package, including LMS, Lifeline, and open entry.

The concern remains that any success Vermont may have will cause other BOCs to push less balanced social contracts through their state legislatures, and the integrity of the idea will be lost.

State as User and Planner and Economic Development

In contrast to perceptions on general state economic development, almost all players agree that there are clear links between use of telecommunications and the state's own efficiency, and there is concrete evidence of such a link. As discussed above, the consultant's report estimates the state can make further improvements based on telecommunications usage and earn a net savings of approximately $450,000 a year for each of the next five years. That is a total savings of $2.4 million, which is more than 16 times the total cost of the recommended planning program.

The VTC interactive video system is another concrete link between telecommunications and economic prosperity. Many demonstration projects have shown the economic and social value of using telecommunications to extend educational and other services into rural or underdeveloped areas. Vermont's investment in the interactive video link and other similar projects that enhance education and state delivery of services will net clear, identifiable payoffs that will benefit the general public as well as businesses in their capacity as taxpayers and in their needs for a well-trained work force.

In only one respect is there disagreement about the state's role as user and planner. Senator Hoff added an amendment to the legislation that requires the state to survey all telecommunications users in the public and private sectors and forecast the state's needs for the next ten years. Many in the industry and in state government believe there should be no intermingling of public and private planning. The consensus seems to be that the industry has done a good job at planning its own network and that government planning of the public network is unwarranted. Only the state has fallen short in planning for its own needs.

Although it is a small, rural state, Vermont has adopted an aggressive approach to telecommunications policy. Vermont regulators have a history of facing issues directly, and the state has taken steps which lawmakers hope will accentuate the benefits of competition in telecommunications while minimizing the drawbacks. At the same time, the state is taking an active role in telecommunications planning and utilization. Although at this time Vermont has not written telecommunications policy into an overall state economic development plan, that connection has been made by the public and private sector, and, as a result, policy-planning agencies are beginning that implementation. Vermonters have embraced the notion that a modern, innovative telecommunications infrastructure is linked to economic development as well as to the efficient operation of state government.

Yet Vermont must be cautious. Except for education and other state-delivered services, any links between telecommunications and economic development are largely based on rhetoric. Vermont may be taking drastic action that will net little of the intended payoff. Critics of the social contract idea may be proven correct in their fears that residential ratepayers are not fully protected and that NET has been given too free a rein.

It is not only Vermont that must be cautious. A successful VTA that brings growth to the state while winning the approval of residential ratepayers will draw attention to the social contract approach. In fact, price caps and other versions of the social contract are already being discussed in other states.

The VTA is the product of much study and debate. It is crafted to address Vermont's specific needs, such as SPF and a highly rural population. It also follows several policy decisions that are also unique to the state, such as mandatory LMS and intraLATA competition. Although other states are grappling with many of the same changes in their telecommunications markets, these new tools forged by policymakers in Vermont may be inappropriate, or even detrimental, to the social and economic goals of other states.

NOTES

1.   U.S. Bureau of the Census, State and Metropolitan Area Data Book, 1986 (Washington, D.C.: U.S. Government Printing Office, 1986), Table C, p. 546.

2.   State of Vermont, Office of Policy Research and Coordination, New England Economic Project Forecast, prepared by Michael Wilson (Montpelier, November 1987), p. 2.

3.   "Kunin Calls for Action on Growth," Burlington Free Press, January 13, 1988, p. 1.

4.   Argus Research Corporation, NYNEX Corporation: Investment Analysis, vol. 12, no. 54 (August 31, 1987), p. 1.

5.   Correspondence with Michael Dworkin, Communications Counsel, Vermont Public Service Board, Montpelier, March 20, 1988.

6.   Telephone interview with Tom Mills, Manager of Public Affairs, New England Telephone-Vermont, Burlington, October 7, 1987.

7.   Correspondence with Dworkin.

8.   Telephone interview with Louise McCarren, former chair of the Vermont Public Service Board, Burlington, December 3, 1987.

9.   The other two current board members are Rosalyn Hunnenman and Suzanne Rude.

10.   State of Vermont, Department of Public Service, Biennial Report of the Department of Public Service (Montpelier, June 30, 1984), pp. v-vi.

11.   State of Vermont, General Assembly, Report of the Telecommunications Study Committee (Montpelier, January 1987), p. 2.

12.   "Time to Grow Up: Chairman McCarren to leave Vermont Public Service Board," Communications Daily, February 11, 1987, p. 5.

13.   "A Pay Phone in Every Home," Consumer Reports, May 1986, p. 305.

14.   Vermont Public Service Board, Docket No. 4946, In Reference to Petition of Burlington Telephone to the Vermont Public Service Board, Order of February 21, 1986, p. 4.

15.   Ibid., p. 66.

16.   Louise McCarren and Michael H. Dworkin, "State Regulators, State Competitors," The New Telecommunications Era, ed. Herbert Forest and Richard Wiley (New York: Practicing Law Institute, 1985), p. 178.

17.   Ibid., p. 180.

18.   Letter from Michael Dworkin, Communications Counsel, Vermont Public Service Board, to Bill Mares, Vermont State Representative, June 1987.

19.   Ibid.

20.   Interview with Gerald Tarrant, Commissioner, Vermont Department of Public Service, Montpelier, January 14, 1988.

21.   Letter from Michael Dworkin, Communications Counsel to the Vermont Public Service Board, to Bill Mares, Vermont State Representative, June 1987.

22.   Interview with Brian Welsh, Director of Rates and Tariffs, New England Telephone-Vermont, Burlington, January 11, 1988.

23.   Vermont Seminar on Education, "An Educational Telecommunications Transmission Network for Vermont," Montpelier, December 1986.

24.   Ibid., p. 49.

25. State of Vermont, General Assembly, Telecommunications Study Committee, Report of the Telecommunications Study Committee (Montpelier, January 15, 1987).

26. Ibid., p. 2.

27. Ibid., p. 10.

28. To date only NET has negotiated a contract with the DPS.

29. State of Vermont, General Assembly, An Act Relating to Regulation of the Telecommunications Industry (Montpelier, 1987), pp. 2-3.

30. Ibid., p. 3.

31. Michael Fahey, "Vermont OKs Vast Deregulation," Network World, June 15, 1987.

32. Argus Research Corporation, NYNEX Corporation Investment Analysis, p. 4.

33. Michael Fahey, "Vermont OKs Vast Deregulation," Network World, June 15, 1987, p. 5.

34. Interview with Tarrant.

35. Gene Laber, University of Vermont Professor of Business Administration, Prefiled Direct Testimony, testimony submitted to the Vermont Public Service Board Re: Vermont Telecommunications Agreement, Montpelier, 1988, p. 33.

36. Ibid., p. 18.

37. Nina Cornell, MCI Telecommunications Corporation, Direct Prefiled Testimony before the Vermont Public Service Board Re: Review of Telecommunications Agreement, Montpelier, February 23, 1988, p. 24.

38. Ibid.

39. Interview with Welsh.

40. Edward B. Dinan, NET&T Division Manager-Corporate Accounting, Prefiled Direct Testimony Re: Joint Petition of New England Telephone and Telegraph Company and Vermont Department of Public Service, Montpelier, October 1987, p. 24.

41. Laber, Prefiled Direct Testimony, p. 33.

42. Because we were unable to obtain a copy of the revised contract prior to publication, it is unclear to what extent the above conditions have changed, other than for freezes in basic local service, under the new contract. The discussion that follows refers to the original version of the VTA.

43. "Terms of VT. Social Contract Rejected by State Regulators," Communications Daily, July 18, 1988, p. 6.

44. "New England Tel's 'Vermont Social Contract' Renegotiated, Filed with PSB," Telecommunications Reports, September 5, 1988, p. 30.

45. Walter G. Bolter and Richard D. Huriaux, on behalf of the Public Contract Advocate, Vermont Attorney General, State of Vermont, Direct Prefiled Testimony Re: Joint Petition of New England Telephone and Telegraph Company and the Vermont Department of Public Service Requesting Approval of the Vermont Telecommunications Agreement of October 14, 1987, Montpelier, February 24, 1988, pp. 5, 6.

46. Ibid., p. 7.

47. Cornell, Direct Prefiled Testimony, p. 30.

48. Lee J. Globerson, District Manager, AT&T, Prefiled Direct Testimony Before State of Vermont Public Service Board Docket 5252, Montpelier, February 23, 1988, p. 14.

49. Cornell, Direct Prefiled Testimony, p. 5.

50. Bolter and Huriaux, Prefiled Direct Testimony, p. 3.

51.   Interview with Peter Zamore, Attorney for US Sprint, Burlington, January 14, 1988.

52.   Interview with Mitchell Knisbacher, President of Long Distance North, Burlington, January 14, 1988.

53.   Ibid.

54.   Correspondence with Mitchell Knisbacher, President of Long Distance North, Burlington, April 14, 1988.

55.   Vermont Seminar on Education, Educational Telecommunications Transmission Network for Vermont (Randolph Center, December 3, 1986), p. 1.

56.   Ibid.

57.   Ibid., p. 2.

58.   Ibid., p. 10.

59.   Ibid., p. 11.

60.   T-1 circuits are digital circuits that are widely used for intercity voice and data transmission.

61.   Federal Engineering, Inc., Vermont Telecommunications Network Report (Montpelier, December 3, 1987), Section 4.

62.   Ibid., p. ix.

63.   Interview with Gene Laber, Professor of Business Administration, University of Vermont, Burlington, January 14, 1988.

64.   Interview with Tarrant.

65.   Governor's Commission on Vermont's Future, Report of the Governor's Commission on Vermont's Future: Guidelines for Growth (Montpelier, January 1988).

66.   Ibid., p. 24.

67.   Interview with Philip Hoff, Senator, State of Vermont, Montpelier, January 15, 1988.

9

Virginia

Amy M. Korzick and Sehba Sarwar

The Commonwealth of Virginia took a seemingly drastic step in telecommunications policy when the Virginia General Assembly passed legislation enabling AT&T to set its rates competitively, effective July 1, 1984. A closer look at Virginia's economy, political climate, and policy development environment will show that the deregulation was a measured and controlled step. The deregulation of AT&T, and its subsequent effects on the telecommunications industry in, are part of an overall development policy for the state, which is supported by the staff and commissioners at the State Corporate Commission.

Virginia's readiness to deregulate AT&T can be attributed to several factors, including the expanding state economy and the political culture of the state. The Virginia economy has experienced rapid growth over the past decade, particularly in the service sector. This expansion has stimulated growth in the telecommunications industry in Virginia.

Since the time of Jefferson's warnings on unrestrained government, Virginians have traditionally been wary of heavy government interference. This sentiment remains a strong characteristic of state policy today. Aided by the fact that Virginia lacks strong consumer advocate groups, is a "right-to-work" state, and has government officials committed to the principles of competition in business, the conservative "gentlemen's approach" to business has made Virginia a model state for the study of regulatory reform.

Because Virginia was the first state to deregulate AT&T, it can be viewed as a potential test case to provide answers to the questions that currently hold AT&T under regulatory constraints in other states. Despite fears that AT&T would displace its competition in a deregulated environment, AT&T has acted with restraint, perhaps because all eyes are on Virginia. Whatever the motivations of AT&T, a state policy that promotes competition in the telecommunications industry has brought economic benefits to the industry and the state as a whole. This study will investigate the questions resulting from deregulation that now face regulators, telecommunications companies, and consumers.

Table 9.1
Nonagricultural Employment Shares and Annual
Percentage Change in Employment* for Virginia and
the United States, 1980 and 1986
(total employees in 1,000s, share and change in %)

| | Employment Shares | | | | Annual Employment Change | |
| | 1980 | | 1986 | | | |
Sector	Virginia	U.S.	Virginia	U.S.	Virginia	U.S.
Mining	23.7	1.1	16.4	0.8	-5.1	-3.9
Construction	120.2	4.9	168.1	4.9	6.6	1.6
Manufacturing	414.4	22.5	424.2	19.1	0.4	-1.1
Transportation	113.8	5.7	137.3	5.3	3.4	0.3
Wholesale & Ret. Trade	436.6	22.7	580.2	23.7	5.5	2.4
Fin., Ins., Real Estate	104.3	5.7	130.8	6.3	4.2	3.7
Services	379.0	19.6	579.0	23.1	8.8	5.0
Government	505.5	17.8	521.0	16.8	0.5	0.6
Total	20,975	90,657	25,571	99,610	3.7	1.7

* Totals may reflect rounding error.

Source: U.S. Department of Labor, Bureau of Labor Statistics, Employment and Earnings, vol. 34, no. 5 (May 1987), pp. 119-129; idem, vol. 34, no. 5 (May 1981), pp. 120-131.

THE ECONOMY AND THE TELECOMMUNICATIONS INDUSTRY
Economic Profile

Over the past decade, the Commonwealth of Virginia has enjoyed the advantages of a strong economic base: with the exception of a decrease in the mining industry, all other sectors have experienced an increase in employment (Table 9.1). This growth has created an overall economic boom in the state, further enhanced by the proximity of the national capital. In 1987 alone, over 76 manufacturing companies announced new locations in Virginia, while 79 others announced the expansion of existing firms. In this same year, 12 foreign-related manufacturing and nonmanufacturing companies announced new locations in the state, including Opton, Inc., and Raicon, Inc., leading to expectations of $48.9 million in investments.[1]

Table 9.2
Employment Shares and Annual Changes in Employment* of
Telecommunications-Intensive Businesses** for Virginia
and the United States, 1980 and 1984
(share and change in %)

| | Employment Shares | | | | Annual Employment | |
| | 1980 | | 1986 | | Change | |
	Virginia	U.S.	Virginia	U.S.	Virginia	U.S.
InformationServices	8.9	9.1	10.1	9.9	6.5	3.2
Finance	2.7	3.1	2.8	3.3	2.5	3.2
Insurance	1.7	2.3	1.7	2.3	1.0	1.0
RealEstate	1.4	1.3	1.5	1.4	3.4	1.6
Computer/DataProc.	0.9	0.4	1.4	0.6	17.0	13.1
OtherInformationServ.	2.2	2.1	2.7	2.3	12.5	4.5
InformationTechnology	1.6	2.2	1.8	2.3	7.6	2.4
Research & Development	0.5	0.3	0.5	0.3	5.3	2.9
Media	3.5	3.7	3.4	3.7	2.6	0.5

* Totals may reflect rounding error.
** The Telecommunications-Intensive Business categories are defined by Standard Industrial Classification codes as follows:
  1. Information Services: Finance: SIC 60 (Banking), SIC 61 (Credit), SIC 62 (Commodities); Insurance: SIC 63 (Insurance Carriers), SIC 64 (Insurance Agents); Real Estate: SIC 65; Computer/Data Proc.: SIC 737; Other Information Services: SIC 731 (Advertising), SIC 732 (Credit Reporting), SIC 81 (Legal Services), SIC 891 (Engineering and Architectural Services), SIC 893 (Accounting and Auditing);
  2. Information Technology Equipment: SIC 3573 (Electronic Computing Equipment), SIC 361 (Electric Distributing Equipment), SIC 365 (Radio and TV Receiving Equipment), SIC 366 (Communications Equipment), SIC 367 (Electronic Components and Accessories);
  3. Research and Development: SIC 7391 (Research and Development Laboratories), SIC 7397 (Commercial Testing Laboratories), SIC 892 (Nonprofit Education and Scientific Research Agencies);
  4. Media: SIC 27 (Printing and Publishing), SIC 48 (Communications), SIC 735 (News Syndicates), SIC 78 (Motion Pictures).

Source: U.S. Bureau of the Census, County Business Patterns, 1980 and 1984, United States (No. 1) and Virginia (No. 29) (Washington D.C.: U.S. Government Printing Office), Table 1B.

Among the companies already operating in Virginia are established names such as Reynolds Metals, Xerox Corporation, and IBM, which are headquartered in Richmond and Northern Virginia and provide employment to over several thousand individuals.

The Commonwealth of Virginia places emphasis on maintaining and increasing quality in information services. The state employment shares in these areas of growth have increased visibly since 1986 to currently exceed the employment shares in these areas on a national level (Table 9.2). Employment shares in research and development are also considerably higher than the national figures in this area of employment. While the shares for information technology and media are below the national level, Virginia's emphasis on information services and research and development can be seen in the presence of organizations such as the Center for Innovative Technology and the headquarters of national banks such as Crestar, Signet, and Sovran in Virginia. Also based in Virginia are over 100 customer premises equipment (CPE) providers, among which are NEC America, Inc., Northern Telecom, Inc., Comdial, and Rolm Corporation. The large number of such companies is reflected in the figures for the computer and data processing category (Table 9.2), in which the employment shares have not only increased by nearly 17 percent between 1980 and 1986, but are also well over double those at the national level.

Furthermore, Virginia has a large number of universities and institutions that offer technical degrees. These include the University of Virginia and Virginia Polytechnic Institute, which offer degrees in engineering and provide the state with a large number of trained technicians and engineers who are integrated within the service industry in the state. All these factors provide Virginia with a sound economic base that is growing rapidly, at a rate higher than that seen on the national level.

Telecommunications Industry

Rapid growth in the Virginia economy, especially in several telecommunications-intensive sectors, has led to a growing and innovative telecommunications industry that has become incorporated into the state's high-quality service industry. There are 20 local exchange companies (LECs) currently offering services within the state; each operates on a noncompetitive basis within certificated monopoly boundaries that are legislatively defined by the State Corporate Commission (SCC). These LECs are separated into 15 deregulated cooperatives and small investor-owned companies and 5 large companies, which are subject to regulation by the SCC.

The largest LEC providing service in Virginia is the Chesapeake and Potomac Telephone Company of Virginia (C&P), the regional Bell Operating Company (BOC), which holds nearly 80 percent of the market. C&P, a subsidiary of Bell Atlantic,[2] provides access lines to 2,227,036 business and residential customers out of a total number of 2,867,350 access lines in the entire state (Table 9.3). Continental Telephone of Virginia (Contel), the second largest LEC, provides 10 percent of the access lines and operates independently of its parent company, Continental Telephone Corporation. Central Telephone Company of Virginia (Centel) provides 6.6 percent of the access lines, while United Inter-Mountain Telephone Company owns 2.5 percent of the access lines within the state. The smallest of the five regulated LECs, General

Telephone Company of the South, owns only 1.0 percent. The remaining 15 small companies provide less than 2.5 percent, and their telephone lines vary from as few as 100 (Burke's Garden Telephone Company) to as many as 24,345 (Clifton Forge-Waynesboro Telephone Company).

Table 9.3
Local Exchange Carriers and Access Lines
in Virginia, 1986

Local Exchange Carrier	Access Lines	Share of Total (%)*
Chesapeake and Potomac Telephone Company of Virginia	2,222,036	77.7
Central Telephone Company of Virginia	188,397	6.6
Continental Telephone Corporation of Virginia	287,636	10.0
United Inter-Mountain Telephone Company	71,796	2.5
General Telephone Company of the South	27,773	1.0
Others**	64,712	2.2

* Totals may reflect rounding error.

** Includes 15 smaller telephone companies (cooperatives and small investor-owned).

Source: Chesapeake and Potomac Telephone Company, Virginia Telephone Companies (Richmond, January 1987).

As is the case in many other states, the principal provider of long distance service in the state is AT&T, which controls approximately 79 percent of this market in the state. Other competing long distance providers are MCI, which holds 14 percent of the market share, and US Sprint, which holds 5 percent. The remaining 2 percent of the market share is divided between TDX of Virginia, SouthernNet, and ICC, Virginia (Table 9.4).

One of the largest users of telecommunications in Virginia is the state government itself, which is serviced by the State Controlled Administrative Telephone Service (SCATS). SCATS owns its own private network, using a CENTREX system provided by C&P, to access its contracted interexchange carriers, MCI Telecommunications and SouthernNet. Long distance contracts are issued on a three-year basis to interexchange carriers by the Department of

Information and Technology (DIT), which selects carriers during an open-competition bidding session. Prior to the October 1987 SCATS arrangement with MCI Telecommunications and SouthernNet, all long distance services provided to state agencies were offered by AT&T Communications of Virginia. SCATS is discussed in more detail in a later section.

Table 9.4
Market Shares of Long
Distance Carriers in Virginia, 1985-87
(%)

Company	Fiscal Year		
	1985	1986	1987 (First Quarter)
AT&T	94	91	79
MCI	3	5	14
Sprint*	1	2	5
OCCs**	2	2	2

* The figures for US Sprint prior to 1987 represent those of GTE Sprint and US Tel combined.

** The OCCs are TDX of Virginia, USTS of Virginia, and, effective May 1, 1987, ICC of Virginia.

Source: Division of Economic Research and Development, Virginia State Corporate Commission, The IntraLATA Market in Virginia, Second Quarter, 1987 (Richmond, January 1988), p. 1.

POLICY DEVELOPMENT

Virginia's move toward regulatory reform has been accompanied by an increase in the number of competing interests in the continuing telecommunications policy debate. The actors include the 20 LECs, AT&T and the other interexchange carriers (IXCs or OCCs), the Virginia Telephone Association (VTA) equipment manufacturers, state regulators at the SCC, the Federal Communications Commission (FCC), consumers represented by the Assistant Attorney General for Antitrust Affairs, and concerned members of the business community and state and local government.

Conflict inevitably arises from the competing agendas of these participants in the policy debate. The telephone companies desire to maintain acceptable levels of revenue. Consumer interest lies in keeping telephone service affordable, particularly with the new pricing flexibility of the interexchange carriers. State regulators need to balance the goals of competition with the goals of universal telephone service.

Corresponding to the modification of their agendas has been a change in the roles of the major players since deregulation was instituted. The LECs and IXCs must be salespersons as much as service providers. The VTA now provides a forum for discussion in addition to representing the interests of the telephone companies. Most importantly, perhaps, the primary task of the SCC is shifting from regulating to monitoring the telcos.

The following section provides a brief summary and analysis of the major participants in Virginia's telecommunications debate, with an emphasis on their current agendas. The dynamics of these conflicting agendas provide the basis upon which Virginia's telecommunications policy is built and may indicate the direction in which the debate is heading.

Telecommunications Companies

Before divestiture and the ensuing changes in regulation in Virginia, limited choices in telecommunications services resulted in a general lack of interest, and perhaps a lack of knowledge, within the business community about telecommunications systems. Most firms dealt solely with their local exchange company, which installed the wiring, provided the equipment, maintained the system, and made any specific modifications necessary for the firm's operations. Problems with the system were solved by a single phone call to the LEC. Due to the fact that a large number of LECs were a part of the AT&T monopoly, and in part due to the general familiarity with the AT&T name, businesses frequently chose AT&T as their interexchange carrier. Such a situation provided little incentive for the LEC or AT&T to aggressively market their services.

With the advent of competition, however, businesses have become increasingly aware of the variety of options available to them at an equally broad range of costs. Business managers have become telecommunications-savvy as telecommunications departments evolve out of phone systems previously managed by the office receptionist. The telcos, in turn, are faced with a choice: either upgrade systems, design more aggressive marketing strategies, and diversify operations or lose revenues as customers seek better prices and selection from competing interexchange carriers and equipment providers. To the surprise of no one, the telcos have chosen the first option.

Upgrading systems and switching to the latest in telecommunications technologies is a primary objective of all telcos operating in Virginia. Fiber optics and digital switching facilities are necessary if the telcos are to meet the more sophisticated demands of the growing service sector in the state. Most telcos are installing fiber and digital equipment at a rapid rate.

C&P leads the state in deployment of digital technology, with roughly 94 percent of all offices using digital equipment.[3] As of 1986, C&P also had more than 29,000 fiber miles in service, with just about every major urban area within its service area served with fiber.[4] With the greater efficiency of fiber and digital over copper and analog equipment, the telcos would like to see some relaxing in the traditional regulations governing depreciation. C&P requested that it be allowed an increase in depreciation reserves, arguing that this would enable it to upgrade more quickly and provide better service to its customers. The SCC turned down this initial request.

Some of the smaller telephone companies serving Virginia have been unable to upgrade their facilities as rapidly as C&P and the other large telcos.

Unlike the larger LECs, these telcos do not have great incentives for modernizing at a particularly rapid pace. Large investments of capital promise a relatively slow return on investment because the customers of the smaller telcos are primarily residential users.

Equal access to interexchange carriers is dependent upon the installation of digital switching equipment. While state regulators, LECs, and some users emphasize the need for equal access, the move to institute equal access in some of the more rural areas has been slow. The cost of equipment is one factor. Another factor is the relatively few number of long distance calls made in these rural areas.[5] The high cost of servicing rural areas, coupled with the reduced access charges that some OCCs pay due to unequal access, results in OCCs such as MCI and GTE Sprint lobbying in a less than strident manner to serve these areas. The equal access issue does, however, provide certain OCCs, such as Sprint, with evidence for their claims of AT&T's dominance in the state.

Beyond improving the telecommunications infrastructure in the state, the concern of the telcos focuses on the development and marketing of new equipment and services. New technologies and marketing strategies introduce new opportunities for greater market penetration.

The LECs are less involved in the area of research and development of new technologies. The parent companies of the larger LECs and IXCs produce much of the new technologies. C&P, for example, is backed by the resources of its parent company, Bell Atlantic. Bellcore, the research arm of Bell Atlantic, is a major developer of new communications technologies.

Developing new services and marketing both new and old services has become an important concern for telcos trying to maintain acceptable levels of revenue. The loss of revenue to the increased competition in installation and customer premises equipment has been offset partially by the influx of industry into Virginia, increasing the customer base of the telcos. However, the threat of large-scale bypass in addition to greater competition has caused the telcos to place a greater emphasis on service.

This threat is magnified by independent telecommunications companies such as ICC, which is installing systems in "smart" buildings across the Northern Virginia region. The telcos are particularly attentive to large users, such as banks, insurance companies, government, and corporate giants headquartered in Virginia. C&P's Blue Chip program, discussed in more detail below, is one example of an innovative marketing and service strategy targeting larger business customers.

The telcos also offer new services for residential and small business customers. These new offerings generally take the form of optional measured service packages. These include message rate, measured rate, economy rate, and lifeline service. The measured service packages are a convenience for some customers who do not make frequent calls or call outside of a particular area. The telcos also benefit by charging customers based on use.

Mandatory local measured service (LMS) is prohibited in Virginia by state law. C&P attempted to institute LMS throughout its service area in the 1970s but met with strong opposition. The debate ended with legislation passed by the General Assembly that prohibits mandatory LMS for residential customers.

Finally, the telcos have diversified their operations to maintain profits as they lose some business to competition. The smaller LECs are now involved in directory publishing, cable television, and long distance service, to name just a few of these new enterprises. The larger LECs have ventured into real estate as well. The days of the local telephone company offering just plain old telephone service (POTS) seem to be disappearing as the telecommunications marketplace is marked by increasing competition.

Competition in Virginia's telecommunications industry has introduced questions about the effectiveness of traditional forms of regulation. A manager in the Division of Regulatory Relations at C&P has commented that current forms of regulation unfairly hinder the regulated LECs.[6] In the present environment IBM and other equipment providers can negotiate customer-specific contracts at special rates, effectively shutting out the LEC.[7]

Responding to these concerns, the SCC created a task force to look into traditional rate of return regulation and related practices. To date, the SCC has loosened its regulatory hold on the 15 smaller LECs in Virginia by waiving the requirements of filing a rate case before changing rates. These telcos need only give the SCC and their customers 30 days' notice in advance of a rate change. The five larger LECs are seeking similar consideration.

Virginia Telephone Association

The Virginia Telephone Association (VTA) represents the interests of the telecommunications industry in Virginia before the SCC and General Assembly. The association's mandate has changed slightly over the past few years, due to significant changes in the regulatory climate. Not only does it provide a unified voice for telcos operating in the state, but it also serves as an educator and provides a forum for discussing issues and reaching compromises.

Principally an association of the LECs, membership in the VTA is comprised of the twenty member LECs, affiliate members (the IXCs), and associate members consisting of customer premises firms, attorneys and certified public accountants involved with telecommunications, and other related services. The seven major standing committees, staffed by volunteers from the various LECs, have recently been joined by an eighth standing committee, the IXC Access Committee. According to the executive director of the VTA, this committee will be the principal source of interaction between the IXCs and LECs within the formal structure of the VTA.[8]

Over the course of the past three years, the VTA has been successful in helping to gain a greater degree of relaxed regulation for the fifteen smaller telcos operating in the state. A 1985 bill allowing the six cooperative phone companies in Virginia to set rates without filing a rate case was followed in 1986 by the Small Investor-Owned Telephone Utility Act.[9] This act further streamlined the rate-setting procedure to be followed by small, investor-owned companies.

The act allows for companies to make rate changes after thirty days' notice to their customers and to the SCC if neither the customers nor the SCC desires a hearing. "Small, investor-owned" was initially defined as those telcos earning less than $10 million in annual revenues. The General Assembly amended the act in 1987 by broadening the concept to include all telcos earning less than $30 million in annual revenues.[10] This includes all LECs except C&P, Contel, Centel, United, and General.

A change in the activities of the VTA has accompanied the streamlined regulation of the LECs and deregulation of AT&T. The VTA had worked closely with the small telcos to help in preparing rate cases. Now that this is no longer a major concern, the VTA has placed a greater emphasis on educating its members and the public.   A 1986 study on lifeline telephone service, commissioned by the VTA, is one example of the association's commitment to continuing research and education.[11]

In addition to its roles as spokesperson and educator, the VTA provides a forum for all telcos to express their interests and concerns. The addition of the IXC Access Committee is a continued step in the direction of reaching compromises through informal procedures rather than costly and lengthy formal proceedings. The policy debate in Virginia is thus marked by an atmosphere of cooperation, encouraged by the work of the VTA and an annual SCC-sponsored telecommunications summit.

Assistant Attorney General for Antitrust Affairs

Consumer group activism in telecommunications regulation in Virginia is almost nonexistent relative to the other states in our study. The Office of the Senior Assistant Attorney General for Antitrust Affairs, Division of Consumer Counsel, represents all consumers, residential and business, before the SCC.

The bulk of the Division of Consumer Counsel's work is tied to rate cases, specifically to keep rates at a minimum. The recent decline in telephone rates and market adjustments resulting from competition, however, preclude aggressive action for rate reduction by this office. Anthony Gambardella, former Senior Assistant Attorney General for Antitrust Affairs and now General Counsel for the SCC, has commented: "1983 really ended the classic rate work in Virginia."[12]

In keeping with the extensive monitoring that characterizes the policy debate in Virginia today, the Antitrust Affairs office keeps a close watch on AT&T. AT&T would like to deaverage in Virginia, but the terms of deregulation specifically prohibit AT&T from setting rates higher in certain areas, such as the rural sections where AT&T is the sole interexchange carrier, and lower in others.

Although consumer groups have successfully lobbied for changes in telecommunications policy in recent years, the more pressing concern of both large user groups and the Virginia Citizens Consumer Congress is electric utility rates.[13] With the steady decline of telephone rates, consumer advocates have concentrated their efforts on universal service and helped to persuade the telcos and General Assembly to take advantage of the FCC's Link Up America program, which includes full and partial (50 percent) waivers on the subscriber line charge and up to $30 discounted on the installation fee.

Despite the sizable amount of resistance to lifeline service, viewed by some individuals within Virginia's political community as a form of welfare, the Virginia Universal Service Plan went into effect January 1, 1988. The telcos initially reacted negatively, with officials at C&P arguing that lifeline service should be paid for from general state funds.[14] Now that universal service is a reality, however, the telcos are making the best of a situation that has cast them in a positive light with consumers.

State Corporate Commission

All public utilities in the state of Virginia are regulated by the SCC. The SCC is subdivided into various departments that oversee the efficient operation of public utilities, among which are the departments of Communications, Economic Research and Development, and Energy Regulation.

The SCC Division of Communications is responsible for the regulation of rates and services of telephone and radio common carriers. Furthermore, the department deals with administrative interpretations and rulings related to rules and regulation of rates and charges; investigates consumer complaints; provides testimony in rate and service proceedings; develops special studies; monitors construction programs and service quality; and maintains territorial maps pertaining to communications.

The SCC is leading the state's drive for a more competitive telecommunications environment, following the General Assembly's lead in the direction of deregulation and the promotion of a healthy, competitive business climate for all industries in the state. One manager at the SCC states succinctly the commission's agenda: "The SCC strives to insure that Virginia's regulated telecommunications companies remain competitive and financially healthy while providing high quality services at reasonable rates using state- of-the-art technology."[15]

Due to this pro-competitive philosophy, a large number of telecommunications services in the state have been deregulated. The fifteen smaller telcos no longer have to file rate cases due to successive streamlining of regulations during the period 1984-1986. Shared tenant services were deregulated in 1986 after a protracted debate, and effective January 1, 1988, CPE service was fully deregulated. The SCC is currently considering alternatives to traditional rate of return regulation that might lead to deregulation of competitive local exchange services.

In the area of regulating local exchange service within the five LATAs in the state, C&P is the only company that can offer intraLATA service. However, the SCC has broad discretion to determine whether interLATA service should be granted to any company. The SCC has also adopted a rule and compensation plan to ensure that companies granted certificates to provide interLATA service do not encroach on markets granted to the LECs.

State Policy and Regulation

As previously mentioned, the primary aim of the SCC and its Division of Communication is to promote competition to enhance the technological growth of the telecommunications industry in Virginia. The main task that confronted the SCC at the time of the divestiture of AT&T was to assess the market power of AT&T within the state and consequently to formulate policy that would promote the overall objective of increasing competition.

In 1984, the Virginia General Assembly enacted legislation that allowed certificates of public convenience and necessity to be issued to competing telephone companies for the provision of interexchange service "if it was determined by the SCC to be in the public interest." The main idea behind this legislation was to ensure uniform treatment of all competing interexchange carriers. Five companies filed for certificates to provide interLATA interexchange service: SouthernTel of Virginia, MCI Telecommunications, US

Transmissions Systems, TDX Systems of Virginia, and GTE Sprint Communications of Virginia. At the same time, AT&T Communications of Virginia also filed for the authority to set rates competitively in the state.

The SCC was then faced with the primary questions of whether AT&T's market share constituted "dominance" and whether competitive rate setting would allow telcos other than AT&T to operate in a fair atmosphere. In August of that year, the SCC decided to deregulate AT&T's rates and tariffs for interLATA interexchange calling, after reaching the following conclusions:

> AT&T's dominant market share did not bring about its market power, rather the historic monopoly bestowed by legislators and regulators provided its market share and market power. That market power had begun to erode through the processes of technological innovation even before the legal barriers to entry were removed.[16]

In addition, the SCC had decided that open market entry would not only encourage the growth of competition in the long distance telecommunications market, but it would also provide a check on AT&T's pricing. Furthermore, issues such as unequal access and its "effect on brand loyalty and costs of serving rotary dial customers" were seen as business challenges rather than barriers to competition.

In looking for an answer to why AT&T was deregulated so soon after divestiture, we have concluded that it is a combination of the particular political climate of Virginia and the overall economic policies of the state that led to the deliberate, measured deregulation of AT&T. A 1984 study done by the Department of Economic Research and Development in the SCC's Division of Communications showed that AT&T's market share had already begun to erode by the time of divestiture. With strong evidence such as this, deregulation became a foregone conclusion.

The political climate in the state of Virginia is strongly conservative as well as pro-business and pro-competition. The process by which telecommunications policy is decided and effected is marked by what can be called the "gentlemen's agreement," with disputes frequently settled outside of the formal hearing process. In addition, the VTA and SCC each sponsor forums to help foster consensus among the parties in the telecommunications debate. The most noteworthy of these is the annual telecommunications summit, sponsored by the SCC and attended by executives from the telephone companies.

The overall regulation policy of the SCC is thus loosely structured and has, over the years, been moving closer to complete deregulation, a process the SCC terms "streamlined regulation." In 1985 the SCC ruled that companies providing local exchange service did not need to file rate cases; instead, they were to notify the public thirty days in advance of a rate increase. The SCC would intervene in the rate case only if a protest by twenty or more persons was raised against the increase in rates; in such an event, the SCC would "investigate the reasonableness or justice of any or all proposed rates, charges, rules and regulations" for a period not exceeding 150 days from the filing.[17]

Also, in 1986, the SCC challenged the FCC ruling to deregulate inside wire, and in return proposed a three-phase deregulation process to apply to all local exchange companies. Currently, the SCC is in the process of reexamining other methods of regulation, such as rate base versus rate of return method, for reasons of comparison rather than for changing its current policy of regulation.

Telephone Rates in Virginia[18]

Due to the 1984 deregulation act in Virginia, there has been considerable speculation on the trend of telephone rate pricing in the state. However, in spite of the fact that rates have consistently been rising since deregulation, it is difficult to perceive these trends as evidence of the impact of deregulation on rates. According to both the SCC manager of rates and costs[19] and the director of the SCC's Division of Research and Economic Development,[20] the status of deregulation in Virginia is distant enough to be accepted as de facto, yet too recent for any trends to be conclusive.

All telcos in Virginia offer highest flat rates (HFR) and lowest flat rates (LFR), with separate rates set for residential and business customers. However, of the twenty telcos, only seven offer measured service at two separate rates (highest and lowest).

In 1980 C&P's basic residential telephone rates (local service only) were set at $10.10. In 1983 these rose to $11.79, but the increase was not seen until 1984, after deregulation in Virginia. In January 1984 basic telephone rates rose by nearly five dollars to amount to a total of $15.22. In 1985 through 1987, these rates remained stable, and as of January 1988 local service rates were reduced by one dollar to amount to $14.22.

Residential telephone rates in Virginia are set by telcos according to flat rates or by measured service. C&P, with eight rate groups, offers the third most expensive service in the state: the HFR is set at $15.48, while its LFR is $8.87. Contel, the second largest telco, sets the HFR at $14.03 and the LFR at $7.10. General of the South sets the highest HFR in the state at $15.53 and the LFR at $15.02. Among the smaller, rural, and unregulated cooperatives, however, rates vary considerably: the lowest basic rates are set by North River Telephone Company at $4.70, while rates of most of the others range from $6.00 to $12.00.

Business rates in Virginia also vary considerably. C&P, which has the largest number of business customers and derives most of its revenue from these customers, sets the HFR for business customers at $50.43 and the LFR at $27.55. Its highest measured service rate (available only in limited areas) is set at $13.00. Among other larger regulated telcos, HFRs for business customers range from $41.38 (General) to $28.86 (Central). The remaining fifteen companies offer HFRs to business customers that vary from $25.95 (Clifton Forge-Waynesboro Telephone Company) to $7.00 (Burke's Garden Telephone Company).

While these rate comparisons indicate that there is a considerable difference between rural and urban telephone costs, the differences are matched by the variety of services offered in urban areas as opposed to POTS in rural areas. Since deregulation in 1984, C&P rates rose considerably, as did the rates of most other BOCs at the time. But since then, rates have remained fairly stable and were even reduced in January 1988. But from the figures quoted above, it is difficult to form conclusive arguments for or against deregulation in Virginia since divestiture of AT&T in 1984. According to most representatives in the telecommunications industry, answers based on rate studies are impossible to be found at this stage of deregulation. Universal service is discussed further in the next section.

Pending Issues

The telecommunications industry in Virginia, as seen in the previous few sections, is currently at a standstill due to the "watch and wait" stance adopted by the State Corporate Commission. However, beneath the seemingly tranquil surface of open competition in the industry, there are several issues under considerable debate.

Task Force, Access Charges, and Bypass

In June 1987 a task force comprised of members of the twenty LECs, the SCC, the VTA, and the State Attorney General's Office was formed at the request of SCC commissioner Judge Shannon. The objective of this group is a joint study to reassess the current rate base versus rate of return regulation of the five leading LECs. In January 1988 representatives from IXCs operating in Virginia were also asked to join the task force, after they demonstrated that their interests were also at stake. However, prior to the inclusion of the IXCs, an interim report by the first task force was handed in to the SCC for a preliminary review.

In this interim report, the five LECs (C&P, Contel, Centel, United, and General) each requested a change in the current form of regulation, under which they are required to refund all profits exceeding 15 percent of their net income. All five companies offered to place a price cap on rates for the next five years as an alternate form of regulation. In addition, as a further appeasement measure, they offered to reduce access charges to interexchange carriers.

Although this plan is currently still under review, all indications by the Division of Communications of the SCC seem to point to a denial of this request by the SCC.[21] While telephone rates have been decreasing over the past six years, the SCC maintains that when rates were originally raised in 1979, they were far too high; now that the LECs are enjoying relative prosperity in Virginia, they have been consistently lowering rates that were higher than necessary. Furthermore, offers such as lower access charges to interexchange carriers hold little appeal for the SCC, which argues that if LECs can afford to lower rates, the benefits must be reaped by customers rather than by other telcos such as AT&T.

In this situation the question of access charges has become fairly volatile in Virginia, since it is closely linked with the possibilities of bypass. Local exchange carriers are willing to lower access charges to reduce the risk of bypass, which could be caused by current high rates that create an incentive for IXCs to bypass LEC switches. However, the SCC considers access charges at the present rate to be ideal for maintaining a state of equilibrium, and none of the telcos can provide substantial evidence of bypass occurrences.

The recent inclusion of interexchange carriers in the task force has been greeted as a positive step by MCI Telecommunications and US Sprint. In 1984 the SCC ordered all interexchange carriers to pay LECs compensation for any unauthorized intraLATA calls in addition to access charges. GTE Sprint and MCI Telecommunications contested this ruling,[22] but were unsuccessful in their filings. Since this defeat in 1984, both companies have been paying a state-determined amount as compensation for spillover calls (calculated through a percentage of their total market share) to LECs.

The access charge debate is further linked to the question of equal access conversion in the state of Virginia. Representatives of US Sprint charge not only that AT&T was deregulated far too early, impeding the growth of equal competition, but that the compensation plan imposed by the SCC is direct proof that smaller companies such as US Sprint must pay the cost of unequal access.[23] However, this area of debate is no longer as volatile as it has been in the past: information gathered in June 1987 indicated that 84 percent of all access lines in Virginia have been converted to equal access (see Table 9.5). C&P, which serves the most urbanized parts of the state, had converted approximately 96 percent of its lines to equal access, while Contel and Centel had converted 69 percent and 28 percent respectively.[24]

Table 9.5
Equal Access in Virginia,
June 30, 1987

	% of total converted
Chesapeake and Potomac Telephone Company of Virginia	96
Continental Telephone Company of Virginia	69
Central Telepone Company of Virginia	28
Total in Virginia	84

Source: Division of Economic Research and Development, Virginia State Corporate Commission, The IntraLATA Market in Virginia, Second Quarter, 1987 (Richmond, January 1988), p. 1.

Universal Service

In accordance with the FCC's Link Up America plan, the General Assembly passed legislation in 1987 that would enable suitable candidates throughout the state to receive discounted service. The Universal Service Plan of Virginia went into effect on January 1, 1988, too recently for the VTA and the SCC to determine the extent of its effectiveness statewide.

In October 1986 a study was commissioned by the VTA to research whether low- income individuals were closed out of options of telephone service due to cost. The study also investigated issues such as how many telephone users and nonusers would take advantage of lifeline service if it was offered in Virginia.[25] A sample of individuals was selected for a survey on attitudes regarding lifeline service. Ninety percent of those included in the sample had incomes below $15,000, and of this sample 85 percent indicated that they were "willing to pay" for a low-cost phone option. Among those in the income bracket above $30,000, only 14 percent indicated that they were against the concept of subsidizing lifeline service.[26]

The Universal Service Plan that went into effect in 1988 was based on the above-mentioned study, but due to the Virginia's conservative stance on a large number of issues, the new program was named Universal Service rather than Lifeline.[27]   The Universal Service Plan was ruled to be an option to all recipients of the federal Medicaid program in Virginia. The plan allows these recipients discounted installation and monthly charges. Under this ruling over 40,000 Medicaid recipients (out of a total 160,000 without telephones) in the state are entitled to apply for this service. Toward the end of 1987, each LEC, within its territory, sent informational letters to those eligible for the discounted service, but none were able to assess the response in January 1988.

The survey mentioned above yielded results indicating that monthly rates were not as much a deterrent to installation as the cost for initial connection.[28] Therefore, initial connection charges were considerably reduced, while monthly minimum charges of $11.00 per month were reduced to $5.00 per month. In addition, companies such as C&P offer a special reduced cost of connection fee, and a ten cent charge for any additional calls beyond three, a service useful for those with little need for telephone service other than for emergencies.

Despite some initial resistance voiced by the LECs, the plan for universal service was ultimately accepted as an obligatory step. The relatively comfortable economic conditions in the state, the new tax law, and the competitive environment in Virginia facilitated the offering of universal service by the larger LECs. Both the SCC and the VTA hold the optimistic view that soon the program can be enlarged to include more individuals than just those on Medicaid.   Both SCC and VTA officials[29] have indicated that any improvements on the Universal Service Plan would be made based on the results of the initial step, which is viewed as a recognition of the importance of telephone service as an integral part of promoting safety and quality of life.

TELECOMMUNICATIONS AND ECONOMIC DEVELOPMENT
Public Initiatives

The principal concern of the Department of Economic Development is to recruit new industry to locate in the state, to retain firms that are already located in Virginia, and to encourage industry to expand within the state. The following analysis of economic development and its relation to the telecommunications industry and continuing policy debate will rely on this general conception of economic development as recruitment, retention, and expansion.

The state's general economic development policies center around two concepts: economic diversity and a "total package" approach. The first, economic diversity, is important because it provides stability to the state's economy. Virginia's economy is not overly dependent on any one industry, thus placing the state on firmer ground than other states whose economic prospects depend on a particular industry. Texas' dependency on oil and related industry is one such example.

Thus, the Department of Economic Development does not target any one industry specifically. The department does, however, recognize the important individual contributions of particular industries to the state. The "total package" approach capitalizes on these assets. The Department of Economic Development promotes the entire range of services available in the state, working in conjunction with private industry and other government agencies. Thus, while the state includes telecommunications as one of its major assets, it does not recruit new industry by focusing on the favorable telecommunications climate alone.

In recent years the Department of Economic Development has acted as a liaison between incoming companies and the local exchange carriers. Although there is no empirical study of the impact of a strong telecommunications industry on new business, there is an awareness within the Department of Economic Development that a strong telecommunications industry is a marketable resource. In the past, the Department of Economic Development has assisted clothing retail industries, such as Lillian Vernon Warehouse, J. Crew, and Orvis Sporting Goods, to develop a "phone-in" order system in collaboration with C&P of Virginia.

In the area of rural economic development, the Department of Economic Development is just beginning to recognize a connection between telecommunications and regional growth. The department recently requested that C&P locate some of its directory assistance facilities in rural areas of the state, particularly in the south and southwest. C&P will oblige, since directory assistance services are not hindered by geographical location.

Overall, however, the development of telecommunications in rural areas is not a major priority for the state. A recent report by the Southwest Virginia Economic Development Council mentions a need for improvements in utilities, but never mentions telecommunications specifically, highlighting electricity and water instead. The VTA study on lifeline service found that most Virginians in the southwest region who do not have telephone service do not want telephone service. Transportation is the greatest concern for both rural and congested urban areas in the state.

This situation might be called the rural telecommunications paradox. While telecommunications is recognized as a necessary part of a region's development, there seems to be no move to expand telecommunications until there is sufficient demand for improved services in the rural areas. There will be no development in business without development in telecommunications, and no development in telecommunications without development in business.

The state has moved to counter this situation, in part, through the Center for Innovative Technology and its various programs sponsored by Virginia's community college system. This is treated in more detail below.

Private Initiatives

The telecommunications companies in Virginia have been most responsible for the growth of the telecommunications industry in the state. While the contributions of outside factors such as proximity to Washington, D.C., a key position in the middle of the eastern seaboard, and the presence of large corporations already in the state cannot be overlooked, it is the industry's commitment to telecommunications that seems to have had the greatest impact on economic development in Virginia.

The telecommunications companies are aware that growth in the region benefits the telecommunications industry, so these companies are willing to do what they can to promote growth. However, the telcos are not first in the business of economic development. Their primary objective is growth of the company.

C&P recognizes the need to promote growth and development in the region, which fits well with its own need to maintain its share of an increasingly competitive market. To these ends, the company is making a strong commitment to research and development in telecommunications technologies for the region. In addition, C&P demonstrates a strong interest in improving marketing and customer service techniques.

In 1986 the Commonwealth of Virginia signed a contract with C&P to expand its CENTREX system to a fully Integrated Services Digital Network (ISDN) in 1988. This is the first contract for ISDN technology in the state. The contract calls for the service to be installed in approximately 30,000 locations statewide. The state's network is important to C&P because it provides a springboard for other large businesses in Virginia that may be interested in such advanced technologies. In addition, it shows that Virginia is a technologically viable option for telecommunications-intensive businesses interested in locating in the mid-Atlantic region.

C&P has targeted its 150 largest business customers with its Blue Chip Program. Among these are large banks and corporations, such as Signet Bank Corp, Reynolds Aluminum, and Philip Morris Corporation. A team of three persons, made up of a liaison, a technical assistant, and a marketing consultant, is assigned to each of the Blue Chip accounts to provide immediate technical support, project management services, and educational services. This is an important move for C&P, since these companies represent 10 percent of C&P's business but generate 80 percent of its revenues.[30]

While smaller businesses in C&P's service area do not merit as much individual attention as the Blue Chip companies, C&P is expanding its services to smaller businesses by offering high-speed data transmissions over a public data network (PDN). Its success to date has been less than satisfactory. This may be attributable, in part, to the marketing campaign used to sell the new service and to the limited experience that most smaller businesses have had with telecommunications. As smaller companies further implement telecommunications into their businesses, there may be a greater demand for PDN service.

While C&P places a greater marketing emphasis on businesses, residential customers are not entirely forgotten. One marketing scheme that has worked well for the company in recent years has been the use of employee-body sales contests in selling software-driven custom calling options to residential customers. This program has proven quite successful for C&P, its employees, and its residential customers. The demand for such enhanced services is quite great, particularly in the more sophisticated, urban areas. In fact, C&P maintains that most consumer complaints are not that the consumer is paying for enhanced services that they cannot use.[31] Instead, it seems that the impatient consumer cannot get the newest technologies quick enough.

Many of the larger CPE firms, including Xerox and IBM, are planning expansions in the Northern Virginia area, adding to the presence of the 100 CPE firms in the state. And as the smaller telcos expand and upgrade their facilities, it can only mean future development in the more rural areas of the state.

The Center for Innovative Technology

The Commonwealth's greatest policy initiative in the area of telecommunications and economic development since the deregulation of AT&T came in 1985 with the inception of the Center for Innovative Technology (CIT).

Seeking to marshal both the intellectual and industrial resources of the state of Virginia, Governor Charles S. Robb appointed a Special Task Force on Science and Technology to investigate ways Virginia could use these resources to their fullest potential.   In 1983 the task force recommended "the establishment of a Center for Innovative Technology to expand and exploit the capabilities of the State's major research universities in partnership with industry."[32] The following year the Virginia General Assembly took action, enacting the Innovative Technology Act of 1984. This act authorized the establishment of the center as a private, nonprofit corporation.

CIT is comprised of four institutes, each located at a major state university, that coordinate research in high-technology areas. These four institutes are the Institute of Biotechnology at Virginia Commonwealth University in Richmond; the Institute of Computer-Aided Engineering at the University of Virginia in Charlottesville; the Institute of Materials Science and Engineering at Virginia Polytechnic Institute and State University (VPI) in Blacksburg; and the Institute of Information Technology, also headquartered at VPI.

The stated mission of CIT is "to enhance the economic well-being of the Commonwealth of Virginia by marshalling the scientific and technical resources of its universities to meet the needs of industry as well as helping industry make the most effective use of these resources."[33] To do this, CIT enlists industry, both within the state and across the country, to sponsor and conduct research in areas important to the growth and development of high technology.

Some of these industry sponsors have included Control Data Corporation, Digital Equipment Corporation, General Electric, IBM, Hewlett Packard, Texas Instruments, and Xerox. The board of directors of CIT also includes some familiar names: chairman of the board of AT&T, a senior vice-president at General Electric, the president of Comsat Technology Products, and chairman of the board of Wheat First Securities.

The Institute of Information Technology, headed by Roger Ehrich, conducts research important for telecommunications companies in Virginia and throughout the world. This institute received 18.7 percent of the $12 million budget for CIT in 1986, and an additional 3.9 percent in funding was allocated to the newly created Centers for Semi-custom Integrated Systems and Fiber and Electro-optics.

The Institute of Information Technology's research falls into several categories: computing systems, intelligent systems, decision and system science, human and computer interaction, and communication systems. Current projects at the institute include the Automated Local Area Network Performance Measurement. This is a joint project with Intel Corporation to develop automated testing capabilities for measuring the performance of automation networks in offices and factories, with possibilities for further applications. Another project representative of the Information Technology Institute is the Voice Recognition and Visual Telecommunications Technologies project with Philip Morris. This project seeks to develop efficient and inexpensive voice-activated equipment for disabled workers. Similar equipment that is currently on the market is both cost-prohibitive and not readily adaptable.

At the Institute of Materials Science research currently under way is investigating the voice and data transmission quality of certain materials, with wide applicability to telecommunications.

In addition to creating a partnership between scientists and industry leaders in the state, CIT serves some of the more immediate business needs of the state. The center sponsors the Center for Innovative Technology and Virginia Community College Partnership. This program exists to help small businesses in the state upgrade their facilities by aiding them in the purchase and integration of new technologies.

By relying on the expertise of consultants at local community colleges, accessible to most small and mid-sized businesses, the partnership provides free consultation, enabling smaller businesses to choose the right equipment to suit their specific needs. Not only does this help in making industry more efficient and technologically advanced, but the telecommunications industry benefits from an expanded market.

Several new programs were developed in 1987 and are planned for implementation in the near future. Among these new programs are the Commonwealth Technology Information Service, a database of researchers and technology consultants in Virginia, particularly members of university faculties; Technology Transfer Agents, a pilot program at community colleges to provide information on the latest technology developments to small businesses throughout the state; Innovation Centers (incubators), which would provide shared space and equipment as well as managerial, financial, and professional assistance to small businesses to reduce startup costs; and Technology Development Centers, which would conduct research in areas of expertise that have great potential for economic development in Virginia. The flexible structure of the center and its institutes enables CIT to rapidly adjust to new programs or terminate programs that no longer prove salient.

The Commonwealth of Virginia has placed great importance on the links between research and economic development in the state, not just for large industries but small businesses as well. The Center for Innovative Technology is seen as a cornerstone for this policy, particularly in the realm of telecommunications. By engaging large telecommunications companies in research with state universities, Virginia enhances its environment for research and development in telecommunications, which in turn should aid in the growth of the industry within the state.

Governor Baliles has expressed this need for a link between education and industry resources, especially in the area of telecommunications:

We see a direct link between education and economic development and we have a simple goal: To place our students and graduates in the first rank of the science, technology and telecommunications talents of tomorrow, as well as in the traditional disciplines of Jefferson's day which are still powerfully relevant to our own.[34]

State-Controlled Administrative Telephone Service

Prior to 1984, three state agencies, operating under the Department of General Services, dealt with the technological needs of all state departments in Virginia. These agencies were the Department of Telecommunications, the Department for Computer Services, and the Department for Management

Analysis Support. In 1984 the General Assembly of Virginia passed legislation to merge all three agencies to create a new division to meet with the growing technological needs of the state. The new department, the Department of Information Technology (DIT), began operations on January 1, 1985.

The DIT currently provides telecommunications services to 65,000 state users within the state of Virginia through the state-owned network, State Controlled Administrative Network Service (SCATS). SCATS is administered and monitored by the Division of Telecommunications of the DIT, which provides billing and directory services to all state users. Since DIT is controlled by the Department of General Services, it does not have procurement and contracting authority: in order to obtain permission for new purchases, it must submit request for purchase (RFP) forms to the Department of General Services.

State users in Virginia are interconnected by five Electronic Tandem Switches (ETS) located in geographically strategic locations: northern Virginia (Washington, D.C., area), western Virginia (Roanoke), central Virginia (Richmond), eastern Virginia (Norfolk), and northwestern Virginia (Charlottesville). These ETS switches allow state agencies to bypass C&P's intraLATA monopoly. Within the C&P regional area of service, however, C&P provides 29,000 SCATS users with 13 CENTREX systems and a large number of PBXs, which are connected to the ETS switches.

Long distance services to state users are appointed on an equal competitive basis through an open bid, generally held in October every three years. IXCs are contracted for a three-year term. Prior to the most recent bid, held in October 1987, AT&T held the contract for both interLATA and interexchange services. However, in 1987 MCI won the contract to provide interstate services, while SouthernNet was contracted to provide intraLATA services. T-1 switches located at the five ETS switch points allow state users to directly access MCI long distance lines, while the CENTREX and PBX systems are connected by SouthernNet.

Long distance carriers are chosen by DIT based on a cost-benefit analysis of low pricing and high-quality services. While the service quality of an IXC is an important consideration, the larger concern is a low pricing: MCI currently offers SCATS a rate of 15 cents per minute. This comparatively low price played a major part in the awarding of the 1987 contract, for price was a major consideration in contracting long distance providers.[35]

The functioning of SCATS is consistent with the sociopolitical climate of the state, where a "gentlemen's code" prevails, as noted earlier. While C&P complains that SCATS bypasses its intraLATA monopoly, within its regional boundaries C&P provides SCATS with CENTREX switches, which play an important role in maintaining the balance between complete bypass and access charges. On the DIT side, the department stresses that it is not cost efficient to completely bypass C&P. In addition, not only is DIT satisfied with services provided by C&P, it also recognizes the importance of maintaining a positive relationship with the LECs. Therefore, the incentive for DIT to bypass LECs is low, while the possible threat of bypass assures DIT of continued high services being provided by LECs.

SCATS is an elaborate network providing services that are equivalent to those provided by small telcos. Each SCATS user is furnished with a directory that provides information on how to use the CENTREX switches and how to access long distance carriers.[36] In addition to providing such basic functions, SCATS furnishes teleconferencing and video teleconferencing facilities, both of which can either be reserved in advance through telephone attendants or self-originated. Furthermore, SCATS offers an 800 service for social services such as education, consumer services, a child abuse hotline, food stamps, fuel assistance, and an AIDS hotline.

In 1988 the state contracted ISDN services through C&P of Virginia. The program began operations in April 1988 and is expected to be completed by December the same year. Under this contract ISDN facilities will be made available to 29,000 state users within the C&P exchange area. When the contract was finalized in January 1988, DIT was unable to specify the exact number of expected ISDN users in the state, nor were there any specifications as to what particular department would be allotted ISDN facilities. According to the director of DIT, ISDN would initially be operated on a low-scale experimental basis and used additionally depending on its cost efficiency.[37]

In the Commonwealth of Virginia, the state itself has clearly played an important role in using telecommunications. But while the state is a leader in deploying the many services offered by local exchange carriers, particularly by C&P of Virginia, efficient telecommunications networking is taken for granted rather than assessed on the basis of economic development.[38] This situation is illustrated by the fact that while the state is the first user in Virginia to contract ISDN facilities, DIT was unable to furnish particulars of a program of usage three months prior to installation. In Virginia, high technology is used because it is available; it has become an integral part of expectations of high-quality services, and the competitive market in Virginia creates a balance between supply and demand of such services. The presence of an agency like CIT as well as the proximity of Washington, D.C., are all factors that push economic growth. SCATS is only one aspect of high-technology usage in Virginia. Telecommunications is thus not considered to be a separate aspect of technology or development but rather an integral part of an environment in which high technology and competition ensure growth in the business sector.

CONCLUSIONS

This chapter has examined the Virginia response to the new demands of telecommunications regulation resulting from the divestiture of AT&T. The Virginia initiative is marked by the early deregulation of AT&T in the state, setting a precedent that has helped to determine the direction of state telecommunications policy making since 1984. Due in part to the magnitude of the decision to deregulate AT&T, and also to its cautious management style, the SCC has been moving forward with a policy of streamlined regulation for both interexchange and local exchange carriers at a careful and measured pace.

The strong growth in the service sector of the Virginia economy has enhanced the telecommunications environment, opening the way for competition within the industry and diminishing the need to regulate telcos as monopolies. The industry has responded to the demands of this growing service sector without much prompting from the state. Although difficult to quantify, it appears that, rather than leading the recent growth in Virginia's economy, the telecommunications industry has benefited from this expansion.

While a robust economy has been instrumental in developing the telecommunications industry in Virginia, the political climate has been equally indispensable. Marked by the "gentlemen's agreement," the Virginia political culture has enabled a smooth policy transition and removed the adversarial atmosphere that predominates in many other states. This atmosphere is aided by the lack of a strong consumer voice in telecommunications matters and by overwhelming support for competition in the industry. The changes in rates following deregulation have not generated any apparent consumer concern.

The various forums for settling minor disputes before they reach the hearing stage illustrate well how the political climate has impacted on regulatory policy. Virginia is not free of conflict within the telecommunications debate, but all concerned parties recognize the value of working together, striving to build consensus. Working together in such a manner can aid in long-term planning for the industry, and provides a stable base from which to build the industry.

While it is necessary to not overlook the importance of Virginia's deregulation of AT&T, it is difficult to assess the full impact of this regulatory move. Three years may be too short a period to gauge the total effects of deregulation. However, several preliminary conclusions can be drawn from the trends seen in Virginia since 1984.

The decision to deregulate AT&T in Virginia resulted from a growing economy and willingness on the part of regulators and legislators to support a competitive telecommunications environment soon after divestiture. Equally important was the increasing demand for advanced telecommunications services by service-sector industries that wished to capitalize on Virginia's advantageous geographical location. Close monitoring of the interexchange market by the SCC before divestiture provided additional evidence in favor of deregulation. Ultimately, the decision to deregulate AT&T must be seen in its context as a measured policy move to encourage industry growth and development in a technologically advanced economy.

The deregulation of AT&T has not had the impact on telephone rates in the state that opponents of deregulation feared; in fact, AT&T has shown restraint since deregulation. Although the long distance rates have gradually increased since full pricing flexibility was instituted, local exchange rates have decreased. A host of factors has affected these rate changes, making it difficult to determine the specific role of policy reforms. The decline in inflation over the decade, the changes in the tax structure, previous local subsidization of long distance rates, and excessively high rates allowed by the SCC in the past all serve to modify the effects of competition in the telecommunications industry.

It is apparent, however, that rates have remained at levels acceptable to the SCC, opening the way for the present task force to examine the continuation of traditional rate of return regulation. The awareness that current policy hinders a regulated LEC's ability to operate effectively in a newly competitive marketplace has impressed Virginia's regulators with the need to devise new means for balancing the responsibilities of assuring an equitable business environment while promoting universal and affordable service. The outlook for the five LECs still under pricing restraints looks promising, perhaps more so for those services which are now open to competition.

The SCC's rejection of the claim that AT&T's market share constituted "dominance" and subsequent deregulation does not seem to have had profound adverse effects on the other interexchange carriers operating in the state. Indeed, MCI and US Sprint now have a healthy presence in the state, and with over 84 percent of total state lines and over 96 percent of C&P's predominately urban lines converted to equal access for 1-Plus dialing, their customers are no longer inconvenienced.

There is additional evidence that the OCCs have not suffered greatly from the deregulation of AT&T. MCI recently won a three-year contract to provide all interstate long distance service for state government. SouthernNet provides the state with all intrastate long distance service, and more businesses and individuals are opting for one of the OCCs to provide their interexchange service. Other long distance companies that have not fared as well are victims of competition in the free market, and not the SCC's decision to deregulate AT&T.

The General Assembly and the SCC recognize the benefits of making telecommunications services available on a statewide basis. This advocacy is seen best in the recent passage and implementation of the Virginia Universal Service Plan. This move is particularly significant, given that Virginia is traditionally a conservative state with strong sentiments against subsidizing telephone service similar to other welfare programs. The plan indicates that available, affordable telephone service is considered an important part of the overall quality of life for the people of Virginia.

Innovation within the telecommunications industry has been sponsored primarily by private-industry initiatives, in response to the needs of industry, although state government has the potential to aid technological innovation in several ways. First, state government constitutes the largest telecommunications user in Virginia and is usually the first to purchase major new technologies, such as ISDN. Secondly, the state can foster innovation through its joint sponsorship with private industry of research and development programs, such as the programs at CIT. Finally, state efforts at relaxing regulation can promote innovation by making the development and sale of new technologies easier for the telephone companies to manage,[39] one of the concerns of the present task force.

Despite the contract to receive ISDN technology, the DIT does not have specific plans for the use of the technology at this time, nor is it certain how individual state agencies plan to use the technology.[40] This suggests a lack of centralized long-term planning on the part of the state in its capacity as a telecommunications consumer.

Just as the state benefits the telecommunications industry, the telecommunications industry can also benefit the state, primarily as a resource used to promote economic development. To what extent the state has capitalized on these benefits is open to debate. Virginia certainly has reaped the fruits of a growing economy, one that is becoming increasingly telecommunications intensive. The question arises, however, whether this growth in economic development is the result of changes in regulatory policy or a general improvement in the state and national economies.

It is arguable whether Virginia has fully realized its potential, particularly at the executive level, to exploit its growing telecommunications infrastructure to attract high-tech industry to the state. The liaison between the Department of Economic Development and the telephone companies is an attempt to forge a link, and seems to serve its purpose well. However, the Department of Economic Development has made few attempts to explicitly link telecommunications to Virginia's growth and development, in either urban or rural areas. The links that exist are implicit.

Long-range planning goals outside of the SCC do not exist for the telecommunications industry in Virginia. While the SCC is looking ahead to meet the challenges of a competitive industry, the commission can only go so far in its role as watchdog and mediator. Based on recent reports,[41] it seems unlikely that state officials will move to create long-range planning goals specifically for telecommunications anytime soon. And this is not so surprising, given the more pressing problem of the state's transportation needs. However, if Virginia is to maintain some control over this important state infrastructure, government officials would be wise to consider their long-term goals for telecommunications in the commonwealth.

Virginia provides a model form of policymaking for other states considering a policy shift to deregulation. The willingness of the SCC to work with industry representatives and to consider alternatives to more traditional, rigid forms of regulation is instrumental in establishing a healthy policy atmosphere, one of mutual respect. The establishment of informal forums for open discussions of industry concerns and the inclusion of all parties in these discussions aid in consensus building and provide an opportunity for long-range planning. Finally, the SCC's ability to define its goals of universal service and an equitable business environment gives direction and purpose to state policy, providing a stable base from which Virginia's telecommunications industry can move into the 21st century.

NOTES

1.   Department of Economic Development, Economic Developments 1987: A Statistical Survey (Richmond, 1988).
2.   Bell Atlantic is rated as having the largest operating revenue of all telecommunications companies in the country. United States Telephone Association, Phone Facts, 1986. (Pamphlet.)
3.   Interview with William Irby, Manager of Rates and Costs, Virginia State Corporate Commission, Richmond, January 5, 1988.
4.   Chesapeake and Potomac Telephone Company of Virginia, 1986 Annual Report (Richmond, n.d.).
5.   Virginia Telephone Association, Lifeline Telephone Service (Blacksburg: Virginia Tech, October 1986).
6.   Interview with Robert Hardiman, Division Staff Manager of Regulatory Relations, Chesapeake & Potomac Telephone Company of Virginia, Richmond, January 8, 1988.
7.   Ibid.
8.   Interview with Ralph Frye, Executive Director, Virginia Telephone Association, Richmond, January 6, 1988.
9.   Ch. 19, Title 56, Code of Virginia.
10.   56-531, Code of Virginia (1987 Supp.).
11.   Virginia Telephone Association, Lifeline Telephone Service.
12.   Interview with Anthony Gambardella, Senior Assistant Attorney General for Antitrust Affairs, Richmond, January 7, 1988.
13.   Ibid.
14.   Interview with Hardiman.
15.   William Irby, Manager of Rates and Costs, Virginia State Corporate Commission, in a letter to Sehba Sarwar, November 30, 1987.
16.   Division of Economic Research and Development and Division of Communications, Virginia State Corporate Commission, The Effect of Deregulation on AT&T Pricing in Virginia (Richmond, September 1987), p. 4.
17.   56-501.01, Code of Virginia.
18.   All figures in this section are taken from information in correspondence from William Irby.
19.   Interview with Irby.
20.   Interview with Richard Williams, Director of the Division of Economic Research and Development, Virginia State Corporate Commission, Richmond, January 7, 1988.
21.   Ibid.
22.   Reply Brief of Appellant GTE Sprint Communications Corporation of Virginia, GTE Sprint Communications Corporation of Virginia v. AT&T Communications of Virginia, Inc., et al., Supreme Court of Virginia, record no. 841881, (Richmond: Appellate Printing Services, 1985). (Photocopied.)
23.   Interview with Rita Barmann, Regulatory Attorney, US Sprint of Virginia, Washington, D.C., January 12, 1988.
24.   Division of Economic Research and Development, Virginia State Corporate Commission, The InterLATA Market in Virginia, Second Quarter, 1987 (Richmond, January 1988), p. 3.
25.   Virginia Telephone Association, Lifeline Telephone Service.
26.   Ibid., pp. 7-10.

27.   According to Anthony Gambardella, the opposition to naming such a plan "Lifeline" service emanated largely from the conservative segments of the society based on their objection to subsidizing "charity." Interview with Gambardella, January 6, 1988.

28.   Virginia Telephone Association, Lifeline Telephone Service, p. 13.

29.   Interviews with Irby and Frye.

30.   Interview with Hardiman.

31.   Ibid.

32.   Center for Innovative Technology, Center for Innovative Technology (Herndon, 1986), p. 1. (Pamphlet.)

33.   Ibid.

34.   Gerald L. Baliles, "Virginia: New Opportunities in the Old Dominion," Leaders, vol. 9, no. 4 (October-December 1986), p. 134.

35.   Interview with E. J. Meisner, Director, Department of Information Technology, Richmond, January 7, 1988.

36.   Long distance carriers are accessed by dialing 7.

37.   Interview with Meisner.

38.   Ibid.

39.   Interview with Hardiman.

40.   Interview with Meisner.

41.   Southwest Virginia Economic Development Council, Forward Southwest Virginia (Wytheville, July 1, 1987).

10

Washington
Kerry Strayer and David Twenhafel

Telecommunications is increasingly being seen as a strategic tool in Washington. Since divestiture, the state has worked to update legislation and address new issues. The legislature has strengthened the role of the utilities commission. The telecommunications industry has also gained political clout. The connection between telecommunications and economic development has been explicitly recognized by the legislature, by state agencies, and by the private sector.

In response to changing telecommunications technology, the Washington legislature enacted a law in 1985 that allowed telecommunications companies and services in competitive markets to be freed from price regulation. At the time of its passage, every major actor in the process supported the law, including Pacific Northwest Bell (PNB) and AT&T. Since that time, AT&T and many OCCs have been detariffed. Dissatisfied with the implementation of the law toward its interests, however, PNB proposed amendatory legislation in January 1988 that would have statutorily deregulated several services and discarded rate of return regulation in exchange for rate caps. This legislation was defeated. Thus, there seems to be division in the telecommunications industry regarding the efficacy of the 1985 act.

Despite the lack of agreement on appropriate state regulatory policies, the major players have developed a process allowing them to work toward consensus. Policy debates have been characterized by full and free discussion among representatives from the telecommunications industry, the state government, and consumers. This collaborative policymaking process is one of the significant features of Washington's telecommunications environment.

The state has increased its activity in the area of economic development in an attempt to continue the growth in the Puget Sound area and respond to a depressed rural economy. In general, the state has not recognized telecommunications as a primary development tool. However, studies have examined possibilities for revitalizing Washington's distressed rural economy via telecommunications.

The state government also has taken steps to use telecommunications to its own advantage. A new state agency was formed in July 1987 to make the state's use of telecommunications more efficient. Within a few months, the new department was able to reduce costs to the state for data transmission.

Both private- and public-sector organizations promoting economic development have begun to emphasize the superior telecommunications network in Washington. Their efforts have focused on using telecommunications to enhance traditional services such as education, promoting a better business climate, encouraging native businesses to expand, and inducing other businesses to relocate.

Thus, the telecommunications environment is moving toward an explicit state policy while economic development efforts are characterized by diffuse, uncoordinated public and private activities. Some attempts have been made to directly link telecommunications to economic development, but unambiguous results are not yet evident.

THE ECONOMY AND THE TELECOMMUNICATIONS INDUSTRY
Economic Profile

Historically, the Washington economy was built on the four Fs: forestry, fisheries, foods, and, more recently, flying. Its geographic position made it a natural distribution center to the Pacific Rim. Today, the Port of Seattle sees more container shipping than any other port in the country. Overall, the Seattle port ranks 18th in the United States in the value of goods shipped.[1] Both transportation and trade have been growing sectors of the Washington economy, as reflected in their total shares of employment (Table 10.1). Overall, changes in the Washington economy have been similar to those in the United States. Heavy industry, such as mining and manufacturing, have been declining while the services, financial, and government sectors have been increasing their shares of employment (Table 10.1).

David Bell, vice-president of the Seattle-King County EDC, noted that the Puget Sound economy has, in the last 15 years, been turning toward high-technology and electronic goods production. The rapid growth in employment in information technology businesses, particularly electronic computing equipment, is testimony to this change (Table 10.2). The presence of Boeing Aircraft Corporation has been an important factor in developing an industrial goods production sector. Seattle's location relative to the rest of the United States is disadvantageous to consumer goods production because of the difficulties involved in distribution to a mass market.[2]

Transportation equipment manufacturing is the top industry in Washington, attributable primarily to Boeing, the largest maker of commercial transport airplanes in the free world. The production of lumber and forest products is the second most important industry, with Weyerhaeuser Corporation being the industry leader. Agriculture ranks third and is particularly important in the eastern half of the state.[3]

The healthy economy in the Puget Sound area compared with the distressed rural economy has given rise to a description of the state as the "two Washingtons." As traditional industries began to decline, the Puget Sound area was able to diversify its economy, adding high- tech industries and expanding the service sector.   In contrast, the eastern half of the state, with its decentralized population and reliance on an agricultural economy, has not yet made the adjustment.

Table 10.1
Nonagricultural Employment Shares and Annual
Percentage Change in Employment* for Washington and
the United States, 1980 and 1986
(total employees in 1,000s, share and change in %)

| Sector | Employment Shares | | | | Annual Employment Change | |
| | 1980 | | 1986 | | | |
	Wash.	U.S.	Wash.	U.S	Wash.	U.S.
Mining	0.2	1.1	0.2	0.8	-1.6	-3.9
Construction	5.7	4.9	4.8	4.9	-1.1	1.6
Manufacturing	19.1	22.5	17.2	19.1	-0.2	-1.1
Transportation	5.7	5.7	5.4	5.3	0.8	0.3
Wholesale and Retail Trade	23.9	22.7	24.6	23.7	2.2	2.4
Fin., Ins., Real Estate	5.7	5.7	5.9	6.3	2.4	3.7
Services	19.2	19.6	19.4	23.2	1.9	5.0
Government	20.6	17.8	19.7	16.8	1.0	0.6
Total	1,607	90,657	1,770	99,610	1.0	1.7

* Totals may reflect rounding error.

Source: U.S. Department of Labor, Bureau of Labor Statistics, Employment and Earnings, vol. 34, no. 5 (May 1987), pp. 120-137; idem, vol. 28, no. 5 (May 1981), pp. 120-128.

     This dual economy may limit the ability of the state to use telecommunications policy as a spur to economic development. Statewide policies designed to strengthen a weak economy may constrain a healthy one. Thus, the state is exploring several narrowly focused means of invigorating the agricultural regions, a few of which seek to make use of telecommunications. Furthermore, the state is studying the adequacy of the telecommunications infrastructure throughout Washington to identify any areas that may be underserved. These actions are discussed below in greater detail.

Table 10.2
Employment Shares and Annual Changes in Employment* of
Telecommunications-Intensive Businesses** for Washington
and the United States, 1980 and 1984
(share and change in %)

| | Employment Shares | | | | Annual Employment Change | |
| | 1980 | | 1984 | | | |
	Wash.	U.S.	Wash.	U.S.	Wash.	U.S.
Information Services	10.9	9.1	10.1	9.9	-1.5	3.2
Finance	3.0	3.1	3.0	3.3	0.5	3.3
Insurance	2.1	2.3	2.3	2.3	1.9	1.0
Real Estate	1.7	1.3	1.6	1.4	-0.3	1.6
Computer/Data Proc.	0.7	0.4	0.5	0.6	-9.0	13.1
Other Information Svcs.	2.4	2.1	2.7	2.3	3.8	4.5
Info. Technology Equip.	0.7	2.2	1.0	2.3	14.2	2.4
Research & Development	0.4	0.3	0.4	0.3	0.5	2.9
Media	3.4	3.7	3.4	3.7	0.2	0.5

* Totals may reflect rounding error.

** The Telecommunications-Intensive Business categories are defined by
Standard Industrial Classification codes as follows:
    1. Information Services: Finance - SIC 60 (Banking), SIC 61 (Credit),
SIC 62 (Commodities); Insurance: SIC 63 (Insurance Carriers), SIC 64
(Insurance Agents); Real Estate: SIC 65; Computer/Data Proc.: SIC 737; Other
Information Services: SIC 731 (Advertising), SIC 732 (Credit Reporting), SIC
81 (Legal Services), SIC 891 (Engineering and Architectural Services), SIC
893 (Accounting and Auditing);
    2. Information Technology Equipment: SIC 3573 (Electronic Computing
Equipment), SIC 361 (Electric Distributing Equipment), SIC 365 (Radio and
TV Receiving Equipment), SIC 366 (Communications Equipment), SIC 367
(Electronic Components and Accessories);
    3. Research and Development: SIC 7391 (Research and Development
Laboratories), SIC 7397 (Commercial Testing Laboratories), SIC 892
(Nonprofit Education and Scientific Research Agencies);
    4. Media: SIC 27 (Printing and Publishing), SIC 48 (Communications),
SIC 735 (News Syndicates), SIC 78 (Motion Pictures).

Source: U.S. Bureau of the Census, County Business Patterns, United States
(No. 1) and Washington (No. 49) (Washington, D.C.: U.S. Government
Printing Office, 1980 and 1984), Table 1B.

Telecommunications Industry Profile

Pacific Northwest Bell is the largest telecommunications service provider in Washington, with 75.3 percent of the access lines in the state. The five largest companies (PNB, General, Telephone Utilities, United, and Contel) together account for almost 98 percent of the state's total access lines. The remaining 2 percent are provided by 19 independent companies; each has fewer than 15,000 lines (Table 10.3).[4]

Alternate providers in the form of shared tenant services and mobile service providers exist on the local level, but all must enter the network via access through the local exchange companies. Several local area networks exist within such firms and institutions as Boeing, Seafirst Bank, and the State of Washington.[5]

Table 10.3
Local Exchange Carriers and Access Lines in
Washington, 1987

Local Exchange Carriers	Access Lines	Share of Total (%)*
Pacific Northwest Bell	1,653,403	75.3
General Telephone Co. of the NW	349,304	15.9
Telephone Utilities	64,318	2.9
United Telephone Co. of the NW	42,017	1.9
Continental Telephone Co. of the NW	39,110	1.8
Others**	47,950	2.2
Total	2,196,102	100.0

* Numbers may not add due to rounding.

** Includes 18 other local exchange companies.

Source: Washington Utilities and Transportation Commission, The Annual Report on the Status of the Washington Telecommunications Industry (Olympia, January 12, 1987).

According to data from 1986, PNB provided 81 percent of the market for switched access (measured in access minutes of use). The five largest companies provided 97.4 percent of switched access.[6] All 24 local exchange carriers (LECs) provide this service, but most small independents have only one access customer: AT&T. Competition in switched access service is minimal, primarily because most of the interexchange carriers (IXCs) are not competing in the same geographic markets.[7]

In the area of intraLATA toll the majority of toll service is provided by the LECs through a cooperative arrangement whereby they all charge the same toll rates as PNB. AT&T may only participate in this market in the area of special services such as full-state WATS.[8] Although PNB carries 94 percent of the traffic in intraLATA toll, the company feels that the market for large-volume users is effectively competitive. Three percent of these large customers account for 50 percent of the intraLATA toll traffic, a substantial part of PNB's toll business.[9] The Washington Utilities and Transportation Commission (WUTC), on the other hand, continues to regulate intraLATA toll service as a noncompetitive market.

InterLATA toll is provided exclusively by AT&T and OCC resellers. The number of IXCs operating in Washington has risen from 10 in 1985 to 15 in 1986.[10] AT&T controls 82.2 percent of the market, a drop from the 1985 estimate of almost 97.0 percent. The carriers ranked second through fifth have a combined share of 13.9 percent of the market, and the remaining carriers have less than 4.0 percent.[11]

The competition in the interLATA market continues to grow at a healthy pace partly because of the implementation of equal access. Equal access has not been required in the intraLATA market, and competition has grown more slowly.

POLICY DEVELOPMENT

Since 1983, Washington has been home to an ongoing debate about telecommunications policy. The legislature has considered various deregulation measures in 1984, 1985, and 1988. Regulatory policies were changed in 1985, and changes in those policies are under review. The WUTC has been given substantial latitude in its authority. The major actors have not reached consensus on an appropriate state policy. However, they have developed a process that allows them to work toward consensus. The result is continuing refinement of telecommunications regulatory policy.

Environment and Political Culture

The telecommunications policymaking process in Washington has been a collaborative effort. Ongoing participation by all the major actors and a willingness to compromise have characterized the debate. Disagreements about policy and differences on substantive issues exist, of course, but a commitment to thorough and open discussion of the issues has generated a well-informed policy community.

The development of the 1985 Regulatory Flexibility Act is a case in point. The bill went through nine iterations and incorporated the perspectives of Pacific Northwest Bell, the independent telephone companies, AT&T, MCI, US Sprint, resellers, consumer groups, and labor unions. The final product was a compromise acceptable to every party. Almost every interested group had some reason to work for passage of the bill.[12] An appendix to this chapter presents an extended analysis of the debate.

The primary actors in the policy development process have been the state legislature, the WUTC, and the telephone companies. The legislature created the Joint Select Committee on Telecommunications in 1983 to review the state code and propose remedial legislation. Over a two-year period the Select Committee provided a forum for the presentation of a broad spectrum of views. Several members of the telecommunications industry proposed legislation to the committee in 1984 and again in 1985. The committee undertook a study of bypass and network dropoff in Washington. A comprehensive symposium on telecommunications issues in 1984 brought together regulators, academics, legislators, consumers, and industry representatives to exchange ideas and views. The committee also held five public hearings to further discuss issues.[13]

The official life of the Joint Select Committee came to an end in 1987, but it was immediately succeeded by a telecommunications subcommittee in the House. The subcommittee, chaired by Representative Ken Jacobsen, has become an active player in telecommunications issues and has assumed the role of providing a forum for bringing together other interested parties.

A second major player in the state government is the Washington Utilities and Transportation Commission, which is charged with the day-to-day regulation of the telecommunications industry. Sharon Nelson, chair of the three-member commission, was appointed in 1985 after having served as staff director for the Select Committee. Thus, she brings a clear understanding of legislative intent to the WUTC.

The WUTC has the authority to hear rate cases, to initiate hearings, to set maximum allowable rate of return on equity levels, to order refunds to customers of monopoly service providers, and to intervene in the telecommunications industry in other ways. In 1985 it was given the authority to evaluate the competitiveness of both companies and specific telecommunications services within regulated companies and to grant pricing deregulation when it determined that a market was competitive.

In 1985 the WUTC was instructed by the legislature to conduct policy analysis and research. During its hearings, the Select Committee found that the WUTC needed to be more forward looking. The committee felt the commission should be suggesting policy changes and providing clear policy advice. To accomplish these tasks, the Policy Planning Division was created in the commission and was given funding for four new staff positions.[14]

Pacific Northwest Bell is the most active private-sector player in Washington. Indeed, most of the policy debate in the state since 1983 has come at the prodding of PNB. The company sponsored legislation in 1984, 1985, and 1988. PNB has helped draft legislation and, at the commission level, has helped draft rules and regulations.

PNB has consistently sought to have its services deregulated as much as possible. Company representatives put a premium on operational flexibility. To them, that means being able to change prices and, to a lesser extent, to enter and leave markets on a few days' notice. PNB perceives itself to be threatened by competition from AT&T and other common carriers for intraLATA toll, high-capacity private lines, and special access.

AT&T, as the largest common carrier in the state, is another company that has participated in the policy debates of the 1980s. The company claims that it is not competing with PNB for the same markets.[15] However, half of its costs consist of access charges paid to PNB, and AT&T wishes to see those charges kept as low as possible.

MCI and US Sprint have also taken part in the recent policy debates. They are working to gain market share and, like AT&T, are seeking to keep access charges as low as possible.

The Washington Independent Telephone Association (WITA) has taken the lead in representing rural interests in the telecommunications industry. Like PNB, it puts a premium on flexibility but defines the term differently. WITA is interested in much higher rate of return limits. It is also concerned about higher per-line costs and fears losing customers if it is forced to price at cost. Boundary protection is another key concern as well as maintaining high access charges or, in lieu of that, finding a nonbasic rate source of revenue to replace access charges.

Only one consumer group has consistently intervened in the policy debate since 1983. TRACER,[16] an association of large businesses in Washington, believes business is paying more than its fair share for local basic service and seeks to nudge business rates closer to cost. TRACER argues that cost-based pricing for all consumers is not only equitable but will increase economic efficiency in the telecommunications industry. The group has maintained an active role in part because it feels the WUTC is more inclined to favor small consumers. A spokesman for TRACER pointed out that the Attorney General's Office has a public counsel to represent individuals and small businesses but does not have a counterpart to represent large consumers.[17]

A number of other consumer groups have played a lesser role in the development of state telecommunications policies. The Independent Business Association (IBA) represents small businesses. Its goals are to ensure efficient availability of telephone service and to minimize rates.[18]

A managed health care system, Group Health Cooperative (GHC) of Puget Sound, testified against proposed legislation, arguing that its costs would be significantly increased. GHC is comprised of 25 outpatient clinics, 2 hospitals, and numerous contract arrangements with physicians, home health agencies, and hospitals. Telecommunications services are one of GHC's most costly technical resources. In 1987 it paid PNB more than $1.7 million.[19]

Washington Fair Share, a statewide grassroots citizens organization, and the American Association of Retired Persons (AARP) both claim to speak on behalf of low-income consumers. Similarly, the Washington State Grange represents 60,000 people with rural and agricultural interests. Its concerns are focused on consumers with few or no alternatives to the local telephone company.[20]

Most of these major players have taken an active role in the shaping of telecommunications policy in Washington. Thus, the policies that eventually emerged from the legislature incorporated the concerns of industry giants, small telecommunications companies, the regulatory community, and both large and small consumers.

Legislation

Telecommunications regulation in Washington is governed by the 1985 Regulatory Flexibility Act, which comprehensively overhauled previous regulatory policies. (The legislative activity leading to the passage of this watershed act is discussed at the end of the chapter.) As in many states, the regulatory laws in Washington were a hodgepodge of incremental changes dating back to the early 1900s. Prior to the legislation, the WUTC found itself required to enforce laws that had not kept pace with technological advances.[21] The Flexibility Act brought state laws up to date and sought to plan for future changes. The law established the following state policy on telecommunications:

1. To preserve affordable universal telecommunications service.
2. To maintain and advance the efficiency and availability of telecommunications service.
3. To ensure that customers pay only reasonable charges.
4. To prevent cross-subsidization of noncompetitive services by competitive services.
5. To promote diversity in the supply of telecommunications services and products.
6. To permit flexible regulation of competitive telecommunications companies and services.[22]

The law also required the commission to provide the legislature with an annual report on the status of the Washington telecommunications industry. Specifically, the legislature requested information on the competitiveness of all markets, the availability and diversity of telecommunications services in all areas of the state with special reference to rural areas, and the rates for local and interexchange telecommunications service. Furthermore, the WUTC was directed to recommend changes in regulatory policy, including detariffing and deregulation, if such action would fulfill the state's objectives as stated in the law.[23]

Significantly, the legislature wrote into the law a provision requiring "an intensive review [to study] if further relaxation of regulatory requirements is in the public interest."[24] Thus, both by requesting the WUTC to recommend changes and by requiring a legislative review, the legislature explicitly acknowledged that the telecommunications industry is likely to undergo further changes in the near future. The 1985 law ensures that the state will be well positioned to respond to any changes.

In September 1987 the WUTC exercised its authority to suggest changes in its regulatory processes. It proposed two changes in the rate-setting process. The first, termed "regulatory streamlining," would allow the commission to expedite rate increase requests stemming from changes in federal and state policies or other events beyond the control of the local telephone company.[25]

The second, incentive regulation, would modify the traditional rate of return method. Under incentive regulation, the commission would set a range rate of return and establish a series of performance indices. The top of the range would be higher than the single rate currently allowed. As long as a telephone company maintained an adequate level of service, it would be allowed to earn up to the highest rate in the range.[26]

In response to a request for comments, the commission received mostly favorable responses. The WUTC is moving toward adoption of these plans.[27]

Degree of Regulation

The premise of the Regulatory Flexibility Act is quite simple. The WUTC will regulate prices for noncompetitive services but not prices in competitive markets. The commission is charged with determining the competitiveness of markets.

The WUTC can detariff either entire companies or specific services. If the commission finds that all the services a company offers are subject to effective competition, that company may be classified as competitive. Effective competition is defined as an environment in which "the company's customers have reasonably available alternatives and the company does not have a significant captive customer base." Competitive companies are permitted to file price lists effective on ten days' notice.[28] To date, the commission has classified 19 interexchange carriers as competitive, including AT&T, MCI, and US Sprint.[29]

For companies that offer both monopoly and competitive services, the Regulatory Flexibility Act permits the commission to classify specific services as competitive. To prevent companies from using their captive customers to finance competitive services, the law requires that telecommunications companies demonstrate that the rates for competitive services cover their costs.[30] PNB successfully applied for such classification for its Centrex-type services and United for its billing and collection services.[31]

The legislation also allows banded rates for any service. Rates may be set within a range determined by the commission. PNB applied for banded rates for ten services, two of which--Intracalling and Custom Calling Services-- received approval.[32] The commission later accepted a staff recommendation to investigate the need for standards governing the use of banded rates. The commission chose PNB's Remote Call Forwarding (RCF) filing as a vehicle for resolving this question. During the course of the proceeding, guidelines to assist the commission in the evaluation of banded rate proposals were offered by the staff.[33]

In its order, the commission rejected the RCF filing and adopted the staff's recommended standards. According to these standards, companies must file in conjunction with a request for banded rates a business plan outlining the uses for pricing flexibility and an explanation of how the proposal will better serve the public interest than would a conventional tariff. The standards also stipulated that banded rates be allowed only on an experimental basis and have an expiration date. Finally, the current rate for the service must be used as the maximum of the band, and the minimum of the band should not exceed 30 percent of the maximum.[34]

PNB felt these standards gave it little incentive to further develop those services; the process was too cumbersome and the profit margin too small. Consequently, it withdrew its other applications for banded rates.[35]

Significant WUTC Decisions

The WUTC has a great amount of latitude in its authority. Its most recent rate case settlement is a case in point. Since early 1986, PNB has earned at or above its authorized rate of return. The WUTC intervened, ordering a rate case hearing. In May 1986 PNB's rate of return level was decreased 11.22 percent to a range of 9.4 to 10.5 percent.[36] The commission also ordered that PNB refund $51 million dollars to consumers.[37]

A major and controversial area of activity for the WUTC has been the writing of rules to implement the Regulatory Flexibility Act. Sharon Nelson, chair of the commission, and the commission staff have steadfastly maintained that their first priority is protecting consumers. Thus, when evaluating applications for detariffing, the commission demands clear and persuasive evidence that the market is competitive and that cross-subsidy is not occurring.

PNB and, to a lesser extent, WITA and the small independent telephone companies argue that the commission's rules are too cumbersome and its investigative processes too slow. PNB officials note that the commission can take up to 11 months to evaluate an application for banded rates or to have a service ruled competitive and thus not subject to price regulation. In a competitive market, that period of time can be costly to the company.[38]

Similarly, WITA states that several small telephone companies have been deterred from even approaching the WUTC for fear of being compelled to undergo a costly review. The commission can require extensive cost data, which is difficult for small companies to provide. While many independents need to increase revenue, they have not come forward to request rate increases.[39]

PNB's dissatisfaction with the implementation of the 1985 Regulatory Flexibility Act prompted it to propose a new regulatory policy. Since it found the WUTC too cumbersome and too protective of consumers at the expense of the providers, PNB turned to the Washington legislature to seek redress.

Pending Issues

In the 1988 legislative session, PNB drafted and supported the Regulatory Improvement Act. A controversial bill, it would have bypassed many of the provisions of the Regulatory Flexibility Act and dramatically changed telecommunications regulation in Washington. With most of the major actors and many consumer groups opposing it, the bill was soundly rejected by the legislature. PNB's willingness to introduce the bill in the face of certain opposition and its subsequent defeat indicates the fragility of the collaborative process and the fundamental differences of opinion that exist regarding the appropriate role of state regulation.

The bill would have given telephone companies a choice between two regulatory systems. Those opting for the new system would be subject to substantially less WUTC oversight. For companies electing to be regulated under the new system, the bill would have abolished rate of return regulation for noncompetitive services, substituting rate caps in its place. Furthermore, the bill would have statutorily declared a number of services to be competitive and removed them entirely from price regulation.[40]

PNB claimed it was being hurt by competitors in intrastate toll service, high- capacity private lines, high-capacity special access service, and central-office-based services and, furthermore, that WUTC procedures are too cumbersome to allow PNB to respond to market forces.[41] It cites, for example, a six-month wait for the commission to deliver a decision on banded rates for Remote Call Forwarding.[42]

Two themes dominated the testimony of those opposing the PNB-backed bill: the 1985 law provides a remedy for every one of PNB's complaints, and weakening the WUTC is not in the best interest of consumers.[43]

At issue was a reopening of the policy debate that took place between 1983 and 1985. The Regulatory Flexibility Act implicitly declared that the WUTC was the best forum to examine the detailed, technical issues that help determine the day-to-day quality of service and the health of the telecommunications industry. The law acknowledged that regulation is inappropriate in competitive markets but recognized that excessive deregulation--that is, deregulation in insufficiently competitive markets-could cause great harm to consumers. PNB attempted to bypass the commission and sought to achieve its regulatory goals in the legislature.

After the bill's defeat, PNB indicated it would apply to the WUTC for detariffing of services under the 1985 Regulatory Flexibility Act. However, PNB also indicated it would not hesitate to return to the legislature with another bill if the commission proved to be too cumbersome.[44]

The legislative battle of 1988 underscores the fact that telecommunications policymaking is an ongoing process. The collaborative process that developed in Washington did not resolve all the issues; it merely provided a means by which the issues could be fully discussed.

ECONOMIC DEVELOPMENT

Unlike the area of policy in which decisions have been made in an atmosphere of either total cooperation or adversarial relationships, economic development plans have been pursued by various groups largely independent of each other. But whether plans have been initiated by public or private groups, the consensus remains that action needs to be taken.

In contrast to states such as Florida, where growth in the economic sector has encouraged the telecommunications industry toward expansion and growth in new technologies, Washington is dealing with economic difficulties for which telecommunications is one part of a larger solution.

The difficulties faced by Washington's four Fs--fishing, forestry, flying, and foods--were described above. In the last 15 years, as all the traditional industries except aviation became less viable, the market began to diversify. Today, the Puget Sound region supports a large service industry, an active port, and a large government and defense presence. The large rural areas, however, have not adapted as well. In January 1988, 21 of the state's 39 counties were classified as "distressed" with unemployment in the double digits compared with King County's (the Seattle area) rate of 5 to 6 percent.[45]

Consequently, numerous economic development initiatives have sprung up around the state, both to deal with the rapid growth taking place in the Puget Sound area and with the problems of adapting to a changing economic structure in the rural areas. These initiatives have taken many forms and come from both the public and the private sector. While telecommunications is still seen by many as a "second tier" consideration in promoting economic growth, its inclusion in many economic development plans points toward the growing understanding that an explicit link exists between telecommunications and economic development.

Public Initiatives

The chairperson of the Washington Utilities and Transportation Commission, Sharon Nelson, has stated directly that linking economic development with deregulation of monopoly telephone service is inappropriate. Nelson maintains that economic development has been used to support arguments by the telecommunications industry toward deregulation and does not necessarily uphold the interests of the average consumer or promote economic efficiency. Her goal is to allow for deregulation when the market is truly competitive, therefore working to the advantage of the consumer, business, and general economic efficiency.

Nonetheless, cooperation between business and government within the state has allowed for a variety of programs to be formed outside the official auspices of the WUTC. On the state level, the governor, Booth Gardner, has organized an effort toward addressing economic development issues titled Team Washington. Team Washington is a cooperative economic development team composed of leaders in business and government as well as the heads of local economic development councils (EDCs) throughout the state. One goal of the group is to ensure that resources are used appropriately and that existing programs are not duplicated. The team provides a network of support for local EDCs and recruits businesses to locate in Washington by providing pools of investment capital for new businesses and by organizing business assistance programs.

One such initiative on the local level is in the Seattle-King County EDC's Small Business Incubator. Through the EDC's Business Help Center, newly forming businesses have access to a number of services:

> The Center's professional staff can (locate) an incredible amount of information and assistance for King County businesses from a network of government agencies, chambers of commerce, colleges and universities and other groups. They can also draw upon a Professional Services Advisory committee of lawyers, accountants, bankers, venture capitalists and others who volunteer their special problem-solving expertise.[46]

Although the Seattle-King County EDC believes that much of the future development of Washington depends on small "home-grown" businesses, David Bell, vice-president of the EDC, stills sends out over 200 letters a month to existing businesses encouraging them to expand or relocate in the Puget Sound area. Included in the packet of information that accompanies these letters is a colorful, glossy brochure on Pacific Northwest Bell's services. PNB territory is identified and potential customers are assured that PNB can deliver any service.[47]

This brochure and the provision of "telecommunications experts" through the Business Help Center are the most overt references to telecommunications in this arena. The active role of PNB employees in these processes, however, ensures that the role of telecommunications is not overlooked. George Walker, vice-president at PNB, is a member of the Seattle/King County EDC's 34-member Board of Directors and sits on the Education Committee. Victor Ericson, director of economic development for PNB, is an active member of Team Washington. According to David Bell, PNB is one of the most active corporate citizens in the community.

The role of telecommunications in economic development has received attention in other segments of state government as well. A report ordered by the legislature and commissioned through the Washington State Department of Community Development studied the viability of locating branch offices in rural Washington. The study, which looked specifically at the small city of Wenatchee, found that, of the firms surveyed, over 90 percent considered telephone service very important for their business but that most did not require any advanced telecommunications services other than data transmission via a telecommunications system. To this extent, the telecommunications network already in place was deemed sufficient to provide this service.[48] The study determined that "a modern telecommunications system is a necessary but not sufficient condition for economic development" and that labor was the most important production factor. The final conclusion reached toward future development of rural areas is that, while communities of 10,000 or more are potential locations for offices, "opportunities for Washington's smallest free-standing communities are extremely limited."[49]

A number of studies have been produced by Don Dillman.[50] One study, co-authored with Donald M. Beck, makes a number of suggestions for using telecommunications in rural development. First, the study stresses that information is necessary for entrepreneurialism, in and out of the traditional field of agriculture.[51] Dillman and Beck suggest that developing a "rural technical information infrastructure" is no less urgent than providing for transportation and electricity. Finally, they stress that rural areas must develop "human capital," teaching skills in information technologies in particular.[52] They cite as an example a Washington farmer who used a computer link with an overseas broker to establish a market in France for his garbanzo beans. The same farmer later picked up a large order for lentils via a computer link.[53]

Dillman and Beck are not alone in arguing the importance of a strong telecommunications infrastructure. The legislature, adopting a bill sponsored by Representative Ken Jacobsen, ordered the WUTC to examine the existing telecommunications infrastructure and to identify "telecommunications deserts." Although the study results will not presented until 1989, there is already some controversy over potential policy implications. PNB lobbyist Dale Vincent believes that the study's backers expect the state to fund the building of additional infrastructure where a deficit is found.[54] Others, including Representative Jacobsen, maintain that the information will instead be offered to the business community in the hope that telecommunications companies will see the "telecommunications deserts" as opportunities to create new markets.[55]

In view of the variety of activities occurring in or sponsored by Washington state government, it is noteworthy that the state agency most directly involved with development, the Department of Trade and Economic Development, has not pursued the role of telecommunications. Whether this neglect is due to the characterization of telecommunications as a second-tier consideration in development or the lack of explicit problems with the current infrastructure is not known.

Private Initiatives

US West, the regional holding company that operates Pacific Northwest Bell, is considered one of the most aggressive of the RBOCs. The Western States Strategy Center, funded in part by US West and located in Colorado, has produced "Profiles of the West." Each profile is a two-page advertisement in the Wall Street Journal highlighting one of fourteen states in US West's territory. The ads extol the benefits of locating businesses in the state.

Pacific Northwest Bell maintains an economic development division and has initiated a number of economic development programs within the state. Victor Ericson, director of the division, has taken a broad view, arguing that a healthy local economy is one of the most important goals to which PNB can contribute. A robust economy means greater volume for PNB and, thus, eventually lower rates for consumers. It also means a steady flow of tax revenues to state and local governments, a necessary precondition to maintaining public infrastructure systems.[56] Consequently, Ericson has coordinated PNB's participation in a number of activities seemingly far removed from telephone service.

For example, through use of a well-equipped television studio, PNB has produced three videos. The first, "Clallam County," highlights the many resources and the pleasant living conditions to be found in Clallam County, one of the state's distressed counties. The video was distributed in the United States as well as translated into Japanese and distributed in Japan. Since its distribution, a Japanese firm has purchased an ailing paper mill in Clallam County and plans to increase production, doubling employment from 400 to 800 jobs. The firm states that part of the reason it chose this particular mill was the Clallam County video.[57]

The second video produced by PNB is one promoting tourism as a growing industry in Washington. Increased tourism in the state not only enhances the general economy but also creates new businesses that will use the telephone network.

"The 21st Century Awards" is the title of the third video. These awards were given for excellence and innovation in K-12 education. The video presents segments of the awards ceremony and highlights the winning programs in four categories.

PNB considers education crucial to providing the educated work force necessary for an expanding economy, and this theme plays an important part in community outreach. Choices is a program in which volunteers from PNB agree to act as mentors and talk to groups of ninth graders who are contemplating leaving school. The Registry, a scholarship program funded by PNB, provides minority students $1000 a year in a trust toward their college education.

While there is not a single plan for economic development in the state of Washington, there is a lot of activity. Team Washington coordinates programs on a statewide level and oversees many county and local programs. Studies by various groups, with state funding, continue to search for means to use telecommunications toward economic development. Pacific Northwest Bell funds and oversees many individual development programs, particularly in the area of education. Additionally, there are numerous success stories from individual companies that have used telecommunications to enhance or increase their business capacities. A few examples include Seafirst Bank, Boeing Computer Services, and St. John's Hospital in Longview, Washington. While there is not a single track of activity, there does seem to be an increasing understanding that telecommunications is linked with continued, ongoing growth and development in the information age.

THE STATE AS A USER

Economic development efforts extend to Washington's own use of telecommunications. In 1987 the Washington Legislature enacted a law guiding the state toward comprehensive planning in its own use of telecommunications. The state is one of the largest consumers of telecommunications services. With government offices scattered across the state as well as obligations to deliver services to people in every locale, the state had compelling economic reasons to make efficient use of telecommunications.

In July 1987 the legislature created the Department of Information Services (DIS), a cabinet-level agency. It united into one department several telecommunications divisions that had been scattered through various state agencies. The legislation, in creating DIS, described its purpose as providing "for coordinated planning and management of state information services." It further noted that "the legislature recognizes that information systems, telecommunications, equipment, software, and services must satisfy the needs of end users and that many appropriate and cost- effective alternatives exist for meeting these needs." [58]

The creation of DIS stemmed in part from past state policies of decentralized state telecommunications functions. Voice communication needs were being met by nearly 100 switching systems, many dedicated to the needs of a specific interest such as a state prison or a regional agency office. Typically, these systems were managed by the agency involved.[59] In some cases, where different agencies were housed in the same building, as many as six separate data lines had been installed to serve the different offices. Similarly, agencies sought to guard their data to protect their turf.[60]

Another hallmark of the decentralized Washington telecommunications system was its size. Until the National Aeronautics and Space Administration (NASA) became a major agency, Washington owned the largest private telephone network in the United States. Most of the employees were service providers, such as operators, but the state began developing a small cadre of analysts.[61] The state owned many of its switches, a decision justified by the potential to obtain detailed call information. Employee abuse of long distance calling had become a significant problem, and it was believed the call detail would discourage further abuse. Washington had excess capacity on its lines and resold distance services to local governments. The state also had been considering building its own private "backbone" network, a policy against which PNB vigorously lobbied.[62] Throughout the 1970s and early 1980s the state acquired a host of mostly incompatible data equipment.

In 1984 then Governor Spellman ordered a freeze on new telephone system acquisition and commissioned separate studies of the state's voice and data needs. The studies were contracted out. However, the two state officials overseeing the studies, both of the analyst mold, realized that voice and data needs should be considered together rather than separately. To the extent possible, they coordinated the reporting of the studies to encourage joint action.[63]

Both of the studies concluded that the state would save money by consolidating its decentralized system. For data services, cost savings were estimated at $7.8 million over the first seven years and approximately $5 million annually thereafter. Consolidating would have yielded substantial initial costs, but the break-even point would have occurred in three to four years.[64]

The estimated savings were larger on the voice side. Over a ten-year period, the state could expect to reduce costs by $56 million and break even in the second year.[65]

The Department of General Administration, which had overseen the voice study, submitted a detailed design of an integrated voice and data communications network in 1985. The Select Committee supported the idea, both for the potential cost savings and for the opportunity to improve

Washington's image as a state hospitable to high-technology businesses.[66] However, funding was denied at that time and the plans were temporarily shelved.[67] By the 1987 legislative session, increasing state telecommunications costs refocused attention on the potential of an integrated system to increase efficiency.

When DIS opened its doors in July 1987, it had a mandate from the legislature to accomplish the following tasks:

1.   To plan, manage, and operate shared telecommunications and computing networks and data centers.

2.   To increase agencies' awareness of information sharing opportunities.

3.   To establish a process for acquisition of equipment, software, and related services.

4   To establish a process for review of information services from a management perspective as part of the budget process.

5.   To improve recruitment, retention, and training of professional staff.

6.   To assess agency projects, plans, or information processing performance as requested by state agencies, the Office of Financial Management, or the legislature.

7.   To develop statewide telecommunications strategic goals and objectives.[68]

In its first six months, DIS spent the bulk of its effort organizing the department and developing its managerial and business plans.   It also immediately started providing computer services through the divisions DIS had acquired from other agencies. Four months after the consolidation took place, increased volume and other cost-saving measures allowed DIS to reduce its rates for mainframe data processing services by 9 percent. Two months later, it reduced by 10 percent its rates on on-line disk storage and batch processing rates.[69] It also negotiated contracts for large-volume purchases of information processing hardware and software and made this equipment available to agencies at a substantial cost savings.[70]

Washington presents a case study of a long-term commitment to telecommunications planning. The motives have varied--cost containment, better service delivery--but the result has been a move toward a more efficient telecommunications system. Washington's use of telecommunications, while not explicitly directed at economic development, has had beneficial effects. Greater efficiency in service delivery enables the state to reduce its costs and, in some cases, provide better services.

CONCLUSIONS

Washington has developed an explicit policy toward the regulation of telecommunications and is moving toward an explicit link with economic development. The 1985 Regulatory Flexibility Act sets forth a clear state policy on telecommunications.

The legislature declared the preservation of universal service to be its first goal. Furthermore, it adopted a policy of price deregulation in competitive markets and of maintaining traditional rate of return regulation for services provided to monopoly customers. Finally, the 1985 act broadened the authority of the WUTC and gave it greater flexibility. Previously, the commission had operated under a set of strict directions from the legislature. Now the commission has the authority to determine whether markets are competitive and thus to deregulate; to suggest regulatory and legislative changes; and to provide the legislature with expert advice. To enable the commission to carry out the last two duties, the legislature created four new policy and planning staff positions.

Links between telecommunications and economic development have shown up in many forms and in many forums. The legislature has been one source of such efforts. For example, many of Washington's rural areas are economically distressed, and the state is attempting to foster economic development through a variety of means, including telecommunications. The feasibility study of rural office development is one example. While the study concluded that telecommunications alone is an insufficient incentive for businesses to locate in rural areas, it also found that the availability of enhanced telecommunications services is one essential element of a healthy business climate. Although studies such as this one provide recommendations, it is unclear whose role it is to facilitate these suggestions, the state or private industry.

Several state agencies also recognize the link between telecommunications and economic development. The most obvious example is the Department of Information Services. The agency has an explicit mission to make the state's use of telecommunications more efficient. The staff is committed to assisting other agencies, both those that already are major users of telecommunications services and those that are just beginning to discover potential applications. The end result will be to make the state government more efficient, in terms of time and money, in its delivery of services.

Improved efficiency is a form of economic development. The money saved could be applied to other state uses or be returned to residents in the form of lower taxes. Moreover, to the extent that better state services improve the quality of life, Washington will be a more desirable place to live and to locate business.

The private sector, too, is involved in economic development efforts utilizing telecommunications. The Seattle-King County EDC's Small Business Incubator is one example. Companies offer their expertise to help new and expanding businesses use telecommunications wisely. PNB's efforts in community development and education, while not explicitly using telecommunications, help to promote a healthy business climate, which in turn expands PNB's business and enhances PNB's image as a good corporate citizen.

These various efforts indicate a growing awareness of telecommunications as a strategic economic development tool. Implicit in all this activity, however, is a lack of consensus on how best to exploit the connection. On one hand, the various efforts could be interpreted as an uncoordinated amalgam of programs, some perhaps working at cross purposes. On the other hand, the diversity of efforts could be seen as experimentation that may eventually identify promising strategies.

Given the current level of understanding of the technology, many of the major actors in Washington believe that telecommunications is a necessary but insufficient condition for economic development. Thus, a region must take advantage of the resources at hand, such as in Clallam County, or seek to attract new resources, such as locating branch offices in rural areas. Equally important, however, is maintaining an adequate telecommunications system and providing service at a reasonable cost.

One of the most important legacies of telecommunications in Washington is the political process by which major state telecommunications policies have been reached. The Joint Select Committee, the forum for a four-year policy debate, brought together the major players, gave them ample opportunity to voice their views, and ensured full discussion of contentious issues. The product of this debate, the 1985 Regulatory Flexibility Act, was an explicit state policy with the support of every major player, a good example of the consensus-building model that Washington has tried to follow. While this model operated well for the 1985 act, the introduction of new legislation in January 1988 by PNB, without prior discussion with other players, points toward a breakdown in the consensus style. The sound defeat of the legislation, however, indicates that others still believe that negotiation is the path to follow.

Continuity is a second important aspect of the policy process. Sharon Nelson, staff director of the Joint Select Committee, was appointed chair of the WUTC. She brought to the commission a clear sense of legislative intent as well as a working relationship with the telecommunications companies.

Similarly, the House established a telecommunications subcommittee. The subcommittee, chaired by Representative Ken Jacobsen, has been particularly active. By continually addressing new issues, it has assumed the role of providing a policy debate forum previously provided by the Joint Select Committee.

Continuity is also ensured by the sunset provision of the 1985 law. In 1990 the legislature will reexamine its telecommunications policies and adjust them as it sees fit. The past and present participation by major players in the policy debate and the presence of policy staff at the WUTC suggest future debates will be equally well informed.

The process by which policy decisions are reached may be as important as the substance of the decisions themselves. The process in Washington-- deliberate, thoughtful, and with full participation--has created the conditions for further debates. As technology continues to change, reevaluations of state policy will be necessary. The process that crafted the 1985 Regulatory Flexibility Act can craft a new law when the need arises.

CASE STUDY: THE 1985 REGULATORY FLEXIBILITY ACT

In early 1985 the Joint Select Committee on Telecommunications, composed of four senators, four representatives, and two staff members,[71] submitted its 1985 report to the state legislature. The report described activity in the field of telecommunications in terms of innovation and market share as well as the regulatory environment, both nationally and in the state, since divestiture a year earlier.

In the section on state regulation, the report mentioned a number of bills that had failed to pass during the 1983 season. Among these were S.B. 4519 and S.B. 4536, which dealt primarily with detariffing telecommunications services and were proposed by Pacific Northwest Bell. In response to the need for change and a stated desire to work toward "flexible regulation," the committee drafted its own bill, found in Appendix H of the document. The bill called for the continuation of universal service, an end to cross-subsidies, development of competition in the marketplace, and "flexible regulation of competitive telecommunications companies and services."[72] It also set up the procedure under which a company could apply to the commission to have itself, or a specific service, declared competitive. It allowed a company to set up contracts to sell and manufacture through private companies. Additionally, the bill defined the powers of the commission and explained the procedure for filing a complaint. Finally, it required all public service companies to file a statement of gross operating revenue every year.

The committee, in a series of hearings, heard testimony from more than a dozen concerned parties regarding the bill. Pacific Northwest Bell, the dominant local exchange carrier throughout most of the state, voiced its support, going as far as to say that "passage of regulatory flexibility legislation is absolutely essential during this session."[73] PNB went on to say that it would support, and take responsibility for instituting, a "lifeline" program to ensure the continuation of universal service.[74]

Small independent companies, like Peninsula Telecommunications, Inc., voiced concern over the lack of a clause to protect against geographic deaveraging.[75] The Washington Independent Telephone Association (WITA) supported the bill, which allowed even small independents to move quickly toward deregulation and, thus, competition.[76]

AT&T, still the dominant long distance provider, agreed with the bill but recommended the inclusion of a provision requiring that any services not now subject to regulation would be free from regulation in the future.[77] Additionally, AT&T declared that the commission should be granted more explicit power in determining when markets became competitive so that the process would not be tied up in "legislatively imposed guidelines."[78]

MCI and GTE Sprint (now US Sprint), newcomers to the long distance market, actively agreed with the idea of flexible, and thus variable, regulation. This would allow competition by encouraging those without equivalent market share and by providing stricter regulation for "those carriers who dominate the market."[79] GTE Sprint encouraged the committee to toughen provisions necessary to prove a company's competitiveness.[80]

Both NewVector Communications, Inc., a representative of the cellular industry, and the Washington State Cable Communications Association sought for definitional changes that would establish their place in the market and under the law.

WASHPIRG, the Washington Public Interest Research Group, asked that companies be required to submit biennial reports that would outline their plans for submitting items for "competitive" status. The purpose of this proviso would be "to guarantee that the costs of Plain Old Telephone Service . . . do not rise so dramatically as to threaten Universal Service."[81]

Finally, TRACER, which includes many of the telecommunications-intensive companies in the state of Washington, asked for clarification on a number of crucial terms, including "basic telecommunications service," "reasonable charges," and "market." While supportive of the bill overall, TRACER questioned the efficiency of instituting a lifeline program and suggested instead making available a discounted flat rate.[82] TRACER also maintained that, if a lifeline program were instituted, it should be administered through a government agency and funded from tax revenues, not telephone rates.[83]

The noteworthy aspect of the 1985 legislation is that through the process of hearings the concerns of the involved parties were voiced and were, as much as possible, built into the original bill. Before it was introduced to the legislature, S.B. 3305 went through nine iterations. In its final form the bill had the support of all concerned parties. The process demonstrated political consensus-building at its best.

Nearly everyone was granted what they asked. The concept of universal service was retained, flexible regulation was instituted, and a mechanism for the various processes was set up. New definitions were added to the bill in several sections for clarification. Section Four established the test and procedures necessary for classification as a competitive service or company. According to Section Seven, only minimal controls would be placed on new (after January 1, 1985) telecommunications providers in the state. Although no lifeline program was specifically instituted in the bill, such a program has since been instituted.[84] The bill passed through the House and the Senate with only one dissenting vote, and on July 28, 1985, it became law.

Yet despite this successful venture in democratic lawmaking, the afterglow of cooperation has faded. Before the Regulatory Flexibility Act even reaches its 1990 review date, it will have been challenged by a bill proposed by Pacific Northwest Bell. PNB maintains that the 1985 act has been interpreted much too narrowly and that even when it passed, it was, at best, a compromise.

In the hearing before the House Telecommunications Subcommittee in January 1988 on the proposed PNB legislation, one of the people testifying projected a picture of a group of smiling people and offered this comment: "This was the group who drafted the 1985 legislation. These two are from PNB. They were smiling then, what's the problem now?" Yet what this situation illustrates is that, even with occasional cooperation, creating telecommunications policy is a dynamic event. It is not likely to be resolved for good for a long time to come.

NOTES

1.   Interview with David Bell, Vice-President, Seattle-King County Economic Development Council, Seattle, January 15, 1988.

2.   Ibid.

3.   Telephone interview by Joellen Harper with Roe Wilson, Public Affairs Manager, Department of Trade and Economic Development, Olympia, September 29, 1987.

4.   Washington Utilities and Transportation Commission, The Annual Report on the Status of the Washington Telecommunications Industry (Olympia, January 1987), p. 16.

5.   Ibid., pp. 50-51.

6.   Washington Utilities and Transportation Commission, The Annual Report on the Status of the Telecommunications Industry (Olympia, January 1986), p. 35.

7.   Washington Utilities and Transportation Commission, Annual Report (1987), p. iii.

8.   Ibid., pp. 93-95.

9.   Interview with Dale Vincent, Director, Legislative Affairs, Pacific Northwest Bell, Olympia, January 13, 1988.

10.   Washington Utilities and Transportation Commission, Annual Report (1987), p. iii.

11.   Ibid., p. 68.

12.   Sharon L. Nelson, "Washington State's New Regulatory Flexibility Act," Public Utilities Fortnightly, January 9, 1986, p. 30.

13.   Washington State Legislature, Joint Select Committee on Telecommunications, 1985 Final Report, 49th Leg., reg. sess., 1985, pp. 2-3.

14.   Ibid., p. 17.

15.   Interview with Laddie Taylor, Assistant Vice-President, External Affairs, Regulatory Relations, AT&T, Seattle, January 11, 1988.

16.   Telephone Ratepayers Association for Cost Effective and Equitable Rates.

17.   Interview with Arthur Butler, Legal Counsel, Lindsay, Hart, Neil and Weigler, Seattle, January 12, 1988.

18.   Letter from Gary L. Smith, Executive Director, Independent Business Association, to Ken Jacobsen, Washington State Representative, Chairman, House Telecommunications Subcommittee, Olympia, January 8, 1988.

19.   Letter from Darlene Burgess, Director, Governmental Affairs, Group Health Cooperative of Puget Sound, to Ken Jacobsen, Washington State Representative, Chairman, House Telecommunications Subcommittee, January 8, 1988.

20.   Dwight Pelz, Executive Director, Washington Fair Share, Testimony Before House Telecommunications Subcommittee On HB 1268, pp. 1-2; Mike Rendish, Chairman, State Legislative Committee, American Association of Retired Persons, Testimony Before House Subcommittee on Telecommunications, pp. 1-2; Bob Joy, Legislative Director, Washington State Grange, Testimony of the Washington State Grange Before the Subcommittee on Telecommunications of the House Energy and Utilities Committee, pp. 2-3; Olympia, January 8, 1988.

21.   Nelson, "Washington State's New Regulatory Flexibility Act," p. 29.

22.   Washington State Legislature, 1985 Regulatory Flexibility Act, 49th Leg., reg. sess., 1985, S.S.B. 3305, p. 1.

23.   Ibid., p. 26.

24.   Ibid., p. 27.

25.   Washington Utilities and Transportation Commission, "Notice of Inquiry," September 16, 1987, pp. 2-3.

26.   Ibid., pp. 3-5.

27.   Interview with Steve McClellan, Public Affairs Manager, Washington Utilities and Transportation Commission, Olympia, March 28, 1988.

28.   1985 Regulatory Flexibility Act, pp. 5-7.

29.   Washington Utilities and Transportation Commission, Annual Report (1987), p. 1.

30.   1985 Regulatory Flexibility Act, pp. 7-8.

31.   Interview with Joe Hommel, Policy Specialist, Policy and Planning Division, Washington Utilities and Transportation Commission, Olympia, January 13, 1988.

32.   Ibid.

33.   Letter from Joe Hommel to David Twenhafel, April 21, 1988.

34.   Ibid.

35.   Interview with Jane Nishita, Regulatory Affairs Manager, Idaho/Washington, Pacific Northwest Bell, Seattle, January 12, 1988.

36.   Letter from Sharon L. Nelson, Chair, Washington Utilities and Transportation Commission, to Ken Jacobsen, Washington State Representative, Chairman, House Telecommunications Subcommittee, December 18, 1987.

37.   Bill Virgin, "Commission Head Pans PNB's Phone Charge Plan," [Tacoma] News Tribune, December 4, 1987.

38.   Interview with Bob McGinnis, Regulatory Affairs Manager, Washington/Idaho, Pacific Northwest Bell, Seattle, January 15, 1988.

39   Interview with John M. Doyle, Executive Vice-President, Washington Independent Telephone Association, Olympia, January 14, 1988.

40.   Washington State Legislature, House Energy and Utilities Committee, Regulatory Improvement Act, 50st Leg., 2d sess., 1988, H.B. 1268, pp. 1-2.

41.   Ibid., p. 3.

42.   Interview with McGinnis.

43.   Telephone interview with McClellan, March 28, 1988.

44.   Telephone interview with Victor Ericson, Director, Economic Development Division, Pacific Northwest Bell, Seattle, March 31, 1988.

45.   Interview with Bell.

46   Seattle/King County Economic Development Council, "Helping Local Business Is Our Biggest Business," n.d. (Brochure.)

47.   Interview with Bell.

48.   Washington State Department of Community Development, Rural Office Development in Washington State: Its Feasibility and the Role of Telecommunications, prepared by Dick Conway & Associates (Seattle, January 1988), pp. 49-52.

49.   Ibid., p. vii.

50.   Dillman is a rural sociologist by training and is director of the Social and Economic Sciences Research Center at Washington State University in Pullman.

51.   Don A. Dillman and Donald M. Beck, "Information Technologies and Rural Development in the 1990s," (paper presented at Symposium on Telecommunications and Economic Development in Rural America, Denver, Colorado, November 3-5, 1987), p. 24.

52.   Ibid, pp. 26-27.

53.   Ibid, p. 14.

54.   Interview with Vincent.

55.   Interview with Ken Jacobsen, Washington State Representative, Olympia, January 13, 1988.

56.   Pacific Northwest Bell, Statement on Economic Development (Seattle, n.d.).

57.   Interview with Ericson.

58.   Washington State Legislature, 50th Leg., reg. sess., 1987, S.S.B. 5555, p. 1.

59.   Washington Department of General Administration, Telecommunications Division, Introduction to the Integrated Network Study, by Jim Culp (Olympia, n.d.), p. 1.

60.   Interview with Betty Boushey, Director, Telecommunications Division, Washington Department of Information Services, Olympia, January 14, 1988.

61.   Ibid.

62.   Joint Select Committee on Telecommunications, 1985 Final Report, p. 28.

63.   Interview with Boushey; interview with Jerry Wolfson, Telecommunications Manager, Washington Department of Information Services, Olympia, January 14, 1988.

64.   Joint Select Committee on Telecommunications, 1985 Final Report, App. G, pp. 2, 4.

65.   Ibid., p. 7.

66.   Joint Select Committee on Telecommunications, 1985 Final Report, p. 28.

67.   Washington Department of General Administration, Introduction to the Integrated Network Study, p. 6.

68.   Ibid.

69.   Washington Department of Information Services, Report to the Legislature (Olympia, January 1988), p. 21.

70.   Ibid.

71.   The senators were Al Williams, William F. "Bill" Fuller, Dick Hemstad, and Dianne Woody. The representatives were Seth Armstrong, Jeanine Long, Ken Jacobsen, and Darwin Nealey. The committee staff was headed by Sharon Nelson, now WUTC chair, and Steven J. McLellan, now public affairs manager for the WUTC.

72.   Joint Select Committee on Telecommunications, 1985 Final Report, App. H, p. 6.

73.   Thomas R. Beierle, Pacific Northwest Bell, Testimony before the Washington State Legislature Joint Select Committee on Telecommunications, January 13, 1984, p. 1.

74.   Ibid, p. 4.

75.   Jon C. Erickson, Vice-President, Peninsula Telecommunications, Inc., _Testimony before the Washington State Legislature Joint Select Committee on Telecommunications_, January 13, 1984, p. 2.

76.   David D. King, President, Washington Independent Telephone Association, _Testimony before the Washington State Legislature Joint Select Committee on Telecommunications_, January 13, 1984, p. 4.

77.   John E. Dennis, Vice-President, AT&T Communications--Regulatory Matters, _Testimony before the Washington State Legislature Joint Select Committee on Telecommunications_, January 13, 1984, p. 4.

78.   Ibid, p. 5.

79.   Don Eberle, Director of External Affairs, MCI West, _Testimony before the Washington State Legislature Joint Select Committee on Telecommunications_, n.d., p. 3.

80.   Jan Denton, GTE Sprint, _Testimony before the Washington State Legislature Joint Select Committee on Telecommunications_, January 13, 1984, p. 3.

81.   Washington Public Interest Research Group, "Proposed Amendment to the Joint Select Committee on Telecommunications' Staff Draft Regulatory Flexibility Legislation (S-133/85)," n.d., p. 1. (Mimeograph.)

82.   Arthur A. Butler, Telecommunications Ratepayers Association for Cost-Effective and Equitable Rates, Legal Counsel, _Testimony before the Washington State Legislature Joint Select Committee on Telecommunications_, n.d., p. 11.

83.   Ibid, p. 12.

84.   Since the institution of the lifeline program, there has been an overwhelmingly negative public response. Many of the problems with the current program could have been avoided by instituting the suggestions in TRACER's testimony.

11

Conclusion: Perspectives on the New State Role

Janee Briesemeister and John Horrigan

The nine states examined in this study--California, Florida, Illinois, Nebraska, New York, Texas, Vermont, Virginia, and Washington-- demonstrate that telecommunications policy is undergoing rapid and continuous change. Industry structure, services offered, technology used, and type of regulation imposed are all changing at unprecedented speed. Where businesses once saw telecommunications as simply an expense, many now see telecommunications as a chance to enhance their competitive position. Where policymakers once saw the promotion of universal service as the primary goal of telecommunications policy, they are now besieged by competing policy goals from a variety of actors, old and new. Large users of telecommunications services, once dormant in the policy debate, now frequently voice their needs to regulators and legislators. Telecommunications companies, once comfortable in their monopoly roles, now fervently compete with new service providers in the marketplace and before legislatures and regulatory commissions. Finally, different actors--legislators, economic development officials, the telecommunications industry, and the business community--are invoking in different ways the phrase "economic development" to justify their policy demands.

All this is taking place in environments produced by each state's unique political, economic, and social conditions. Nonetheless, study of these nine states yields conclusions about telecommunications policy nationwide that are summarized below and developed more fully in this chapter:

1. States as telecommunications policymakers. The politics of telecommunications has broadened since the divestiture of AT&T. Whereas telecommunications policy was once the primary province of regulators, today legislators, governors, and economic development officials recognize the importance of telecommunications policy to the state.

2. Telecommunications and economic development. Policymakers have begun to recognize that the telecommunications infrastructure is important to

state economies. Often policymakers perceive a link between a sophisticated telecommunications infrastructure, market competition, and economic development.

3. <u>Universal service</u>. Moves toward deregulation and regulatory flexibility have drawn attention to issues of social equity, particularly universal service. Most states, however, have not defined what universal service is in an era of rapidly changing telecommunications technology.

4. <u>States as users of telecommunications</u>. States have begun to take their own role as users of telecommunications more seriously. Many states are purchasing new telecommunications systems, often with an eye toward cutting costs and improving service delivery.

STATES AS TELECOMMUNICATIONS POLICYMAKERS

Three forces have driven state policymakers to take a more critical look at telecommunications policy. The first was the economic problems that most states experienced in the late 1970s and the early 1980s. These problems compelled state policymakers to take a more active role in promoting the economic welfare of their states. The second was a growing understanding that a sophisticated telecommunications infrastructure is necessary to support an economy increasingly dependent on information. The third was the convergence of computer and telecommunications technology, which was largely responsible for the breakup of AT&T and caused a reevaluation of telecommunications regulation.

These three forces have caused the telecommunications policy debate to broaden in most states. In the past, most of the debate over telecommunications policy centered in state regulatory commissions. Their mandate was to ensure affordable service for consumers while allowing telephone companies a fair return on their investment. As telecommunications has assumed greater prominence in our economy, legislators, governors, and economic development officials have entered the policy debate.

The first two forces are closely related: economic crisis precipitated a new concern for the telecommunications infrastructure. In New York, for example, the flight of Fortune 500 companies from New York City resulted in the Teleport initiative as well as a study by the state Department of Economic Development on the importance of telecommunications to the economy. In California, economic stagnation after years of rapid growth has prompted PUC and economic development officials to consider how traditional methods of regulation influence the telecommunications infrastructure. In Nebraska, the crisis in the farm economy forced the state to look for ways to diversify the economy. One result of this effort was the deregulation of telecommunications in the state in the hopes that information-intensive industries would locate in the state. In Texas, the drop in oil prices, the crash in the real estate market, and their devastating effect on the state's economy brought the debate over telecommunications policy into the state legislature. Some of the arguments for regulatory reform in Texas were couched in terms of economic development.

Conversely, in Florida, where the economy has consistently experienced rapid growth, policy has demonstrated little concern for the telecommunications infrastructure. This is not because the importance of the telecommunications infrastructure is not recognized but rather because the infrastructure is fairly advanced, a result of overinvestment by the industry in the 1970s and 1980s.

Thus, there has been little need for the state to address the issue. In Illinois, where the loss in manufacturing jobs in recent years has resulted in state economic development initiatives, the presence of an advanced network meant that new development initiatives need not be concerned with inadequate telecommunications systems.

Table 11.1
Summary of Telecommunications Policy Recommendations for State Governments

---

-- Establish nonadversarial forums in which all parties can discuss the future direction of telecommunications policy, focussing not on narrow short-term issues, but rather on global issues such as how the telecommunications network can assist economic development.

-- Gather data evaluating the effects of more competition in the telecommunications industry on state economies.

-- Economic development agencies should tap into the telecommunications expertise at regulatory commissions so that telecommunications can be better used in economic development efforts.

-- Economic development agencies should serve as information resources for small businesses on the benefits of new telecommunications technologies.

-- Define more precisely universal service in the face of advances in telecommunications technology. All stakeholders should be involved in this process.

-- Survey the telecommunications needs of rural users to see what kinds of services are necessary for rural development and the costs rural users can bear in procuring new services.

-- Engage in more strategic planning when purchasing telecommunications systems for state government in order to generate greater cost savings from new telecommunications systems and more efficient service delivery.

The third force, the convergence of computer and telecommunications technology, radically altered the stakes of telecommunications policy. No longer was policy concerned solely with the price of a service. Policy had to be reoriented to account for the fact that the telecommunications infrastructure had become vital to the economy. The consequences of this force, the divestiture of AT&T, is readily visible in regulatory policy. State policymakers could not avoid reevaluating regulatory policy in light of the breakup of the Bell System. Although each state had its own approach to regulatory reform, these efforts reflect different forms and degrees of regulation. Examples of form are the social contract, flexible regulation, incentive regulation, and rate of return regulation. Degree refers to the extent to which the regulation is closer to PUC control or deregulation.

Illinois has chosen to pursue competition through regulatory flexibility. The Universal Telephone Service Protection Act of 1985 was based on the premise that more competition in the telecommunications industry would economically benefit the state. Carriers can declare a service competitive on their own initiative, based on a definition of competitive services that is less strict than in other states. The burden of proof as to whether or not a service is competitive is on the Illinois Commerce Commission rather than the carrier.

Two states have clearly chosen deregulation as a policy option: Nebraska and Virginia. In these states, LECs are virtually deregulated and are able to set rates without filing rate cases with regulatory agencies. Furthermore, in both Nebraska and Virginia, AT&T has been completely deregulated, with a desire on the part of state regulatory agencies to see an increase in interexchange competition. These may represent extremes in degree and form.

Approaches adopted by regulators in Washington, Vermont, and New York represent responses to competitive pressures. In Washington and Vermont the large proportion of rural users has made universal service a fundamental goal in achieving statewide benefits of telecommunications. Vermont has enacted a social contract, which, although controversial, clearly states universal service as a top priority while eliminating rate of return regulation. Universal service is also a goal in incentive regulation in Washington. New York presents a different situation. New York City dominates the telecommunications market in the state. Regulators are faced with a substantial disparity in development between New York City and the rest of New York State. The states in which PUC control is more apparent are California, Florida, and Texas. In each of these three states the regulatory climate is considered fairly conservative, yet there is a growing trend to increase flexibility in regulation. In each of the three states, AT&T is still considered a dominant carrier and is urging regulatory agencies to adopt deregulation or devise new means of regulation in response to competition in the market.

In viewing these patterns among states, two points about telecommunications policy initiatives should be kept in mind. The first is that initiatives in each state bear the distinct stamp of the state's personality. In Virginia, the political tradition of the state militates against open conflict in the policy process. More often disputes are settled in a genteel fashion in which all parties emerge feeling unscathed by the battle. In Vermont, the "social contract" emerged as a result of the state's emphasis on consensus among groups; legislation was developed and passed in the spirit of a town meeting. Quality of life and social goals are high on the agenda in Vermont, and attempts are made to incorporate these into the policy. Texas, on the other hand presents a different story. Political conflicts are often heated in Texas, with negotiation conducted in informal settings rather than in the statehouse. Many groups feel they are shut out of this process.

The second point is that most policy initiatives have come from the industry, either directly or indirectly. For example, in Texas and Nebraska telecommunications bills have been drafted by the industry and sponsored by sympathetic legislators. In California and Vermont the initiative has come from the regulators, but undeniably in response to pressure by the industry. Indeed, the skill with which the telecommunications companies seized the policy initiative after divestiture is a point not lost on other observers of the industry.[1]

Although a variety of new actors have entered the telecommunications policy arena in recent years, what remains lacking in most states is any type of institutional response to the changing policy environment. The debate about telecommunications policy is moving beyond regulatory commissions, but much debate about policy continues to occur in adversarial regulatory proceedings over cost issues. Few states have any forum in which to address broader issues of telecommunications policy, such as the role of telecommunications in a society increasingly reliant on information.

We recommend that states consider the costs of the adversarial process, not only in terms of dollars spent on litigation but also in terms of opportunities lost for innovative and forward-looking telecommunications policy. States should be encouraged to establish a nonadversarial forum in which all parties can discuss the direction in which telecommunications policy should go.

TELECOMMUNICATIONS AND ECONOMIC DEVELOPMENT

As discussed in Chapter 1, there are at least two perspectives on state economic development efforts. One view might consider traditional state economic development activities, which involve efforts to retain or attract businesses to a state or foster new firm formation. A second view might consider economic development in terms of efforts to enhance the productive capacity of the economy, such as through infrastructure provision. How states might integrate telecommunications into these approaches has not been articulated clearly in policy in the states studied. The lack of any explicit link between telecommunications and economic development policy should not be confused with no link at all, however. On a more subtle level, most states in this study have recognized that their economic welfare is related to an advanced telecommunications infrastructure.

How this recognition translates into policy varies greatly across different states. Although there are a number of public initiatives linking the telecommunications infrastructure to economic development, a factor limiting public action in some states is that the telecommunications infrastructure is provided by the private sector. This differs from infrastructure like roads or bridges, which are usually provided by government. Due to the private sector's large role in telecommunications, there are many joint public and private initiatives that link telecommunications and economic development. We will therefore discuss both public initiatives as well as joint public and private initiatives identified in the states studied.

Public Initiatives

Only occasionally did this study find economic development agencies in the nine states actively using telecommunications to attract service or manufacturing firms. If a state is attempting to recruit a business that relies heavily on telecommunications, the state economic development agency may contact the local telephone company to make sure the necessary services are available. This reflects a case-by-case approach to telecommunications and economic development, not a systematic and coherent policy response.

There is, however, an implicit understanding within some state economic development agencies that new businesses can be recruited by marketing telecommunications as a location incentive. Some agencies have worked with carriers to market their state, while others do not seem to recognize and appreciate the existence of a telecommunications base in publications designed to promote their state. Although the approach is varied and the stated linkages few, there is a growing awareness of the importance of telecommunications technology overall.

Perhaps the most prominent public initiative linking telecommunications and economic development has been the movement toward regulatory flexibility and deregulation. After divestiture some states, such as Virginia and Illinois, equated deregulation with innovation and hence economic development, even though there was little empirical evidence supporting or refuting the proposition. Other states, like Vermont, California, and New York, did not deny the link, but have adopted a more cautious approach toward regulation. These states questioned the economic promises of rapid deregulation and its subsequent impact on universal service. Their regulatory posture attempts to address both sides of the scale. Recently, it should be pointed out, California's new interest in economic development has led policymakers to consider the economic benefits of regulatory reform. Still other states, such as Florida-- which is experiencing rapid economic growth--have not moved so quickly in granting flexibility or deregulation of the telecommunications industry.

Economic development is often used by the proponents of deregulation as justification for the policies they advocate, and is written into the policy statements of legislation passed recently in several states. It is important to note, however, that economic development is a politically popular (although rarely defined) concept that has been invoked as justification for everything from repealing bans on interstate banking to laws allowing pari-mutuel betting.

Although state policymakers believe a link exists, states have been cautious in using this link as a policy instrument to promote economic development. Some states seem to have decided, in the short term at least, to let the market respond to the needs of users in an increasingly communications-dependent economy. The regulatory flexibility laws in Illinois and Vermont, for example, are not permanent; they will be evaluated for renewal at the end of 1991. Other states, such as New York, are assuming a more active role and encourage private and public initiatives. For now it seems that some states are permitting more competition in the hopes of spurring economic growth, while others, like California, are still sorting out what the state policy response to new conditions in the telecommunications industry should be.

In summary, states are exploring how they might use telecommunications in a traditional way to attract and retain business or as infrastructure that might expand the productive capacity of the economy. The emphasis in some states, such as Illinois, Nebraska, and Virginia, seems to be on encouraging the development of the infrastructure by promoting competition within the industry. Within these states and others, there is some recognition, although not often reflected in programs, that low cost and sophisticated services will make the state a more attractive place for business to locate or stay. But most of these initiatives are cautious, in part because there is little empirical data establishing a link between telecommunications and economic development.

We recommend that states gather data to evaluate the effects on the state economy of more competition in the telecommunications industry. Laws encouraging competition have had a chance to operate for several years and soon sufficient time will have passed to permit evaluation of these laws. It is imperative, however, that data collection be initiated now.

There are other ways for states to address the perplexing question of how telecommunications can be used in economic development. One is to establish better communications between economic development agencies and regulatory commissions. We recommend that economic development agencies tap into the telecommunications expertise available at PUCs. Although we found some evidence that economic development agencies recognize the importance of the telecommunications infrastructure, there is little telecommunications expertise in economic development agencies, a situation in need of remedy.

While it is difficult to predict precisely the benefits of a dialogue between PUCs and economic development agencies, small businesses are likely to be beneficiaries. Debate about business usage frequently centers on large users. Large users often lobby for approval of expensive and sophisticated services. Telephone companies often argue that approval of these services are vital to the whole network, since large users may bypass the local exchange to get these services elsewhere. Bypass, argues the telephone companies, will result in higher residential rates. But lost in this debate are the needs of small businesses, which may not have access to information on the costs and uses of new services. State economic development agencies have, in recent years, been encouraging small business creation, since much new job creation occurs in small businesses.

We recommend that, as part of establishing better lines of communication between PUCs and economic development agencies, some sort of information clearinghouse be set up to enable small businesses to find out how telecommunications could benefit their operations.

Joint Public and Private Economic Development Initiatives

Various public and private projects that tie telecommunications with economic development have emerged in the states studied. In some, state government plays an important part in developing technology, while in others, large businesses prompt innovative projects in telecommunications technology and business recruitment.

The breakup of the Bell system and the merging of computer and telecommunications technology seem to have sparked interest in the private sector of the potential economic benefits of telecommunications. In many states the first response to the divestiture was establishment of a research center or some other institution to serve as a think tank for examining the long-term needs of the state. Some examples include Florida's Information Resource Commission and the Joint Committee on Information Technology (1983); Virginia's Center for Innovative Technologies (1985); and New York's Center for Advanced Technology at Polytechnic University (1983). Typically these research centers involved industry, academia, and the state. In states such as Virginia and New York, these centers for telecommunications were extensions of high-technology research systems. In California a separate center was not established; rather the think-tank role was incorporated in long-range planning projects like Vision California 2010 and other studies. The date of establishment of these research centers would suggest they were created in response to the AT&T divestiture. Their establishment also signals an acknowledgement that telecommunications technologies opens up new possibilities for economic growth.

Beyond these centers, there are few examples of public and private economic development programs with a substantial telecommunications component. One major exception is the state of New York. In New York, perhaps due to the nature of its telecommunications-intensive service economy, the link between telecommunications and economic development is well recognized. This realization, compounded with a tradition of active state participation in economic development through joint public- and private- sector projects, has resulted in projects with substantial telecommunications components. The most ambitious is the Teleport, a public and private venture formed with the objective of stimulating economic development by enhancing the telecommunications infrastructure of the region. A major motive for establishing the Teleport was to prevent the flight of transaction-intensive portions of New York-headquartered corporations to other states. By combining state-of-the-art telecommunications services with real estate development, the city hopes to retain corporate back-office functions. Another substantial New York project is NYSERNet, a high-speed data communications network linking universities, industrial research labs, and government facilities throughout the New York state. The goal is to give greater access to computing and information resources, which will aid in improving economic competitiveness. NYSERNet is run by a not-for-profit company formed by a group of New York state educators, researchers, industrialists, and the telephone companies.

The project that comes closest to New York's Teleport is San Antonio's efforts to market itself as a telecity. The city has worked with telecommunications providers to build and market a telecommunications infrastructure specifically designed to attract businesses to the area. Originally conceived as a business park developed around a teleport, the telecity concept grew out of an inventory of telecommunications facilities and services available in the city. The business park concept failed to materialize precisely because telecommunications capabilities were readily available throughout the city. Another project with a telecommunications emphasis is the Bay Area Teleport in California. However the BAT differs from New York's Teleport and San Antonio's telecity project in that high-technology growth in the Bay Area preceded the development of the BAT by at least 20 years. Therefore, the argument could be made that the BAT was developed in Alameda to take advantage of existing businesses rather than to generate new economic development.

A project of special interest in California is the attempt to introduce telecommuting as a method to decongest the overcrowded urban areas. The Southern California Association of Government has recognized telecommuting as a possible solution to resolve part of the traffic problem in Southern California. Thus, economic growth is encouraged, but its negative side effects are minimized.

Another private initiative in telecommunications has been the establishment of economic development divisions in the BOCs. In 1978 Illinois Bell was the first Bell company to establish such a division, although now 17 of the 22 BOCs have them. The main focus of their developmental activities is not telecommunications. The primary strategy that Illinois Bell uses for economic development is to establish regional organizations to assist communities in attracting and retaining businesses. Telecommunications technologies and services are not used as incentives in this regional approach; instead, through promotion of general business development, the company will expand the number of customers and increase revenue. In February 1988 NYTel created its own department of economic development. This was in response to the

Omnibus Economic Development Act of 1987, which established the Department of Economic Development at the state level. Even earlier NYTel was working closely with various economic development agencies, community boards, and chambers of commerce. The creation of a sperate department would provide a better focus to NYTel's own initiatives. Like Illinois Bell, the department's activities do not involve telecommunication. In Nebraska, Northwestern Bell recently created its own Economic Development Office. Unlike Illinois Bell, Northwestern Bell's Economic Development Office emphasizes telecommunications to a degree, partly because telemarketing is significant to Nebraska's economy. Even in Nebraska, however, telecommunications is considered to be just a part of the big picture of economic development. In Nebraska that picture includes a strong business climate, a progressive legislature, strength in natural resources, ample land and space, a stable infrastructure, a central location, and a midwestern work ethic. In Texas, the link made by Southwestern Bell's Economic Development Division is somewhat more explicit. Established two years ago, Southwestern Bell's Economic Development Division has been active in educating chambers of commerce about the technical capabilities of the network and ways in which business might use it. The economic development activities of the BOCs reflect the fact that these companies are among the largest businesses in each state and depend upon the ability of the state to grow.

UNIVERSAL SERVICE

The changing character of regulation at the state level is marked by a new emphasis on universal service, especially in rural areas. Moves toward regulatory flexibility or deregulation in efforts to achieve economic development goals are often seen as a threat to basic service. Critics of deregulation might argue that regulation is better at leveraging telecommunications investment. Because telecommunications competition is centered in major markets, rural areas fear they will be left in the backwater of the Information Age. Erosion of universal service has clearly been identified as a potential problem of new regulatory schemes. Policies set by many states therefore make explicit attempts to balance traditional universal service goals with innovation and competition in the telecommunications industry. This may be in the form of policy language only, through the establishment of lifeline programs, or in cost-allocation decisions regarding access charges, short-haul long distance rates, and other factors. Several states, including California and Texas, have active consumer organizations and offices of public counsel. Vermont has developed a social contract that is an explicit attempt to protect residential ratepayers while giving the BOC some freedom on the pricing and introduction of services. Florida's PSC is considered pro-consumer. Its orientation is to keep residential rates low; it has not followed the trend of moving nontraffic-sensitive costs to end users for that reason. This policy has not created political confrontation because rapid growth in the state has permitted the telecommunications companies to thrive even with low local rates and the threat of bypass.

Threats to Basic Service

Many regulators, lawmakers, and consumer advocates have expressed concern over the threat to basic service posed by regulatory flexibility and deregulation. The issue centers around the fact that basic service is a monopoly service provided to captive customers. There simply are not alternative providers for local residential phone service. Regulation was imposed on the telephone industry in the early part of this century because phone service was believed to be a natural monopoly. Subscribers had to be protected from the pricing abuses possible from a monopoly provider.

Today the situation is less clear-cut. Aspects of the industry--long distance, customer premises equipment, business services--operate in a competitive market. Presumably market forces work to keep prices close to marginal cost and supply at levels to meet demand. It is basic local service that poses the problem. Not only is basic local service still a monopoly, but it is provided by the same firm engaged in competitive ventures. The monopolistic and competitive functions are similar in nature in that they share the same network, the same overhead, and often the same packaging. The potential for abusive cross-subsidization is obvious and thus difficult to ignore. Consumer groups and competitors alike are afraid the BOCs will use rates paid by customers of monopoly services to underprice competitive services. In addition, policies that promote competitive services, such as moving NTS costs to end users, disproportionately increase costs for residential customers.

The states studied have taken several different approaches in promoting universal service. For some states, a policy declaration in support of universal service stands as the only recognition of universal service as a goal. For others that policy statement is augmented with a lifeline program. California operates one of the nation's oldest lifeline programs. The Moore Universal Service Telephone Act was passed in 1983 and is funded through a tax on long distance carrier revenue.

In states with minimal deregulation, like Florida, cost allocation schemes and other policies are used to keep basic rates low. In California, the CPUC prices intraLATA toll calls above cost in order to keep basic rates low. Elsewhere, capping basic service rates is a new and controversial attempt to foster both competition and universal service. Vermont will soon implement, and Washington is considering, a cap on basic rates (with mechanisms for some type of yearly increases) and elimination of rate of return regulation. Supporters believe the rate caps solve the cross-subsidization dilemma and force BOCs to be more efficient in their operations in order to earn higher profits. Opponents--who primarily represent the residential customers who are supposed to benefit from price caps--believe rate caps set in place rates that are already too high and allow for automatic rate increases in a declining-cost industry.

Although states strive to protect universal service, rarely do they define what it is. There seems to be no common definition of universal service and it is clear that a more precise definition of universal service is needed. With advances in telecommunications technology, states must decide whether universal service is a dial tone, ISDN capability, or on-line access to information. The National Governors' Association has already taken steps in this direction and recently held hearings to determine how universal service should be defined.

Rural Issues

The inequities between rural and urban telecommunications systems are coming to the fore as a hot political issue. One of the selling points of telecommunications has been that it can make considerations such as proximity to resources, markets, and transportation networks largely irrelevant in the location decisions of many businesses. For this reason, telecommunications may increase the attractiveness of rural areas, with their lower land values and higher quality-of-living factors, as places to do business. Yet there is much concern that rural areas will become backwaters of the information economy as competition is concentrated in urban areas, where the high volume of traffic makes telecommunications investment more profitable.

Under full regulation, rural areas benefit from price averaging, which keeps rates in low-density areas affordable while allowing local exchange companies to profitably string wire and invest in and maintain plants there. Local exchange companies that are eager to participate in competitive telecommunications markets have been calling on regulators to allow them to move prices closer to cost. Local telephone company executives believe cost and price structures are skewed, with certain classes of customers subsidizing others. If prices were deaveraged and NTS costs placed on end users, the prices would drop on services for which demand is highly elastic. Price deaveraging works against most rural areas, harming their ability to take advantage of the freedom of location telecommunications should offer.

States with significant rural populations have taken different approaches to this issue. Vermont's social contract approach includes a provision for upgrading nearly all BOC facilities to digital lines and electronic switches by 1991. Technologically Vermont's most remote areas will be on a par with its most urban centers. Whether competitors move to serve those areas is another question. Nebraska's detariffing legislation includes a provision to deaverage rates by 1991, although many in the state believe this particular provision will be removed because of its impact on rural areas. Washington's legislature has instructed the commission to emphasize rural areas when conducting its annual report on the telecommunications industry in the state. Specifically, the legislature is interested in whether there are any "telecommunications deserts" in the state.

Fears by rural customers about price and quality of service seem well-founded. They represent a minority of most states' populations and a much smaller share of most telephone companies' revenues. This may well be a case in which the imperatives of market competition clash with notions of distributional equity. The economist may know that the elasticity of demand for rural users is very low, perhaps lower than that for urban users; thus deaveraging of rates is the economically efficient choice. The policymaker, however, is faced with the broader question of whether society wants rural residents to pay more for service that may be inferior in quality to service available to urban dwellers. To help elucidate the needs of rural users more clearly, states should survey rural users' needs to find out what these users want in terms quality and what they can afford in terms of price.

STATES AS USERS OF TELECOMMUNICATIONS

The trend in all of the states is for more planning in the purchase and use of telecommunications services for the state itself. Since the divestiture of

AT&T, many states have found it necessary and desirable to reevaluate their own patterns of telecommunications use. Prior to the divestiture only the regulated telephone company provided service to the state. Now CPE, interexchange service, and some local services are available from a variety of providers. States have found that decentralized telecommunications decisions often left them with incompatible systems and higher overall costs. Not only could savings be achieved through coordinating or centralizing the purchase of services and equipment, but the efficiency of the state's service delivery and internal administration systems could be significantly improved.

State Coordination

Coordinating bodies such as offices of telecommunications, executive-level agencies, and legislative oversight committees have been established in most states to manage state telecommunications services, billing, and purchase of equipment. Typically these offices are designed to centralize the state's purchase of telecommunications services and equipment. This includes CPE, PBX, or Centrex systems, private lines, data lines, and video. Most states bypass the public network at least in part and have leased or purchased their own networks. Often telecommunications offices are also charged with developing a comprehensive statewide strategy for telecommunications use and management.

Cost savings have also been achieved through using telecommunications in the administration of government. In Vermont telecommunications is linked with the data processing system to tie all agencies into a central purchasing system that speeds up purchase orders and eliminates paperwork. Yearly budget requests will also be put on a similar system. These types of efficiencies have been estimated to save individual states millions of dollars each year in tax dollars. Florida has developed value-added databases through which businesses can access information collected by the state.

Service Delivery

Telecommunications is also used by state governments to cut costs in service delivery. One way this is done is to link social service field offices with the central office. Applications for food stamps, AFDC, Medicaid, and other programs can be entered into a terminal at the field office and processed the same day. Law enforcement agencies have long used communications systems to communicate with dispatchers and run checks on drivers licenses, vehicle registration, and the like. Today these agencies are making use of more sophisticated communications services such as 911, data transfer, and video conferencing.

Education is an area in which telecommunications is being used in innovative ways. Florida sees a link between telecommunications and economic development in that telecommunications offers enhanced capabilities for education. In particular, telecommunications is seen as the conduit necessary for providing distributed educational resources. Although in this view telecommunications has a support function, it is very important to Florida's overall economic agenda, for education and job training are cornerstones of Florida's economic program. Texas has a satellite-based TI-IN network operated out of San Antonio and used by about 80 school districts throughout the state. Many of these are in small and rural communities, which cannot afford to hire sufficient teachers to meet their needs. Instructional programming as well as in-service training for teachers is distributed via satellite to participating schools. The schools use telephone lines to communicate with the instructor at a central site. The Vermont Video Link also uses telecommunications to extend the reach of vocational courses to the most rural areas of the state. Tele-education in Vermont has been pushed by the private sector, which desires a highly trained work force and opportunities for retraining.

Some states have used education to stimulate the telecommunications industry. In Nebraska the Center for Telecommunication and Information helped create the curriculum for a degree program in telecommunications management at Kearney State College. New York has initiated a program within the state university system to train personnel specifically for the telecommunications industry.

The states approach to using telecommunications to improve service delivery is to provide agencies with the most advanced telecommunications technology available that the state is willing to purchase. It is then up to the agency to use its creativity to solve service delivery problems using the network. As a result of this strategy of decentralization, agencies may become service delivery laboratories in which the most innovative agencies serve as models for other agencies within state government.

On balance, however, there is considerable disparity among states as users of telecommunications in their approach to the rapidly changing marketplace. Some states have gathered considerable expertise in the process of upgrading their telecommunications systems while others see themselves only as procurement agencies and show little interest in how agencies will use the network. Rarely do those state personnel in charge of the telecommunications system communicate their needs and policy concerns to regulators and other policymakers. It is not clear what kind of impact this information would have on policy, but states, as a large users of telecommunications, certainly have an interest in the price and availability of services. What is needed in some states is greater strategic thinking within procurement agencies on how telecommunications could be used for better service delivery.

THE FUTURE OF STATE TELECOMMUNICATIONS POLICY

Revived concern about economic development among states has been an important environmental factor in broadening the telecommunications policy debate. While there has been no public perception of a crisis in telecommunications, the economic crisis that most states experienced in the early 1980s has forced many states to reevaluate how policy affects the economy. In some states (California, Nebraska, New York) this reevaluation has included telecommunications policy. Anticipating the future of state telecommunications policy, however, is difficult because states are pulled by a variety of forces in the policy environment: the desire to promote competition and thus economic efficiency, foster network innovation, protect universal service, and use the network to promote economic development. Only one state in our study, Illinois, operates as if these goals are compatible; most struggle with the real and perceived trade-offs inherent in them. One prevailing assumption is that competition will lead to innovation in the industry. Although a widely held position, it is a notion worthy of critical evaluation. Some have argued that monopoly profits enable firms to accumulate the resources to invest in new products and processes. It is the threat of competitive entry which drives innovation by the firm, not a state of perfect competition in which prices reflect costs.[2] Whether or not one agrees with this position, it is important that states examine the assumptions underlying options under consideration, particularly since so little empirical evidence is available on the subject.

Another prevalent idea is that economic efficiency and economic development are consistent goals. Although this view is not shared by all states, the possibility that these goals might diverge deserves more scrutiny. For example, one might consider telecommunications first as a service to be purchased in the marketplace and then as infrastructure important to our economy. If one sees telecommunications only as a service, arguments that policy should encourage economic efficiency are powerful. Prices should reflect costs, and only those willing and able to pay such prices should have access to telecommunications services. If one sees telecommunications as infrastructure, an argument for using telecommunications to promote economic development might require a departure from economic efficiency. The telecommunications infrastructure then becomes analogous to the transportation infrastructure; both are crucial to the economy, but the market operating on its own may not supply sufficient quantities of the service in question. Telecommunications may take on characteristics of a public good, meaning that government may be justified in encouraging additional production of the good even when market signals for such production do not exist. The issue that best captures the public good notion in telecommunications is universal service. It is interesting to observe that several states (California, New York) which have begun to see telecommunications as infrastructure are also quite sensitive to preserving universal service and have been somewhat more willing than other states to depart from economic efficiency in policy. Even in these states, however, the public good character of telecommunications services is limited to the dial tone; states do not often consider the public good features of advanced telecommunications technology. Indeed, building telecommunications infrastructure and making services available to the public before demand in the market exists is a strategy not often discussed explicitly in this country. It is worth noting that it is a strategy used in other countries, such as Japan and France.

Although states will continue to struggle with these trade-offs in different ways, one common thread runs through all nine states in this study: states are encouraging competition in the telecommunications industry. A recent policy statement by the National Governors' Association reinforces this view: the NGA has declared that states should experiment with new forms of regulation which remove unproductive barriers to competition or entry into the telecommunications market..[3] Granted, the timing of pro-competitive policies varies considerably, from early moves toward competition in Virginia, Nebraska, Illinois, and Washington to states like California, which is only now considering pro-competitive policies. But it is clear that competition and deregulation have cast a long shadow over telecommunications policy at the state level.

The reasons why states move toward competition vary. Some states, like Virginia, Illinois, and Nebraska, moved swiftly toward competition believing that structural changes in the industry made competition inevitable and that the possible economic benefits of competition made it desirable. Others, like New

York, Florida, and California, were more cautious. The variety of reasons for and different timing of deregulation brings us to the question of whether states, in telecommunications at least, serve as laboratories for policy experiments, the most successful of which are adopted by other states and the federal government. In telecommunications, how well the laboratory thesis works is unclear. To a great extent, state policy encouraging competition was driven by federal actions--namely, FCC policy favoring competition and the MFJ. Some states have taken bold action in response. It is not clear, however, whether states have taken action based on well-grounded analysis or simply responded to the fashion of competition. The fact that there is no empirical evidence demonstrating the benefits of competition suggests that states may be responding to a trend they see as inevitable rather than as successful policy.

Thus states seem to have substantially ignored the question of the size of the benefits of competition and to whom those benefits might go. Much of the rationale for pro-competitive policies has stemmed from the belief that policies promoting economic efficiency are good public policies. Implicit in this belief is the idea that power in the marketplace is fully reflected in the political arena. The urban versus rural issue demonstrates this starkly. Rural residents comprise a minority of the electorate but an even smaller minority of telephone company revenues; their economic power in the telecommunications debate is less than their political power. If policy follows only the imperative of economic efficiency, the costs of rural service should, by this criterion, increase dramatically as rates are driven to costs. Lost will be the question of distributional equity, such as whether society feels rural dwellers ought to have access to certain services at certain prices. Our point is that economic efficiency and equitable public policy may be two different things, a notion struggling to be heard in some states as the wave of deregulation continues.

While the future course of state policy remains uncertain, it is certain that state policy will have great influence on the nation's telecommunications network. The study of these nine states suggests to us that the whole of state telecommunications policy is greater than the sum of its parts. Because telecommunications is a network, spanning states and even countries, policies in one state, if taken in concert with policies in another, may create benefits greater than would result if the same policies were taken independently or at different times. The introduction of a new service is an example. If a carrier introduces a service oriented to users with multiple locations, approval by different states at different times, or approval in some states and not others, may decrease the service's attractiveness in the market. Approval in one state may be meaningless, or at least less beneficial than it might otherwise be. In this and other ways, state policies do not act in isolation from one another but instead substantially shape the nation's network. As competitive advantage in a global economy becomes more dependent on quick and efficient transmission of information, state telecommunications policies will inevitably affect our country's economic position in the world.

For this reason, the steps taken by the National Governors' Association to coordinate state telecommunications policy are good ones. Yet, in the absence of empirical data, we are not ready to give an unqualified endorsement to competition as the future of telecommunications policy in states, particularly in the presence of monopoly at the local exchange level. Policymakers must be careful not to take competition as the only goal of telecommunications policy. Future telecommunications policy may well lie beyond the debate over deregulation and rate of return regulation, but instead focus on the growing role the telecommunications infrastructure plays in all sectors of the economy. The growing dependence of our economy and society on information has made telecommunications policy a matter not just for regulators, but for legislators and governors concerned about the future of their states' economies. Ensuring a state-of-the-art telecommunications network has become a policy priority for all states since divestiture, not just for the present benefits the network can offer the economy but also for the unforeseen benefits such a network is likely to bring in the future.

NOTES

1.   Gerald R. Faulhaber, <u>Telecommunications Policy in Turmoil: Technology and Public Policy</u> (Cambridge, Mass.: Ballinger Publishing Co., 1987), p. 144.

2.   See Joseph Schumpeter, <u>Capitalism, Socialism, and Democracy</u> (New York: Harper and Row, 1942).

3.   <u>Draft Telecommunications Policy</u> (Washington, D.C.: National Governors' Association, May 20, 1988), p. 4.

Telecommunications Glossary

Access charge -- A special fee to compensate the local exchange company for use of its network to connect to the long distance network; recently a fixed fee for access has been authorized to be charged to U.S. telephone customers.

AM -- Amplitude modulation (see Modulation).

Analog -- Representations that bear some physical relationship to the original quantity: usually electrical voltage, frequency, resistance, or mechanical translation or rotation.

Antenna -- A device used to collect and/or radiate radio energy.

Artificial intelligence -- Computer programs that perform functions, often by imitation, usually associated with human reasoning and learning.

ASCII -- (pronounced ask-ee). American Standard Code for Information Interchange. The binary transmission code used by most teletypewriters and display terminals.

Band -- A range of radio frequencies within prescribed limits of the radio frequency spectrum.

Bandwith -- The width of an electrical transmission path or circuit, in terms of the range of frequencies it can pass; a measure of the volume of communications traffic that the channel can carry. A voice channel typically has a bandwidth of 4000 cycles per second; a TV channel requires about 6.5 MHz.

Baseband -- An information or message signal whose content extends from a frequency near dc to some finite value. For voice, baseband extends from 300 hertz (Hz) to 3400 Hz. Video baseband is from 50 Hz to 4.2 MHz (NTSC standard).

Baud -- Bits per second (bps) in a binary (two-state) telecommunications transmission. After Emile Baudot, the inventor of the asynchronous telegraph printer.

Bell-compatible -- Essentially this means that a modem conforms to the standards of the Bell Telephone System.

Binary -- A numbering system having only digits, typically 0 and 1.

Bit -- Binary digit. The smallest part of information with values or states of 0 or 1, or yes or no. In electrical communication systems, a bit can be represented by the presence or absence of a pulse.

BOC -- Telephone jargon for Bell operating company, used to refer to divested companies.

Booster -- Amplifier in a communications system that increases the power of a signal for retransmission to a further point in the system.

Bridge -- In teleconferencing, a device used to interconnect three or more phone lines in different locations.

Broadband carriers -- The term to describe high-capacity transmission systems used to carry large blocks of, for instance, telephone channels or one or more video channels. Such broadband systems may be provided by coaxial cables and repeated amplifiers or microwave radio systems.

Broadband communication -- A communications system with a bandwidth greater than voiceband. Cable is a broadband communication system with a bandwidth usually from 5 MHz to 450 MHz.

Buffer -- A machine or other device to be inserted between other machines or devices to match systems or speeds, prevent unwanted interaction, or delay the rate of information flow.

Bypass -- A telephone industry term meaning service that avoids use of the local exchange company network, such as a customer connecting directly into the long distance network or buying a direct line between offices instead of using the public
network.

Byte -- A group of bits processed or operating together. Bytes are often a 8-bit group, but 16-bit and 32-bit bytes are not uncommon.

Cable television -- The use of a broadband cable (coaxial cable or optical fiber) to deliver video signals directly to television sets in contrast to over-the-air transmissions. Current systems may have the capability of receiving data inputs from the viewer and of transmitting video signals in two directions, permitting pay services and videoconferencing from selected locations.

CAD -- Computer-aided design. Techniques that use computers to help design machinery and electronic components.

CAI -- Computer-assisted instruction.

CAM -- Computer-aided manufacturing.

Carrier -- Signal with given frequency, amplitude, and phase characteristics that is modulated in order to transmit messages.

Carrier signal -- The tone that you hear when you manually dial into a computer network.

Cathode ray tube -- Called CRT, this is the display unit or screen of your computer.

CCITT -- Consultative Committee for International Telephone and Telegraphs, an arm of the International Telecommunications Union (ITU), which establishes voluntary standards for telephone and telegraph interconnection.

Cellular radio (telephone) -- Radio or telephone system that operates within a grid of low-powered radio sender-receivers. As a user travels to different locations on the grid, different receiver-transmitters automatically support the message traffic. This is the basis for modern cellular telephone systems.

Central office -- The local switch for a telephone system, sometimes referred to as a wire center.

Channel -- A segment of bandwidth that may be used to establish a communications link. A television channel has a bandwidth of 6 MHz, a voice channel about 4000 Hz.

Chip -- A single device made up of transistors, diodes, and other components, interconnected by chemical process and forming the basic component of microprocessors.

Circuit switching -- The process by which a physical interconnection is made between two circuits or channels.

Coaxial cable -- A metal cable consisting of a conductor surrounded by another conductor in the form of a tube that can carry broadband signals by guiding high-frequency electromagnetic radiation.

Common carrier -- An organization licensed by the Federal Communications Commission (FCC) and/or by various state public utility commissions to supply communications services to all users at established and stated prices.

Computer word -- A string of characters or binary numbers considered as one unit and stored at a single computer address or location.

COMSAT -- Communications Satellite Corporation. A private corporation authorized by the Communications Satellite Act of 1962 to represent the United States in international satellite communications and to operate domestic and international satellites.

CPE -- Telephone jargon for customer premises equipment, which may often be distinguished from telephone company-owned equipment.

CPU -- The central processing unit of a computer.

Cross-subsidy -- A telephone term meaning that funds from one part of the business (e.g., long distance) are used to lower prices in another (local service).

A controversy is how to prevent cross-subsidy between regulated and unregulated parts of the telephone business.

CRT -- See Cathode ray tube.

Database -- Information or files stored in a computer for subsequent retrieval and use. Many of the services obtained from information utilities actually involve accessing large databases.

DCE -- Data communications equipment, computer components that are designed to communicate directly to data terminal equipment (see DTE).

Deaveraging -- Changing telephone rates so as to reflect true cost differences, thus making rates vary in different parts of a state. (Local rates are typically regulated so that telephone service is not much more expensive in some parts of a state than in others, although the costs to the providers may vary greatly; rates are kept at an "average" by having a pool so that high-cost areas are subsidized by low-cost ones. Typically rural telephone companies are against deaveraging because it could cause a major increase in their rates.

Dedicated lines -- Telephone lines leased for a specific term between specific points on a network, usually to provide certain special services not otherwise available on the public watched network.

Demodulate -- A process in which information is recovered from a carrier.

Depreciation -- As usually defined, the tax "write-off" or giving credit in some way for the declining value of equipment investments; in the telephone business, depreciation variations are an important variable in setting rates.

Digital -- A function that operates in discrete steps as contrasted to a continuous or analog function. Digital computers manipulate numbers encoded into binary (on-off) forms, while analog computers sum continuously varying forms. Digital communication is the transmission of information using discontinuous, discrete electrical or electromagnetic signals that change in frequency, polarity, or amplitude. Analog intelligence may be encoded for transmission on digital communication systems (see Pulse code modulation).

Direct broadcast satellite (DBS) -- A satellite system designed with sufficient power so that inexpensive earth stations can be used for direct residential or community reception, thus reducing the need for a local loop by allowing use of a receiving antenna with a diameter that is less than one meter.

Divestiture -- The breakup of AT&T into separate companies.

Dominance -- A telephone industry term meaning whether a company serving an area has such a high percentage of the business that it drives out competition; a current challenge is in how to define and measure dominance.

Downlink -- An antenna designed to receive signals from a communications satellite (see Uplink).

Download -- To receive information from another computer and store it into your computer memory or disk files.

Dumb terminal -- See Terminal.

Duplex -- The condition when information can flow two ways simultaneously in a communication link. This condition is often called full duplex as contrasted with one-way communications or half duplex. For most computer communication services, a full duplex condition is necessary.

Earth station -- A communication station on the surface of the earth used to communicate with a satellite. (Also TVRO, television receive-only earth station.)

Elasticity -- How one variable may be subject to change given changes in a related variable; "demand elasticity" in the telephone business is how much the quantity of service demanded may vary with changes in price.

Electronic mail -- The delivery of correspondence, including graphics, by electronic means, usually by the interconnection of computers, word processors, or facsimile equipment.

Encryption -- To change from a plain text to an encoded form requiring sophisticated techniques for decoding. Digital information can be encrypted directly with computer software.

Equity -- In the telephone business, this refers mainly to the availability of low cost service to all groups of customers, including the poor, handicapped, elderly, or rural.

ESS -- Electronic switching system. The Bell System designation for their stored program control switching machines.

FAX -- Facsimile. A system for the transmission of images. It is a black and white reproduction of a document or picture transmitted over a telephone or other transmission system.

FCC -- Federal Communications Commission. A board of five members (commissioners) appointed by the president and confirmed by the Senate under the provision of the Communications Act of 1934. The FCC has the power to regulate interstate communications.

Fiber optics -- Glass strands that allow transmission of modulated light waves for communication.

Final mile -- The communications systems required to get from the earth station to where the information or program is to be received and used. Terrestrial broadcasting from local stations and/or cable television systems provide the final mile for today's satellite networks.

FM -- Frequency modulation (see Modulation).

Frequency -- The number of recurrences of a phenomenon during a specified period of time. Electrical frequency is expressed in hertz, equivalent to cycles per second.

Frequency spectrum -- A term describing a range of frequencies of electromagnetic waves in radio terms; the range of frequencies useful for radio communication, from about 10 Hz to 3000 GHz.

Full duplex -- See Duplex.

Gateway -- The ability of one information service to transfer the user to another one, as from Dow Jones/News Retrieval to MCI Mail.

Geostationary satellite -- A satellite, with a circular orbit 22,400 miles in space, which lies in the satellite plane of the earth's equator and which turns about the polar axis of the earth in the same direction and with the same period as that of the earth's rotation. Thus, the satellite is stationary when viewed from the earth.

Gigahertz (GHz) -- Billions of cycles per second.

Half duplex -- Message flow is only one-way at a time (see Duplex).

Handshaking -- Jargon for the electronic exchange of signals as one computer links with another.

Hardware -- The electrical and mechanical equipment used in telecommunications and computer systems (see Software).

Hard wire modem -- Or direct modem; as contrasted with an acoustic modem, this equipment plugs directly into a telephone jack.

Headend -- The electronic control center of the cable television system where weaving signals are amplified, filtered, or converted as necessary. The headend is usually located at or near the antenna site.

Hertz (Hz) -- The frequency of an electric or electromagnetic wave in cycles per second, named after Heinrich Hertz, who detected such waves in 1883.

Host -- The main computer or computer system that is supporting a group of users.

IEEE -- Institute of Electrical and Electronic Engineers, a professional society.

Information utility -- A term increasingly used to refer to services that offer a wide variety of information, communications, and computing services to subscribers; examples are The Source, CompuServe, or Dow Jones News/Retrieval.

Institutional loop -- A separate cable for a CATV system designed to serve public institutions or businesses, usually with two-way video and data services. Also called I-net.

Interface -- Devices that operates at a common boundary of adjacent components or systems and that enable these components or systems to interchange information.

I/O -- Input-output. The equipment or processes that transmit data into or out of a computer's central processing unit.

ISDN -- Integrated Services Digital Network; a set of standards for integrating voice, data, and image communication; a service now being promoted by AT&T and some regional telephone companies.

IXC -- Interexchange carrier; telephone companies (e.g., AT&T, MCI, Sprint) that connect local exchanges and local access and transport areas (LATAs) to one another; a highly competitive part of the business.

Kilobyte (Kb) -- 1024 bytes of information, or roughly the same number of symbols or digits.

Kilohertz (KHz) -- Thousands of cycles per second.

LAN -- See Local area network.

Laser -- Light amplification by simulated emission of radiation. An intense beam that can be modulated for communications.

LATA -- Local access and transport area; a telephone service region incorporating local exchanges, yet usually smaller than a state; typically are serviced by a given telephone company for local services, and interexchange carriers for some intraLATA and all interLATA service.

Local area network (LAN) -- A special linkage of computers or other communications devices into their own network for use by an individual or organization. Local area networks are part of the modern trend of office communication systems.

LMS -- Local measured service; a method of telephone rate calculation that is sensitive to amount of usage as against a flat rate.

LEC -- Local exchange company; the telephone company that supports local calls (non long distance); typically a regulated monopoly. LECs are within larger areas called LATAs (Local access and transport areas).

Loop -- The wire pair that extends from a telephone central office to a telephone instrument. The coaxial cable in broadband or CATV systems that passes by each building or residence on a street and connects with the trunk cable at a neighborhood node is often called the "subscriber loop" or "local loop."

LSI -- Large-scale integration. Single integrated circuits that contain more than 100 logic circuits on one microchip (see VLSI).

Mainframe -- The base or main part of a large computer, as contrasted with mini- or microcomputers. Usually refers to the actual processing unit.

Mass storage -- A device that can hold very large amounts of information cheaply with automated access on demand.

Megahertz (MHz) -- Millions of cycles per second.

Memory -- One of the basic components of a central processing unit (CPU). It stores information for future use.

MFJ -- Short for modified final judgment which set AT&T divestiture in motion.

Microchip -- An electronic circuit with multiple solid-state devices engraved through photolithographic or microbeam processes on one substrate (see Microcomputer; Microprocessor).

Microcomputer -- A set of microchips that can perform all of the functions of a digital stored-program computer (see Microprocessor).

Microprocessor -- A microchip that performs the logic functions of a digital computer.

Microsecond -- One millionth of a second.

Microwave -- The short wave lengths from 1 GHz to 30 GHz used for radio, television, and satellite systems.

Millisecond -- One thousandth of a second.

Minicomputer -- In general, a minicomputer is a stationary computer that has more computer power than a microcomputer but less than a large mainframe computer.

MOU -- Minute of use; a usage measure used in the telephone business to calculate certain rates.

Modem -- Short for modulator-demodulator. The equipment used to link a computer to a telephone line.

Modulation -- A process of modifying the characteristics of a propagating signal, such as a carrier, so that it represents the instantaneous changes of another signal. The carrier wave can change its amplitude (AM), its frequency (FM), its phase, or its duration (pulse code modulation), or combinations of these.

Monitor (Video) -- Usually refers to the video screen on a computer, but has more technical meanings as well.

Multiplexing -- A process of combining two or more signals from separate sources into a single signal for sending on a transmission system from which the original signals may be recovered.

Nanosecond -- One billionth of a second.

Narrowband communication -- A communication system capable of carrying only voice or relatively slow-speed computer signals.

Network -- The circuits over which computers or other devices may be connected with one another, such as over the telephone network. One can also speak of computer networking.

Node -- A point at which terminals and other computer and telecommunications equipment are connected to the transmissions network.

Off-line -- Equipment not connected to a telecommunications system or an operating computer system.

On-line -- A device normally connected to a microcomputer that permit it to run various programs and handle scheduling, control of printers, terminals, memory devices, and so forth.

Optical fiber -- A thin flexible glass fiber the size of a human hair which will transmit light waves capable of carrying large amounts of information.

Packet switching -- A technique of switching digital signals with computers wherein the signal stream is broken into packets and reassembled in the correct sequence at the destination.

Parallel interface -- Refers to a computer communications connection where the bits code for a symbol is sent simultaneously as contrasted with serial interface, where the symbols are sent in sequence.

PBX -- A private branch exchange which may or may not be automated. Also called PABX (private automatic branch exchange).

Peripherals -- Units that operate in conjunction with a computer but are not a part of it, such as printers, modems, or disk drive.

Pooling -- "Revenue pooling". A telephone industry term meaning setting up special collections of funds for intended cross-subsidy, as in averaging rates between high-cost rural services and less expensive urban ones.

Port -- A place for a communication signal to enter or exit a computer.

POTS -- Jargon for "plain old telephone service."

Program -- A set of instructions arranged in proper sequence for directing a computer to perform a desired operation.

Protocol -- A description of the requirements for enabling one computer to communicate with another.

Public switched telephone network -- The more formal name given to the commercial telephone business in the United States; includes all the operating companies.

PUC -- Public Utility Commission, usually the entity that sets telephone rates in a state.

Pulse code modulation (PCM) -- A technique by which a signal is sampled periodically, each sample quantitized, and transmitted as a signal binary code.

RAM -- Random access memory. A RAM provides access to any storage or memory location point directly by means of vertical and horizontal coordinates. It is erasable and reusable.

Regional holding companies (RHC) -- The companies formed to take over the individual Bell System operating companies at divestiture; there are seven (e.g., Pacific Telesis).

Return key -- A holdover from the carriage return of a typewriter keyboard, the return key is used to tell a computer to execute what it has received. It is sometimes called an enter or execute key.

Robotics -- The use of electronic control techniques, as programmed on microprocessors and microcomputers, to operate mechanical sensing and guidance mechanism or robots in manufacturing and assembly processes.

ROM -- Read only memory. A permanently stored memory which is read out and not altered in the operation.

RS232 -- An interface between a modem and associated data terminal equipment. It is standardized.

Separations -- A telephone industry term meaning methods for dividing costs, revenues, etc. between different types of carriers, especially long distance versus local exchanges.

Slow-scan television -- A technique of placing video signals on a narrowband circuit, such as telephone lines, which results in a picture changing every few seconds.

Software -- The written instructions that direct a computer program. Any written material or script for use on a communications system or the program produced from the script (see Hardware).

Systems program -- As contrasted with an applications program which accomplishes specific tasks (e.g., word processing), this supports the basic operating system of the computer, for example, in allocating memory storage and operating peripherals.

Tariff -- The published rate for a service, equipment, or facility established by the communications common carrier.

Telco -- Jargon for "telephone company."

Telecommuting -- The use of computers and telecommunications to enable people to work at home. More broadly, the substitution of telecommunications for transportation.

Teleconference -- The simultaneous visual and/or sound interconnection that allows individuals in two or more locations to see and talk to one another in a long distance conference arrangement.

Telemarketing -- A method of marketing that emphasizes the creative use of the telephone and other telecommunications systems.

Teletext -- The generic name for a set of systems that transmit alphanumeric and simple graphical information over the broadcast (or one-way cable) signal, using spare line capacity in the signal for display on a suitably modified TV receiver.

Telex -- A dial-up telegraph service.

Terminal -- A point at which a communication can either leave or enter a communications network.

Terminal emulator -- Use of a personal computer to act as a dumb terminal; this requires special software or firmware.

TIBS -- Telecommunications-intensive businesses.

Timesharing -- When a computer can support two or more users. The large computers used by the information utilities can accommodate many users simultaneously who are said to be timesharing on the system.

Transponder -- The electronic circuit of a satellite that receives a signal from the transmitting earth station, amplifies it, and transmits it to the earth at a different frequency.

Trunk -- A main cable that runs from the head end to a local node, then connects to the drop running to a home in a cable television system; a main circuit connected to local central offices with regional or intercity switches in telephone systems.

Twisted pair -- The term given to the two wires that connect local telephone circuits to the telephone central office.

Uplink -- The communications link from the transmitting earth station to the satellite.

Upload -- To transfer information out of the memory or disk file of your computer to another computer.

Videotext -- The generic name for a computer system that transmits alphanumeric and simple graphics information over the ordinary telephone line for display on a video monitor.

VLSI -- Very large scale integration. Single integrated circuits that contain more than 100,000 logic gates on one microchip (see LSI).

WATS -- Wide area telephone service. A service offered by telephone companies in the United States that permits customers to make dial calls to telephones in a specific area for a flat monthly charge, or to receive calls collect at a flat monthly charge.

Index

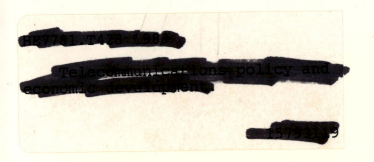

DATE DUE
